Dancing in My Dreams

LIBRARY OF RELIGIOUS BIOGRAPHY

Mark A. Noll, Kathryn Gin Lum, and Heath W. Carter, series editors

Long overlooked by historians, religion has emerged in recent years as a key factor in understanding the past. From politics to popular culture, from social struggles to the rhythms of family life, religion shapes every story. Religious biographies open a window to the sometimes surprising influence of religion on the lives of influential people and the worlds they inhabited.

The Library of Religious Biography is a series that brings to life important figures in United States history and beyond. Grounded in careful research, these volumes link the lives of their subjects to the broader cultural contexts and religious issues that surrounded them. The authors are respected historians and recognized authorities in the historical period in which their subject lived and worked.

Marked by careful scholarship yet free of academic jargon, the books in this series are well-written narratives meant to be read and enjoyed as well as studied.

Titles include:

An Odd Cross to Bear: A Biography of Ruth Bell Graham
by Anne Blue Wills

A Heart Lost in Wonder: The Life and Faith of Gerard Manley Hopkins
by Catharine Randall

Oral Roberts and the Rise of the Prosperity Gospel
by Jonathan Root

Strength for the Fight: The Life and Faith of Jackie Robinson
by Gary Scott Smith

We Will Be Free: The Life and Faith of Sojourner Truth
by Nancy Koester

For a complete list of published volumes, see the back of this volume.

Dancing in My Dreams

A Spiritual Biography of Tina Turner

Ralph H. Craig III

WILLIAM B. EERDMANS PUBLISHING COMPANY

GRAND RAPIDS, MICHIGAN

Wm. B. Eerdmans Publishing Co.
4035 Park East Court SE, Grand Rapids, Michigan 49546
www.eerdmans.com

Book design by Lydia Hall

Printed in the United States of America

29 28 27 26 25 24 23   1 2 3 4 5 6 7

ISBN 978-0-8028-7863-2

Library of Congress Cataloging-in-Publication Data

A catalog record for this book is available from the Library of Congress.

To my ancestors who carry me *On Silent Wings*:

Alene M. Bonds
Baderinwa Ain
Gamaliel A. Bonds
Lattie Blanton
Ralph H. Craig Jr.
Rebecca B. Ross
Robert Bonds Sr.
Scarlett M. Blanton

and to

Lelia B. Bell, my mother and partner-in-crime,
and the enduring legacy of Tina Turner,

all of whom have, by their example, taught me the meaning
of Nichiren Daishonin's maxim, "If one lights a fire for others,
one will brighten one's own way"

Contents

Foreword by Jan Willis   ix

Acknowledgments   xv

Introduction   1

1   **Motherless Child**   11

2   **Becoming "Tina Turner"**   42

3   **Tina's Prayer**   72

4   **Becoming Tina**   99

5   **Wildest Dreams**   143

6   *Beyond* **and Beyond**   189

Epilogue   217

A Note on Sources   221

Notes   223

Index   261

Foreword

One evening in Amsterdam, in September 1996, I stood among at least 50,000 souls, shoulder to shoulder, sweaty with anticipation of the return of Tina Turner and her new show, the Wildest Dreams concert and tour. As the lights dimmed and then came up, the band members ran onto the stage and took their places, followed by Turner and three dancers. And there they were: those smooth, taut, beautiful thighs, the dancers, the excitement, the energy, the lady herself, and that voice! Turner's live show was pure adrenaline and pure power. It felt like I had died and gone to heaven!

To say that Tina Turner's live shows in the late 1980s and 1990s were a "phenom" would not be doing them justice. They were communal gatherings to which people flocked to get revived, rejuvenated—even healed—by the sheer exuberance and loving energy that was moved between performers and audience. If you were anywhere within reach of her live performances in those days, you wanted to be there!

Ralph H. Craig III begins this wonderful book with Turner's Wildest Dreams Tour. In preparation for the tour, he writes, "Turner appeared on *Saturday Night Live*, *The Late Show with David Letterman*, and *The Oprah Winfrey Show*, in addition to her appearance on *Larry King Live*. To King, Turner declared that the Wildest Dreams Tour could be her best tour ever . . . faithful audiences were encouraged to buy her albums, watch her life story in the film *What's Love Got to Do with It?*, read her autobiography, or see her live on tours like the Wildest Dreams Tour—where her concerts become opportunities to participate in Turner's religiosity." During that tour, aged fifty-seven and fifty-eight, Turner performed 255 concerts witnessed by more than three million people across five continents over the course of sixteen months!

As Tina Turner fans, we have heard and read about her triumphant reemergence following the years of physical and sexual abuse meted out by her former husband, and musical partner, Ike Turner. We have watched and witnessed as she clawed her way back to become a world-famous solo artist who never publicly seemed to lose that inner strength that enabled her. Indeed, with that gorgeous smile, she offered that strength to all who would listen and have the discipline to follow.

Tina Turner's life of overcoming obstacles and giving strength to women the world over has been chronicled in countless written interviews, in documentaries, in the movie *What's Love Got to Do with It?*, in interfaith children's recordings, and, most recently, onstage, in *Tina: The Tina Turner Musical* and not one but *three* best-selling autobiographies and memoirs of her life—*I, Tina: My Life Story* in 1986; *My Love Story* in 2018; and, most recently, *Happiness Becomes You: A Guide to Changing Your Life for Good* in 2020 (the latter explicitly about her spiritual journey).

Even so, and fortunately for us, Craig has, in *Dancing in My Dreams: A Spiritual Biography of Tina Turner*, placed Turner's spirituality at the center of her story. Centering Turner's spirituality makes an enormous difference in the interpretation of Turner's life and work. And Craig has accomplished this with heart, with insight, and with near encyclopedic knowledge of anthropology, theology, music history and aesthetics, psychology, ritual, and religious studies. He has thereby given us a much richer, more nuanced, and more holistic *context* for the continuity and constancy of the spiritual arc of Turner's life wishes and the various "expedient" or skillful means, the spiritual tools and aesthetics, she employed to attain them.

As noted by Craig, Tina Turner's "wildest dreams" were *twofold*: the first was to become a world-renowned solo performer who filled arenas and stadiums. In this, she more than succeeded, selling, by some estimates, "more concert tickets than any solo performer in history."

Her second wildest dream was to become a Buddhist teacher. Since her 2009 retirement from performing, she has been focused on this specific dream. In addition to the narratives of her life, she contributed to an audio series called *Beyond* on which she recites prayers, intones various mantras, and gives practice instructions for doing certain Buddhist and other spiritual rituals and practices. She has given interviews in which she explains her faith in Soka Gakkai Nichiren Buddhism and provides details about how she practices it. While she may not be the most prominent Black Buddhist living today (and many of her fans do not know that she *is* Buddhist), she is certainly one of the most well-known Black musical performers to claim Buddhism as her own. Owing to Craig's book, for example, we are privy to the vibrant jazz scene of the 1970s and 1980s in LA where musicians like Herbie Hancock, Wayne Shorter, Pharoah Sanders, and other jazz greats were all also practicing, or dabbling with, Nichiren Buddhism.

In a 1993 *Vanity Fair* cover profile and interview, Tina Turner called herself a "Buddhist-Baptist." She told her interviewer, "I do something about my life besides eating and exercises and whatever. I contact my soul. I must stay in contact with my soul. That's my connection to the universe. . . . I'm a Buddhist-Baptist." Today, hyphenated or dual identities are commonplace. Indeed, not knowing about the earlier Turner description at the time, in my own memoir, *Dreaming Me: Black, Baptist and Buddhist*, I referred to myself as a "Baptist-Buddhist" and commented that I felt this to be a true description of who I am since, when situations seem dire, I am likely to draw on *both* traditions in my life. It is a deep response.

Craig illuminates here how the "Buddhist-Baptist" identity fits into what he terms Turner's "combinatory religious repertoire," how she combined her childhood Baptist and Pentecostal experiences, and what she learned from her maternal grandmother's knowledge of spells, conjure, reading signs, and root work with what she would later learn from other practices—of consulting with readers and psychics, and especially from her practice of chanting according to Nichiren Buddhism. Ultimately, she fashioned a balance that worked for her. Employing all these religious threads as "skillful means" helped Turner to find and to strengthen her spiritual life—her health and energy, her fortitude and determination, and her sanity. A psychic told her in London in 1996, "You will be among the biggest of stars, and your partner will fall away like a leaf from a tree"; these words kept her going despite the traumas of her abusive relationship with Ike until she found, and converted to, Nichiren Buddhism in 1973.

Soka Gakkai Nichiren Buddhism, a thirteenth-century Japanese form of Mahayana Buddhism founded by a priest named Nichiren, first appeared in the United States in 1960, when its head and chief propagator, Daisaku Ikeda, arrived in Los Angeles with the specific aim of popularizing and spreading Nichiren's teachings. The most fundamental Nichiren teachings call for three practices: (1) *chanting* the name of the Lotus Sutra in the form of an invocation, or mantra, namely *Nam-myoho-renge-kyo* before a boxlike altar called the *butsudan*, twice daily, morning and evening; (2) *chanting* while maintaining a mind of *faith* (*shinjin*), and (3) *propagating* the teaching of Nichiren by studying it and teaching it to others. Followers of Nichiren Buddhism are trained to become teachers of the doctrine. Thus, propagating the teachings (called *shakubuku*) is one of its highest aims. Given this trajectory of practice, there is little wonder that this became one of Turner's "wildest dreams"! In *Dancing in My Dreams*, Craig deftly illustrates how and why this dream originated and developed. Moreover, the practice of Nichiren Buddhism is a little like Tantric Buddhism, in that if one doesn't see and experience it from the "inside," one doesn't really understand it. We are, once more, fortunate to have Craig as our guide since his unique insider vantage point makes this book even more valuable—to students not only of Buddhism but of American religion more broadly.

The addition of Soka Gakkai's chanting practice to Turner's growing medicine chest of spiritual aids created exactly the magic potion she had been searching for. As she said, chanting was like singing for her. It was also like prayer. In *Happiness Becomes You*, Turner has said, "I have chanted and prayed before each show, focusing on the happiness of each person who came to see me. I visualized my audience and prayed that I could be whoever each person needed me to be that day in order to inspire their dreams, invigorate their hope, and recharge their souls. I prayed to spark in them a joyful revolution of the heart." Craig notes that Turner "chanted up to an hour before each show." Now, that is genuine behind-the-scenes preparation before a performance! And it is the compassionate action of a Buddhist bodhisattva.

In September 2022, the night before I was flying out of Spain heading for my next teaching engagement in Europe, I looked up to see, adorning an adjacent building, a gigantic, three-paneled advertisement covered with huge images of Turner performing. It was an ad for the still-ongoing onstage production of *Tina: The Tina Turner Musical*. At eighty-three years of age, the "queen of rock 'n' roll" is still *Rollin'*!

This marvelous book is an indispensable complement to music history, to religious and ritual studies, to Tina Turner studies, and to a much deeper understanding, and appreciation, of her. Read it with pleasure.

JAN WILLIS
Professor of Religion, Emerita,
Wesleyan University, Middletown, CT
Author of *Dreaming Me: Black, Baptist, and Buddhist*
and *Dharma Matters: Women, Race, and Tantra*

Acknowledgments

I wanna take you higher; said I wanna light your fire! Tina Turner sang these words in her live rendition of "I Want to Take You Higher." I could not have written this book without the guidance and community of friends, colleagues, and family who have surrounded me over the years. Their support continues to take me higher and light my fire.

First and foremost, this book would not exist without the wonderful team at Wm. B. Eerdmans Publishing. Heath Carter, Kathryn Gin Lum, and Mark Noll have been amazing editors, and any merits this book may have are deeply indebted to their collective critical acumen. I could not have asked for a better acquisitions editor in Lisa Ann Cockrel. A special thank you as well to David Bratt and Laura Bardolph Hubers, both of whom were involved with this project in its early stages. Tom Raabe and Laurel Draper, as copyeditors, you have done the Lord's work; thank you! Many thanks as well to the marketing team. A huge thank you to Joseph Stuart for indexing this book. To the anonymous reviewers, whoever you are, I offer a deep bow of gratitude; you read the first draft and took it higher.

My colleagues and professors at Stanford University have enriched my scholarship immeasurably. My advisors Kathryn Gin Lum and Paul Harrison have served as model mentors, offering crucial insights every step of the way. Alexis Wells-Oghoghomeh listened (and listens) to me talk about Tina Turner for hours and pointed me in the direction of critical resources. Ariel Evan Mayse uplifted me and kept me going when my spirits flagged. I am grateful to the faculty and fellows of the American Religions in a Global Context Initiative. Their constructive feedback and generous sharing of their knowledge and resources were integral to the completion of this manuscript.

I am especially grateful to Chanhee Heo, Daniel N. Gullotta (whose chance tweet initiated this project!), Esiteli Hafoka, jem Jebbia, and Johanna Mueller. They commented on chapter drafts, shared their own painstaking research with me, and provided much-needed encouragement. Johanna Mueller read multiple iterations of the full manuscript; without her critical eye and incisive comments, this manuscript would have suffered immensely.

Other members of my intellectual community also read full versions of the manuscript and likewise made it much stronger. A special thank you goes, again, to Kathryn Gin Lum. She is a great person, a brilliant scholar, and an unparalleled advisor. I am deeply grateful to Adeana McNicholl. In addition to commenting on earlier drafts, she paused her own work to read the full manuscript at the eleventh hour and helped me cross the finish line. She made this book better. Paul Harvey gave me writing advice when I was stuck and pointed me toward key secondary research. I cannot thank Vaughn A. Booker enough for his feedback, resources, inspiration, and generosity of spirit. Rima Vesely-Flad was and remains an insightful conversation partner. Levi McLaughlin, thank the heavens for you. When I could not bring myself to write, Pamela Ayo Yetunde listened to me on the phone and then said, "I'll tell you how you'll do it: you'll go step by step." I followed her advice to the end; Ayo remains a guiding light.

Other teachers have served as mentors and inspirations over the years: Anthony Recasner; Bill Batty; Christopher and Maureen Chapple; Jay Altman; John Campbell; Julia Carson; Karen Enriquez; Matthew Pereira; Quin Clemons; Peter Masteller; and Richard Freeman and Mary Taylor. I am endlessly grateful for the mentorship of Kim R. Harris. All of them have supported me in my journey, pushing, inspiring, and challenging me.

Several institutions made my research possible. Irene Lin and Stephanie Lee of the Ho Center for Buddhist Studies at Stanford University provided critical funding for this project. Sonia Outlaw-Clark of the West Tennessee Delta Heritage Center and the Tina Turner Museum helped arrange my stay in Brownsville, Tennessee. Not only did she make the resources and archives of both institutions available to me, she also drove me to sites associated with Tina Turner's early life. Achana Jarrett opened Woodlawn Missionary Baptist Church to me, shared archival material, and played the piano as we sang our hearts out. She made sure I understood the local history of Nutbush and made sure I had a good time doing it. Robbie Ewing, a longtime member of Woodlawn Missionary Baptist Church, shared her love of that church and knowledge of its history. Achana Jarrett, Ms. Robbie Ewing, and Sonia Outlaw-Clark have become members of my extended West Tennessee family. And I cannot thank them enough. I am also grateful to the staff of Brownsville Public Library and of the Tennessee State Library and Archives in Nashville.

Tina Turner has a global network of fans and associates, without whom I could not have carried out this research. Julia Szwaczka, Michael Wallace Jr., and Sean Jackson talked with me informally, sat for formal interviews, and continued to send me anything they thought might be humorous or relevant to my research. Ben Piner, Dan Lindsay, and T. J. Martin provided key insights into Turner's life. I am especially grateful to Taro Gold for his time, patience, and eye for detail. A special thank you goes to Jacquline R. Bullock. And thank you to Tina Turner herself.

Another deep bow of gratitude to Soka Gakkai International (SGI) president Daisaku Ikeda, and to the many warm members of Soka Gakkai International-USA. A special thank you to: Adin Strauss, Bobby Debozi, Danny Nagashima, Jason Goulah, Jesse Goins, Kathy Lucien, Ken Valderrama, Maria Lucien, Maryam Molstad, and Matilda Buck. Matilda Buck, especially, provided insight into the history of the organization and its development in the United States. May your warmth and compassion continue to shine in this world.

Portions of this book are reprinted and adapted from my article "Some Will Hear: Tina Turner, African American Buddhist Teacher," *American Religion* 4, no. 1 (Fall 2022): 1–33. Many thanks to the journal for allowing me to use this material.

My friends have seen me through: Aina and Justin Walker, Akil Spooner, Alex Radisich, Alex Topper, Arielle Maugé, Arnold Sobers, Beth Loh, Carl Lindstrom, Constance and Martin Tarantino, Delia Flanagan, Derek and Jody Lipkin, Eliza Davis, Erika York, Jasmine York, Jen Garcia Beyer, Jensi Rovang, Josh and Paulina Gardner, Keysha Baynes, Laura Chesney, Laura Watson, Lina Goujjane, Mia Buckland, Nia Spooner, Nina Friedly, Reine Paradis, Sarah Balgooyen, Scott Cohen, Sharon Cromer, Simone Sobers ("my sista"), and Steven Green. I have so much gratitude and appreciation to the other two of the "Three Kings": Donovan Saddler and Robert "Esho Funi" Fisher. Get yourself some friends like them.

Writing a book is undoubtedly a family affair, and my family has been there from the beginning. I owe my love of music history to my brother Miguel Bonds. My brother Cornelius "Muff" Collins Jr. is my true champion. Thank you to my best-cousin-friend Kristen Bonds, our weekly CST (cousin standard time) call is lively, love-filled, and more than a little therapeutic. My endless love and gratitude goes to Anita Johnson, Annie Archie, Betty Sims, Charles Johnson, Dorothy Thompson, Justin Schief, LaQunia Banks, Latanya-Sims Barbarin, Morgan Bonds, Nikki Harris, Porché Bonds, Raymond "Reecy" Delaney Jr., Regina Thompson, Reginald Thompson, Rhonda Bonds, Robert Bonds III, Robert Bonds Jr., Russell "Ricky" Seymour, Shaka Shabazz, Shekeva Bonds, Tikelanna Dutton, Trenice Varnado, and Trevis Dutton. Much appreciation goes to Francisco "Chico" Medina, Mary and Ruben Polanco, and Nichole "Snow" and Heath "Magic" Shore. My deep love goes out to "The Sibz": Eric Boyd, Laura Boyd, and Lindsay Walter. And to Aprilan F. Woolworth and Larry and Michelle Walter. Dawn and Walt Boyd, I thank you from the bottom of my heart for your relentless support.

My mother, Lelia B. Bell, gave me life. She is a source of light, *deep* wisdom, and rollicking good cheer. It might have seemed, to her, that at times she worked just to buy Tina Turner memorabilia. I can only say thank you. And I can assure her that all of that memorabilia made it into this book as archival material.

My wife, Kelly Craig, is my rock. In the beginning of our relationship, she patiently (or by force) endured a "Tina Turner Appreciation" drill, five mornings a week. Little did she know, that too was a part of my research. She has read every draft of this book and her keen editorial eye has touched every part of it. This project has been a long journey, and I hope that she is proud.

I deeply apologize to all those whom I may have forgotten, but know that I appreciate you nonetheless.

Beat is gettin' stronger, beat is gettin' longer too. Take your places, I wanna take you higher!

Introduction

O n February 21, 1997, Tina Turner appeared on CNN's *Larry King Live*. Larry King and Turner sat across from each other in front of King's trademark cityscape backdrop. Arrayed on King's desk were his interview notes, a phone switchboard to take calls from viewers, and Turner's mug (likely for tea, as she had given up coffee at the time). In this wide-ranging interview, King asked Turner questions about why she stayed with her infamously abusive ex-husband, Ike Turner; why she moved from the United States to Europe; and why she converted to Buddhism. The latter topic provided space for Turner to affirm her identity as a Buddhist, give a demonstration of her chanting practice, and explain how chanting works.

Larry King: Buddhism . . . is also a way of living isn't it, right? It's more than a faith.

Tina Turner: Yes . . . how I view it is that it . . . it is something that one depends on like, I think, like I need my refrigerator, I need the clothing on my back, I need shelter, and chanting takes care of that spiritual side, that subconscious mind, that I tap into. My reality is God has given us the faith, but we have to find it, we have to work on it to find the God within us, that . . . say that coin [inside], and when you chant, when you get into the rhythm, the sound. . . .

LK: Is the chant to God?

TT: It is to the coin, let's say, within us, which is the subconscious mind. . . .

LK: . . . those are not words, but they are prayer, right? They're . . . they're . . . what are they? What is it? Just sounds?

TT: It's sounds, and the sounds resonate the chakras, and starts the wheels turning there, and that is the whole vibration, that makes the contact actually with the subconscious mind. They are words . . . they . . . it reads similar I would say in some way like the Bible. We have translations now of what [LK: really?] it . . . but it reads, it's scientific kind of, it reads . . . you must be able to just take it in to understand it.[1]

Where Turner had previously demonstrated the chanting of *Nam-myoho-renge-kyo* for interviewers, she now performed for King the extended liturgical practice of *gongyo*, chanting excerpts from *The Liturgy of the Soka Gakkai International*. Turner then explained the practice to King, drawing upon language that referenced her Black Baptist Christian upbringing, drawing on the metaphysical language of chakras, sound vibration, and the notion of contacting the subconscious mind to explain the mechanism of chanting's efficacy. Throughout the interview, Turner references astrology and her confidence that the world would be transformed in the new millennium, all hallmarks of metaphysical religious beliefs. At the end of the interview, Turner briefly discusses her conviction in her past life as Hatshepsut. In so doing, Turner—whose appearance on *Larry King Live* took place as a part of the promotional tour for the American leg of Tina Turner's Wildest Dreams Tour 1996–1997—displayed for a live audience her identity as a combinatory religious practitioner and foreshadowed her future role as a spiritual teacher.

Tina Turner's Wildest Dreams Tour had much to live up to. Her previous tours had broken global box office records, shattered overall concert attendance records, and supported multiplatinum albums. Now, at fifty-six years old, Turner had to promote an album that had yet to achieve the level of success of her earlier, career-defining albums and get through to global markets she hadn't reached before. This was a tall order for any tour, but that was not all. The concerts also needed to be carefully calibrated to convey what the icon's brand had come to represent: show-business longevity, a rags-to-riches narrative of resilience, and a religious belief in the power of dreams to overcome all obstacles. Rehearsals for the shows took place in South Africa, followed by some of the first concert performances of the tour. The tour then moved to Europe, where the set list of songs was finalized for the remaining concert dates. In each country in which she performed, Turner carried out promotional interviews that appeared in print and on radio and television. In the United States, among other television shows, Turner appeared on *Saturday Night Live, The Late Show with David Letterman,* and *The Oprah Winfrey Show,* in addition to her appearance on *Larry King Live.* To King, Turner declared that the Wildest Dreams Tour could be her best tour ever in America. She reiterated this message in each promotional interview, nearly always accompanied by a discussion of her religious beliefs and practices. Beyond these promotional appearances, Turner's faithful audiences were encouraged to buy her albums, watch her life story in the film *What's Love Got to Do with It?,* read her autobiography, or see her live on tours like the Wildest Dreams Tour—where her concerts become opportunities to participate in Turner's religiosity. Regardless of how her brand's message was consumed, it was highlighted for a broad audience that Turner was a role model for others, particularly women, who had used the foundation of religious practice to make her wildest dreams come true. By implication, the message was conveyed that attentive consumers of Turner's brand could follow her and make their own wildest dreams come true.

Tina Turner herself harbored two "wildest" dreams. The first was to become a commercially successful artist who could fill arenas and stadiums as a solo artist. She began accomplishing this dream following the success of her multiplatinum album of 1984, *Private Dancer.* That album spawned a major concert tour in which she filled arenas around the globe and paved the way for subsequent arena- and stadium-filling tours. During the Wildest Dreams Tour, which concluded in the summer of 1997, Turner performed 255 concerts witnessed by more than three million people across five continents over the course of sixteen months. The tour further consolidated her reputation as a successful, headlining arena and stadium commodity. Highlighting the importance of this tour, elements of its stage design and set list recur on Turner's final two concert tours: Tina Turner Twenty-Four Seven World Tour 2000 and Tina Turner's Fiftieth Anniversary Concert Tour 2008–2009. And further, by reinforcing Turner's message of religious belief in the power of dreams, the tour also transformed Turner into a model of personal transformation. She never failed to mention that her success was the result of her religious beliefs and practices. Specifically, as a Buddhist, a central element of that practice is the understanding that a significant aspect of Buddhist praxis is the imperative to spread the teachings to others. In other words, the ultimate fulfillment of Buddhist practice is to become a teacher. So, Turner's second "wildest" dream was to use the platform that she created with her commercial success to become a religious teacher. After her retirement from live performing, she released a series of interfaith albums with the Beyond Foundation, which initiated her turn to teaching. She completed this turn with the release of her 2020 memoir, *Happiness Becomes You*.

"Ladies and Gentlemen: Tina Turner!"

My own journey to writing a religious biography of Tina Turner began, in a sense, in my childhood. *What's Love Got to Do with It?* was among the VHS tapes that we had at home. My cousins Kristen, Porché, and I would perform the film's musical numbers for our older cousin Charles. Despite this, I did not connect the character in the movie to any actual living person. I considered Angela Bassett, as Tina Turner, to be simply another character, on par with Bassett's portrayal of Katherine Jackson in *The Jacksons: An American Dream*. However, I made the connection between the life portrayed in *What's Love Got to Do with It?* and Tina Turner as an actual historical, living person in December 2000. I sat with my brother Cornelius as he flipped through television channels. On CBS we saw a commercial advertising a concert special: *Tina Turner One Last Time Live*. This was an advertisement for a concert recorded on the Tina Turner Twenty-Four Seven World Tour 2000. I begged my brother to let me watch it; and together, we watched the entire concert special.

"Work like you don't need the money," James Earl Jones recited, quoting Rumi to introduce Turner. He continued: "Love like you've never been hurt. Dance like nobody's watching. Ladies and gentlemen: Tina Turner!"[2] With that the curtain opened, and I was reintroduced to the legend that is Tina Turner. By the time the special ended with Turner on a platform extended over the audience singing "Nutbush City Limits," I was determined to learn more about her. From that time, I avidly collected her albums, memorabilia, and autobiographies. Eventually, I saw Turner live on the Fiftieth Anniversary Concert Tour 2008–2009. As Oprah Winfrey said about her own experience seeing Turner perform, I caught the spirit (see chap. 5 below)! At the same time, I began studying Buddhism. Even as I came to understand that Turner herself is a Buddhist, it became increasingly clear to me that other religious traditions also played prominent roles in Turner's life. I was curious about the development of Turner's religious beliefs and the role they played in her career.

As I started to research Turner's religiosity from an academic perspective, I realized that the accounts of Turner's life I read neither sufficiently emphasized religion (since those accounts were often concerned with promoting Turner's career, religion served as one discussion item among many in her promotional agenda) nor distinguished the intertwined threads of her religious life. Those accounts also failed to notice that throughout her career Turner had taken every available opportunity to discuss her religious beliefs, explain her practices, and name her aspiration to become a religious teacher. This latter aspiration was itself a part of the larger wildest-dreams message at the center of Turner's iconic brand. *Dancing in My Dreams: A Spiritual Biography of Tina Turner* corrects these oversights.

Tina Turner's remarkable life begins as the story of a young Black woman who rose from the cotton fields of Nutbush, Tennessee. Her early life, as the daughter of sharecroppers with her horizons proscribed by Jim Crow racism, was a story common to many young southern Black children in the 1930s. Born Anna Mae Bullock in 1939, Turner moved constantly in those early years after being abandoned by her parents.[3] Like many young Black southern women growing up in church, she had a talent for singing that she honed by singing at picnics, in a church choir, and along to the radio. Radio programs and films revealed to her the possibility of a world outside of West Tennessee, and she began to harbor dreams of seeing that world herself.

Turner reunited with her mother in 1956 in St. Louis, and there she met early rock pioneer Ike Turner. She began singing with Ike Turner, and by 1960 she had formed half of the Ike & Tina Turner Revue. Over their sixteen-year partnership, Ike and Tina Turner released a string of memorable songs, including "A Fool in Love," "River Deep, Mountain High," "Proud Mary," and "Nutbush City Limits." Their marriage would become one of the most infamous in music history when Turner revealed in a 1980 interview that the reason they divorced in 1978 was that Ike Turner had physically and mentally abused her for most of their time together. After working for eight years to establish herself as a solo artist, Turner reemerged with 1984's *Private Dancer* album and staged one of the most well-known comebacks in popular music history. Turner retired from live performances in 2009, having established herself as a commercially successful recording and performing artist.

Turner's story has been told in three memoirs, *I, Tina*; *My Love Story*; and *Happiness Becomes You: A Guide to Changing Your Life for Good*; the major motion picture *What's Love Got to Do with It?*; and the stage musical *Tina: The Tina Turner Musical*. It has also been told in innumerable media profiles, interviews, and documentaries over the course of a career that spans six decades. Turner's tale is most often presented as a classic rags-to-riches narrative, or a heroic myth, but this obscures the central place of religion in Turner's life. Turner's story is fundamentally a religious story.

Turner's Religious Background

Turner grew up in the milieu of Black southern religious culture in the early decades of the twentieth century (chap. 1). Turner was born into a Baptist family that worshiped at local churches in the Nutbush and Spring Hill communities of Brownsville, Tennessee (Turner also briefly attended a Black Pentecostal church). For Turner's religious upbringing, the most important of these churches is Woodlawn Missionary Baptist Church. Today designated as a historical site, Woodlawn was established by the Reverend Hardin Smith in 1866. Turner dutifully attended Woodlawn under the watchful eye of her paternal grandmother, perhaps the most devout member of her family. However, church was not the only site of Turner's religious development. Turner paid particular attention to her maternal grandmother, who was spiritually attuned to the natural landscape of Brownsville, Nutbush, and Spring Hill. Turner's maternal grandmother, then, represents another stream of Black southern religious culture. This stream included a complex of supernatural beliefs and practices that included conjuring and hoodoo, mystical ideas about the natural world, and the importance of dreams, visions, and signs. The importance of these elements in Black southern religious culture has led some scholars to refer to a uniquely African American mysticism.[4] Whether explicitly iden-

6

tified as such or considered more broadly, the mystical and supernatural elements of Black southern religious culture are themselves a subset of the broad stream of American metaphysical religion.[5] Turner's maternal grandmother is indicative of this stream, and both grandmothers would have a major influence on Turner's early religious sensibilities.

Like many Americans, Turner was influenced by the countercultural movements of the sixties and seventies (chap. 2). In 1966, Turner began a lifelong practice of consulting with psychics, from whom she learned principles of inner and outer correspondences and learned to appreciate psychic phenomena. Such a lifelong practice is indicative of Turner's own participation in American metaphysical religion. I contend that Turner's early religious experiences, especially with her maternal grandmother, primed her for an attraction toward the beliefs and practices of American metaphysical religion. In 1973, Turner was introduced to the practice of Soka Gakkai Nichiren Buddhism, under the auspices of the Nichiren Shoshu Soka Gakkai of America organization (chap. 3). Turner's ability to attend the organization's local Buddhist meetings was all but completely curtailed by Ike Turner. Nonetheless, members of the organization were able to visit with Turner and help her develop her practice. Turner officially converted to Soka Gakkai Nichiren Buddhism on August 8, 1976, when she received her own *gohonzon*, Soka Gakkai's central object of devotion (chap. 4). Even as Turner converted to Buddhism, she worked to incorporate into it metaphysical beliefs in astrology and past lives, alongside her work with psychics. Thus, rather than renounce her Black Baptist Christian and metaphysical religious beliefs, Turner made Soka Gakkai Nichiren Buddhism the cornerstone of her religious repertoire.[6] Given the combinatory nature of Turner's religious repertoire, how do we understand her statement on *Larry King Live* that she is "converted" to Buddhism? What does conversion mean for Turner?

While notions of religious change have remained central topics of discussion in most religions, the idea of conversion as a dramatic and complete break with one's prior religious orientation describes a distinctly Christian phenomenon. Many scholars in religious studies have drawn attention to the fact that when understood in this way, conversion does not accurately capture many people's understanding of their own religious adherence.[7] Indeed, Turner's use of the language of conversion to describe her identity as a Buddhist requires a more expansive conception of conversion. Turner's Buddhist practice developed gradually, as detailed in chapter 3 below, through encountering others who practiced Soka Gakkai Nichiren Buddhism. When she received her *gohonzon* in 1976 and formally became Buddhist, this was the culmination of her gradual development. As chapters 3 and 4 show, becoming Buddhist started a new gradual process of inculcating the teachings into her life in the context of carrying out the Soka Gakkai Buddhist practice of chanting. As this book makes clear, and echoing the experiences of other Black Buddhists (chap. 4), converting to Buddhism did not preclude Turner from incorporating her previous religious beliefs. That is to say, Turner's practice of Soka Gakkai Nichiren Buddhism interweaves beliefs drawn from her primarily Black Baptist Christian upbringing, elements of the supernaturalism and mysticism that inhere in Black southern religious culture, and elements of what religious historian Catherine Albanese has termed American metaphysical religion. Based on this understanding, I argue that conversion for Turner means an institutional commitment to the doctrines and practices of one religious tradition (Soka Gakkai Nichiren Buddhism) but in the context of forming a religious repertoire that combines elements of Afro-Protestant Christianity and American metaphysical religion. Thus, even as each element of Turner's combinatory religious repertoire is separated out and discussed in the pages that follow, we must not lose sight of the holistic nature of Turner's religious life.

Tina Turner as Black Buddhist Teacher

Afro-Protestantism, and specifically notions of the "Black church," has dominated the study of African American religious history. Recently, scholars have convincingly argued that the African American religious experience has been marked by greater diversity.[8] Scholar Anthony B. Pinn, for example, has repeatedly called attention to the "religious pluralism" that has marked African American communities.[9] Indeed, throughout American history, African Americans have affiliated with or incorporated ideas derived from Africana religions, Asian religions, metaphysical beliefs, and more. Tina Turner's combinatory religious repertoire demonstrates this exactly. In Turner's religious life, Black southern religious culture in both its institutional forms and its supernatural manifestations (which often intertwine and display fuzzy boundaries), American metaphysical religion, and Buddhism combine to produce a complex religious orientation. Careful study of Turner's life and career from a religious perspective brings a necessary focus on "overlooked but vital dimensions and schemes of African American life."[10]

By examining the place of religion in Turner's life and career and charting her trajectory from popular entertainer to religious teacher, *Dancing in My Dreams: A Spiritual Biography of Tina Turner* reveals trends in twentieth- and twenty-first-century American religious history more broadly, and African American religious history and the history of Buddhism in the West specifically. Like many Black Americans, Turner was raised in a religious culture shaped by forms of Afro-Protestant Christianity. Yet, Turner's own religious trajectory stands outside of Afro-Protestant Christianity because of her incorporation of metaphysical ideas into her beliefs and her eventual conversion to Buddhism. This captures the religious pluralism that has characterized African American religious experience specifically and American religious experience more broadly.

As a religious authority figure, Turner is specifically a Black Buddhist teacher, as is her Soka Gakkai Nichiren Buddhist practice. By dispensing her teachings in a written memoir, Turner has contributed to the growing body of twenty-first-century Black Buddhist writings. These include the published memoirs of Jan Willis and Faith Adiele, and the writings of Lama Rod Owens, Ruth King, bell hooks, Reverend angel Kyodo Williams, Zenju Earthlyn Manuel, and others. The memoirs, writings, and academic publications have established these figures as prominent Black Buddhist teachers. While Turner joins them as an author, she also differs from them in a significant way. As a recording and performing artist with a global platform, Turner's reflections and teachings are disseminated on a wider scale. Turner has recorded her teachings on albums, evoked them in a staggering number of media profiles, had her religiosity represented in film and theater, and used her religious faith and practice to craft global concert tours that function as arenas of spiritual experience for millions of fans. Her career success—the success of her brand as Tina Turner—augments and partially constitutes her religious authority. In this regard, Turner might be considered one of the world's most prominent Black Buddhist teachers.

In this context, Turner's public sharing of her story of abuse, abandonment, and ultimate triumph, precipitated by her conversion to Buddhism, has done much to bring Buddhism to the fore of American popular culture and American religious history. More than a figure of popular culture, Turner has been a significant catalyst for changes in American religion, bringing greater awareness and acceptance of Buddhism to the mainstream through the commercial projects and media profiles that have centered her religious beliefs. Buddhism is a vital dimension of African American religious life. Turner has contributed immensely to this vitality. Scholarship on the history of Buddhism in the West and in the United States has often noted how the voices, presence, and significance of African Americans have been regularly neglected in these histories.[11]

Toward the end of their conversation, Larry King asked Turner if she believed that she had been "here before." In other words, did Turner, as a Buddhist, believe that she herself had lived previous lives? With a smile, Turner answered in the affirmative and explained that in a previous birth, some 3,500 years ago, she had been the Egyptian queen Hatshepsut. At this, Turner and King shared a laugh; they went on to conclude the conversation with Turner's hope-filled vision of the coming millennium based on the Buddhist principle of cause and effect. Turner's response to King's final question drew upon the full spectrum of her combinatory religious sensibilities. In *this* life, Turner's religious beliefs found their origins in her early life in West Tennessee. To understand Tina Turner's religious journey, we start there, in the small community of Nutbush.

1

Motherless Child

I felt like a complete outsider, the only one of my kind. So I just went off by myself, out in the world, to walk in the pastures and be with the animals. I was lonely, but I didn't dwell on it. I just said, "Okay," and I became accustomed to it, I guess. I had my own other thing going, my own world. And that was the beginning for me. I didn't have anybody, really, no foundation in life, so I had to make my own way. Always. From the start. I had to go out in the world and become strong, to discover my mission in life.

—Tina Turner, *I, Tina*

Located just off Highway 19 in Brownsville, Tennessee, Woodlawn Missionary Baptist Church stands today, as it did in the 1940s and 1950s, as an imposing redbrick building with white columns. A set of stairs leads up to the glass front doors, through which a small foyer leads to the sanctuary. In the 1940s, many families from the surrounding communities of Nutbush and Flagg Grove worshiped at Woodlawn. The Bullock family—comprised of Floyd (Richard), Zelma, and their two daughters, Alline and Anna Mae—was one of the families that faithfully attended church services at Woodlawn.

In those days, church services would start anywhere between eleven and eleven thirty in the morning and end sometime around one thirty or two o'clock in the afternoon. While the core of Sunday services was the preacher's sermon, music was an integral part of the program at Wood-lawn. The church featured both a junior choir and an adult choir, accom-panied by a single piano. The choir would sing traditional hymns, and as newer gospel songs were released, they would incorporate those songs into their repertoire. As a member of the junior choir, the youngest of the two Bullock girls, Anna Mae, was known for having a strong, beautiful voice that could sing alto, soprano, or even tenor parts as necessary. During some services, Anna Mae would take the lead part of a song with the choir backing her up. "I know a man from Galilee," she might sing. "If you're a sinner he'll set you free," she would continue, before building toward the song's chorus, which was driven by the rhetorical question, "Do you know him?" During other services, the choir would sing standards, such as "Amazing Grace" and "Jesus Keep Me Near the Cross." The hymns and gospel songs that were a regular feature of services at Woodlawn Mission-ary Baptist Church—and other local churches like the nearby Spring Hill Baptist Church—would have a long-lasting effect on Anna Mae Bullock when she grew up to be Tina Turner.[1]

Tina Turner was born Anna Mae Bullock on Sunday morning, Novem-ber 26, 1939, in Brownsville, Tennessee. Evidence of the combinatory sensibilities that would characterize her religious life was already starting to emerge in her early years. Turner lived much of her early life between worlds. In the first of these, she was alienated and insecure. Her parents, Zelma Priscilla Currie and Floyd Richard Bullock (Richard), constantly fought at home, and she felt ignored and unwanted. But in the world of her imagination, out in nature and free of the difficulties at home, she felt a peace and belonging all her own. Outside, she roamed the pastures, climbed trees, and played with animals, using the natural environment of Nutbush and her imagination to construct a personal spiritual world, and found a peace there that was absent in her family. This inner peace mirrored the tranquillity of Nutbush's rural environs, and it would precip-itate a lifelong affinity for exploring correspondences between her inner world and the external world around her. Though she later explained that she had nobody, and no basis in life, she found that in nature she could be her own foundation. Much later, she would discover that being her own foundation was akin to the concept of buddha-nature as espoused by Soka Gakkai Nichiren Buddhists, but at this early stage it remained a simple assurance that she had herself, if no one else. And in the world of church performances, she hit her stride, singing in the choir and at local picnics, where she was allowed to be her energetic and expressive self. Picnics and church were stages before which she found receptive audiences, unlike at home, where myriad forces combined to shrink the amount of attention available for a young child.

In many ways, Turner couldn't help but be torn by forces bigger than herself. She was born at the end of the Great Depression, which had ripped through Tennessee, and on the eve of World War Two.[2] The war effort would eventually see her parents move to Knoxville for work opportunities, further fracturing her already contentious home life. After their move, Alline Bullock, Turner's older sister, was sent to live with their warm, maternal grandparents. Turner landed with Roxanna Bullock, her strict, Black Baptist paternal grandmother. Her parents returned, but their domestic situation rapidly deteriorated and eventually both parents abandoned each other and their children. As Turner shuffled from relative to relative, she later described herself as feeling alone, like an outsider. One day, she imagined, her worlds would combine into a foundation that would serve as the platform to carry her beyond the cotton fields of Nutbush, Tennessee, to some other stage, perhaps even a world stage.

Nutbush, Haywood County, Tennessee

Located in Haywood County, Tennessee, Nutbush was a small agricultural town in the early decades of the twentieth century, situated approximately seventy miles northeast of Memphis and nearly two hundred miles southwest of Nashville. Today, Haywood County's official website describes it as "a progressive community that has learned from its historical past about growing a thriving community." For Black people in 1940s' Haywood County, their historical past was shaped by the legacy of slavery. During the antebellum period, Black people were brought into nearby Brownsville via the Hatchie River, itself connected to the Mississippi River, as slaves. Farther south, Shelby County was established in 1819 on land acquired by the United States government from the Chickasaw. The town of Memphis was established the same year and incorporated seven years later. To supply labor for the farms of Haywood County, Memphis created a slave trade with enslaved people transported from St. Louis, New Orleans, West Virginia, and North Carolina.[3] In 1865, the US institution of slavery officially ended. During the Reconstruction Era that followed, cotton's importance in the postwar economy grew, even as the South struggled to control the loss of Black labor. The exploitative system of sharecropping arose to fill this gap.[4] Many African American families found themselves entering sharecropping arrangements with white landholders in Haywood County.

Black Southern Religious Culture

Though the sharecropping system ensured that racial inequality remained a defining feature of their lives, African Americans still made unprecedented gains during the Reconstruction Era, with the help of organizations like the Freedmen's Bureau. They endeavored to reconstitute their families, marry, and acquire land for farming, and to build institutions.

Churches were among the most crucial of the institutions that African Americans sought to build. "During Reconstruction," American religious historian Paul Harvey explains, "churches provided an indispensable public forum where African American men and women could advocate, organize, and agitate in their own defense."[5] These churches were founded across the upper and lower South. Along with founding independent churches, African Americans also founded denominational institutions, such as mission societies and publishing boards (77). Black churches often combined African American religious practices that arose during the antebellum period, including the chanted sermon, the practice of the ring shout, and spirituals (49), with the worship styles prevalent in Black denominations, especially Black Baptist churches (69). Black church membership grew steadily toward the end of the nineteenth century. By 1906, one organization, the National Baptist Convention, claimed more than half of all Black church attendees (72).

An important element in the success of these churches was the preacher. Some preachers were well educated and institutionally minded, like Hardin Smith—discussed in detail later—who founded several churches (and schools) in Haywood County, including Woodlawn Missionary Baptist Church. Other preachers across the upper and lower South bore little to no education but effectively guided congregations nonetheless. The preacher's sermon was at the core of their church services. The content of these sermons was as varied as the preaching styles used to deliver them, distinguished mainly by the way the preachers paced their sermons, their sense of sermonic timing, the inflection of their words, or the musicality of their speech.[6] Emphasis could be placed on the last of these to such a degree that the sermon would be whooped in the form of the "chanted sermon."

Historian of African American religion Albert J. Raboteau explains that a chanted sermon has three distinct movements. The first sees the preacher "speaking in conversational, if oratorical and occasionally grandiloquent, prose." In the second movement, the preacher "gradually begins to speak more rapidly, excitedly, and to chant his words in time to a regular beat." Finally, the preacher reaches "an emotional peak in which his chanted speech becomes tonal and merges with the singing, clapping, and shouting of the congregation."[7]

That emotional peak is the place where, as scholar of homiletics Evans E. Crawford aptly summarized, "meter and message not only meet but celebrate."[8] As a celebration, the chanted sermon, combined with the call-and-response model of participation common in Afro-Protestant churches, rendered the preacher's sermon into a communal event in which the entire church participated.[9]

As central as preachers and their sermons were to church services, it was the laity, especially older Black women, who formed the backbone of Afro-Protestant churches.[10] American religious historian Anthea Butler explains that older African American women, known as "church mothers," were (and remain) as "much of a fixture as the role of preacher" in Black churches, though this fact is often "obscured by traditional roles of preaching and patriarchal leadership within the black church."[11] As fixtures of the Black church, church mothers often serve as spiritually authoritative figures within their religious communities.[12]

Within the institutional structure of the Black Baptist church, African American women organized in 1900, under the auspices of Nannie Burroughs, the Woman's Convention, an auxiliary to the National Baptist Convention. Burroughs also ran a training school that aimed to instruct African American women in the virtues of the Bible, the bath, and the broom, emphasizing the morality of cleanliness.[13] Burroughs and other African American women wove together biblical teachings and ideas about cleanliness, self-help, self-respect, and professionalism into what eminent historian Evelyn Brooks Higginbotham called "the politics of respectability."[14] With this politics of respectability, Black Baptist women sought to make manners and morality the primary weapons with which to counter negative portrayals of African Americans in the white supremacist structures of American society.[15] Even as the institutional force of Afro-Protestant Christianity—with its two primary axes of authority in the preacher and the church mother—held sway across the American South, religion in a Black southern context was not limited to institutional expressions.

Traditions of conjure and root work, and the importance of dreams, visions, and divination practices, permeated Black southern religious culture. Yvonne P. Chireau defines "conjure" as "a magical tradition in which spiritual power is invoked for various purposes, such as healing, protection, and self defense."[16] Central to the practice of conjure was the conviction that spirits and other supernatural entities could be called upon by a practitioner possessing extraordinary powers.[17] Chireau identifies such supernatural beliefs as a part of the "composite of cultural practices that emerged in the context of slave religion," which persists into the twenty-first century.[18] Similarly, root work was performed by specialists and "folk doctors" with knowledge of the natural world's plants and herbs, often for healing purposes. Conjure and root work functioned alongside careful attention to dreams, visions, and signs that signaled omens and foreknowledge of future events to lend a persistent orientation toward the supernatural in Black southern religious culture. While some interpreters of Black American religion have seen magical or supernatural beliefs as being antithetical to institutional forms of African American Christianity, supernatural beliefs often complemented and infused institutional forms, especially in rural southern areas such as Nutbush, Tennessee.

The elements of Black southern religious culture discussed above—the place of preachers and their sermons in Black Baptist churches; the role of church mothers as authoritative figures in the Black church; and the persistence of supernatural beliefs and practices—were ubiquitous features of the religious life of African American families in the towns and counties of West Tennessee on the eve of the Second World War. Tina Turner's family, the Bullocks, was one such family.

The Bullocks

In Nutbush, the Bullock family lived on the farm of a local white man named Vollye Poindexter. They worked the Poindexter farm as sharecroppers, with Turner's father, Richard, serving as one of the farm's overseers. While the Bullock family had a relative degree of material comfort on the Poindexter farm, this comfort existed within the social and political boundaries defined by the segregationist policies of Jim Crow, which ensured that Black people knew "their place" and stayed in it. Like what occurred in other cities across the Jim Crow South, the consequences for transgressing the limits of racial place were often lethal. Turner later wrote about the example of Elbert Williams, one of the first organizers for civil rights in the Haywood County area.[19] In 1940, Williams attempted to register Black voters. For his efforts, Williams became the last documented lynching victim in Tennessee.[20] Full participation in the political life of the county, like unrestrained participation in the social realm, remained a distant goal.

Still, Richard and Zelma were valued employees of the Poindexter family, and their congenial relations with the Poindexters made for hospitable circumstances for the Bullocks. Their wooden house was not far from the Poindexters' brick home. They maintained a shotgun-style home with a garden that seemed to the young Turner to cover an acre or so, replete with cabbage, onions, sweet potatoes, tomatoes, and watermelons. The family also kept their own animals nearby: cows, pigs, chickens, and horses. Thus, in Turner's estimation, her family was not necessarily poor, especially when compared to the other families she knew. For those families, she recalled dirty houses filled with children and the *smell* of poverty.

Regardless of the relative circumstances of each individual family, everyone's lives followed the rhythms of the land, in particular the cotton-planting and -harvesting seasons. Although Turner enjoyed the freedom she found outdoors, the realities of an agricultural economy were confining. In her first autobiography, *I, Tina*, Turner wrote,

One thing I couldn't fit into any kind of dream was picking cotton. God, I hated that—hated it. I mean, that wasn't glamorous at all, right? The cotton would have to be cultivated first, with the sharpened hoe and all, and then in July we'd have to pick it out of the husks. It was hot, and hard, and I was never very good at it; a sixty-pound bag was the most I was ever able to fill—half as much as a grown-up. We'd pick strawberries, too, a seasonal thing: When the crops came in, the people that owned the strawberry fields around there would hire the whole community to come and pick them, and we'd all make a little extra money from that. And there was corn to be cut, which the men did. But everybody worked on the cotton. I can still see those fields, the rows of cotton, the struggle of the country. Anna Mae out there, with her dreams.[21]

Nonetheless, the wilderness of Nutbush could also provide vital communion with the wonders of the natural world.

Turner would later recall with joy and fondness walking roads lined with honeysuckle, wrestling with horses and mules on the farm, and swinging over mud-water creeks. In the backwoods of Nutbush Turner dashed about, taking risks but doing her best to avoid snakes and other harmful creatures.[22] To her, the bright, hot noon sun was a source of beautiful light, while the night sky was filled with wonder and mysticism. These feelings of delight would have to sustain her through the domestic chaos of her home life.

By the time Turner was born, Zelma and Richard's relationship was breaking down. Their fights would begin as screaming matches and turn into violent rows. Turner later told Oprah Winfrey that she remembers her mother fighting her father with "sticks of wood and everything."[23] Their fighting also affected the way they dealt with the children. Turner felt her mother to be affectionate with her older sister, Alline, but less so with her. When Zelma combed Alline's hair, it was a soft, tender moment of mother-daughter bonding; when she combed Turner's hair, her manner was gruff, her touch was rough. When Alline committed some infraction or another, the whipping switch was slow to come; for Turner, it seemed that even the most minor trouble would lead to a swift lashing. She later wrote: "It was all right when Alline came along—even if she was the reason they had to get married—but then the marriage went bad, and when my mother all of a sudden became pregnant with me . . . well, today it would be abortion time, I think."[24] Zelma explained, "My husband and I weren't getting along too good. But, I had her . . . and I'm proud of her."[25] Turner surmised that she arrived at a difficult time in her parents' marriage. In her estimation, the problem was that Zelma was in the process of trying to leave Richard when she discovered she was pregnant again. This stymied her plans to leave and rendered Turner an unwelcome pregnancy. The continuous cycle of violence and perceptions of being unwanted rendered her home environment less than ideal. So, Turner turned to the natural environment.

Turner's turn to the natural world connects her to the "wilderness experience" of African American women, named by womanist theologian Delores S. Williams. In *Sisters in the Wilderness*, Williams defines the wilderness experience as representative of a "near-destruction situation in which God gives personal direction to the believer and thereby helps her make a way out of what she thought was no way."[26] Drawing on the biblical story of Hagar, who twice flees into the wilderness, encountering an angel the first time and God the second time, Williams explains that the wilderness experience for Hagar and Black women means "standing utterly alone, in the midst of serious trouble, with only God's support to rely on," and it symbolizes a "risk-taking faith."[27] Wilderness, in this understanding, becomes a place of encounter where African Americans, especially Black women, gain the knowledge necessary to survive both social and personal experiences of suffering. Williams sees Hagar and the wilderness as a model for understanding the womanhood of non-middle-class Black women. The politics of respectability promulgated by Black Baptist women like Nannie Burroughs shunned nature and developed from Victorian notions of true womanhood. Yet, this was an educated, elite, middle-class-to-upper-middle-class model. To Williams, it does not account for Black women who, like Hagar, turned to nature to find solace and guidance.[28]

Consequently, the respectability model of Black womanhood cannot account for Tina Turner's experiences in the backwoods of Nutbush, Tennessee. Indeed, Turner's paternal grandmother, Roxanna Bullock, was a stark representative of the respectable Black Baptist woman who did not endorse wild behavior and would not have accepted Williams's notion of the wilderness. Contrary to her paternal grandmother, Turner described nature as "the only place where I always felt welcome and enjoyed a sense of belonging—my truest childhood home."[29] Statements like these show that Nutbush's rural backwoods served as sites of the wilderness experience for Turner. However, Turner never alludes to Nutbush's wilderness as a site where she finds God, unlike the experience Williams names. The wilderness seemingly remains for Turner a place where she communes with nature itself and thereby communes with herself. Tellingly, she linked this love of nature not to her paternal grandparents but rather to her maternal grandparents, Josephus Cecil Currie and Georgianna Flagg. It was from Georgianna Flagg that Turner's spiritual affinity for the natural world began to form.

The Flaggs

Josephus Cecil Currie was born in August 1883 in Madison County, Tennessee, and Georgianna Flagg was born in February 1887 in Haywood County. They had seven children and looked after many of their grandchildren, including Turner herself at different points over the years. Josephus Currie worked the farm on which they lived in various capacities, while Georgianna Flagg—whom Turner affectionately called Mama Georgie—was a domestic worker. "Oh, Mama Georgie," Turner recalled. "She wore men's shoes, and a shirt over the top of her dress, and she looked totally Indian—had the layered look before anyone thought to call it fashionable."[30] The family legend went that Georgianna, Zelma, and others on that side of the family were primarily of Native American ancestry. Given their physiognomy—high cheekbones, straight black hair, and sharp features—and their proximity to central Tennessee, originally the Cherokee Nation, it seemed to them only natural that they were more Native American than African American. To Turner, this also explained Georgianna Flagg's affinities for "mother nature."

Turner felt her grandmother, as a Native American woman, possessed a special sense of oneness with nature; and she steadily hummed, creating a peaceful atmosphere regardless of life's vicissitudes. Turner explained to a journalist that Flagg "was spiritual, although she did not go to church, but she had the hum. She used to tell me stories of the rivers."[31] As Georgianna Flagg taught her about rivers and nature, Turner developed a sense that there were "unseen universal forces" around her, and that by communing with those forces, she could develop her own intuition.

Turner's memory of Georgianna Flagg's aesthetic, the stories she told, and the lessons she taught closely tied Flagg to the land of Nutbush and its surrounding communities. Turner's reflections accord with the ways that other African American women have perceived their own mothers and grandmothers. For example, compare Turner's reflections on Flagg to those of activist and spiritual teacher Rosemarie Freeney Harding (1930–2004) regarding her own mother. In Harding's memoir, *Remnants*, she wrote that her mother's and great-grandmother's "manner in the world pointed toward rootedness, a very old strength. They were trusted women. They were healers." Through their "rootedness" they taught Harding "to recognize the reality of spirit in the world through those stories passed to her, in the southwest Georgia woods, by her elders like Grandma Rye."[32] In moments of difficulty Harding found that her mother would go quiet, and, like Turner's grandmother, she would hum subtly. Just as Turner's grandmother would tell stories of the rivers dotting West Tennessee's delta landscape, so too would Harding's great-grandmother spend time at the river, fishing quietly.[33] As Harding observed the women in her family, their moments of quiet, their understanding of nature, their careful attention to signs, dreams, visions, spirits, and liminal boundaries,[34] she named a "streak of unspoken mysticism" in their bloodline.[35] Elsewhere, Harding considered these to be the features of an African American mysticism that pervades African American religious history, especially in a Black southern context.[36] Harding's understanding is an alternate way of expressing the persistence of supernatural beliefs and practice in Black southern religious culture. For Turner, this streak of Black southern religiosity that runs in her family, most pronounced in the person of her grandmother Georgianna Flagg, was attributable to her Native American ancestry.

And yet, later research into their family's DNA and ancestry, done by historian Henry Louis Gates Jr., showed that in fact Turner herself was only 1 percent Native American, of an indeterminate tribe. Gates's research returned surprising results: "Her admixture test clearly indicates that the family legend is just that: legend. She is 66 percent sub-Saharan African, 33 percent European, and 1 percent Native American. . . . If both of Tina's maternal grandparents had been three-quarters Native American, the ad-mixture test would have indicated a 37 percent result, not a 1 percent result. One percent Native American ancestry means that Tina has one great-great-great-great-grandparent who was Native American. This person probably lived around 1770, maybe earlier. That is simply not a significant amount of Native American ancestry, despite the family legend."[37] Gates painstakingly explained to Turner that Native Americans and African

Americans had only three periods of significant interaction: the early colonial era, the mid-1700s, and again throughout the eighteenth century.[38] In Turner's DNA, except for that single distant grandparent, interaction was nonexistent. Thus, the aesthetic features that they identified as Native American likely came from white settlers and slave owners, and the illicit and often violent sexual relations that occurred during slavery. Rather than see Flagg's humming, spiritual attunement to the natural world and her wisdom stories as evidence of Native American heritage, as Turner herself believed, Flagg is instead better seen as exemplifying the mystical and supernatural tendencies that pervade Black southern religious history.

When Gates conveyed this information to Turner in August of 2007, she was shocked, but Georgianna, Josephus, and Zelma were long gone. The information never affected their self-identification, and the legend of their family's Native American ancestry continued. Perhaps the specificity of the familial legend of their ancestry persisted for Turner because of what it and Georgianna Flagg came to represent to her: comfort, home, peace, acceptance. No DNA test is powerful enough to shift that.

Roxanna Bullock

Turner's paternal grandmother, on the other hand, was Black Baptist. The stiff atmosphere that prevailed at Alex and Roxanna Bullock's home was an anxiety-producing contrast to the open, relaxed, nature-loving atmosphere at Georgianna and Josephus's house. Alex Bullock Jr. was born in Haywood County on November 23, 1882; Roxanna Bullock was born in March of 1888. They had thirteen sons and one daughter. This provided a host of cousins for Turner when she eventually came to live with them in the 1940s.

With the United States' full engagement in World War II, new opportunities arose for Black Americans. By 1942, the United States was struggling to develop a nuclear weapon before the Nazi government could develop one, under the auspices of the Manhattan Project. Research for the Manhattan Project started in 1939, but in 1942 a sense of urgency was added to the project, and a diffusion plant was constructed in Oak Ridge, Tennessee. With the construction of the plant came an increased demand for labor both in the plant and in the adjacent factories: builders, janitors, domestic help, and so forth. Zelma and Richard sought to take advantage of these opportunities and moved 350 miles east of Nutbush to Knoxville, Tennessee, near Oak Ridge. Just before they moved, they sent their daughter Alline to live with Georgianna Flagg and Turner to live with Roxanna Bullock. Zelma never gave any indication of why the sisters were separated or the rationale for which grandparents received the girls. In this case, Alline was the more fortunate of the two. Turner recalled that "Mama Georgie was great. She'd never beat us if we were bad; she'd just hit us on the elbow with a stick of wood, or pop us on the head with a spoon, and we'd go, 'Wowww!' It didn't really hurt, but just the same, you wouldn't want to let her get near you with that spoon, or the stick. She was fun, mainly. I loved her. There was a lot of love there with the Indians, just natural affection, and that was where I wanted to be."[39] But Turner was sent to live with Richard's parents, where things were decidedly different:

> Mama Roxanna was a big woman with fair skin and long hair mingled with silver, and she was a church woman—wore Dr. Scholl's shoes, and the hair pulled back in a ball. She was a seamstress, and in her house dresses stayed washed, starched, and ironed. And the house was spotless, of course. All I ever wanted to do was get out of there—out in the fields, out with the animals. But she held me prisoner. She'd always make me sit in some damned chair. I hated it. I was never one for sitting still, and I was never one for a dress, either.[40]

Roxanna's husband, Alex, was a hard-living, drinking man, a bit of a rolling stone. He had no particular religious beliefs, at least none that Turner could identify. She thought his most dapper day was his own funeral in 1954.

Roxanna Bullock, though, was a devout Baptist and zealous attendee of Woodlawn Missionary Baptist Church. And she epitomizes the politics of respectability that Higginbotham theorized as characterizing the women's movement in the Black Baptist church between 1900 and 1920. In this model, as explained above, manners or decorum and morality were seen as the tools that African American women had to counter negative stereotypes about Black people in American society. Life at Bullock's home, particularly Bullock's emphasis on prayer, decorum, and cleanliness, echoed the training in the three *B*s—bible, bath, and broom—that were the hallmarks of Nancy Burroughs's training school. The three *B*s index a host of virtues like self-reliance, self-respect, and professionalism seen as constitutive of the ideal Black woman. As Higginbotham explains it, "By claiming respectability through their manners and morals, poor black women boldly asserted the will and agency to define themselves outside the parameters of prevailing racist discourses."[41] By keeping an orderly home and participating in church, Bullock likely sought to internalize a subjectivity worthy of respect in line with the ideals of the women's movement of the early twentieth century. Under Bullock's roof, Turner would be forced to internalize these same values. And through Bullock, Turner was introduced to *church*.

Woodlawn Missionary Baptist Church

The Bullock family worshiped at Woodlawn Missionary Baptist Church, where her father, Richard, served as a deacon. When the church began, its congregation met and worshiped under the canopy of a brush arbor.[42] State of Tennessee House Joint Resolution 1026, put forward by Representative Craig Fitzhugh, whose district includes Haywood County, acknowledged the 150th anniversary of the church's founding, noting that the current building dates to 1928, with bricks used from its original incarnation.[43]

The church was first established as the Woodlawn Colored Baptist Church, out of the efforts of the Reverend Hardin Smith. Born as a slave in Virginia in March 1829, Hardin, his mother, and six siblings were sold to a landowner in Haywood County around ten years later. Smith was taught to read in secret by his owner's wife. At the age of sixteen, Hardin was given permission to minister to slaves in night services at the all-white Woodlawn Baptist Church in Nutbush. At the same time, in clandestine meetings near Brownsville's Hatchie River, he preached and taught a slave congregation.[44] Receiving his training from New York City's Baptist Home Mission Society, a forerunner of today's American Baptist Home Mission Societies, Hardin was able to acquire a combined estate of $700 by 1870.[45] He used these resources and joined forces with both the Freedmen's Bureau and the white residents of Nutbush to form the Woodlawn Colored Baptist Church, which became Woodlawn Missionary Baptist Church.[46] Hardin also founded other churches in the area, including Spring Hill

Baptist Church, where the Bullock family sometimes worshiped. For Hardin, who contributed substantially to the educational development of the county, church, school, and communal uplift were the keys to creating a thriving Haywood County. Tina Turner's grandmother Roxanna Bullock participated wholeheartedly in the legacy left by Hardin Smith.

In Turner's eyes, Mama Roxanna was in church every day and "on her knees every night praying, and in the morning, too. Praying and praying. Just a full-on Baptist."[47] In contrast, Papa Alex "was a drunk." His weekends were reserved for drinking until he fell unconscious and Turner, her cousins, and Alline when she was visiting would use the opportunity to put "makeup on him, lipstick and everything, and paint little faces on his head."[48] At their home, Turner's carefree, nature-loving inclinations were sharply curtailed. She had to attend church and Sunday school, every Sunday. It left such an impression on her that later, in 1973, she emphasized the lyric "go to church *every* Sunday in ole Nutbush" in her autobiographical song "Nutbush City Limits."

Just as Roxanna Bullock regulated Turner's behavior in the home, she also watched over Turner and the other children during services at Woodlawn. As an elder and long-standing member of Woodlawn, Bullock was a church mother who sat in the "mother's corner" of the women's side of the church. The church had two main aisles dividing the pews into three sections. Congregants were separated by gender so that men sat on one side of the church and women sat on the other side, with children seated in the middle. Placed between their parents and other adults of the community, the children were carefully observed for any signs of misbehavior. Bullock and the other mothers would ensure that the children held to the standards of Black Baptist respectability. But her granddaughter was observed even more carefully. Turner was expected to be a model of orderly comportment for other children since she was a member of the junior choir. Instead of being seated with the other children, Turner sat directly in front of the mother's corner, along with her friend Robbie Ewing (née Brack).[49]

Ewing fondly remembers those years at Woodlawn with Turner. Sitting in front of Roxanna Bullock and the other church mothers, Ewing knew that "good children" kept still for the duration of church services. The adults too knew the requirements of respectable comportment: congregants dressed neatly in their Sunday best; female ushers wore clean white dresses with white gloves; the men sported black suits with neat ties. The Sunday service at Woodlawn followed a regular sequence: a deacon, kneeling before the altar, "resting on [his] knees to pray to God," led a prayer. Readings from the Bible followed. After this, the choir—accompanied by a single piano—would sing traditional hymns and whatever new gospel songs had made their way to Nutbush from Chicago, Memphis, or Nashville. Then the preacher would preach his sermon. Between 1942 and 1956, while Turner and the Bullock family attended Woodlawn, the church was pastored by the Reverend A. J. Caldwell (tenure from 1942 to 1954) and then by the Reverend B. T. Hopkins (tenure from 1954 to 1961).[50] The former was particularly formative for both Ewing and Turner.

Congregants at Woodlawn knew Rev. Caldwell as a rousing preacher who often led them to an emotive frenzy in the chanted sermon style of delivery discussed above. His sermons began in an orderly manner with a clear outline. Caldwell frequently preached about the Ten Commandments, taking time to dwell at length on each commandment. Robbie Ewing gauged that this was because "we really needed to know God and not put anything before him." He also preached at length about the Lord's Prayer as a model for Baptist faith and practice. As Caldwell's sermons progressed, he laid greater stress on the musicality of his sermon, approaching the chanted style of delivery, supported by the pianist. Ewing remembers church attendees responding to Caldwell's chant with fervent "amens" and becoming "very emotional." Occasionally someone would shriek, "Glory hallelujah!" amid tears of joy. Evans Crawford explained that when this happens during a sermon, the congregation is "expressing the joy of feeling with all their heart that the spirit has worked through the preacher and themselves to bring them into the joyful, redemptive presence of God."[51] Ewing remembers that even as a young girl she could feel the power of Caldwell's sermons: "[Caldwell's sermons] really struck a note with me and from that time on I always respected God as my personal savior; I've never put anything before him." Caldwell also holds particular significance for Ewing, as it was under him that she and Turner received their "blessings from God." In other words, Caldwell baptized them.[52]

As a child, Turner experienced the Baptist church as hot and boring. The church building had no air-conditioning, and she found the preacher's sermonizing to be inscrutable: "it was baffling to my young mind that everyone got all dressed up just to go and sit in a hot oven and listen to someone lecture. I never understood what the preacher was talking about, since no one bothered to explain it to the children."[53] Her grandmother's constant praying stayed with her, though, as she later told Gates: "I can relate to the praying, because I kind of picked it up in life and it got me through. But she was the real thing."[54] Still, if that was all church was, there wasn't much for her to attach to. However, while her parents lived in Knoxville, Turner was introduced to a new worship style in the form of a sanctified church.

The Pentecostal Experience

Zelma and Richard brought Alline and Turner to live with them during the summer of their second year in Knoxville. In Knoxville, Zelma also sang in a church choir.[55] For Turner, who was almost five, and Alline, who was almost eight, the city was a new world. Where Nutbush had dirt and gravel roads, Knoxville had paved streets. Nutbush had wooden, shotgun houses; Knoxville had two-story brick homes. While horses were still the common means of transportation in Nutbush, Knoxville had cars everywhere. Though she still felt that her mother was cold toward her, Zelma would sometimes take her and Alline shopping in Knoxville. Turner recalls the shop attendants and sales associates giving her money for making up songs and singing in the store. Looking back, she saw them as her first paying audience. To Turner, Knoxville shined with an aura of fun and newness. Even the worship was different there. Knoxville, of course, also had Black Baptist churches, but while Zelma worked as a domestic laborer and Richard worked at the plant at Oak Ridge, they left their daughters in the care of a Mrs. Blake, a friend of the owner of their residence in the Knoxville area. Mrs. Blake was Pentecostal, and would take the girls to a sanctified, Pentecostal church with her. "I didn't know what 'sanctified' meant, but I loved that it was totally different from our Baptist church back in Nutbush," Turner later recalled.[56] Signs of this difference grabbed her attention as congregants at the sanctified church "got . . . the 'Spirit,' they danced, clapped their hands, and sang at the top of their lungs."[57] In other ways, she found that these "sanctified people were a little weird—they'd fall out and go into spasms and things. I didn't know what that was about. I just thought, 'Well, they must be real happy.'"[58] Nonetheless, she saw that, weird or not, "they were possessed by God and music." With the latter she could definitely join in, singing and dancing with them. Zelma later remembered that her young daughter "could really do that holy dance. Picked it up just like that, you know? She was always quick to catch on to things"—a comment that showed that her mother was not as inattentive as Turner imagined.[59] When Turner would attend Woodlawn with Roxanna Bullock in Nutbush, she had to be respectable, she had to sit still and model good behavior to others. At the Pentecostal church with Mrs. Blake in Knoxville, on the other hand, Turner could express her natural propensities to run by joining in the "holy dance" in the aisles of the church.

The anthropologist and folklorist Zora Neale Hurston coined the phrase "sanctified church" to describe the wide variety of churches that emerged from the nineteenth-century Holiness Pentecostal movement.[60] These churches emphasized being "'filled with the spirit' after conversion and expressing their rapture through bodily trances, speaking in tongues, and enthusiastic music."[61] The Spirit-filled, ecstatic worship experience is exemplified by Charles Harrison Mason. Mason began his career as a Baptist minister in Mississippi. He wandered as an itinerant folk preacher before eventually participating in the 1906 Azusa Street revival in Los Angeles, under William J. Seymour. Praying through the night, Mason had a vision of himself being possessed by the Holy Spirit. As a result of this possession, Mason drew spiritual images and wrote inspired messages, and he spoke in tongues. Filled with the Spirit and employing his considerable skill as a preacher, Mason made a name for himself and eventually established the Church of God in Christ (COGIC) in Memphis, Tennessee. COGIC became the largest and most influential Black Pentecostal organization.[62]

As both Chireau and Harvey have noted, Black Pentecostal churches carried forward many of the supernatural traditions of Black southern religious culture.[63] Chireau explains that "Pentecostal belief revolved around invisible forces, beings, and powers in the spiritual realm, and like the Conjure practitioners, Pentecostalists viewed unusual events as signs of divine or satanic intervention in the physical realm."[64] In addition to the invocation of spiritual powers and healing, Spirit possession, dreams, and signs all found a place in the nineteenth-century African American Holiness movement and in the twentieth-century Pentecostal movement. The enthusiastic music that Harvey discussed encouraged the incorporation of the ring shout practice of enslaved African Americans as the holy dance.[65] While Black Pentecostal church services held much in common with mainline African American Protestant churches, their services were distinguished by the emphasis on ecstatic worship and supernatural beliefs.

Just as in Black Baptist churches, women were central to Black Pentecostal churches. In addition to their role as church mothers, older African American women served in a variety of authoritative capacities in Black Pentecostal churches. "Women's voices in the pulpit," Harvey explains, "in prophesying, and in church leadership were far more common in what were perceived to be fringe sects" like COGIC.[66] Though Charles Harrison Mason rejected the ordination of women as bishops, women were able to exercise authority in other areas of the church.

In *Women in the Church of God in Christ*, Anthea Butler argued that through belief in the notion of sanctification—the holiness obtained through the creation of moral authority as a result of fasting, prayer, and other practices—COGIC women exercised power through their own purity, and thus often did not seek authority derived from ordination.[67] Beyond this, because COGIC services also incorporated new musical instruments like the guitar, new performative possibilities arose for women. In Church of God in Christ services, women gave moving testimonies and sang. Cultural historian Jerma A. Jackson explained that as COGIC women "raised themselves before the congregation to sing and share their personal experiences of the Holy Spirit, sanctified women developed critical, musical, and leadership abilities."[68]

Ecstatic worship, including inspired utterances and holy dancing; women in a variety of authoritative roles; and enthusiastic music incorporating novel instruments—these were the differences that Turner saw before her at the sanctified church in Knoxville. Turner encountered new performative possibilities there, and a freedom of expression that seemingly undermined the respectable strictures of worship at the Black Baptist churches of Nutbush.

However, appearances can be deceiving. Since Turner only briefly attended the Pentecostal church in Knoxville and was a young child, she did not know that the performative possibilities she saw at sanctified churches belied a world of controlled behavior and theological strictures. Because of their belief in sanctification, Black Pentecostal women, like those in COGIC, were "unbounded in worship yet bounded in behavior and appearance" even as they shifted away from mainline African American Protestant churches' attempts to emulate staid white church cultures.[69] Had Turner known that Black Pentecostal women engaged in fasting, strict biblical study, and intensive periods of prayer in order to live in a state of holiness, a state as much cultural and aesthetic as it was theological,[70] she would have seen that they had more in common with her grandmother Roxanna Bullock and Black Baptist respectability than first meets the eye. Regardless, her worship experiences in Knoxville would have a lasting impact on her understanding of the possibilities of church, music, and performance.

Eventually, Alline and Anna Mae returned to their grandparents' homes in Nutbush. For Turner, it was back to the strictures of Mama Roxanna, Baptist church, and Sunday school. Recalling her feelings about church as a child, Turner felt that, at least from what she could glean of the theology—a "bearded old white man in space, monitoring activities here on Earth"—neither the "Pentecostal experience" nor "the quieter Baptist services" resonated much, but that at least the former was "fun."[71] Undoubtedly, though, her feelings changed, as she would later describe herself as Buddhist-Baptist; recall the influence of Roxanna Flagg Bullock; and fondly discuss her Black Baptist upbringing in *Happiness Becomes You*. Therefore, whatever Turner's childhood feelings about Black Baptist and Pentecostal theology, her experiences in church were formative for her.

Nonetheless, when her parents returned to Nutbush from Knoxville, she no longer had to live with Roxanna Flagg and her strict Baptist ways. Eventually, the family moved to Flagg Grove, adjacent to Nutbush, before they settled in Spring Hill. Inspired by her experiences with Mrs. Blake at the sanctified church, Turner looked forward to singing in the choir at Spring Hill Baptist Church. At eight or nine years old, she remembers being the youngest singer in the choir, and surrounded by teenagers. The choir sang traditional hymns such as "Onward, Christian Soldiers" and "Amazing Grace." In Spring Hill's choir, she sang solos and danced, much as she did in Knoxville. Turner's choir antics were dramatized in the opening scene of *What's Love Got to Do with It?*, the 1993 Oscar-nominated biographical film based on her 1986 autobiography, *I, Tina*. When the movie begins, the viewers see a young Anna Mae Bullock (played by Rae'Ven Larrymore Kelly) dragged out of church by the choir director for overdelivering while singing "This Little Light of Mine," with her head swinging and shoulders bobbing up and down. Dramatized though the scene may be, one wonders how the more reserved choir and congregation at Spring Hill Baptist Church viewed the "sanctified" performance style that she learned in Knoxville.

Turner's Early Education

If church proved to be a permanent fixture in her life, school was decidedly less so. Turner attended several schools through the late forties and early fifties, and her elementary school itself illustrates the surprising connection between Turner's family and the land of Haywood County. She attended Flagg Grove Elementary School, housed in the Flagg Grove School House in Nutbush. Unbeknownst to her, the school was situated on land that once belonged to Benjamin Brown Flagg, Georgianna Flagg's uncle, and thus Turner's great-granduncle. In his research into her ancestry, Gates discovered that George Flagg, Georgianna's father, was born in May 1858 as a slave in North Carolina. Gates also discovered "a land deed filed January 26, 1889, which indicated that Benjamin B. Flagg, George Flagg's older brother, sold one acre of land that he owned in Haywood County, Tennessee, for twenty-five dollars in cash to a group of men identified as the trustees of the Flagg Grove School House. Now, at that time the going rate for land in Tennessee was approximately seventy-five or eighty-dollars an acre."[72] As Gates explains, Benjamin Flagg sold his land below the market-value rate of seventy-five or eighty dollars an acre. In so doing, he made it possible for the formation of Flagg Grove Elementary School. Flagg's acquisition of land can be seen against the larger backdrop of the efforts of Black Americans during the Reconstruction Era to advance after the end of slavery, as detailed by Gates. His sale of that land a decade or so after Reconstruction for the establishment of a school should be seen in the same light. Flagg Grove School served first as a subscription school and then became part of the public school system. The school remained active until the late 1960s.[73] However, Turner was unaware of this history. When she attended in the 1940s, it was fairly unremarkable in her appraisal: "Like other rural schools at the time, the Flagg Grove School in Nutbush was one big room, made of clapboard, and shared by three classes that were taught simultaneously."[74] When their family moved to the hamlet-like community of Spring Hill, she attended Johnson Grade School Annex, next to Lauderdale High School in Ripley, Tennessee. At age fourteen, she entered Lauderdale High School. Shortly after that, when she returned to Roxanna Bullock's house, she transferred to Carver High School in Brownsville.

In high school, she found new audiences, as she excelled in sports. Growing up, she described herself as a tomboy who would hunt alongside her father. This blossomed into a facility with any sport she tried. To Roy Bond, her principal at Brownsville's Carver High School, it seemed that she was fully involved in every aspect of the school. As he described her: "She was involved in everything. Basketball, cheerleading—she'd be on the court playing, and then she'd go put on a cheerleader's uniform and come back out and lead the cheers for us. If there was a track meet, she'd run track. She would have played football, too, if it had been allowed. She was a leader, an organizer—parties, sock hops, class trips. She might not have been an A student, but she made up for it with her energy."[75] His final comment is telling. Academically, she struggled with most subjects. Though she tried to compensate for her difficulties by taking harder subjects, she felt her studying was to no avail. She recalled occasionally being called to the blackboard to solve math problems and feeling "ashamed"; she added, "ashamed that I was standing there in front of all the other kids, failing, with numbers blurring in front of me because of my tears. My brain didn't have that ability."[76] This scene played itself out repeatedly throughout her educational life, convincing her that she was simply "not smart." This feeling stayed with her for much of her life, and she explained that she suffered because, she said, "I believed I had to hide my stupidity from my family and friends and, when I got older, my coworkers and managers." Years later, after suffering a stroke in 2013 at the age of seventy-three, she became interested in cognitive science. It was then that she learned she suffered from dyslexia and that the frontal lobes of her brain were damaged. Her doctors told her, as she put it, "The creative part of my brain was ablaze and working overtime, but I would never be good at counting or reading." Through her own research, she also learned that "when a person is raised in an environment of chronic instability and dysfunction, the synapses in the brain don't form optimally."[77] And indeed, her family life was a locus of instability and dysfunction.

Changing Family Dynamics

By 1950, Zelma and Richard's dysfunctional marriage was rapidly deteriorating. Ten-year-old Turner could feel something in the air, and then it happened. Zelma left Richard for good, leaving both children behind with their father. This left Turner depressed, dispirited, and resentful. While Zelma hadn't been affectionate, and her daughters had been passed around to various relatives over the years, at least she was *there*. But no longer. Turner hoped her mother would come back for her and went to the mailbox every day anticipating a letter sending for her; it never came. "How many years had I watched her acting like a real mother with Alline; . . . when she was happy; watched her in the kitchen on Sundays, sitting in the window, just staring out? Then one day she wasn't in that window anymore. And she was never in it again."[78] For his part, Richard quickly remarried and moved his daughters, new wife, and stepdaughter to the town of Ripley. When Richard attempted to beat his new wife, she fought back, as Zelma had, and even stabbed him. Then she took her daughter and left. Richard became depressed, and he stopped attending either of the family's churches, Woodlawn and Spring Hill Baptist. A shifting number of relatives were moved into the home to help with his daughters. Finally, in 1952, Turner's father left and moved to Detroit, which meant that Turner and Alline were placed in the care of yet more family members. As Turner neared her thirteenth birthday, she was now without both parents, and her sense of abandonment grew to an almost unbearable crescendo. She relied most heavily in this period on her connection to her cousins.

One cousin in particular, Margaret Currie, acted as a mother figure to the teenaged Turner. Since Margaret was older than Turner, she would often share stories of her exploits and experiences in the local towns of Brownsville and Ripley, such as going out to drink, party, and attend sports games. Turner mostly lived vicariously through Margaret's vivid retellings of her exploits, but occasionally Turner herself went into town. Ripley, Tennessee, had an area called "the Hole," which functioned much as Beale Street did in Memphis: it was the center of African American life in the town. There were movie theaters, juke joints, and food shacks down in the Hole. To Turner, the Hole was filled with the sights and sounds of a life more exciting than that offered in Nutbush. Being a young teenager, she gravitated mostly toward the blues music coming out of the juke joints and the glamorous world presented in movies she saw there, rather than the racier fun enjoyed by many. Margaret and Turner's older half sister, Evelyn, were no strangers to those racier elements. Soon Evelyn became pregnant, followed by Margaret in short order. This shocked Turner, because, though her cousin spent time in risqué environments, she always seemed so careful. Regardless, Turner relied upon Margaret as a dependable mother figure, and she followed her cousin's developments with interest.

One night, coming home late from a basketball game, Evelyn, Margaret, another cousin, and their driver were involved in a car accident. The driver of the car in which Turner rode had been drinking heavily, and he, Margaret, and Evelyn were all killed. Death was a new experience for Turner. Though Turner was thirteen when her grandfather Alex Bullock Jr. died in 1954, her conception of death had been childlike, and the significance of death escaped her. She mused: "I had been to Papa Alex's funeral, but I just thought he looked great in the casket, better than in life—all done up in a suit and tie, not acting crazy like he always did."[79] The accident left her half sister and cousin disfigured, and there was little the mortician could do to disguise this, so their joint open-casket funeral presented a gruesome sight. The mortuary sent their ripped and bloodied clothing back to their grandmother Georgianna Flagg, who kept the clothing as a sad memorial to her lost grandchildren. Seeing them in their caskets side by side, Turner began to understand the finality of death. She explained, "With Margaret and Evelyn, it was the first time I realized how cold death really was."[80] Margaret, her cousin and mother figure, was gone. Even as Turner was left shaken by the magnitude of these losses, she tried to carry on with the stabilizing force of high school. However, when her father stopped sending money to the relatives then caring for her and Alline, Turner was involuntarily returned to Mama Roxanna's home.

Roxanna Bullock was as strict and churchgoing as ever, so Turner was forced to return to her old routine of church and choir. Living with Mama Roxanna put her back in Haywood County, and she transferred from Lauderdale High School to Carver High School in Brownsville. At Carver, Turner's teachers and the principal, Mr. Bond, took an interest in her. Whenever she got into trouble, they reminded her that they expected better of her, and she took their advice to heart. Mr. Bond's daughter, Carolyn Bond, and Turner became fast friends. Carolyn experienced firsthand how insecure her friend was, as Turner struggled with her appearance, feelings of inferiority as a country girl, the death of her cousin, and Mama Roxanna's stern demeanor. Soon, she sought to counter these feelings by moving to Georgianna Flagg's house.

By the spring of 1956, Turner was sixteen years old and had neither seen nor heard from her mother, Zelma, since 1950. Zelma's mother, Georgianna Flagg, was supporting many of her grandchildren, including Turner, in her household. Zelma and her siblings often didn't return once they deposited their children with Flagg. To lighten her grandmother's load, Turner began working as a nanny for a white family in Ripley, who allowed her to live with them on the weekends. Turner traveled with the family to Dallas, and she relished the chance to experience a new city; however, the trip was curtailed when Turner received word that Flagg had suddenly died. When Turner returned to Nutbush for the funeral, she found herself face-to-face with her own mother, Zelma. For Turner, who later shared with interviewers that it was only after her mother left that she realized how much she loved her, and how much she hated her, this must have been an emotional reunion. Whatever emotions she felt, she must have been startled when her mother offered her an olive branch, and a chance at a new life: Would Turner consider moving with her to St. Louis? Alline had already moved there, after living for a time with their father, Richard, in Detroit. Turner weighed her options—Ripley and the bleak prospects of life in Haywood County without the grounding love of her grandmother, or big-city life and a chance to connect with her mother—and moved to St. Louis.

In St. Louis, she transferred to yet another high school, Sumner High School, and started spending more time with Alline. Alline coached her sister, with her rustic sensibilities, in the ways, dress, and manners of city life. Together, they would go out and experience nightlife in St. Louis and across the Mississippi River in East St. Louis, Illinois, frequenting bars and clubs to watch local bands perform. The nightlife in St. Louis, and in grittier East St. Louis in particular, must have reminded Turner of her time in the Hole with her late cousin Margaret. Even as Turner put her schoolwork on hold for weekends out with Alline, she deepened her interest in music and her own talents.

Music

Music had remained a constant in her life through the changes at home, through the deaths, and through loss. In addition to the choirs back home, Turner would often sing at local picnics in Nutbush. On occasion, she drew a crowd by singing and dancing along to the Bootsie Whitelow String Band, named for the trombonist frontliner Bootsie Whitelow. A handwritten obituary identified Whitelow, born in 1858, as a freed slave.[81] Whitelow himself had been a member of Woodlawn Missionary Baptist Church's band, where he would play his horn, and the band played in the church and at picnics. His string band consisted of himself and a drummer who would play swing and blues, while the young Turner was encouraged to sing along. Biographer Chris Welch summarized Turner's deepening musical ambitions that arose from this context, writing, "As well as singing swing at picnics, and later hot gospel in church, Anna began to absorb the blues music she heard regularly on the local black radio stations. She loved the famous 'King Biscuit Hour,' a show sponsored by the biscuit company and hosted by Sonny Boy Williamson. Listening to him made her think she might be able to pursue a career as a singer, rather than pickin' cotton."[82] Turner herself had said that she couldn't fit picking cotton into "any kind of dream," but as Welch explained, she was increasingly paying attention to the music that surrounded her.

In *I, Tina*, Turner wrote that while her family didn't have a record player, they had a radio that they listened to constantly, and that she mostly recalls listening to country and western music, which she liked, and blues music: "Papa Joe always listened to WDIA, the black station out of Memphis, and I remember hearing B. B. King on there . . . [and] a few women, like Faye Adams with 'Shake a Hand,' and LaVern Baker with 'Tweedle Dee.' Women with a certain style: the hair pulled back, the mole on the cheek, just so. I didn't care that much for the blues, but I did learn to sing 'Tweedle Dee,' because it was fast."[83] WDIA is regarded as the first radio station in the United States that was programmed entirely for African Americans. WDIA was a white-owned radio station started in 1947 by John Pepper and Bert Ferguson. The following year, they hired a local deejay in Memphis who began to shift the programming toward blues, gospel, and artists in the Delta region. By 1950, the station's programming was aimed almost exclusively toward African Americans, and it became the premier Black radio station in the region.[84]

Cultural anthropologist Maureen Mahon lists LaVern Baker as one of the original "Black Diamond Queens," African American women who made significant contributions to (rock) music history in the 1950s and 1960s.[85] Like the notion of a religious repertoire, these women formed musical repertoires by taking their early experiences singing in church and at family gatherings and merging them with contemporary musical trends to forge distinctive singing styles. Eventually Anna Mae Bullock herself would do the same and, as Tina Turner, would take her place as a black diamond queen. But at this early age, she was only listening to those like LaVern Baker who came before her.

It was the middle of the 1950s, Turner was living in St. Louis, and new trends in music were all around. Kurt Loder, music journalist and coauthor of *I, Tina*, summarized these trends:

The blues—a raw secular outgrowth of the call-and-response style of black gospel singing—spread throughout the cotton fields and turpentine camps of the South by itinerant singer-guitarists. . . . In New Orleans, Dixieland bands combined the harmonies of the blues with the rhythms of ragtime, then added a spirit of improvisation and began (along with musicians in many other cities) to create jazz, the soundtrack of the Roaring Twenties. [In 1935,] the swing years began. . . . Gifted bandleaders such as Duke Ellington and Count Basie maintained an improvisational spark, but in the hands of more pop-inclined white orchestras, jazz was processed into simple dance music.[86]

Loder's depiction of the blues as "a raw secular outgrowth" of gospel has been challenged by scholars and theologians alike.[87] Instead, the blues is better seen as drawing from the same font that would also produce gospel. Further, the boundaries between blues, gospel, and spirituals are fuzzy and amorphous.[88] And yet, Turner herself was in many ways emblematic of these changing music styles. She listened to and eventually sang gospel music at both Woodlawn Missionary Baptist Church and Spring Hill Baptist Church; at home, she listened to country and western music on the radio; and then, at picnics, she would sing and dance to the faster rhythms of the Bootsie Whitelow String Band. Thus, like the trends noted by Loder, Turner was progressing from singing gospel to simpler and faster dance music. Loder further explained: "With America's entry into World War II, many swing stars began to ebb. Black jazz musicians began reclaiming the field with hot black R & B groups that applied the horn playing of the big bands to stripped-down combos led by frantic saxophonists and blues-shouting vocalists."[89] The music of these ensembles was captured on record and sold in the burgeoning "race markets" industry. This music was also broadcast in live radio shows across the Delta. It was these rhythm and blues groups that Turner began listening to on the radio and seeing perform live in St. Louis.

The backgrounds of both the rhythm and blues and gospel artists Turner listened to were similar to her own. For example, gospel artist Mahalia Jackson (1911–1972) was born into a Black Baptist family in New Orleans. Like Turner would later do, she drew musical inspiration from the worship music coming out of Holiness and Pentecostal churches in New Orleans. Jackson saw the fervor and spiritual enthusiasm prevalent in those churches as a powerful and expressive form of music.[90] Another figure whom Turner would later cite as an influence, Sister Rosetta Tharpe (1915–1973), was born in Cotton Plant, Arkansas. Tharpe's mother had been a missionary in the Church of God in Christ. As seen above, Black Pentecostal churches like COGIC incorporated new musical instruments in their worship. These included the guitar, the tambourine, and eventually the Hammond organ.[91] Tharpe developed her talents for singing in the church and learned to play the guitar from her mother. Her guitar-playing skills and sanctified style brought her renown as she increasingly played in secular venues. Tharpe came to exemplify the contribution of African American Protestant women to the historical development of rock 'n' roll, especially women from Black Pentecostal backgrounds. Black gospel artists like Mahalia Jackson and Rosetta Tharpe, Delta string instrument bands like the Bootsie Whitelow String Band, and blues artists like B. B. King and LaVern Baker would all contribute to Turner's developing sense of musical taste and style.

"I Am a Motherless Child," a blues song that Turner wrote in 1969, clearly demonstrates her indebtedness to this legacy of blues and gospel artists. Written for the album *Outta Season*, this song captured Turner's feelings about the early years of her life.[92] This song is the only track Turner wrote for that album, which was mostly written by blues artists including B. B. King and Sonny Boy Williamson II. Like nearly all the songs Turner wrote during her tenure with the Ike & Tina Turner Revue, "I Am a Motherless Child" is an autobiographical composition. She begins the song humming plaintively to Ike Turner's bluesy guitar chords. "Sometimes I'm exhausted and driven, Lord," Turner sang, giving voice to how tiring emotional distress can be. She had moved all around Haywood and the surrounding counties of West Tennessee as a child; as a teenager she moved even more frequently, before finally settling in St. Louis with her emotionally indifferent mother. This whirlwind of changes left her with a sense of placelessness, and she lamented, "sometimes I don't know where to go." Turner plainly stated the indifference of her parents toward her when she intoned, "My mother and father won't own me." The final line of the first verse, "So I'll try to make heaven my home," echoes the place of heaven in spirituals like Mahalia Jackson's "A City Called Heaven," from which Turner likely drew some of her lyrics. In both songs, heaven is presented as a home for those who can't find home *here*. This verse and the rest of the song express the exhaustion, abandonment, and sense of rootlessness that colored her early life in Haywood County, Tennessee, and beyond. Composed with lyrics drawn from Mahalia Jackson's gospel catalogue and recorded in the gospel-blues style, Turner's composition places her firmly in the legacy left by African American blues and gospel music.

Conclusion

While Turner would speak of herself as being a motherless child, she was certainly not grandmotherless. As Turner described her grandmothers, they embodied two aspects of Black southern religious culture. Turner's maternal grandmother, Georgianna Flagg, embodies the mysticism and supernaturalism that pervade Black southern religious culture. Turner perceived Flagg as being otherworldly. Flagg's constant humming, her telling of stories of the rivers, the abiding sense of peace that she seemed to find in West Tennessee's rural environment, and her aesthetic sensibilities all conveyed to Turner lessons about the natural world and the value of quiet. Roxanna Bullock, Turner's paternal grandmother, was a devout Black Baptist woman. When not in church, she could be found in prayer at home. Her house and person were kept clean and orderly. In Bullock's home, Turner was expected to be well behaved, just as she was expected to be a model of good behavior while sitting in front of the mother's corner at Woodlawn Missionary Baptist Church. In many ways, Bullock enshrined in herself the respectability politics of early twentieth-century Black Baptist women. As Turner described it, Bullock was determined to inculcate the same values in her granddaughter. Turner's reflections on her grandmothers show that in the early years of her life, her religiosity is best captured in the womanist notion of grandmother theology.

Womanist theologian Yolanda Pierce defines grandmother theology as that subset of womanist theology that explores the generational wisdom and theological reflections of Black grandmothers. Grandmother theology is dispensed in all places inhabited by elder African American women: in churches, in hair salons, in kitchens, and in gardens.[93] It is also dispensed in church by the Black church (grand)mothers discussed above. In Black Baptist churches, grandmother theologians may be those church women who exemplify virtue, morality, and cleanliness—the hallmarks of Black Baptist women's respectability. In Black Pentecostal churches, grandmother theologians may be paragons of saintliness, derived from the doctrine of sanctification. Grandmother theology is not limited, however, to these institutional forms. Grandmother wisdom may also be found in those grandmothers who embody features that might be associated with mystical or supernatural religiosity. In this case, their generational wisdom may be drawn from their knowledge of roots and herbs, signs revealed in dreams and visions, or attentiveness to the natural world. This theology pays attention to any or all of these sources of the wisdom and instruction of Black grandmothers. Grandmother theology names the theological learning that Tina Turner received from both of her grandmothers.

At Woodlawn Missionary Baptist Church and at Spring Hill Baptist Church, both in Nutbush, Tennessee, Turner honed her vocal talents in the gospel music tradition. At a Black Pentecostal church in Knoxville, Tennessee, Turner also heard gospel music augmented by new instruments such as the guitar, organ, and tambourine. Not content to simply hear gospel music, Turner participated by singing in the choir at her family's churches. In the Black Pentecostal church, she participated by performing the holy dance. Turner's experience of music, though, was not confined to church. She also heard music at local picnics and on the radio. Once she moved to St. Louis, Turner also began frequenting clubs where she could hear popular music from the radio performed live.

In St. Louis, Turner was in her final years of high school. Listening to blues, gospel, and rhythm and blues songs on the radio, and perhaps inspired by the live acts she saw at nightclubs, she began to dream of a life as an entertainer and recorded that dream under her high school yearbook photo. At one East St. Louis club in particular, Club Manhattan, she would meet early rock pioneer Ike Turner. This meeting, and the relationship that came of it, would have a lasting impact on the course of her life.

2

Becoming "Tina Turner"

> *The only thing that kept me going in those years was the*
> *readers. Whatever cities we played—here in Europe,*
> *wherever—I would always try to find a reader to go to.*
> *Some of these people read cards, some read palms, some*
> *read the stars. Some read tea leaves and coffee sediments.*
> *Some of them weren't for real, but others gave me some-*
> *thing to hold on to, some insight into what was going on in*
> *my life. I was exploring my soul for the first time.*
>
> —Tina Turner, *I, Tina*

"Y ou will be among the biggest of stars, and your partner will fall away like a leaf from a tree." A psychic spoke these words to Tina Turner in London in 1966.[1] The Ike & Tina Turner Revue were in London to support their album *River Deep, Mountain High*, as an opening act for the Rolling Stones. In addition to opening for the Stones' twelve-date concert tour, which ran from September 23 to October 9, the Revue played their own club dates for their growing British fan base.[2] The group also made appearances on English television shows, including *Ready! Steady! Go!* During the taping of their set, Turner befriended a woman named Vicki Wickham, and she confided in Vicki about her abusive relationship with Ike Turner. Wickham saw the physical effects of Ike's abuse when Turner came to work with her face swollen and bruised. By 1966, Turner was four years into her marriage to Ike, and six years into her role as half of the Ike & Tina Turner Revue. The couple's fighting was increasing in frequency. It was Vicki Wickham who took Turner to see her first psychic. The psychic's words gave Turner much needed hope and context about her abusive and unhappy marriage to Ike Turner.

Tina Turner had first seen Ike Turner and his band, the Kings of Rhythm, at Club Manhattan, then located at 1312 Broadway Street in East St. Louis, Illinois, in 1956. Club Manhattan was an African American–owned club that competed with white clubs across the river in St. Louis, such as George Edick's Club Imperial. Ike Turner was one of a number of blues, early rock, and rhythm and blues musicians who played at the club and later became well known, including Chuck Berry, Little Milton, and B. B. King. Turner later recalled her first experience seeing Ike and his band, explaining that "he got up onstage and picked up his guitar. He hit one note, and I thought: 'Jesus, listen to this guy play.'" As Turner tells it, once Ike started playing, the club came to life and people came in to listen: "And that joint started rocking. The floor was packed with people dancing and sweating to this great music, and I was just sitting there, amazed, staring at Ike Turner. I thought, 'God, I wonder why so many women like him? He sure is ugly.' But I kept listening and looking. I almost went into a trance watching him."[3] For Turner and her sister, Alline Bullock, seeing Ike Turner perform became a regular part of their weekend.

Ike Turner and the Blues

In many ways, when Anna Mae Bullock met Ike Turner, she was meeting someone who was immediately legible to her. His background was similar to hers: Ike Turner was born Ike Wister Turner, in Clarksdale, Mississippi, a town in the Mississippi Delta, on November 5, 1931. Like Nutbush, Clarksdale in the 1930s was a rural, segregated southern town situated along the Sunflower River, a tributary of the Yazoo River, which ran into the Mississippi River. Clarksdale served as a key train hub where cotton was brought from the nearby cottonfields and the cotton gins farther out to be compressed and stored before being sent out. These railroad tracks, which transported Mississippi's contribution to the region's precious "white gold" commodity, also served as Clarksdale's racial dividing line. Black people lived on the east side of the railroad tracks, separated from Oakhurst and other white sections of Clarksdale. Crossing racial boundaries, intentionally or otherwise, had bodily consequences, as Ike Turner's father experienced firsthand.[4]

Ike Turner's father—Izear Luster Turner—was a pastor at Clarksdale's Centennial Baptist Church, at 200 Fifth Street, on the corner of Fifth and Yazoo.[5] No record of the sermons he preached or of his tenure as pastor survives, but given his church's location near the blues "juke joints" of Clarksdale, his preaching and performance style may have followed that of preachers like C. L. Franklin, whose preaching "possessed an undeniable blues sensibility."[6] Explaining the affinities between Black preachers like Franklin and blues artists, historian Nick Salvatore writes that "At the very center of the sacred and secular performances by these talented soloists, an ability to improvise in word and tone allowed each to seek the emotional core in their audience."[7] The central ritual in both the blues artist's and the preacher's performance was the "intimate pattern of call and response, where audience and artist sought to draw out—to elongate—the essence of the other in a joined search for deliverance, [which] underscored the very communal nature of the performance."[8] Izear Luster Turner may have used call-and-response and inflected his preaching with a "blues sensibility" to reach congregants at Centennial Baptist Church. And we might wonder if, like other Mississippi-born preachers who looked up the nearby Highway 61—linking Clarksdale to Memphis and beyond—and dreamed of a more lucrative, northern career as a preacher, Izear Turner had similar dreams.[9] Whatever his dreams or preaching style may have been, his life was cut short when he was brutally beaten by a gang of white men for crossing racial boundaries by having unspecified relations with a white woman.[10]

Though Ike Turner remembers his mother pushing him to attend revivals and get baptized, Centennial Baptist Church faded from his life after his father succumbed to injuries sustained in the racially charged beating.[11] Nevertheless, a woman from the church did introduce him to the piano, which proved fruitful. Initially, his mother paid for him to have piano lessons, but Ike was introduced to the rapid-fire, boogie-woogie style of piano playing. Unbeknownst to her, he was receiving extracurricular lessons in the piano stylings of an early blues artist. In the thirties and forties, Clarksdale was a hotbed of blues musical activity and blues artists who would in time come to national prominence could easily be encountered around town. One figure in particular, Pinetop Perkins, was to have an immense influence on Ike.

When he died in March 2011, then-governor of Mississippi, Haley Barbour, memorialized Joe Willie "Pinetop" Perkins by saying that "Mississippi lost one of the last, great Delta blues legends" and that he would be "remembered for his immense talent and the decades of music he created and performed."[12] Perkins was ninety-seven years old when he died and had played blues piano for more than eight decades. Perkins was born in Belzoni, Mississippi, in 1913, and his father, like Ike Turner's father, Izear, was a preacher. Partially inspired by the piano playing he heard in church, Perkins learned to play, and eventually came to play alongside major Delta blues figures such as Sonny Boy Williamson II, B. B. King, Howlin' Wolf, and, later, Muddy Waters. Alongside Williamson, he performed on the *King Biscuit Time Radio Show*, which broadcast on KFFA-AM, out of Helena, Arkansas, in the forties, and both rehearsed for the show in Clarksdale, not far from Centennial Baptist Church. In later interviews, Perkins recalled that the music played in the juke joints and the music played in churches were so close that "the church and the juke flowed back and forth."[13] They rehearsed in the home of one of Ike Turner's neighborhood friends, and Ike remembered first hearing Perkins play his famous "boogie-woogie" piano style there. Eventually, Ike Turner began an apprenticeship under Perkins. Ultimately, Perkins, like other blues artists, joined the northern migration up Highway 61 to Memphis, and beyond to Chicago.[14] Highway 61 was not the only route out of Clarksdale, though; the trains that passed through Clarksdale's train depot were another. Together with the freight train depot, churches like Centennial Baptist Church where Ike Turner's father pastored, and the bluesy juke joints frequented by Pinetop Perkins and other musical mentors of Ike Turner, these locales triangulate defining images of Black religion in the Delta region.

In the Mississippi Delta, the freight train and the railroad held a "cultural meaning" as a saving vehicle for African Americans, as John M. Giggie explains in *After Redemption*.[15] Though the trains themselves were heavily segregated, they could carry African Americans away from the oppressive conditions of Black life in the Delta to major cities west, north, and northeast, where it was hoped that life would be better. This image of the railroad served as a source of inspiration for the chanted sermons of reverends like J. M. Gates and his famous recorded sermon "Death's Black Train."[16]

It also served as an inspiration for the song lyrics of early African American blues artists. With the image of the train as a vehicle leading toward freedom in blues songs, and with blues musicians thinking through the problems of the world and deliverance from them, some have argued that "the blues are an African American form of theodicy that attempts to reconcile the existence of evil in a world ruled and controlled by God, who is good."[17] As performers, some early blues artists "performed in ways that loosely resembled a minister delivering a Sunday church sermon," from song themes to their heavy reliance upon improvisation and frequent usage of call-and-response.[18] The train and elements of church come together in the blues of the Delta region.

Beyond mimicking and incorporating the delivery styles of Black preachers, blues artists and their music also embraced elements of the supernaturalism permeating Black southern religious culture. "From the country styles of the Mississippi delta songsters to the urban blues performers of the post–World War II era and beyond," Yvonne Chireau explains, "black bluespeople utilized the rhetoric of Conjure in their songs."[19] These "bluespeople" also continuously referenced figures like Marie Laveau, the "Voodoo Queen," and other conjurers, diviners, and healers in their songs. Features of the conjuring tradition and supernaturalism—magic, healing, and harming—were constant themes in the blues.[20] Chireau concludes that as the blues evolved into a form of popular entertainment, it became "a powerful medium by which performers articulated personal tribulations and conveyed them to a receptive audience. Blues singers were storytellers whose listeners affirmed and participated in Black experience."[21] Storytelling, preacherly delivery, and elements of Black supernaturalism, all delivered via guitar and rapid-fire piano playing, were characteristic features of the blues that Ike Turner was mentored in.

Thus, despite Ike Turner's minimal affiliations with and memory of the church, church music infused the ubiquitous Delta blues of Pinetop Perkins and others who served as his mentors.[22] By 1945, Ike himself was working as a disc jockey at Clarksdale's WROX radio station. While still in school, he formed a band called the Tophatters, out of which came his later band, the Kings of Rhythm. The band mostly played radio covers in local gigs as Ike honed the piano stylings taught to him by Perkins. But, in 1951, Ike followed his blues mentors north to Memphis, at the behest of B. B. King, where the Kings of Rhythm recorded for record producer Sam Phillips at Sun Studios. Today, Sun Studios and Sam Phillips are most famous for the "discovery" of Elvis Presley in 1954. However, three years before this he recorded Ike Turner and the Kings of Rhythm and their composition "Rocket '88." The song, which Tina Turner's coauthor Kurt Loder described as a "crudely pulsating tune," was crafted by both Ike Turner and his bandmate Jackie Brenston, and the song's intro features Ike's Pinetop Perkins–trained boogie-woogie piano. Phillips licensed the song to Chess Records, but instead of crediting the song to Ike Turner and the Kings of Rhythm, he credited it to Jackie Brenston and a nonexistent band called the Delta Cats. "Rocket '88" became a *Billboard* number 1 hit on June 12, 1951; eventually sold over half a million copies; and is considered one of the first rock 'n' roll songs. While the song was a lucrative hit for Phillips and Chess Records, Brenston received roughly $900, with Ike Turner and the other uncredited members of the Kings of Rhythm receiving $20 apiece. Though this pattern of African American recording artists being taken advantage of by white record producers and executives would play out countless times for innumerable artists, the scars from this could prove devastating and could, as they did with Ike Turner, remain with them for the rest of their lives.[23]

Nevertheless, Sam Phillips and B. B. King introduced Ike to Joe Bihari of Modern/RPM Records, who hired Ike as a talent scout. Together with Bihari, Ike traveled the Delta region recording and sometimes accompanying the blues artists who had served as his friends and mentors.[24] In 1954, Ike moved to St. Louis and began performing in East St. Louis, Illinois, with the Kings of Rhythm. During this period, Ike shifted from piano to guitar as they performed local gigs around St. Louis and East St. Louis. Two years later, the band had another regional rhythm and blues hit with the song "I'm Tore Up." As with "Rocket '88," "I'm Tore Up" was credited to its lead singer—Billy Gayles—who, on the success of the single, promptly left Ike's band to work as a solo artist. Nevertheless, Ike Turner and the Kings of Rhythm were becoming a local sensation. In St. Louis, the band would play up to fourteen jobs a week, at predominantly white clubs like George Edick's Club Imperial, and the band had a reputation for strict decorum. Edick would later recall that he had the band perform on Tuesday, Thursday, and Friday nights to packed crowds of around one thousand people. Of Ike himself, Edick later said, "[He] was the strictest man I knew. Ike's band had to be dressed—they wore suits and ties. And he wouldn't let them have drinks up on the bandstand. There was no drinking at all.

He used to rehearse at my place sometimes, and if one of his men was late or something, he would raise holy hell with him. That's why he changed musicians so much—he would just get rid of guys if he had trouble with them."[25] Likely owing to his experiences with "Rocket '88" and "I'm Tore Up," Edick recalls that Ike was a workaholic and a strict businessman.[26] In East St. Louis, the band played predominantly Black clubs and had a large following. But East St. Louis was rougher than St. Louis, and consequently the band had a more pugnacious reputation there.[27] Both of these reputations—the Kings of Rhythm as an impeccably dressed band, with Ike as talented guitarist, strict bandleader, businessman, and workaholic; and the band's rougher reputation—would be repeated for the Ike & Tina Turner Revue, featuring Anna Mae Bullock ("Little Ann") as lead singer.

Ike and Tina Turner

When Anna Mae Bullock first saw Ike Turner, she was a sixteen-year-old junior at St. Louis's Sumner High School. Aesthetically, Ike Turner was much like other men in her life: dapper, church reared, and influenced by the dictates of the politics of respectability. Yet, like Anna Mae's father, Ike had a rough edge that enabled him to make his way above the poor economic and social conditions of southern Black people. There was also social and domestic violence in Ike Turner's upbringing, and Ike was domineering, like her father. Nevertheless, Ike Turner represented success, and with his Kings of Rhythm band he gave her the idea that singing could be a way out of the simple future she foresaw.

Turner related to Kurt Loder in detail about how she "wanted to get up there [on stage with Ike Turner and the Kings of Rhythm] so bad." But she also acknowledged that she was only one of *many* women who wanted to sing with him.[28] One night, she got her wish. During an intermission, members of the Kings of Rhythm went outside to escape the smoke-filled air of Club Manhattan. Ike put away his guitar, sat at the piano, and began to play a melody. In interviews throughout her career, Turner consistently recalls the song as B. B. King's "Darlin' You Know I Love You." Ike admits that this is possible, but that it could have been another song.[29] Whatever the song, when the drummer placed the microphone in front of her, Anna Mae Bullock began to sing, and what Ike Turner heard that night convinced him that "that girl" could indeed sing.[30] Increasingly, Ike allowed the teen that he called "Little Ann" to sing along to his accompaniment during intermissions. Before long, she was a regular vocalist and sang with the band on weekends while in high school, first appearing on record in 1958 on the song "Box Top," where she is credited as a vocalist, under the name "Little Ann." With its simple melody and instrumentation, Turner's voice—though only singing backup—comes through distinctly.

The developing vocal style of "Little Ann" was influenced by gospel great Mahalia Jackson, gospel-blues pioneer Sister Rosetta Tharpe, Ray Charles, and Sam Cooke. Her performance style had resonances with Little Richard, who had a similar Black Pentecostal background. When "A Fool in Love" became a hit in 1960, with Little Ann mistakenly on lead vocals, Ike changed her name to "Tina Turner," adding his last name and trademarking the name so that if she tried to leave him, she wouldn't be able to use the name.[31] Though Ike Turner maintained that the name "Tina" and the image he developed of her were derived from the comic book heroine Sheena, Queen of the Jungle,[32] it is clear that his fascination with his own father's engaging preacherly delivery, and Ike Turner's close association with other postsanctified performers such as Little Richard, also influenced the image Ike and Tina constructed together. The dynamic performance style that Tina Turner cultivated during her tenure with the Revue that would earn her the moniker "queen of rock 'n' roll" can be broadly linked to the tradition of "postsanctified" performers who followed in the wake of singers like Tharpe. Sister Rosetta Tharpe, like Turner, was born in a rural town, raised in the Black Pentecostal tradition, and developed a distinctive style characterized by dynamic performance antics and a vocal blend of gospel and blues.[33]

Excited by the success of "A Fool in Love," Ike scheduled a theater and club date tour, and when "Tina Turner" protested, Ike beat her for the first time with a wooden shoe stretcher. This began a pattern of abuse that endured to the end of their relationship.[34] With hindsight, Turner said,

> To control me psychologically, Ike worked several angles. Before our relationship became sexual, he preyed on my better nature by begging me to be loyal to him. In his hangdog way, he told me that every time he wrote a song for someone, if it became a hit, they left him. I was grateful for everything he did for me—if Ike liked you, he would give you the

shirt off his back—so I promised him that I was different, that he could trust me, that I would never, ever leave him. As long as I can remember, I was always honest and never told lies. It was just my way. When I said something, I meant it. A promise was a promise, and that was it. My promise to Ike meant something to me and I intended to keep it.[35]

Turner's promise to never leave Ike was formalized when the couple married, in 1962. That same year, Ike and Tina moved their young family to a home on 4263 Olympiad Drive in the View Park neighborhood of Inglewood, California. Their family now consisted of four children: Ike Turner Jr. and Michael Turner, Ike's sons from a previous relationship; Craig Raymond Turner, Tina Turner's son with saxophone player Raymond Hill; and Ronnie Turner, Ike and Tina's son. Speaking of their early married life, Turner explained: "The best part was that I got to sing professionally. Back in Tennessee, if you enjoyed singing, you had three options: singing along with the radio, singing at a church, or singing at a picnic with Mr. Bootsy Whitelow [all of which Turner herself did]. But this was the real thing, performing on a stage, with a popular band. Ike taught me all about music *and* he paid me to sing. When we weren't performing, we lived and breathed music, whether we were rehearsing or making late night rounds of the clubs."[36] With the chart success of "A Fool in Love," the Ike & Tina Turner Revue, now replete with a troupe of backup singer-dancers that Ike named and trademarked as the "Ikettes," launched a tour consisting of a series of one-nighter concert dates in the same kind of small venues and "juke joints" that Turner had seen in Ripley, Tennessee, and Ike had seen in Clarksdale.

On these tours, the Revue performed two to four concerts a night in small venues, punctuated by occasional dates at major venues—at the circuit of theaters where African American artists could perform across the South, Upper Midwest, and Eastern Seaboard. They also established a home base around which to perform. After moving to Los Angeles, the Ike & Tina Turner Revue would spend "three months on the road, then three months working six or seven days a week in places within driving distance of L. A., and Ike considered San Francisco, which was almost four hundred miles away (and parts of Arizona, for that matter), to be within driving distance!" Turner added, "After three months at home, we'd go back on the road and the cycle would begin again."[37] Included on this circuit were places such as the Apollo Theater in Harlem, New York; the Howard Theatre in Washington, DC; Club DeLisa in Chicago; and the Blue Note in Tampa, Florida. This route came to be called the Chitlin' Circuit.

Race, Civil Rights, and the Chitlin' Circuit

The Chitlin' Circuit's origins lay in the racialized vaudeville performance circuit of the twenties, which remained enmeshed in the racial context of the United States forty years later.[38] On the circuit, each act would be booked on a bill with other "Black acts," including rhythm and blues acts, gospel performers, comedians, and more. For example, a typical advertisement for a performance at the University of Dayton's Wampler's Ballroom reads "Sunday, Oct. 14—9:00 p.m. till 1:00 A.M. Ike and Tina Turner Revue The Ike ettes [sic] Aretha Franklin *And many other Recording Stars.*"[39]

Segregation, a perverse, divisive force in society, was a unitive force for performers on the Chitlin' Circuit. Black performers were prevented from staying at most hotels and had only one housing option available to them in each location. This meant that in addition to being advertised on the same bill, blues, rhythm and blues, gospel, and soul acts, alongside touring preachers and comedians, all stayed at the same hotel. This led to collaboration, competition, and after-hours fraternizing.[40] Members of the Revue later spoke of this fraternizing aspect of the circuit. "On the chitlin' circuit," recalled Jimmy Thomas, a vocalist in the Revue from 1960 to 1966, "you know you are down with the dregs, but it's the place where everybody goes."[41]

Neither Ike nor Tina Turner ever spoke of the communal realities of the Chitlin' Circuit, but both later spoke of the careful ruses that they maintained to stay in segregated hotels. Often, they had their white road assistant go in first to ensure their stay. In later interviews, Turner wrote about the racial difficulties of the circuit and how while traveling in the South they were often forced to sleep outside. They were also forced to get dressed and do their makeup in janitorial closets and other hidden areas within venues—this was far from the life of stardom she imagined as a sixteen-year-old meeting Ike Turner.[42]

Each performer on the circuit, Ike and Tina included, performed energetic shows against a backdrop of racial tensions and the expanding civil rights movement. Some of these performers, like Aretha Franklin, were active participants in the movement, using their rising fame on the circuit to bring attention to social issues. For their part, the Ike & Tina Turner Revue sometimes entered performance contracts with explicitly social activist groups like the Black Panthers. Ike Turner later explained that when the Black Panthers booked the Revue, he signed the contract under a different name because of his reluctance to get involved in racial conflicts. Of the Black Panthers, Ike said, "They were thinking race; we [were] just thinking of music and having fun." Explaining his position further, Ike related that, though he didn't belong to any Black or white organizations, he "made [his] stand" where he deemed it necessary and "paid [his] dues just like Stokely Carmichael and all the [r]est of them." He added, "But I did it my way."[43] Perhaps the Revue's resistance to overt participation in the civil rights movement bespoke a concern that taking a more activist stance would prevent audiences from hearing their music *as* music. Instead, their music could be perceived as alluding to the social and political struggles of the day, thereby limiting their reach, which would affect the group's record sales, a primary concern of Ike Turner. Indeed, he wrote in his memoir that he had advised other artists, like Janis Joplin, to tone down their public criticisms of the government; the powers that be, he said, "don't like you when you are doing" things like that.[44] This attitude is likely what precluded the group from taking part in any American State Department efforts at musical diplomacy, like the "jazz diplomacy" tours that began in the 1950s.[45] (This did not, however, prevent the Revue's participation in the 1971 *Soul to Soul* concert held to commemorate Ghana Independence Day.)[46] Other members of the Revue, though, took their lack of involvement differently, understanding themselves as taking a more removed, "cool" approach to the social movements.

Revue vocalist Jimmy Thomas explained their philosophy: "We were instrumental in keeping the situation cool. We were brave enough to go out during the marches and protests, when other bands like ours would only play black universities."[47] Thomas maintains, though, that the Revue would still "fight for what we knew, in our own way."[48] This cool approach did not always endear the group to activist groups who, according to Thomas, targeted the Revue for their lack of involvement.

Yet through all this, the Ike & Tina Turner Revue forged a unique act and distinctive style with Turner and the Ikettes as the visual and sonic feature. While the Revue released many albums during this time, most failed to reach the success of songs like "A Fool in Love" and "I Think It's Gonna Work Out Fine." However, their relentless touring and appearances on popular television shows brought them to national prominence, and to the attention of record producer Phil Spector.

"River Deep, Mountain High"

By the time Phil Spector[49] met Ike and Tina Turner, he had already recorded a string of *Billboard* hits with vocalist Darlene Love and groups including the Ronettes, the Righteous Brothers, and the Crystals. With the Righteous Brothers, Spector had four top ten hits, the last of which was his biggest chart success, "You've Lost That Lovin' Feelin'," from 1965. Because of his chart success in the early sixties, Spector built a reputation as a genius, if mysterious, record producer. Retrospective reviews of his career often detailed the amount of effort he put into crafting records with his signature "wall of sound" production technique. This description of his working style in a 1977 *New York Times* profile is typical: "Working for days to get the right instrumental combination, orchestrating with the recording console by bringing up some instruments while obliterating others, piling detail on detail only to reduce his elaborate instrumentation to a dull roar when he mixed his records, Spector was a perfectionist who took his art seriously at a time when most pop record makers were only in it for the money."[50] Spector applied this same seriousness to searching for new musical acts to produce. At the Galaxy Club in Los Angeles, he saw Ike and Tina Turner perform and later reported, "Their in-person act just killed me."[51] Spector signed on to produce the Larry Peerce–directed concert film *The Big T.N.T Show*, featuring performances by the Byrds, Ray Charles, and others. He hired Ike and Tina Turner to perform on the show as well, and during the show's taping in November of 1965, he was sufficiently impressed with Tina Turner that he contacted Bob Krasnow, label head at the Turners' record label, Loma Records, to request that she be allowed to work with him, without Ike. The next year, in 1966, Spector cowrote "River Deep, Mountain High," imagining Turner as the lead vocalist. Krasnow contacted Ike Turner, who made all creative and business decisions for the Ike & Tina Turner Revue, and put him in touch with Spector. A deal was worked out between them, and Turner was "licensed" to Spector. With the details of the deal confirmed, Turner went to Spector's home to begin working on the song without Ike.[52]

Phil Spector lived in the Hollywood Hills, so Turner commuted from her home in Inglewood to Spector's home for two weeks of daily rehearsals. Each day, Spector worked with Turner on her vocal phrasing and the melody of the verses, patiently coaxing the performances he wanted out of her voice. In some ways, Spector's working style was like Ike's in that he was exacting and controlling. And yet, Turner found major differences between their song-crafting styles. As Turner herself explained:

> I loved that song ["River Deep, Mountain High"]. Because for the first time in my life, it wasn't just R and B—it had structure, it had a melody. You see, Ike would always have me screaming and shouting on his songs—selling them, you know. Because there wasn't really much to them: I'd always have to improvise and ad-lib. But with Phil ... well, one day, when we were about finished rehearsing at his house, I started really feeling this song, and I went into my old routine—"Whoaaaahhhh"—the way I'd been taught by Ike. But Phil said, "No, no—I just want you to stick to the melody." ... It was my voice he liked, not the screaming. He told me I had an extremely unusual voice, that he had never heard a woman's voice like mine, and that that was why he wanted to record me.[53]

Turner is likely referring here to the opening lines of the 1960 hit "A Fool in Love," which opens with Turner's distinctive, guttural wail. She would later say Ike favored a preacher's style of delivery for her.[54] Spector was asking her to sing in a new way. While utilizing her wail for the choruses, he expected Turner to maintain the melodic structure of the song during the verses. Others, from music critics to Ike himself, had made similar comments about her voice's unusual quality. But Spector's coaching sounded different to her. On the one hand, in asking her to stick to the melody of the song, he was asking her to adhere to his vision of the song and controlling her performance as Ike did, but he was simultaneously reminding her that her voice was unique and worthy of being featured in its own right. Recording with Spector confirmed for Turner that she could do more with her vocal talent than Ike allowed.[55]

Spector considered "River Deep, Mountain High" to be his master-piece, anticipating that the song would be his next *Billboard* hit.[56] Instead, the song failed to reach the Top 40, peaked at number 88 in June 1966, and quickly fell. While it was a chart failure in the United States, the song became a number 3 hit on the British charts in July and spent nearly four months in the Top 50. In the May 1971 issue of *Ebony* magazine, Ike Turner gave the following reason for the song's poor performance in America: "The black radio stations kept telling me, 'It's too pop' and the white stations claimed that it was 'too r and b' (rhythm and blues). Black artists are always branded r and b, so therefore there's little or no chance of breaking into the Top 40 market."[57] In other words, as Ike saw it, the song flopped because of the segregation of US radio. The fact that it flopped in America but was successful in England confirmed for Turner that she had given a vocal performance on this song unlike anything she and Ike had ever done. The song's success in England also brought the Ike & Tina Turner Revue, and specifically Tina Turner, to the attention of the Rolling Stones, who invited them to be an opening act on their 1966 tour. Summarizing the impact of this tour on British audiences and on Ike and Tina Turner's career, cultural anthropologist Maureen Mahon explained that the tour connected Ike and Tina Turner to the blues revival then taking place in England; it also gave "the Turners visibility in the United Kingdom and started a long-lasting alliance between Tina, British rock musicians, and the British record-buying public."[58] For Ike, the tour opened his eyes to the kind of success that was possible but had eluded the Revue in America. Turner remembers, "Ike looked out from behind the curtain and said, 'I want Ike and Tina, just Ike and Tina, to fill this place,' which sounded like a pipe dream."[59] For Turner, though, England was to be the beginning of a spiritual awakening.

Cultural Universalism and the Beginning of an Awakening

To this point in Tina Turner's life, religion, with grandmother theology at its foundation, was largely in the background. She had internalized the mystical, nature-based spirituality of her maternal grandmother, Georgianna Flagg, and had retained the deep respect for the healing powers of nature that she had learned from her.[60] Turner had also internalized what she learned from the strict Black Baptist adherence of her paternal grandmother, Roxanna Bullock, and indeed Turner said that during this period she "prayed every night." But she was a long way from both grandmothers. Flagg died in 1956, prompting her move to St. Louis to live with her mother, Zelma Bullock, and she hadn't lived near Roxanna Bullock in a decade. Now, she was "Tina Turner," traveling the United States, Europe, and beyond as half of the Ike & Tina Turner Revue. The Revue's rehearsal, recording, performance, and travel schedule consumed much of her time, and the remainder of her time was devoted to taking care of the couple's four children. Until her conversion to Soka Gakkai Nichiren Buddhism in 1973, neither Turner nor Ike had any known religious affiliation aside from their Black Baptist upbringings. Given her close relationship with both grandmothers in the absence of her parents, Turner must have felt a significant religious void during this period. At this point, in 1966, Turner was six years into her relationship with Ike Turner. His womanizing continued, as did his abuse. This void and Turner's unhappiness with her situation created an opening for a new friend to introduce her to the world of psychics.

After doing twelve shows with the Rolling Stones, the Ike & Tina Turner Revue continued their own tour of England, France, and Germany. While in England, the Revue was featured on the English television show *Ready! Steady! Go!*, and backstage, Turner befriended one of the show's employees, Vicki Wickham. Turner confided the details of her difficult relationship with Ike, and Wickham could see the physical effects of Ike's abuse on Turner, after she and Ike had a bad fight in London one night. "Ike really kept me down and gave me a good whammin'—and the next day I was all swollen. That's when Vicki started feeling sorry for me."[61] Wickham introduced Turner to a psychic card reader, and the reader told her that one day she would be "among the biggest of stars . . . and [her] partner will fall away like a leaf from a tree." This produced a mixed reaction in Turner: "Well: 'among the biggest of stars'—I liked that! I felt kind of bad about the other part: like 'Oh, poor Ike,' you know? Felt a little guilty. But that's how I was then. Sometimes Ike would beat me, and he'd get so crazy afterwards, I'd feel sorry for him—can you imagine? I was all mixed up. But I held on to what that reader said."

For those in abusive relationships, this feeling of guilt is common. Especially because, as in Ike and Tina Turner's relationship, one person is dependent upon the other and the abuser alternates between abuse and moments of affection. For Ike and Tina, this pattern began after their first physical altercation in 1960 over the success of "A Fool in Love," after which Ike made Turner have sex with him and bought her gifts immediately after. She was also unhappy with their professional relationship, describing a lack of agency that she felt in both their personal and professional lives. So, despite the guilt that she felt about Ike "falling away like a leaf from a tree," the psychic's pronouncement that she would be "among the biggest of stars" gave her hope that she would one day be independent of Ike. As Turner explained: "[The psychic] had seen a six, so I held on for six months, and then I held on for six years, and after that I just kept holding on—seeing other readers every place we played, knowing my time would come, knowing that someday I'd be free of this life I was leading. Through it all I held on to what that lady in London told me."

Beyond England, the Revue also traveled to Continental Europe, going to France and Germany. For Turner, that first tour abroad was akin to coming home. French culture particularly resonated with her, and the distinct way in which French people pronounced her name changed her view of herself. She later explained to Loder: "It was the first time I'd ever heard my name pronounced beautifully before—this name I had hated up until then. With Ike it was always *Tee-nuh*. Real . . . kind of crude. But the French people said *Tee-nah*. It sounded pretty, and after that I started to like it. *Tee-nah*."[62] Recall that the name "Tina" had been given to her by Ike, as a form of ownership. What's more, Ike had essentially changed her name without discussing it with her. Almost overnight, an entity was created—"Tina Turner"—as distinct from Anna Mae Bullock. The name remained separate from her, and its origins were tied to the first instance of domestic abuse she experienced at the hands of Ike. In that incident, several transformations took place: she went from being Anna Mae to being "Tina"; she went from being Ike's sisterly friend to his (unequal) partner; and her feelings of brotherly love became inseparable from fear. Thus, her name caused her constant consternation. Her friends and family continued to call her "Ann," never Tina. But, hearing her name pronounced with a French accent opened the possibility that her name *could be* beautiful. Just over a decade later she would divorce Ike and take full ownership of "Tina Turner" as *her* name. At the same time, she began to consider cultural belonging anew. Though neither she nor Ike could speak French, and she believed that Ike "couldn't communicate with anybody," she felt that she could "get through to people somehow." Maybe, she wondered, her real home was abroad:

And that was when I started thinking that maybe I had been there before—that maybe this *was* my real home. Now, don't misunderstand me: I'm black. I mean, nobody's hair is nappier than mine, you know? But I think being of mixed blood . . . helped me communicate with the French. So on that first trip to France, that's when I began to feel, deep down inside, that maybe I was French, too. Or had been—I didn't know about reincarnation then. And I got to thinking that maybe I was such a mixture of things that it was beyond black or white, beyond just culture—that I was universal! I had never had these feelings before, but they were real, and they felt right. Naturally, I didn't tell Ike about any of this—that kind of talk scared him, I think.[63]

Turner displays a simultaneous acknowledgment of her racial specificity and a dawning sense of cultural universalism, linking her experiences abroad to those of other African American artists who traveled abroad at this time and developed expansive notions of culture and belonging. Artists including Nina Simone and James Baldwin would also identify France, in particular, as a place of belonging free of the racial discrimination that marred life in the United States for Black Americans.[64] Like them, Turner would eventually move to Europe: first to England and France, later to Germany and Switzerland.[65] After the Ike & Tina Turner Revue's initial tour in 1966, the Turners returned to tour Europe each winter, eventually adding Australia, Japan, and Southeast Asia to their touring schedule. Each subsequent trip increased Turner's sense of globalism and belonging.

Psychics

Around this time, Turner also met the Dutch psychic Peter Hurkos. Born in 1911 in Holland, Hurkos moved to Los Angeles in 1956 to participate in experiments of psychic phenomena. Hurkos claimed to have discovered his psychic abilities around the age of thirty when he fell from a ladder, suffering a brain injury. According to Hurkos's obituary in the *Los Angeles Times*, four days after falling from the ladder he regained consciousness and discovered that he "possessed psychic powers—an ability to see into the future, to exercise artistic and musical talents he had never exhibited before, and to trace missing persons by 'psychometrizing,' or tuning into their psychic vibrations by touching clothing and other personal possessions."[66] In his biography, authored by Norma Lee Browning, *The Psychic World of Peter Hurkos*,[67] Hurkos explained that he could see pictures in his mind when he touched objects. His *New York Times* obituary reports that he first "gained widespread attention in 1964 when Attorney General Edward W. Brooke of Massachusetts said he had come 'uncannily close' to describing the person suspected of strangling 11 women in Boston," and he was convicted of impersonating an FBI agent that same year.[68] Later, Hurkos appeared nationally in profiles on CBS and *The Johnny Carson Show*, as well as internationally.

Turner consulted Hurkos frequently and brought Hurkos to meet Ike. In his own memoir, Ike recalls Turner convincing him to consult Hurkos when nearly $100,000 in cash was stolen from him in Paris.[69] Though Turner repeatedly stated after their divorce that she had no freedom during her time with Ike, it appears that he did allow her to explore her interest in psychics, as Peter Hurkos was only one of many psychics that she would turn to throughout their relationship.

Though Turner saw her first psychic in England and Peter Hurkos himself was Dutch, both Turner's and the American media's interest in psychics like Hurkos highlights a broader fascination with psychic phenomena in American religious history. In the latter half of the nineteenth century, as historian of science and medicine Alicia Puglionesi has shown, there was "an overwhelming popular interest in liminal states, psychic force, and mental permeability; the persistence of American Spiritualism; and the development of psychology as a scientific discipline claiming objective knowledge of the mind."[70] Trance, hypnotism, clairvoyance, and so on were all studied as a part of an emerging scientific discipline known as psychical research. Puglionesi sees liminal states and contested experiences as being at the core of psychical research. While psychical experiences could occur during the space between, for example, sleeping and waking, such experiences could also occur after accidents or extreme duress. Hurkos typifies the development of psychic capacities after suffering injury, as he discovered his abilities after falling from a ladder. In Puglionesi's estimation, spiritualists viewed themselves as mediators between competing interpretations of these liminal spaces through their sensational demonstrations of trance mediumship.[71] Toward the end of the nineteenth century, the American Society for Psychical Research (ASPR) was established, in part by the pioneering American philosopher and psychologist William James, to organize and systematize psychical research (showing the connection with similar trends in Europe, a Society for Psychical Research was founded in England a few years prior).[72]

Yet, due in no small part to institutions like the ASPR, overall, the voices of African Americans and Native Americans were often left out of historical narratives surrounding psychical research. Such organizations often presumed a "universalized white mind" in their discourses around psychical phenomena, even as the ideas of African Americans and Native Americans often shaped these discourses.[73] That African American ideas helped to shape these ideas is readily apparent to the discerning reader of the religious context of Turner's early religious life. The previous chapter showed that the liminal states and contested experiences Puglionesi identified as being at the core of psychical research were also core elements of the religious experiences of southern Black Americans (and southern white Americans).[74] For Black southern Americans prior to and including Turner's generation, these liminal states consisted of dreams and the discernment of signs derived therefrom, and even included the liminal space of the wilderness. Their contested religious experiences played out in debates that arose in African American communities about the relationship between institutional forms of religious expression and more ecstatic, supernatural forms. Recognizing this is a step toward the restoration of African American contributions to the discourses and phenomena that institutions like the ASPR made it their mission to classify and systematize.

Although criticism of experiences that fall under the heading of psychic phenomena has persisted since the seventeenth century, interest in such experiences has persisted in American religious history through the twentieth century and continues today into the twenty-first. Psychical phenomena, the research conducted under the guise of the ASPR, and the American public's fascination with figures like Peter Hurkos are themselves constitutive elements of the stream of American metaphysical religion, named by historian Catherine Albanese (see below).

Beyond psychics and new religious ideas, the Ike & Tina Turner Revue's 1966 tour of England, France, and Germany exposed Turner to new cultures and new audiences. But back home the following year, her personal and professional relationship experienced setbacks. Personally, Turner recounted that Ike engaged in extramarital affairs with a variety of women, from the Revue's groupies to the wives of his own musicians. Worse still for Turner, during this period Ike was introduced to cocaine, and, while he had always had a violent temper, cocaine quickened his emotions and made his outbursts worse. Many of his violent outbursts were directed at Turner herself.[75] Professionally, the Revue had no chart hits during 1967, though they were still touring and performing constantly to larger crowds. To generate income in the absence of album sales, the Revue returned to Europe for another concert tour in the spring of 1968. While in London, Turner discovered that both she and her friend Ann Thomas, an Ikette, were pregnant with Ike's children. Turner explained to Kurt Loder that upon realizing that both she and her friend were pregnant, she "lost all feeling" for Ike as her husband. At that point, she explained, she became depressed, and when they returned to Los Angeles, though she attempted to maintain their normal work and domestic routines, she struggled. Before one show, she attempted suicide and was rushed to a hospital in Inglewood. She recalls that Ike visited her in the hospital only once, and when she was released, his only comment to her about the suicide attempt and resulting health complications was, "It serves you right. You wanna die? Then *die!*" Turner explained that that was when she developed hatred for Ike.[76]

The failed suicide attempt, an increasing reliance upon psychics, her developing cultural awareness, and commercial needs led Tina Turner to begin exercising her own creative agency in the Ike & Tina Turner Revue. In 1969, she took her first album production credit when she coproduced the album *Outta Season* on Blue Thumb Records, with Bob Krasnow. The album included a cover, by Ike and her, of the Otis Redding song "I've Been Loving You Too Long," which reached number 68 in May 1969.[77] The album also contained "I Am a Motherless Child," the song, written by Turner herself, in which she voiced her struggles with abandonment caused by her parents' departure. On the Revue's next album for Blue Thumb, *The Hunter*, Turner cowrote the song "Bold Soul Sister," which peaked on the *Billboard Soul Singles* chart at number 22. These successes made Turner herself pay attention to music charts and new kinds of music, including rock music, which she perceived as fundamentally different from the blues and rhythm and blues that the Revue played. She pushed the Revue to incorporate covers of rock music. The Revue covered the Beatles' song "Come Together" and the Rolling Stones' "Honky Tonk Women" for their *Come Together* album, on Liberty Records.[78] When the Rolling Stones announced a US tour for November of that year, the Ike & Tina Turner Revue joined them as an opening act. The resulting reception from the Rolling Stones' white fan base allowed the Revue to finally achieve crossover success.

Much of this success was driven by Turner herself, and, as Loder understood, she was "clearly making some kind of move."[79] For Turner, it seemed as if the predictions of the psychic in London that she would be among the biggest stars and her consultations with Hurkos were starting to come true. And professionally, Turner was becoming more comfortable working in multiple genres. Indicative of the multiple genres that the Revue worked in, profiles in the *New York Times* would variously categorize the group as "rhythm and blues," "soul," "rock," and "rock-soul." This genre crossing would remain a mainstay of Tina Turner's solo career, even as Ike Turner rebranded himself solely as a blues guitarist. Slowly, she was becoming conscious of herself as an independent, creative entity.

"Proud Mary"

One of the fruits of the Revue's explorations was their 1970 cover of "Proud Mary." The song was composed by John Fogerty of Credence Clearwater Rival, in that band's trademark bluesy, swamp-rock style.[80] While Ike Turner reportedly did not like the song, Tina Turner heard it when another band covered it and became interested in doing her own version.[81] The Ike & Tina Turner Revue began performing "Proud Mary" in their shows toward the end of 1968, before finally recording it. Turner's usage of language on the track can be contrasted with her 1969 composition of the blues song "Motherless Child," which captures the feelings of her earlier life, and her 1973 composition "Nutbush City Limits," which details the quotidian nature of life in rural Nutbush, Tennessee. While each song that Turner composed can be broadly construed as autobiographical, each of her compositions is marked by different uses of voice and pronoun. For example, "I Am a Motherless Child" takes a plaintive tone and features "I" and "my."

Sometimes *I'm* exhausted and driven, Lord
Sometimes *I* don't know where to go
My mother and father won't own *me*
So *I'll* try to make heaven *my* home.[82]

Closely following the inspiration of one of her gospel idols, Mahalia Jackson, Turner's early composition stands firmly in the gospel-blues tradition. These usages of "I" and "my" lend a pointed sense of personal longing and despair to the haunting track. Compare this to "Nutbush City Limits." This song is also autobiographical but takes an impersonal voice to narrate the details of life in her hometown of Nutbush.

You go to the fields on weekdays
And have a picnic on Labor Day
You go to town on Saturdays
But go to church every Sunday.[83]

This song presents a realist depiction of life in Nutbush. Even as "Nutbush City Limits" is delivered in an impersonal style of address, it draws on Turner's intimate familiarity with her hometown. As chapter 1 detailed, Turner grew up going to the fields, picnics, and churches that she sings about. "Proud Mary," though, is distinguished from both songs in several meaningful ways.

"Proud Mary" was released on the 1970 album *Workin' Together*, which featured some of the Revue's most message-heavy songwriting and covers of funk, rock, and soul music. The song features a spoken-word introduction, composed by Turner herself.

You know, every now and then
I think you might like to hear something from us
Nice and easy but there's just one thing
You see, we never ever do nothing nice and easy.[84]

Turner employs a colloquial style of speaking, opening with "You know, every now and then . . ." and sets up what initially appears to be an *us*-versus-*them* dynamic: "I think you might like to hear something from *us* nice and easy." The terms are ambiguous: Does "you" refer to a general listening public or a white listening audience, who is perceived as the target of this crossover music? Does "us" refer to the Revue or to Black artists attempting to crossover? There is a similar ambiguity in her usage of "we": "*We* never ever do nothing . . ." Is this "we" referring to Black people, to the Revue, or to both? The introduction ends with Turner finally resolving that she will do the song both ways: nice and easy *and* nice and rough.

Cultural critic Emily Lordi's analysis of the choices and discursive work conveyed when an artist covers another artist's song in *Black Resonance: Iconic Women Singers and African American Literature* is pertinent in discussions of how "Proud Mary" functions as a cover song. Lordi explains that in covering a song, an artist expresses agency and creativity.[85] On "Proud Mary," Tina Turner is revealed as a masterful cover artist, rich composer, and agentive performer. Yet, this is not solely or even primarily an act of expression for Turner. She was facing increased pressure and abuse from Ike because of his perception of the group's dwindling fortunes and lack of chart successes, so she was writing not to express herself, as Lordi understands it, but to help the Revue overcome their commercial slump and stave off Ike Turner's physical abuse. Here, we are reminded of Audre Lorde's reflections in "Poetry Is Not a Luxury": composition was not a luxury for Tina Turner, it was a consequential act of survival.[86]

As with Turner's creative efforts on *Outta Season*, *The Hunter*, and *Come Together*, "Proud Mary" and the *Workin' Together* album were immense successes. "Proud Mary" became a gold-selling single, and the Turners won a Grammy Award in the Best R&B Vocal Performance by a Group category.[87] While the song was a crossover success,[88] it was also a success among Black audiences, partly because of the song's resonance with earlier blues traditions; Craig Werner argues that the Black "listeners who made Ike and Tina Turner's remake of 'Proud Mary' a major R & B hit heard more than a touch of the blues in Tina's incendiary performance."[89] If Black audiences heard "more than a touch of the blues," they also heard an invitation to the emotional frenzy of an ecstatic Black church service embodied in her delivery. Stylistically, Turner's delivery on "Proud Mary" brings an echo of the climactic emotional frenzy that preachers in African American Protestant churches could sometimes work up in their congregants.

The "frenzy" was named by W. E. B. Du Bois in reference to the shout or holy dance performed particularly in the context of Black southern churches.[90] American religious historian Wallace Best estimated that in some African American Protestant churches in the rural South, the shout was "second only in importance to the sermon and was the centerpiece of emotionally frenzied worship," and that the 1930s and 1940s saw a "rise of emotionalism" even in Black churches in urban centers like Chicago.[91] The frenzy was often elicited in congregations when preachers moved from the prepared text of a sermon to extemporaneous preaching, with their volume steadily rising. Eventually the orderliness of preacher and congregation would give way to the emotional frenzy.[92]

Tina Turner echoes this elicitation of emotional frenzy in "Proud Mary." In the song's introduction, Turner begins speaking in a slow-paced, conversational prose, then shifts to a slightly faster, higher-note delivery of the first two verses and chorus, before the song finally changes to a fast-tempo rhythm and blues song. In this final movement, Turner brings her listener to the frenzied climax. Thus, as another instance of Lordi's "black resonance," the song's success was due in part to its resonance with this familiar aspect of ecstatic Afro-Protestant church worship. As we have seen, the intertwined nature of blues and Afro-Protestant Christianity, in particular, infused both Ike's and Tina's musical backgrounds. With "Proud Mary," Turner drew upon her experiences in Black Baptist and Pentecostal churches, her familiarity with the delivery modes of Black preachers, and her association with other postsanctified performers in the process of developing her career as a rhythm and blues singer, and as a rock performer.

The success of "Proud Mary," with Tina Turner's original introduction, and albums like *Come Together* and *Workin' Together*, propelled the Ike & Tina Turner Revue into the seventies. Ike Turner was able to realize his dream of opening a recording studio, which he named Bolic Sound Studios.[93] Each success brought the need for further success, a need that Ike felt acutely and was compounded by what had become a serious addiction to cocaine. Desperation and addiction fueled Ike's intensifying physical violence against Turner. During this period, solo work opportunities poured in for Turner. She released several albums produced by others, continued covering rock music, and expanded into new genres with country and gospel albums. She also added a film credit to her catalogue with a solo cameo appearance as the "Acid Queen" in the 1975 film *Tommy*, directed by Ken Russell. While business arrangements for these projects were handled by

Ike Turner—in effect licensing her to others, as he did for 1966's "River Deep, Mountain High"—they still represented increased independence for Turner. She explained: "Now that I was spending more and more time outside the bubble, I think Ike sensed that he was losing his hold on me. . . . I was distancing myself from 'Ike and Tina.'"[94]

Metaphysical Religion

The more time Turner spent away from Ike, working on solo projects, the more reflective she became. Of Ike's own religious sensibilities, Turner explained: "By this time we were playing places like the Fillmore in San Francisco, and Ike was starting to meet these white hippie girls. They'd be turning him on to cults and things, and telling him he was like a god—it got real crazy. Ike would be walking around saying things like, 'Caesar did cocaine!' And I'd be thinking, 'Great, Ike—Caesar's dead.'"[95] But, fueled by her reliance on psychics, Turner was starting to reflect on her life and her own religiosity. She explained: "I had always held on to the bible and the things I'd learned as a little girl—the Lord's Prayer, the Ten Commandments. And I prayed every night, you can believe that." She continued, "But now I was really seeking a change, and I knew that it had to come from the inside out—that I had to understand myself, and accept myself, before anything else could be accomplished. The readers—the good ones—helped me do that. I'm not talking about fortune-telling or witchcraft. I was looking for the truth of a future that I could feel inside of me.[96] As Turner's understanding of her own religiosity developed, psychic readers, Peter Hurkos foremost among them, were a therapeutic resource for her and a source of hope. Even as she disavows any association to practices of fortune-telling or witchcraft, Turner's consultations with psychics connects her back to the supernaturalism permeating her early religious life in West Tennessee.

In the context of Black southern religious culture, healers, conjurers, and diviners played an important role as professional supernatural specialists who could be consulted by members of their communities. "Some early-twentieth-century blacks," explains scholar LaShawn Harris, "viewed supernatural consultants as intermediaries between the spirit world and God and human beings; they believed that hoodoo and conjure practices and other supernatural rituals and paraphernalia were potentially beneficial to their daily lives."[97] These supernatural consultants included psychics and diviners, those who could draw on extrasensory perception, dreams, or other forms of foreknowledge to provide guidance to those who sought it. Perhaps like some others from Nutbush and surrounding communities, Turner fit Hurkos and other psychics into a framework that did not exclude her Black Baptist (and Pentecostal) background, but instead further deepened it. About her explorations, Turner said, "[I] also felt my chains lifting when I started paying attention to matters of the spirit and the soul. I'm a seeker, so I've always been drawn to psychics and readers."[98]

Around the time the Ike & Tina Turner Revue released Turner's composition "Nutbush City Limits," her spiritual reflections intensified.

Well, by the time "Nutbush City Limits" hit, I was turning thirty-four years old. I think when a woman reaches those mid-thirties, her thinking starts to change; I know mine did. I started thinking about this career I had, about how when I'd started out I thought it would be such a glamorous life. But there was nothing glamorous about it. It wasn't even my career—it was Ike's career. And it was Ike's songs, mostly, and they were always about Ike's life—and I had to sing them. I was just his tool. Then I started thinking about my marriage.[99]

Processing these feelings led Turner to devote further attention to her spiritual development. At the same time, Turner's ruminations echoed broader changes in the religious and cultural life of America in the sixties and seventies. Her statements align her with the "spiritual seeker," an archetype that emerged—as explained by cultural historian Jane Iwamura—in the tumult of the sixties:

The 1960s was a watershed period in American history—a time of unusual social, political, cultural, and religious transformation. The period saw the popular recognition of "alternative" lifestyles and spiritual experimentation, as well as a new tolerance toward "peoples of color" (in the form of the Civil Rights movement and the 1965 Immigration Act). At the same time, this transformation was underwritten by a sense of loss—a loss configured by the wounds of war, the impact of technology and global capitalism, domestic racial strife, and growing disillusionment with traditional forms of religious faith and worship. Out of this context emerged the archetype of the American religious subject as a "spiritual seeker" who journeys in search of new religious ground for reconciliation and healing.[100]

While the broad outlines of this American cultural transformation, sketched by Iwamura and others, are no doubt accurate, Turner's life also enables a nuancing of the details. For example, religious and cultural shifts occurred for African Americans as they moved out of the South and into urban cities in the North during the Great Migration in the early decades of the twentieth century.

As African Americans experienced difficult living conditions in cramped urban environments, they formed cultural establishments that "tempered the vagaries of black people's urban existence" and became sites for the "survival of supernatural practices." Some of these, like Black spiritualist churches, enabled specialists in supernatural practices to earn a living as "mediums, psychic readers, and spiritual healers."[101] Yvonne P. Chireau notes how press advertisements in Black newspapers from the 1920s and 1930s emphasized the credentials of these specialists. They also referenced their skills in numerology, palmistry, astrology, and so on. At the same time, these newspapers show an influx of new identities, especially identities of professional supernatural specialists from India and other parts of Asia. In this context, "theosophy, astrology, and European spiritualism," alongside "the influences of various Asian philosophies in American culture at the turn of the twentieth century," came to influence Black supernatural practices like conjure and magic.[102] These trends continued in African American life into the middle decades of the twentieth century and beyond.[103] For Black Americans, then, the spiritual-seeker identity and the predilection for religious experimentation that attends it did not emerge in the sixties and seventies. Instead it emerged in the early twentieth century.

Nonetheless, from the countercultural movements of the sixties came a flourishing of nontraditional religions, and by the end of the seventies, the seeker could engage in a wide variety of practices drawn from an equally wide array of religious traditions.[104] Such spiritual seekers emerged around the United States, but California, in particular, served as a key locale for spiritual seekers' explorations. Living in Los Angeles during this time of cultural transformation, Turner was taking advantage of this variety of spiritual resources.

The picture of Tina Turner's religiosity that emerges during this period, constituted by reliance upon psychics and a developing intuition that change must come from within, can best be captured by the label "metaphysical religion." American religious historian Catherine Albanese explains that metaphysical religion represents one of three types of American religiosity. The first type, labeled "evangelical," "favors the cultivation of strong emotional experience that is felt as life-transforming." Its underlying mentality is "built on a sense of separation from the source of spiritual power (historically, in Christian America, God or his son and emissary Jesus) that needs to be overcome."[105] For Turner, this form of American religiosity held limited theological appeal because she did not accept the abstract notions of God that she learned about in her early Black Baptist church experiences.[106] The second type, labeled "liturgical," is based in "communally organized ceremonial action." The liturgical type, represented by mainstream-denominational traditions, also emphasizes separation from the source of spiritual power but overcomes this through a series of "inner correspondences" between oneself and the divine, where the operative notion is grace.[107] Turner's experiences at Woodlawn Missionary Baptist Church and Spring Hill Baptist Church in Nutbush and Spring Hill, Tennessee, respectively, fall under this type of religiosity. Albanese understands the third type, the "metaphysical" form, or metaphysical religion, to privilege "the mind in forms that include reason but move beyond it to intuition, clairvoyance, and its relatives such as 'revelation' and 'higher guidance.'"[108] As Albanese describes, throughout American religious history, metaphysical religion has been able to encompass ideas and practices from Europe, Asia, and Africa, as well as those native to this continent. By the twentieth century, metaphysical religion embraced many who saw themselves as members of the group that Iwamura identified as "spiritual seekers." This group includes the Black professional supernatural specialists discussed above.[109] Both Turner's devotion to psychics and her self-understanding as a "spiritual seeker" utilizing a variety of religious tools fit in this category. Additionally, Turner's religiosity in this period evidences a "vernacular religion" in which "*everybody* glosses a tradition in one way or another to put life's pieces together. In the religious vernacular, *everybody* creates; *everybody* picks and chooses from what is available to constitute changing religious" repertoires.[110] Albanese sees this American metaphysical religion, inclusive of the notion of the religious vernacular, as a fundamentally combinatory force that combines a wide array of religious phenomena into a coherent religious repertoire. The combinatory nature of the religious sensibilities that Tina Turner forged during the six-year period from her first encounter with a psychic in 1966 to the eve of her introduction to Soka Gakkai Nichiren Buddhism in 1973 is in this sense best captured by American metaphysical religion.

Conclusion

Tina Turner was enacting this American metaphysical vernacular religion to construct a religious repertoire of tools—including those of Black Baptist and metaphysical religion, itself inclusive of the trends of supernaturalism and psychical experiences—to assimilate a series of personal crises and transformations that occurred over the fifteen-year period between 1957 and 1972.[111] In 1958, she had become "Little Ann," an occasional vocalist for Ike Turner and the Kings of Rhythm band. Two years later, with the success of "A Fool in Love," she became "Tina Turner" and the band became the Ike & Tina Turner Revue. In the Revue's early years, Tina Turner had limited freedom or creative control within the band. As the band became more successful, Ike Turner's physical violence against and control over Turner increased. In 1966, buoyed by the British success of the Phil Spector-produced song "River Deep, Mountain High," Turner traveled with the Ike & Tina Turner Revue to England, France, and Germany for the first time. There, her religious world expanded through an introduction to psychics, even as her cultural world diversified. From 1966 to 1972, she relied on psychics, who instilled in her the hope of an independent future. The sense of confidence that resulted fueled her creative output as she wrote her first songs and pushed the Revue into new directions.

In this period, Turner never gave evidence that she saw a distinction between her pursuit of metaphysical beliefs and her Afro-Protestant upbringing. Rather, to her, it was all an "exploration of the soul," characteristic of her self-identification as a spiritual seeker. This likely owes to the persistence of supernatural beliefs and practices in the religious culture of her upbringing. As we saw above, Turner's religious explorations fall under the third type of American religiosity, called metaphysical religion. Through these explorations she sought to understand her traumatic experiences with Ike Turner, and their successes and disappointments, and to incorporate an increasingly globalized understanding of the world gained on international tours. As a category, American metaphysical religion encapsulates diverse strands in Turner's religious life up to 1973, and it bridges the gaps in her life between her Afro-Protestant upbringing, her psychical and supernatural inclinations, and her conversion to Soka Gakkai Nichiren Buddhism.

3

Tina's Prayer

I was born into a Baptist family, and I'd still pray the Lord's Prayer. But Buddhism gave me other words, Nam-myoho-renge-kyo, another spiritual system, and it worked. It gives me the clarity and wisdom to change what is in my power to change.

—"The Queen of Hope: Tina Turner," *Living Buddhism*

Tina Turner converted to Soka Gakkai Nichiren Buddhism in 1973. Turner's conversion did not come about *ex nihilo*. Rather, she was primed for her conversion to Buddhism by her self-identification as a "spiritual seeker." As a spiritual seeker Turner had developed a religious repertoire that combined her Afro-Protestant background (alongside the supernaturalism and mysticism of Black southern religious culture) and American metaphysical religion. Friends like Vicki Wickham had already introduced Turner to a psychic in 1966. After this, Turner frequently consulted with psychics like Peter Hurkos. As the previous chapter described, the Ike & Tina Turner Revue was surrounded by groupies who followed the Revue on tour. Specifically, these groupies followed Ike Turner, telling him about mystical spirituality and occult ideas. Thus, when Turner encountered Buddhism, it was only one set of religious ideas among the many she was hearing about. But when a sound engineer, her son Ronnie Turner, and Valerie Bishop each separately told Turner about Soka Gakkai

Nichiren Buddhism and its chanting practice, Turner took notice. Bishop, in particular, taught Turner how to practice and eventually brought Turner to her first Buddhist meetings.

First Two Encounters with Buddhism

In *Happiness Becomes You*, Turner recalled that, in addition to Ronnie, a recording engineer at Ike Turner's Bolic Sound Studios told her about chanting. "Tina, you should try chanting. It will help change your life," the sound engineer explained. Turner may have quickly forgotten about this encounter, since she did not ask the engineer to explain further what he meant.[1] It wasn't until her son Ronnie "came home carrying what looked like a lacquered brown wooden rosary" that she learned more about chanting.[2]

In 1973, the Turner family was still living in the View Park neighborhood of Inglewood, just south of Los Angeles. Inglewood served as the headquarters of the entire Turner organization, which, at this time, comprised the Ike & Tina Turner Revue, including Ike and Tina; their backing band called the Family Vibes; and the Ikettes, their three-person troupe of backing singers and dancers. Together, the Ike & Tina Turner Revue mostly rehearsed and recorded near the Turners' home, at Bolic Sound Studios, located at 1310 La Brea Avenue. When not in Inglewood, they toured extensively, playing small local clubs as well as prestigious gigs in venues like the Las Vegas Hilton Hotel and Madison Square Garden in New York City, and undertook major international tours to Canada, Europe, Japan, Australia, and the Middle East.

The Turners' home life mirrored their work life in intensity. In *My Love Story*, Turner described their home life as a "mockery of a 'normal' relationship: defined by abuse and fear, not love, or even affection."[3] Before Ike built Bolic Sound, he had a recording studio in the living room of the family home. While the Revue maintained its intensive touring schedule, Ike and Tina employed several nannies to watch their four children: Craig, Ike Jr., Michael, and Ronnie. When they weren't touring, Turner remembers, Ike spent his time recording at home at all hours of the night, with minimal interaction with the children.[4] Even as Ike Turner was hands-off with the children, Turner explained that she tried her best to instill the manners she had learned from living with her grandparents and the Henderson family in the

Brownsville area of West Tennessee. At the same time, she tried to provide a semblance of normalcy for the children, which was missing from her own upbringing.[5] Still, the children's home life was marred by witnessing their mother and father's volatile relationship. Ike Turner Jr. and Michael Turner have rarely spoken in public about their parents' relationship. Turner's oldest son, Craig, told Kurt Loder that his stepfather would "sometimes just be out of his mind."[6] In the 2021 HBO and Lightbox Films documentary *TINA*, Craig recounted that when Ike came home he would take Turner into their bedroom, from which the children could hear Turner's screams, and the children would pull the covers over their heads to drown out the screams.[7] Ronnie, their youngest son and the only child of both Ike and Tina, recalled that Turner would sometimes take him with her to Bolic Sound so that she would have an excuse to leave, and that he was aware of how unhappy she was.[8] It was Ronnie who first explained the practice of chanting to Turner.

One day, in their View Park neighborhood, Ronnie was approached on the street by someone who told him that chanting *Nam-myoho-renge-kyo* could help you "get anything you want."[9] Ronnie returned home carrying the prayer beads that Turner described as being a "lacquered brown wooden rosary," but he explained to his mother that they were in fact Buddhist chanting beads and that if she chanted, she too could "have anything [she] wanted."[10] In effect, Ronnie had experienced the "street-corner *shakubuku*" conversion tactics that were prevalent in the sixties and early seventies, in Nichiren Shoshu Soka Gakkai of America.

Soka Gakkai Nichiren Buddhism

Soka Gakkai was founded in 1930 as the Soka Kyoiku Gakkai (Value-Creating Education Society), by the Japanese educators Tsunesaburo Makiguchi (1877–1944) and Josei Toda (1900–1958). Makiguchi spent much of his youth on Japan's northernmost island of Hokkaido and began his teaching career there. Eventually he moved with his family to Tokyo, where he worked as a principal and developed his educational theories around culture, geography, and the role of the state. Makiguchi grew increasingly dissatisfied with the Japanese educational system in the early years of the twentieth century, and he formed the Soka Kyoiku Gakkai as a group of like-minded educators focused on reform.[11] With the help of his disciple, fellow educator Josei Toda, Makiguchi published his own educational theories in a work titled *The System of Value-Creating Pedagogy*, on November 18, 1930.[12] Two years prior to the publication of this work, both Makiguchi and Toda converted to Nichiren Shoshu Buddhism.

Like other sects of the Nichiren-shu, the teachings of Nichiren Daishonin are based on the *gosho*, or the collected writings of Nichiren Shonin ("Nichiren the Great Sage," 1222–1282). Nichiren was a thirteenth-century monk in Japan who lived during the Kamakura period (1185–1333).[13] Originally ordained in the Buddhist Tendai sect, he publicly broke with the sect in 1253 over what he saw as doctrinal errors on the part of his contemporaries. Due to his subscription to the idea that the people of his day were living in *mappo*, or "the latter day" of the Buddhist teachings, Nichiren proclaimed that these doctrinal errors were the direct cause of the political, social, and economic instability of Kamakura-era Japan.[14] Rather than accept the erroneous teachings promulgated by other schools, Nichiren urged people to adhere to the teachings contained in the *Saddharma-pundarika-sutra*, or the "Teaching of the Lotus Blossom of the Wonderful Law" ("Lotus Sutra" hereafter). Specifically, he declared that chanting the title of the text in the form of the mantra *Nam-myoho-renge-kyo* (known as the *daimoku*, or "title") was the most efficacious Buddhist practice for people living in the latter day of the Buddhist teachings. Eventually, Nichiren codified his teachings into a schema known as the *three great secret laws*: "1) The *Gohonzon*, or mandalic representation of awakened reality, 2) the *Daimoku* of Nam-Myoho-Renge-Kyo, and 3) the *Kaidan*, or place where the *Gohonzon* is enshrined."[15]

Nichiren Shoshu teachings are distinguished from other branches of the Nichiren-shu in their view of Nichiren, the *gohonzon*, and the tracing of their lineage. Nichiren Shoshu understands Nichiren to be the Buddha of the latter day of the teachings. In other words, for this sect, Nichiren and his teachings supersede the teachings of Shakyamuni, the historical Buddha. They uphold the worship of a *gohonzon* housed at their head temple, Taisekiji, as the focal point of their practice. They also understand Nichiren's disciple Nikko to be the originator of their lineage. Following Nikko's death in the fourteenth century, a succession of high priests led the Nichiren Shoshu sect from its base at the foot of Mount Fuji in Japan.

From the fourteenth century to the early years of the twentieth, Nichiren Shoshu remained a marginal sect, but their fortunes began to change once the Soka Kyoiku Gakkai joined the sect as a lay organization and increased their membership through their propagation activities. Even as both grew, their expansion occurred against the backdrop of an increasingly militarized Japanese state. By 1941, the Japanese government had begun close surveillance of religious organizations via Japan's Special Higher Police. Invoking the 1925 Peace Preservation Law, the government prevailed upon all religious organizations to enshrine talismans to the sun goddess, revered as an imperial ancestor. At the same time, the government was encouraging (as a precursor to requiring) Buddhist denominations to merge. Nichiren Shoshu was no exception to this, and they urged their lay organizations, including Soka Kyoiku Gakkai, to comply with the government's directives. Makiguchi, Toda, and the leadership refused to enshrine the talisman, seeing it as an infringement on their religious freedom, and Makiguchi in particular urged Nichiren Shoshu's clerical body to refuse the request to merge with other Nichiren sects.[16] By July 1943, Makiguchi, Toda, and the entire leadership of the Soka Kyoiku Gakkai had been arrested and the educational and lay Buddhist organization, disbanded. While Makiguchi would die in prison on November 18, 1944, at age seventy-three, Toda experienced two spiritual awakenings in prison and was released from prison on July 3, 1945. He reformulated the organization as the Soka Gakkai—henceforth a religious organization, rather than an educational study society—and became its second president on May 3, 1951.[17]

During Toda's presidency, Makiguchi's theories were brought into greater alignment with the philosophy and practice of Nichiren Shoshu Buddhism, lending Soka Gakkai a distinctively modernist take on Buddhism. Summarizing Toda's understanding of Nichiren Buddhism, Richard Seager explains, "Toda's Buddhism was both a restatement of and an expansion upon Makiguchi's hybrid philosophy. He deepened its traditional aspects by an increased dependence on the Lotus Sutra, Nichiren's *Gosho*, and Nichiren Shoshu doctrine. He also strengthened its modernist elements by identifying the Buddha with the life force and by teaching Buddhism as a transformative force in culture and politics."[18] Toda became known for a pragmatic style that sought to convey Buddhist concepts in simple, everyday language. For example, rather than providing abstruse technical discussions of the *gohonzon*—the central object of practice in Nichiren Buddhism—Toda often explained that the *gohonzon* was a "happiness producing machine." Daisaku Ikeda quoted Toda as saying, "With much trepidation lest I am thought blasphemous, I compare the Gohonzon to a machine that produces happiness." Toda carried his analogy further and included a discussion of the prescribed daily practice, explaining that "Its operation is quite simple. You only have to observe morning and evening gongyo every day and strive to convert ten people each year."[19] Toda's words also evince the focus on propagation of Nichiren Buddhism, or *shakubuku* (see below), that he bequeathed to Soka Gakkai. By the time of Toda's death in 1958, the Soka Gakkai had substantially passed Toda's goal of converting 750,000 member households.[20] In 1960, Toda's disciple Daisaku Ikeda became the third Soka Gakkai president.

Daisaku Ikeda (1928–) met Toda at a Soka Gakkai meeting in August of 1947 and joined the organization soon thereafter. Ikeda took Toda as his mentor and started working for Toda's various companies. At the same time, Toda drew on his background as an educator to privately tutor his disciple, who had quit school to work for him.[21] Toda gave Ikeda his first leadership responsibilities in the Soka Gakkai in 1952, and by June of 1959 (a year after Toda's death) Ikeda had been appointed as both Soka Gakkai's general manager and head of the board of directors, becoming the organization's third president a year later, on May 3, 1960.[22] Levi McLaughlin explains that, just as Toda built on Makiguchi's ideas to expand the organization, Ikeda, as the Gakkai's new president, "built on Toda's initiatives in response to the priorities of the postwar generation. In 1960, many in the country were eager to embrace a new rhetoric of internationalism and Japan's return to the company of powerful nations, this time as a harbinger of peace."[23] Taking advantage of this new zeitgeist and endeavoring to organize the group's scattered membership abroad, Ikeda set out to globalize the Soka Gakkai. In October of the same year, Ikeda embarked on his first overseas trip to the United States, Canada, and Brazil—all places where several Japanese members had moved.

Members of Soka Gakkai first came to the United States in the fifties. While the organization claimed a substantial following in Japan, its presence was marginal in the United States. These members were mostly "the Japanese wives of American military men."[24] The early members struggled due to language barriers between these Japanese-speaking women and their English-speaking neighbors, isolation from other members, and a lack of organizational support in the absence of Soka Gakkai community centers or Nichiren Shoshu temples.[25] After the election of Ikeda in 1960, propagation efforts increased around the world. That same year, Ikeda, accompanied by a team of organizational leaders, traveled to the United States and established Nichiren Shoshu Soka Gakkai of America (NSA) in Los Angeles. Once NSA was established, the members were encouraged to expand their conversion efforts. Initially they targeted fellow Japanese immigrants, but by 1963 they were able to conduct portions of their meetings in English. During his visit in 1960, Ikeda placed a young immigrant named Masayasu Sadanaga in charge of the nascent American branch of the organization.[26] In 1985 Sadanaga—who had changed his name to George M. Williams to appeal to hippies and other young people—published *Freedom and Influence: The Role of Religion in American Society* to reflect on the twenty-five-year development of the NSA organization, in the context of American religious history.

According to his book, Williams joined Soka Gakkai in 1953 under President Toda. His practice developed under both Toda and Ikeda before coming to the United States in 1957, to study at the University of California, Los Angeles (UCLA).[27] Williams experienced firsthand the isolation of members from each other, as members often did not know there were other Soka Gakkai members near them. While Toda had been interested in Soka Gakkai members abroad and the organization's Japanese daily publication, *Seikyo Shimbun*, occasionally featured profiles of members abroad, the organization was centered in Japan.[28] In July 1960, Ikeda established the Overseas Branch to organize support for Soka Gakkai's international membership. In his 1969 study of Soka Gakkai's Japanese and American members, James Allen Dator used the *Seikyo Shimbun* and the *Seikyo Graphic*, two of the Gakkai's Japanese-language publications, to make a general classification of the organization's members abroad. Dator found that these members fell into four categories: Japanese women married to American military personnel and residing in the United States or on American military bases, Japanese emigrants to South America (and to a lesser extent North America), representatives of Japanese business firms who moved abroad, and Japanese students in the United States and Europe.[29] Williams fell into the last category, as he studied first at UCLA and later at Georgetown University. In the bureaucratic structure of the

Soka Gakkai, Ikeda initially established the American organization as the American General Chapter, with Williams as its leader. In 1963, on Ikeda's second visit to the United States, NSA opened its first community center in the Little Tokyo neighborhood of downtown Los Angeles. That same year NSA was registered as a nonprofit religious corporation in the United States.[30] With NSA's formal establishment, propagation efforts began in earnest. At Ikeda's behest, Williams spearheaded efforts to propagate Nichiren's teachings. Nichiren had taught that there were two means to spread Buddhist teachings: *shoju* and *shakubuku*. The former refers to the "method of expounding Buddhism in which one gradually leads another to the correct teaching according to that person's capacity and without refuting his or her attachment to mistaken views."[31] For Nichiren, this meant introducing teachings to the person slowly, and in a manner that does not conflict with beliefs the person already holds. By contrast, the latter method refers to refuting erroneous views people might have and "eliminating their attachment to opinions they have formed. [It] thus means to correct another's false views and awaken that person to the truth of Buddhism."[32] According to Nichiren, *shakubuku* was the primary means for teaching Buddhism. Toda, mentor of Ikeda and second president of Soka Gakkai, encouraged members of the organization in Japan to aggressively share the practice with others, while setting membership goals for his followers. As a result of what some perceived as aggressive, heavy-handed recruitment tactics, and their entry into politics, the organization gained a negative reputation in Japan that persists to this day.[33] In the United States, *shakubuku* took the form of the aforementioned "street *shakubuku*," wherein members went to parks, stood on street corners, rode public transportation, and wandered neighborhoods. This tactic, which had been successful in Japan, was seen by Williams and others as the best way to introduce an unfamiliar religion into a new land.[34] As detailed in Williams's book, through *shakubuku* and understanding American religious history, NSA consciously sought to create an American religious organization. Williams summarized this effort by explaining that "NSA has steadfastly maintained the fundamental teachings of Nichiren Daishonin ['the Great Sage'] and the organizational principles of the Soka Gakkai which support them, while carefully designing a format for activities that would be suitable for American members."[35]

Nichiren Shoshu Soka Gakkai of America (later rebranded as Soka Gakkai International–USA, hereafter SGI-USA) made calculated accommodations to aspects of American culture. As Hammond and Machacek explain:

> Where other new religions of the 1960s decried American materialism, Soka Gakkai embraced it. To the communal religions of the period, for example, attachment to material goods only distracted people from their focus on higher goals, and led to selfishness and competitiveness. Soka Gakkai, alternatively, interpreted material success as evidence of the efficacy of the practice. Competitiveness and the achievement of specific, identifiable goals were portrayed as evidence of human revolution taking place in the individual's life. Instead of tuning in, turning on, and dropping out, Soka Gakkai members got focused, dove in, and got on with life. The general tactic, in other words, has been one of accommodation to American culture.[36]

This conscious accommodation contributed to SGI-USA's long-term success in the United States. Hammond and Machacek point out that as the organization changed its tactics from the aggressive proselytizing methods charted above, combined with consumerist accommodations, the organization's rapid growth slowed down. At the same time, they ceased holding large-scale parades and public festivals and shifted to sponsoring more "neutral" activities such as "sponsoring art and cultural exhibits, local performances, and subscription drives for SGI publications."[37] With this changed focus, the organization also streamlined its vertical leadership structure, where members are appointed to leadership positions responsible for larger areas at each ascending level. This is balanced by horizontal connections between members in each area or district. It is this model of lay participation that emboldens the practitioners of SGI-USA to take on leadership roles in the organization, which also entails taking on roles as teachers. SGI-USA calls on each practitioner to *shakubuku* others, which, as we have seen, essentially means to teach others about the practice. To do so, members attend Buddhist meetings to discuss the practice, share experiences of the efficacy of chanting, and study the teachings of Nichiren and the first three presidents of the organization: Makiguchi, Toda, and

Ikeda. In the meetings, members and sometimes their guests take on various roles such as emcee and presenter. In fulfilling these roles, members learn to study and communicate Buddhist teachings and ideas. Thus, each member is trained to be a lay Buddhist teacher.

On that day in 1973 when Ronnie Turner began to tell his mother about the practice, he was attempting to engage in the practice of *shakubuku,* as taught in the SGI-USA Buddhist meetings. Turner recalls her son explaining to her that the practice of chanting was "mystical, but it all makes sense," and that while he couldn't explain the practice, she should accompany him "up the street to a chanting meeting and learn more."[38] But she did not attend any meetings with him because, she said, "By that time, I was basically a prisoner in my own home; I couldn't go anywhere without Ike's permission. He rarely allowed me to go on my own to places other than the grocery store or the recording studio."[39] Thus, much like the engineer's attempt to introduce the practice to her, Ronnie's attempt proved futile. Instead, Turner was left to continue her explorations with psychics and astrology.

Astrology

Turner's interest in astrology is yet another marker of her embrace of American metaphysical religion. In both European and American religious history, astrology has maintained an interpretive role for understanding the universe and the human being's place in it. Astrology held an important place in the complex of Rosicrucian, hermetic, and other metaphysical ideas that flowed from Continental Europe and England to seventeenth-century Anglo-America. "In a cosmology of resonances and replications," Albanese explains, astrology was called into service to explain how astrological signs connected people to the four elements of earth, air, water, and fire.[40] Here, celestial bodies evoke the different elements and are assigned to the astrological signs. When combined with theories of bodily humors and speculation on the mysteries of time, astrology became an effective interpretive model that explained correspondences between the macrocosmic universe and the microcosm of the natural world and human life (49–50). Astrological speculation filtered through the British colonies such that Albanese could conclude, "Throughout the colonies, the pervasive presence of almanacs [filled with astrological content] alongside Bibles ...

spelled out a combinative astrological Hermeticism that had survived the British Atlantic passage and continued to be a familiar feature of vernacular culture in the eighteenth century and after" (78). The "and after" of astrology's place in American religious history would see it play a role in nineteenth-century religious movements like Mormonism (144–48), mingle with derivative forms of Native American religiosity (471–72), function as a key knowledge base in an African American economy of supernatural professionals and metaphysicians in the twentieth century (472–73), and form a cornerstone of New Age metaphysical religious beliefs into the twenty-first century (473–75). Tina Turner's explorations of astrology in the late 1960s and early 1970s, then, confirm once again her commitment to foundational ideas in American metaphysical religious history.

In contrast to the psychics Turner worked with, however, she never named any specific astrologers that she consulted. She did though often mention her interest in astrology and referred to astrological signs to describe her own behavior and that of others like her mother and Ike Turner. And by 1973, her career with the latter was her central focus.

Ike and Tina Turner's Professional Life (1973 to 1975)

In the fall of 1973, Ike and Tina released the album *Nutbush City Limits*. The album was a significant success for the Turners. In the United States it reached its highest chart position on *Billboard*'s Hot 100, peaking at number 22 on November 17, 1973.[41] The album was also a success in European markets. *Nutbush City Limits* received near universal praise in reviews. After noting that the Ike & Tina Turner Revue's recent albums contained "only two or three credible cuts," a *Los Angeles Times* album brief went on to say, "But this new one is brimming with gems. Most of the cuts are stormy upbeat numbers and are all well suited to Turner's delightfully hysterical style. Given first-rate material, as she is here, shrieking Turner is an unbeatable soul singer."[42] *Billboard* chose the album as one of its "Top Album Picks" in the pop category and, taking a tone similar to that of the *Los Angeles Times*, described the album as "featuring far more good original material and less filler than is Ike's wont."[43]

What the *Billboard* review seems to have missed is that half of the "far more good original material" was composed by Turner herself, *not*

Ike. Continuing the creative streak that began with her songwriting on 1969's *Outta Season,* Turner is credited with writing five of the ten songs on *Nutbush City Limits.* Like the title track, "Nutbush City Limits," written about her hometown in West Tennessee, most of the songs remain in the biographical vein. For example, the song "Club Manhattan" is written about the club where she first saw Ike Turner and the Kings of Rhythm perform, the same club where she first began to sing with Ike back in St. Louis in 1956. Thus, nearly twenty years later, she was still writing about the experiences of her earlier life.

And yet, one of Turner's compositions on the album, the second track titled "Make Me Over," stands out for the way she expresses her growing dissatisfaction with the state of her life. This guitar-and-drum-driven funk-soul song begins with Turner's urgent voice calling out in the first verse:

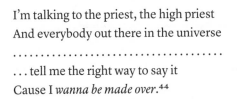

> I'm talking to the priest, the high priest
> And everybody out there in the universe
> ....
> . . . tell me the right way to say it
> Cause I *wanna be made over.*[44]

In this verse, we see Turner's appeal to whatever authority figures there might be "out there in the universe," to guide her with the right words so that she can be "made over." The reference to the "priest" and the "high priest" could be to the ministerial authority of the preachers she had known at Woodlawn Missionary Baptist Church and Spring Hill Baptist Church in Nutbush. It could also be understood as an oblique reference to the psychics she was consulting on a regular basis in Los Angeles and on international tours, including Peter Hurkos. As Turner explained, "The only thing that kept me going in those years was the readers. Whatever cities we played— here in Europe, wherever—I would always try to find a reader to go to. Some of these people read cards, some read palms, some read the stars. Some read tea leaves and coffee sediments. Some of them weren't for real, but others gave me something to hold on to, some insight into what was going on in my life. I was exploring my soul for the first time."[45] Before this search would turn inward with her third introduction to Buddhism from Valerie Bishop, Turner's explorations were still based on reliance on external authorities in the form of "psychic readers," as she expresses in "Make Me Over." As the song progresses, though, Turner clarifies that, ultimately, she is appealing to the "Lord." Each verse mixes spiritual desires for power, love, and beauty in her heart with more mundane concerns to go places, to "do some things," and to be smart, desirable, and voluptuous. While the emphasis she places on most of these desires is equal, the discerning listener can hear the way she underlines the desire for liberty in the second stanza. The song reads as a litany of desires in the form of a prayer. And indeed, later releases of the song would be called "Tina's Prayer."[46] This song presents Turner's bold quarrel with her circumstances, but in language that alludes to her spiritual seeking. And indeed, Turner was beginning to reach the end of her rope with Ike Turner. But first, Ike Turner would inadvertently precipitate her third and lasting encounter with Soka Gakkai Nichiren Buddhism.

Third Encounter with Buddhism

In the fall of 1973, during the success of the *Nutbush City Limits* album, Turner noticed that her thinking was changing. With the approach of her thirty-fourth birthday on November 26, she found herself more pensive and reflecting on her marriage and family anew. She came to realize that rather than being seen as a partner to Ike, and an equal partner in their career, she was "nothing more than a tool" to him. Comparing her real marriage with Ike with her earlier ideas about marriage, she wrote: "I remembered what marriage had meant to me when I was a girl—the loving husband and wife, the happy children. My God, I thought, how had things gone so wrong? The kids would all run and hide when Ike came home, the man was so mean."[47] Even still, she could see that Ike had his issues to deal with, and she went on to explain to Loder that Ike was aging, experiencing the effects of intensive cocaine abuse, and obsessively focused on the recording studio, spending most of his time at Bolic Sound. Turner was beginning to see that, for good or for ill, this was her life; she added, "And I was starting to see it real clearly now."[48]

Sometime after Ronnie gave her a limited introduction to the practice of chanting, Turner was given a more formal introduction by Valerie Bishop, an NSA member who was working for Ike at Bolic Sound. One day Ike brought Valerie to the house so that she could meet Turner:

So he brought this woman in, and he says to me, "Know anything about *chantin'*?" I said no, but didn't it have something to do with witchcraft? That's when he introduced the girl. Her name was Valerie Bishop, and she was a Jewish woman who was married to a black jazz musician. There was a group of mixed-marriage couples in L. A.—Herbie Hancock's wife Gigi, who was German; Wayne Shorter's wife, Anna, who was Portuguese; and also my friend Maria Booker was married to a black musician. Valerie was one of those. And she was also a chanter. I don't know how Ike met her, but he was interested in all these kind of occult things, and he thought chanting was just another one, just something to play with, then forget about. . . . She explained that it wasn't witchcraft, that it was Buddhism—Nichiren Shoshu Buddhism. And she told me about *shakubuku*, which is the first phase of teaching somebody.[49]

While Turner initially had no interest in meeting Bishop, she recognized her as one of the diverse faces that she had seen in the Ike & Tina Turner Revue's orbit. Many of these jazz musicians that Turner named had joined NSA during its conversion drives. Like Ike Turner's reasons for entertaining these kinds of "occult practices," some of them, like Herbie Hancock, would later explain that they were looking for ways to expand their musical horizons. In his memoir, *Possibilities* (2014), Hancock described a particularly moving performance that caused his band to explore more spiritual terrain. This led him and his bandmates to "hit the bookstores in various cities, reading up on all kinds of belief systems, from Transcendental Meditation to Sufism to Eastern mysticism and even the occult. We all wanted to discover whether we could somehow conjure up again what we'd felt that night onstage. . . . Finding a spiritual path seemed the way to do it, because the music itself felt so spiritual."[50] Bishop herself was married to jazz pianist Walter Bishop Jr. (1928–1998).[51]

As Bishop began to explain chanting to Turner, she realized "a gift" was being given to her, and that since this was the third time someone explained it to her, she should try the practice herself.[52] Before leaving the house, Bishop gave Turner a book with information about the practice and prayer beads, and taught her to chant *Nam-myoho-renge-kyo*.[53] In both *I, Tina* and *My Love Story*, Turner recalls having to read the material Bishop gave her and develop her practice in secrecy, as she feared that Ike would not approve of her doing it, although he himself had inadvertently introduced the practice to her. Initially, she would recite the words five times after saying the Lord's Prayer. Like her understanding of psychics, she saw chanting as consonant with her Black Baptist training from her grandmother: "I grew up saying the Lord's Prayer, so I was open to the idea of chanting, which is just another form of prayer."[54] Eventually, she increased her chanting to ten minutes, then fifteen, and finally half an hour to an hour each time.[55] From chanting, Turner immediately saw "proof" of the practice.

Central to Buddhist practice, in Soka Gakkai's understanding, is the notion of "actual proof." In Soka Gakkai Nichiren Buddhism, "actual proof" is the third of three forms of proof that Nichiren outlined to understand the value of Buddhist teachings. In one of his writings, Nichiren explains: "In judging the relative merit of Buddhist doctrines, I, Nichiren, believe that the best standards are those of reason and documentary proof. And even more valuable than reason and documentary proof is the proof of actual fact."[56] The proof of reason, often called "theoretical proof," refers to whether a doctrine makes logical sense. Documentary proof refers to whether or not a particular doctrine is locatable in Buddhist texts. Contrasted with theoretical and documentary proof, actual proof refers to whether or not there are concrete results when a teaching is put into practice. In the philosophical understanding of Tsunesaburo Makiguchi, the first president of Soka Gakkai, actual proof of practicing Buddhism is gained when one experiences benefits from the practice, which relates to his philosophy of value. Richard Seager explains that under the second president, Josei Toda, it was understood that "benefits could be both spiritual and material. At his urging, Soka Gakkai members learned to chant for vitality, courage, and mental and physical health; adequate food and housing; a decent job; a good spouse; and a happy family."[57] Such benefits are thought to increase faith and conviction in the practice. During the efforts of NSA members to *shakubuku* and convert others, they often emphasized that chanting brought actual proof in the form of tangible benefits. As with Ronnie's earlier claim that you could "get anything you want" from chanting and Valerie Bishop's explanation, Turner's introduction to the practice also focused on actual proof.

As Turner practiced, she started to experience both the spiritual and material benefits of chanting. In *I, Tina* she relates a story about searching for a brand of makeup that had been discontinued. After she started chanting, she received a call from Bloomingdale's that not only did they have the makeup but they had it on sale. Trivial though it may seem, for Turner this was actual proof that chanting worked: "Now, this sounds kind of silly, but I knew it was the chant—that it was helping me to rearrange my place in the universe. Makeup—I know: a small thing. But it was a start." Alongside the material benefits, she also noticed internal changes: "Chanting, I discovered, removed uncomfortable attitudes from my thoughts. I started to think differently. Everything became lighter."[58] She concluded that the more she chanted, the stronger she felt: "I could feel myself becoming stronger—becoming less and less afraid."[59]

For all the benefits she was experiencing in the practice, she still had to hide her practice from Ike. Since Ike spent much of his time in the recording studio, Turner bought candles, incense, and other material for a Buddhist altar, which she set up in a spare room of the house. Aside from these details, Turner never provided an exact description of her altar in the nascent stages of her Buddhist practice. Regarding their altars, Soka Gakkai practitioners were instructed to set up *butsudans*, or "Buddha altars," in their homes. Fabio Rambelli, a scholar of Japanese religious and cultural history, describes *butsudans* as having a three-tiered structure: the highest tier contains the object of worship; the second tier usually has copies of religious scriptures, and offerings such as food and water; and the lowest tier contains personal effects, such as written prayers, prayer beads, and so on.[60] For Soka Gakkai members, the *gohonzon*, the Soka Gakkai's object of devotion (about which see the following chapter), hangs in the center of the *butsudan* above the top tier. Just below the *gohonzon* and to either side, some members place cranes or lotuses, both important Nichiren Buddhist symbols. The second tier usually contains a cup for water offerings, a copy of Soka Gakkai's liturgy book, and possibly food. Below this is usually an incense burner filled with aromatic incense powder (usually an accumulation of ash from the burning of incense during each practice session), candles, and a vase of fresh evergreen leaves. Most practitioners also have a bell of variable size on an ornate cushion, which is rung at specifically demarcated points in the liturgy. Beyond these ceremonial items, practitioners might also keep a list of their prayers. The significance of each feature of the *butsudan* was often communicated from one Soka Gakkai member to another directly, and in

Soka Gakkai publications.[61] While there was (and is today) considerable variety in the kinds of *butsudans* practitioners keep in their homes, some altars could be elaborate, adding substantial increases in the *butusdan*'s height and depth. Still others could be minimal, maintaining only the three tiers (or having all religious objects on more or less the same tier). Given that Turner describes her first *butsudan* as being hidden in the back of a spare room in the home that she and Ike shared, it was likely of the smaller, more basic variety. Nonetheless, there, she would chant on her own.

While Soka Gakkai members practice on their own, they are also encouraged to chant in community with other members and regularly attend meetings. The monthly discussion meeting served then, as it does today, as the primary communal meeting. This meeting was originally established under Makiguchi and Toda as a forum for the study of Buddhist teachings, the sharing of members' experiences, and the introduction of new members to the practice.[62] Under Ikeda, these meetings were established in countries around the world, including the United States under the guise of SGI-USA. During the street *shakubuku* movement organized by George M. Williams, they attracted diverse groups of people in and around major urban areas like Los Angeles. Though Ike and Tina lived in Inglewood, and Ronnie Turner was *shakubuku*-ed there, Valerie Bishop practiced in the Brentwood area of West Los Angeles, where the local organization was known as Brentwood Chapter. If Turner had freedom to attend meetings, she would have attended them there. But Ike prevented her attendance.

"Although I wanted to chant with my sangha, the local community of practitioners, I was still married to Ike, and he was afraid of my chanting because he thought I might be able to put a curse on him or something," Turner later explained.[63] In an interview featured in the VH1 show *Behind the Music*, she spoke of Ike's reaction to her chanting: "He had forbidden me to do it actually, a few times I got beaten up about it."[64] When Ike came home one day unexpectedly and discovered Turner chanting in front of the altar she had set up, "he blew up," and told Turner in no uncertain terms to "Get that motherfucker out of this house!"[65] As she understood it, his reaction was about his fear of anything he could not control. In the same VH1 documentary, Ike mocked the practice and recalled being "really really mad" that she was chanting in a foreign language instead of learning songs to pay the bills. He thus forbade her from practicing. But, in his reaction, she saw fear in him. Consequently, even as Ike forbade it, she increased her practice. She chanted whenever she could: "Because now I could feel the power deep inside me, stirring up after all these years. And I would think about Ike's face, and how funny it was to finally see *him* scared: to know that he wasn't all-powerful, that he wasn't God, that there was a little piece of God inside each of us—inside of me, too—and that I could find it, and it could set me free. That's when I *really* started chanting."[66] Turner would follow the Soka Gakkai practice of chanting twice a day, morning and evening, in secrecy whenever Ike was away from the house. On occasion, Valerie Bishop and other Buddhist women would come to the house and chant with her. Turner later referred to these women as her "brave chanting friends." One of these friends was Maria Lucien, the sister of Ana Maria Shorter, who was married to jazz saxophonist Wayne Shorter. While performing in the same venue in New York, Turner met Wayne and Ana Maria. Turner intended to introduce Ana Maria to the practice of chanting but found out that she and Wayne were already chanting, they knew Valerie Bishop, and they hosted chanting meetings in West Los Angeles. When Turner described her life with Ike to Ana Maria, she recalls her saying, "Since we first met, I've had your name in my prayer book and have been chanting for your true happiness."[67]

Turner considered chanting, meeting these women, and being supported by them to be indications that her place in the universe was indeed being rearranged. The confidence that this generated in her also spilled over into her career.

Turner's Career and Family

The remaining two years of Ike and Tina Turner's relationship, from 1974 to 1976, were business as usual. Following *Nutbush City Limits*, the duo sought to explore gospel music on their next album, *The Gospel according to Ike and Tina*. The album featured their version of gospel standards such as "Amazing Grace," "Take My Hand, Precious Lord," and "What a Friend We Have in Jesus." Their cover of this last song, alongside other tracks on the album, prompted biographer Mark Bego to suspect that the album was Ike Turner's attempt to capitalize on the success of Aretha Franklin's best-selling gospel album *Amazing Grace*. Bego points to the album's relative lack of chart success as evidence that the decision to record a gospel album was an "odd choice" on Ike and Tina's part.[68] Bego's reading, however, ignores the successful reviews that the album received. *Billboard* chose it as one of its top picks for the week of April 27, 1974, and the accompanying review called the album "a strong and successful attempt to bring the commercial world of soul music to the church. Not the church to soul music as is usually the case." However, the review goes on to say that the album is "commercial, not pure gospel, so it can be stocked with the Turner's [sic] other soul products." *Record World*, a music industry trade magazine, placed the album on its May 4, 1974, "Hits of the Week" list. The accompanying review says: "Mr. & Ms. Rockin' Soul transform traditional religious songs into commercially viable compositions" and praises both Ike's and Tina's performances on the album.[69] That same week, another major industry trade magazine, *Cash Box*, chose the album as one of its top picks in the pop category and praised the album, saying, "The religious background that's so often a part of the music of today's biggest stars emerges here on Ike and Tina's latest UA [their record label] LP, a collection of gospel oriented material that sparkles with deep feeling and righteousness." The review goes on to praise Ike's vocal performance and predicts that the album will be a major seller.[70] Thus, while at least one industry magazine—*Billboard*—acknowledged that the album was made for a commercial audience, the industry response to the album was positive, regardless of the commercial motivations that those like Bego saw for the album. Recall that both Turner and Ike have strong roots in Black Baptist churches, which has infused much of their music.

The gospel record was followed by *Sweet Rhode Island Red*, half the songs of which were again composed by Turner herself. Later in 1974, Ike and Tina embarked on an international tour to promote the album. Turner also expanded into a new genre with the release of a country album, *Tina Turns the Country On*. The album was produced with an outside producer and is often considered her first solo album (*River Deep, Mountain High* was produced without Ike, but credited to both Ike and Tina).

Earlier in 1974, a producer working on the musical film *Tommy* (based on the Who's concept album of the same name) contacted Ike Turner about the possibility of Turner playing the role of the "Acid Queen" in the film. She would appear in the movie alongside Elton John, Ann-Margret, Eric

Clapton, and other musicians. After Turner met with Ken Russell, the movie's director, she was cast and went to London to work on the film. Turner, who had no familiarity with drugs outside of Ike's cocaine dependence and the usage of marijuana by some members of the Revue, was shocked to learn on set that the *acid* referred to in her character's name was LSD.[71] When filming finished, Ann-Margret invited Turner to remain in London and perform on her television special. Both the film *Tommy* and Ann-Margret's television special were released in 1975, and Turner embarked on a solo press tour to promote the projects. In these press interviews and magazine profiles, a new, more confident Tina Turner was emerging. Two magazine profiles stand out.

The April 24, 1975, issue of *Jet* magazine featured both Ike and Tina on the cover, but the headline read "Tina Turner Talks about Ike and 'Tommy.'" The article juxtaposes an image of her onstage in the film *Soul to Soul* and a still from *Tommy*, with images of her with Ike, with the children, and washing dishes. While the profile is careful to emphasize that she is "strictly Mrs. Isaac Turner [*sic*], housewife," that her "family is her first love," and that "Ike's opinion is essential to her," Turner and her performance in *Tommy* are the focus of the profile's first half.[72] The second half of the profile is subtitled "Tina Turns to Buddhism Religion for Guidance." Turner is quoted as saying that in their relationship, Ike can be difficult to work with, and that she deals with her situation with Ike "as best as I can, as comfortably as I can, so that I'm happy."[73] Here, Turner is beginning to speak publicly about their relationship and the difficulties that it entailed. The article lists her as one of many entertainers who have turned to Buddhism. The spiritual seeking that began in London in 1966 continued into the seventies, and she is quoted as saying: "I had been searching for a religion and I found I could relate to Buddhism." She then explained that she had been reading on Buddhism, presumably from the books given to her by Valerie Bishop and her "brave chanting" friends, and that she connected with what she read. She explained these beliefs to Brown: "We are all little gods within ourselves. Our eyes open by day, which is the day of the universe; they close by night; we cry tears, there's rain; we breathe air, there's air in the universe. And by saying *Nam-Myoho-Renge-Kyo*, you're saying 'I'm me, myself.'"[74] These teachings evince the correspondence theories that religious historian Catherine Albanese sees as a defining feature of American metaphysical religions, and are an almost verbatim echo of Daisaku Ikeda's comments on the notion of correspondence between the universe and the human body, as found in Nichiren's writings and embodied in Buddhist concepts like *ichinen sanzen*.[75] Though she has accepted Buddhist beliefs, she clarifies in the article that she has not made permanent changes to her diet and she desires to act in a "biblical movie" in the future.

The following month, Turner was featured in the May 5, 1975, issue of *People* magazine. This article's title boldly declares, "Tina Turner Sizzles in a Solo Act." Like the *Jet* profile, the article places solo images of Turner onstage and in film alongside images with Ike, with Ike's son Ike Jr., and of Turner in the kitchen. Though the profile also tries to emphasize that she is a housewife under the control of Ike, it focuses largely on Turner's solo projects: *Tina Turns the Country On* and *Tommy*. But this article goes a step further: it hints at Ike's infidelities, it shows Turner lamenting the lack of time she spends with their children, and it highlights her impending departure from the group. She is quoted as saying, "I don't want Ike to feel like I'm leaving him behind . . . but, I've always been in there helping him and now, in *Tommy*, I've learned I can do things without him. Ike'll be proud . . . but he's gonna miss me."[76]

In both profiles, which are typical for this time, Turner is displaying a much more independent attitude. Already, Turner explained that after years of being afraid of Ike, she was starting to feel her own power emerge, a power that she likened to the emergence of a "God inside each of us." This evokes the notion of spiritual benefits emphasized in Soka Gakkai's Buddhist teachings. Increasingly, through solo projects such as *Tina Turns the Country On*, the film *Tommy*, and Ann-Margret's television special, the public was getting used to seeing Tina Turner without Ike. Of course, it must be noted that each of these deals was brokered by Ike Turner as her manager.

In August of 1975, Turner released her second "solo" album, *Acid Queen*, featuring a side of her cover of songs by the Who, the Rolling Stones, and Led Zeppelin, with the second side featuring songs written by Ike. This album would be Ike and Tina Turner's last album together. The success of these projects, and the relative lack of success of Ike and Tina's joint album output at this time, was a constant source of conflict. By now, when the group wasn't touring, Ike was spending much of his time in the recording studio. Ike already had a habit of rerecording old Ike and Tina songs to produce new versions to release as singles and album filler tracks. As new recording technology became available, he retrofitted Bolic Sound Studios with new equipment and continued to record new versions of old songs. His extended studio sessions were largely fueled by cocaine and a desire to keep the Revue on the album charts. Turner was expected to be on call at any time, day or night, to come to the studio and record. Ike's violent assaults at home continued unabated in the studio. For Turner:

> It was real hard by then. Ike got worse and worse. You never knew what you were getting hit for; only Ike knew. He'd just say you were "messing" with him. He'd lock the door, and then you knew you were going to get it. One night in the studio, he threw boiling hot coffee in my face. Said I wasn't singing the way he wanted, that I wasn't trying. When the coffee hit me, it felt like ice—and then it started *burning*, and I started screaming. I grabbed at my neck, where most of it had hit, and the skin just peeled right off. I had third-degree burns on my face. That scared Ike. And you know what he did? He started *beating me*. It was like, "Goddamn it, *she* made me do this...."⁷⁷

Scenes like this played out repeatedly at home and in the recording studio. And Turner would later describe in gruesome detail how often these beatings would end in rape. The success of *Tommy* and the continued press focus on "solo Tina" exacerbated these violent assaults, as Ike would often bring up these solo projects, sometimes reaching back to 1966's *River Deep, Mountain High*, as examples of how Turner was attempting to "mess with him," presumably by having an independent career. The irony, in Turner's view, was that it was Ike who made all of her "solo" deals: "I was never consulted. I guess that probably made him even madder."⁷⁸

Through chanting *Nam-myoho-renge-kyo*, reading Buddhist literature, and spending time outside of the Ike and Tina "bubble," Turner's patience for Ike Turner was reaching its limits. While some around her mourned the state of her life, others, like onetime Ikette Lejeune Richardson, noticed Turner becoming more confident and independent. In the HBO Films Documentary *TINA*, Richardson recalled that during this time it became clear that "she wasn't putting up with any of it anymore." In the same documentary, Turner herself said that through chanting she "started becoming much more confident, not even caring what Ike thought."[79] One solution that came to Turner was the idea of writing letters to Ike. The letters explained in detail to Ike how she was feeling and why she could no longer take the beatings and sexual violence. Turner's rationale was that if she wrote what she had to say in a letter and left it where he could find it, he would have time to "cool off" before seeing her. But the letters did not work: "Two days later I'd have a black eye again. My left eye pretty much stayed black, and my nose was always swollen."[80] Next, with the realization that she could "take his best lick," that she had already "had it all—the broken ribs, the broken jaw"—Turner started to leave Ike. She had left a few times before, but Ike would always find out where she was and beat her. This time, though, Turner was gone for two weeks and stayed with Ana Maria Shorter's sister Maria. Rather than Ike finding her, this time Turner went back of her own accord, since things with Ike "had to be settled somehow." But, to Turner's surprise, Ike did not beat her when she returned; he simply listened to what she had to say. After that the frequency, if not the intensity, of their fights decreased.[81] Around this time, author and music photographer Bob Gruen, who spent much time shooting footage of Ike and Tina throughout their career, recalled to Kurt Loder having a conversation with Ike about Turner wanting to leave (Gruen's wife had just left him) and the fact that Turner was talking to him in ways that she had never done before. Gruen remembers trying to explain "the new feminist movement to Ike" and the zeitgeist of women's liberation. In Gruen's estimation, Ike did not understand and emphasized that Turner had "never acted like she was feeling bad before."[82] Though Turner herself told Loder that she couldn't connect to the feminist movement, her thinking and attitudes—as reflected in interviews—resonate with the spirit of the movement. Whether Ike or even Turner realized it or not, their sixteen-year relationship was coming to an end.

Independence (1976)

In winter 1975, the Ike & Tina Turner Revue embarked upon an international tour, first across Europe, then to Australia, China, and Southeast Asia. While the tour proceeded without difficulty in England and Germany, receiving positive reviews from critics and audiences alike, they experienced issues in other locales. In Paris, Ike reported that nearly $100,000 was stolen from him when the briefcase carrying the money "disappeared." Despite reporting the alleged theft to Parisian authorities and even consulting Turner's psychic Peter Hurkos, Ike never got the money back.[83] In January 1976, the band forfeited thousands of dollars' worth of equipment when Ike refused to perform five concert dates in Djakarta, Indonesia, which caused the band to have to leave the country. Ike often booked the Revue's shows months in advance, so the group had concerts booked around the United States for the rest of 1976. In April, they were scheduled for a prestigious residency at the Las Vegas Hilton; in June they were scheduled to play the Temple University Music Festival in Philadelphia, alongside Aretha Franklin, Lou Rawls, Muddy Waters, and other soul artists. They were scheduled to finish the month of June performing in Memphis, before returning to Los Angeles and continuing to Dallas for Fourth of July shows. The latter shows were expected to be especially big events to celebrate the US Bicentennial.[84]

Although a plethora of tour dates had been booked, their schedule was thinner than in previous years, and everyone in the Ike and Tina orbit felt Ike's anxiety about the Revue's future ratcheting up. As the group returned to the United States to begin their concert dates, key employees left the Turner organization due to the hostile working environment. The first to leave was Rhonda Graam, a trusted employee who held multiple roles in the organization: secretary to Ike Turner, booking agent for the Ike & Tina Turner Revue, and erstwhile personal assistant to both Turners. One by one, people in the Turner organization displayed a decreasing tolerance for the environment of drugs, adultery, partying, and violent abuse, all of which created a chaotic and unstable environment at Bolic Sound Studios.[85] Turner herself was bearing the brunt of Ike's abuse, and her tolerance too had reached its limit, and she began to weigh her options:

Ike was getting very uptight and putting a lot of blame on me, as usual. If I would just sing the way he wanted me to—whatever way that was— then we would have hit records. It was hopeless. I still didn't know where I could go—my mother lived in Ike's house in St. Louis, looking after that, so I couldn't go back to her; and Alline, who lived in Baldwin Hills, was just as scared of Ike as everybody else, so I couldn't go to her either. But I knew I was going somewhere—by now, my determination was outweighing my fear of this man. What did I have to lose anymore?[86]

Estimating that she in fact had *nothing* to lose, and with her sons under the watchful eyes of family and nannies, Turner prepared to embark on what would become her final tour with Ike.

I, Tina and *My Love Story* present slightly different accounts of the sequence of events that precipitated Ike and Tina Turner's final, relationship-ending altercation. Nonetheless, the major details are the same: After a five-day cocaine binge, Ike Turner was on edge. En route to the Los Angeles airport, Ike and Tina were in a limousine with members of their entourage, including at least one of the girlfriends that Ike was openly seeing. Ike was eating a melting chocolate bar that he insisted Turner try. When she refused to eat the melting chocolate because of the white Yves Saint Laurent suit she was wearing, Ike hit her with "one of those backhand licks." Bolstered perhaps by nearly three years of chanting and a growing sense of self-assurance, Turner's response to this act of violence was different from her previous responses: "And this time, I got mad. I didn't think, 'Uh-oh, better be careful, I'm gonna get it.' I thought, 'Today, I'm fighting back.' And from there, everything I'd been holding in for sixteen years started coming out." Once on the plane, Ike and Tina continued their back-and-forth. When the plane landed in Dallas, Ike hit Turner again in the limousine on the way to their hotel. "Another one of those backhand licks. And then I start fighting back. He kept hitting me, but I didn't cry once." Ike repeatedly punched Turner and cursed her out; she cursed him back while fighting for her life. No matter what he did, she kept fighting him. "I didn't care what he did, because I was *flying*—I knew I was gone."[87]

"I *really shocked* him," Turner recalled. She returned each of Ike's blows because "It felt really good to fight this person who had been so rude, vulgar, and abusive for so long." By Turner's account, they fought from the Dallas–Fort Worth International Airport "all the way to the Statler Hilton," roughly twenty or so miles away. When they reached the hotel, Ike explained to the receptionists that he and Turner had been "in an accident" to stave off the gaze of concerned onlookers. Dazed, their entourage checked into their respective rooms with Ike and Tina going to their own, shared room. They were scheduled to play a show that Saturday, the night of July 3. So, Turner mimed her preshow routine: "I pretended to be the same old Tina: the wife who was understanding and forgiving; the one who was concerned about Ike's needs—his headache, his bloody nose, his exhaustion, his pain." She also ordered his dinner, massaged him, and urged him "to take a little nap." When Ike fell into a deep sleep, Turner's adrenaline kicked in. With a scarf on her head and a purse of toiletries, she "got the hell out of that room and out of that life."[88]

The rest of Turner's escape narrative has become a part of popular cultural history: afraid that members of the Ike & Tina Turner Revue would see her, she runs through the hotel and into a back alley. She takes a moment to compose herself in the alley before eventually running nearly a mile and crossing Dallas's Highway 30 on foot. On the highway, she is nearly run over, but she keeps going until she reaches the Ramada Inn. With a mixture of pride, because she was doing something completely on her own for the first time, and fear, because she realized anything could happen to her in the hotel, Turner asked for the manager and explained who she was and that she had run away from her husband and didn't have any money. "But I swore I would pay him back if he'd give me a room for the night." The manager gave her a suite and food, placed security at her door, and left her alone to her mixture of feelings as she finally began to process what she had just done.

Conclusion

In the beginning of the seventies, the Ike & Tina Turner Revue had finally become a commercially viable, mainstream act, finding album and touring success both abroad and in the United States. In 1973, they crowned that success with the release of their *Nutbush City Limits* album, featuring songs written by Turner. While "Nutbush City Limits," written about her hometown, is the most famous track of the album, the song "Make Me Over," later called "Tina's Prayer," is the most revealing track. In its simple verses, Turner further claims an identity for herself as a spiritual seeker but now with a specific aim in mind that is announced in the chorus: to be "made over." The same year that this song was released, Turner was introduced to Soka Gakkai Nichiren Buddhism, first through a recording engineer, then through her son, and finally through Valerie Bishop, all of whom had experienced the conversion tactics of Soka Gakkai's American organization, SGI-USA. Bishop in particular taught Turner the tradition's signature practice of chanting *Nam-myoho-renge-kyo* and gave her the material to practice, such that by 1975, Turner could publicly declare herself to be Buddhist. From there, as Turner expanded into new genres musically, releasing gospel and country albums, she began to display increasing independence in solo projects and press profiles like *Jet* and *People* magazines.

Thus, when in the midst of yet another tour she escaped from Ike Turner after their final fight, it was the culmination of a process that had in some ways begun in 1966 but was brought to maturity in 1973. And so, now Tina Turner sat in a suite at the Ramada Inn in Dallas, "terrified" but "also excited" on the precipice of an independent future.

4

Becoming Tina

While I was facing the hardest challenges of my life, I was
also dreaming the biggest dreams I ever imagined, and I
was chanting several hours a day to achieve them.

—Tina Turner, *Happiness Becomes You*

America celebrated its bicentennial on Sunday, July 4, 1976. As the
country began its celebratory festivities, Tina Turner woke up in an
unfamiliar hotel suite in Dallas, Texas. The day before, she had struggled
against Ike Turner's violent assault and fought for her life before fleeing
in the night. When she woke up on July Fourth, she faced an uncertain
future. And yet, she was resolved. "If I told you that I woke up in a panic
the day after my escape—that I doubted I would be able to figure out how
to live, how to support my kids, how to survive Ike's wrath, how to go on—I
would be lying."[1] Instead, she had taken the first steps of her own liberatory
journey, and so she was determined.

Return to Los Angeles

Determined though she may have been, she had to be careful. She had
performed with Ike Turner since she was seventeen years old, was a member
of the Ike & Tina Turner Revue since its inception in 1960, and had
been married to Ike since 1962. In the nearly twenty years that had elapsed
between their meeting and her escape, every person in her life was tied in

some way to Ike Turner. Any wrong moves or wrong calls would quickly end her liberative journey before it began. Indeed, she learned this immediately when the first person she called for help, Mel Johnson—a car salesman and longtime friend of Ike Turner—called Ike to tell him he had heard from Turner. She needed to think of someone who knew her situation with Ike but had sufficient distance from both of them. So she called Nate Tabor, Ike's attorney.[2]

Tabor had connections in Texas and arranged for her to return to Los Angeles; he provided her with money, arranged for friends to pick her up, and paid for a return ticket. The friends Tabor sent to take Turner to the airport, an older white couple, were prejudiced toward her and would neither speak to her nor sit with her in the airport as she waited for the plane, but Turner paid them no attention, perhaps remembering her days back in Nutbush and Brownsville and her touring days on the Chitlin' Circuit. She concluded, "Fine—I know what that's about." Once on the plane, and nearing Los Angeles, Turner's determination momentarily turned to fear that Ike might already be back in Los Angeles waiting for her. She recalled a previous time she had tried to leave Ike and he had figured out that she would probably go to St. Louis. He tracked her bus schedule, met the bus at a rest stop, and took Turner home to beat her with a wire hanger. While she sat on the plane, she remembered: "[I] was really getting scared, because I didn't underestimate him at all." Then her fear turned to resolve again as she figured, "Well, if he is there, I'm just going to scream and yell until the police come—because there's *no way* I'm going back to him again." Nonetheless, when the plane landed, she recalls "running slowly across that tarmac" and not stopping until she reached a cab. "'Safe,' I thought." And yet, the cab driver instantly recognized that his passenger was none other than Tina Turner. Fortunately, the cab driver drove her to Tabor's home without incident.[3]

Once back in Los Angeles, Turner was constantly on the move, staying with several people. While at the Tabors', Turner and Tabor discussed her next steps, and she made clear to him that she had no intentions of returning to Ike, so she resolved to "get a divorce, whatever that will mean." Thus, with Tabor's counsel, Turner filed a petition for divorce on July 27, 1976, at the Los Angeles Superior Court.[4] When Tabor called Ike to inform him of Turner's filing, Ike responded by threatening Tabor and his family for sheltering Turner. So she left Nate Tabor's home and moved in with Maria Booker Lucien. Together, Lucien and Turner would chant twice a day, following the Soka Gakkai daily liturgical practice of *gongyo*. She couldn't stay there long. Ike knew Lucien, and he would likely come looking for her there. So she went to live with Lucien's sister, Ana Maria Shorter, and her husband, Wayne Shorter. While Turner was moving between the Tabors, Luciens, and Shorters, her family and members of the Turner organization responded to her leaving in various ways.

At Bolic Sound Studio, Turner's disappearance increased the chaos that had prevailed since Rhonda Graam and others left in March of 1976. A staff member at Bolic Sound, who later worked as a personal assistant to Turner, recalls that Ike called the studio repeatedly for at least two days after she left him in Dallas, asking if any of them had heard from her. When Ike and the Revue returned to Los Angeles, he went into the studio to personally question each staff member and musician to see if they had information on Turner's whereabouts. He also made calls to Turner's mother, Zelma, and sister, Alline, to see if Turner had contacted them. She had not contacted any member of her family, and thus they could not aid in his search. Since no one had any information, Ike became increasingly frantic.[5] This atmosphere prevailed until Nate Tabor called to speak on Turner's behalf.

Outside of the studio, Ike Jr., Craig, Michael, and Ronnie—Ike and Tina's sons—also had to be sorted. Most immediately, Turner "decided to leave the kids with Ike at the house for the time being."[6] As she was constantly on the move, she felt it would be too destabilizing to move the children from place to place, as she knew from her own experiences after both of her parents left her and her sister in the care of relatives. Decades later, Turner explained her rationale for leaving the kids behind. In the May 2005 edition of *O, the Oprah Magazine*, Turner explained to Oprah Winfrey: "You have to take care of yourself first—and then you take care of your children. They will understand later. Your children are blessed. They possibly have good karma, or someone will take them in. People take care of children. But they don't always take care of you."[7] And indeed, this was proven by her own experience: she knew that Zelma, Alline, and an assortment of housekeepers were helping with her sons, while she was left to deal with her situation with Ike herself. At the same time, she reasoned that her sons were themselves no longer *kids*. Craig and Ike Jr. were approaching the age of seventeen, Michael was turning sixteen, and Ronnie was fifteen. As teens, and with support, they could take care of themselves, leaving her free to take care of *herself*.[8]

Taking care of herself, for now, meant acting as a maid to her friends. For two months, Turner moved continuously, staying with friends. Without any source of income, she could only repay her friends by cleaning their houses for them. For Turner, "cleaning was one form of therapy,"[9] and she needed to "think," she said. "And I just couldn't *sit* there and think, I needed to think on my feet!" (According to Maria Lucien, Turner "*never* stopped moving! She was always cleaning or doing something.")[10] So, she worked off her energy, as she "moved junk and stored stuff away and put out the trash and cleaned cupboards and washed dishes and scrubbed stoves."[11] She summed up her attitude at this time when she wrote that it was better "to be someone else's maid than Ike Turner's wife."[12]

The Shorters

Even as she moved around, she spent most of her time at Wayne and Ana Maria Shorter's house and eventually remained there. The Shorters lived on Lookout Mountain in the Laurel Canyon area of the Los Angeles Hollywood Hills. Since Wayne Shorter was on tour with his band Weather Report, Turner slept on the floor in Wayne's home office. In her authorized biography of Wayne Shorter, *Footprints: The Life and Work of Wayne Shorter*, Michelle Mercer relates that Wayne came home from the tour to find "soul diva Tina Turner scrubbing his kitchen floor."[13] Wayne explained to Mercer that Turner "had nothing, during those four months she stayed with us." He went on, "I was going in and out, on tour and recording. She was so quiet, you didn't even know she was there."[14] While Turner was quiet, she also relished this time because, she said, "I finally had my freedom—God, how I'd dreamed about it for sixteen years. And my own friends, too, for the very first time."[15] Wayne recalls his wife and Turner "doing some intense things" like chanting four hours at a time.

"It was important for me to think clearly during this terrifying time," Turner said. "I started chanting four hours a day—two hours in the morning and two in the evening—to help me focus."[16] These chanting sessions were sometimes done on her own, and at other times with Ana Maria, Maria

Booker Lucien, Susie Sempers, and other chanting women. As Turner understood it, "The chant brings you into harmony with the hum of the universe, that kind of subtle buzz at the center of all being. Close your eyes and you can hear it all around you. Anna [*sic*] Maria had a *gohonzon*, so I stayed indoors all day and just chanted and chanted, building up my spirit for the trials I knew still lay ahead."[17] One such trial would present itself immediately when Ike discovered that Turner was staying with the Shorters.

Ana Maria asked Turner to accompany her to the grocery store. Unbeknownst to either of them, while Ike continued his interrogations of family and friends at the recording studio, he had also hired a private investigator to search for Turner. En route to the store, Ana Maria and Turner noticed a car following them, and that the car's driver was trying to look inside their car. The car followed them to the market, and the driver confirmed Turner's identity. That night, while Ana and Turner were doing their evening chanting, it occurred to Ana that it might be prudent to turn on the sprinkler system so that if anyone approached the house, they would either be deterred by the system or get wet on approach. Eventually there was a knock on the door, which prompted Turner to get the .38 caliber handgun that she had taken to carrying with her, knowing that Ike would eventually look for her. Ana, who was Portuguese, answered the door, speaking in broken English in pretense of being a maid. While she did this, Turner looked out the window. At the door was former Ikette and friend to Turner, Robbie Montgomery. But, looking out the window, Turner could also see Ike and a full entourage. Knowing that Turner and Robbie were close friends in the early days of the Ike & Tina Turner Revue, Ike had presumably sent Robbie to the door hoping to lure Turner outside. Ana continued her pretense, and Turner called the police. When they arrived, she explained the situation to them, that she was Tina Turner and that the man at the door was Ike. "I left him, and I'm *not* goin' back." To this, the police told Ike, Robbie, and the entourage that they had to leave, citing the fact that this was the Shorters' private property.

That all of this occurred during their evening chanting practice lent spiritual significance to the sequence of events. Turner later acknowledged that it was a practical mistake to go to the market, but the fact that it occurred to Ana to turn on the sprinkler system and pretend to be a maid was evidence of spiritual guidance derived from chanting, since chanting "tunes you in" and "makes you alert."[18] Wayne, who was in the studio when this happened, also understood the blend of the practical and the spiritual at work that night, explaining to Mercer: "Ana Maria went to acting school. . . . And she'd learned how to use the functions of the universe to protect herself. She channeled them like a magnet. She showed me how to do it, too."[19] With Ike now aware of where Turner was and with "protective forces" on their side, she began leaving the house more. This, in turn, enabled her to finally start freely attending the Soka Gakkai's NSA Buddhist meetings that Ronnie told her about three years prior, and that her chanting friends had brought her to clandestinely over the intervening years.

Turner's Conversion

It was Valerie Bishop who brought Turner to some of her first Buddhist meetings. One of these was in the Brentwood area of West Los Angeles and led by Matilda Buck. Born in Arizona in a Christian family and baptized Episcopalian at a young age, Buck had been introduced to the practice while in an African goods shop and went to her first NSA meeting in 1972. Initially she ignored the entreaties of NSA members, much as she did the Hare Krishnas who were also a major presence in Westwood, around UCLA and Brentwood. However, finding that she was just as unhappy in her second marriage as in her first, she decided to try the practice of chanting *Nam-myoho-renge-kyo*. At the meeting, she recalls being impressed both by the "equality among people of different walks of life at meetings" and by "seeing the practical application of the practice to people's lives." The impression she got from NSA members was that their attitude in difficult situations was "you better chant and determine to break through."

As Buck's own practice grew, so did NSA's Brentwood organization. In the NSA's bureaucratic structure, Brentwood was established as a district in 1972. In 1973, due to an increase in membership during *shakubuku* conversion drives, Brentwood District grew to become a chapter, the designation for a larger unit. Brentwood Chapter met both in Laurel Canyon, where Turner was staying with the Shorters, and in the San Fernando Valley, where Maria Booker Lucien lived. Thus, Brentwood Chapter served as the location of Turner's first Buddhist meetings. Buck remembers that in those first meetings Turner attended, sometimes having no more than five people, Turner sat "quietly and took it all in."[20] The meetings included an introduction to the practice, the sharing of experiences with chanting, and guidance from the organization's leaders on personal matters, all of which were established in the Soka Gakkai's early days under Tsunesaburo Makiguchi and Josei Toda in Japan. Also at these meetings, attendees formally joined the organization and converted to Buddhism by receiving their own *gohonzon*.[21] In the context of Buddhism in America, the notion of conversion requires some discussion, as the concept is understood differently for many American Buddhists.

In his 2001 article "Describing the Elephant: Buddhism in America," Buddhist studies scholar Peter Gregory called attention to the difficulty of determining who is a Buddhist, since the parameters of Buddhist identity vary "from one group to another, and there is no single belief or practice that is common to all Buddhists."[22] Given this complexity, Gregory proposes the following definition for a convert in American Buddhism:

It refers to Americans (regardless of ethnicity) who are not Buddhist by birth but who take up various forms of Buddhist practice without necessarily undergoing a dramatic experience that could be characterized as a religious conversion. In other words, their Buddhism does not necessarily imply a radical shift in identity, and many in this category may not even self-identify as Buddhists—especially in the case of practitioners of insight meditation. Indeed, many American Buddhist practitioners who would fit in this category would not recognize themselves in this label. Rather, I suspect that they would be more comfortable with the term "practitioner."[23]

In *Be the Refuge: Raising the Voices of Asian American Buddhists*, author Chenxing Han accepts Gregory's definition of a convert for some of the Asian American Buddhists that she interviewed, but she notes that none of her interviewees "use the term *conversion* to describe their journeys."[24] Instead, many of Han's interviewees found the language of conversion to be too Christian and unable to capture their experiences with Buddhist practice. These experiences, like Han's own experience with Buddhism, are better understood as gradual processes that unfold over the course of many encounters with Buddhism. Consequently, Han proposes several alternatives to the notion of conversion, including the language of affinity.[25]

Gregory's definition of conversion also captures Black Buddhists. Many Black Buddhists, though, as highlighted by religious studies scholar Rima Vesely-Flad, also incorporate elements from non-Buddhist traditions into their practice of Buddhism. In *Black Buddhists and the Black Radical Tradition: The Practice of Stillness in the Movement for Liberation*, Vesely-Flad uses the notion of interweaving to name this phenomenon. She cites Zenju Earthlyn Manuel's description of her incorporation of hymns and chants to Haitian spirits into her Soto Zen Buddhist ceremonies. Vesely-Flad argues that this is a way of "making a religious tradition familiar and personally meaningful."[26] Larry Ward, another prominent Black Buddhist teacher, explained to Vesely-Flad that he found value in incorporating Christianity and indigenous ritual into his teaching.[27] The interweaving of non-Buddhist traditions into their practice does not preclude Manuel and Ward from self-identifying as Buddhists. In line with conversion as Gregory understands it, for Manuel and Ward, as for many Black Buddhists, identifying as Buddhist neither entails a radical change in their identity nor does it foreclose the possibility of engaging with other religious traditions, two assumptions at the heart of Protestant Christian notions of conversion. This understanding also aligns with that of many who begin practicing Soka Gakkai Nichiren Buddhism by receiving the *gohonzon*.

Just over a month after leaving Ike in Dallas, Turner received her own *gohonzon* on August 8, 1976.[28] While attending these meetings, Turner learned the doctrines of Soka Gakkai Nichiren Buddhism.[29] In Soka Gakkai's teachings, the *gohonzon* is a mandalic scroll, with "Nam-Myoho-Renge-Kyo" inscribed down its center. Daisaku Ikeda explained that "The Buddha's enlightened state of life is expressed as the Gohonzon." Further, when individuals accept the *gohonzon*, their "lives as entities of Nam-myoho-renge-kyo—comes [*sic*] to shine. The wisdom of the Buddha inherent in our lives wells forth. The courage to take compassionate action arises in our hearts, and we enter the golden path of happiness."[30] As such, chanting *Nam-myoho-renge-kyo* before the *gohonzon* enables one to bring forth one's own capacity for Buddhahood. Doing so is understood to have a transformative effect on a person's karma, explained as "actions in the past or present that manifest themselves as various results in the present or future."[31]

The process of bringing forth one's Buddhahood, and the pragmatic benefits that Makiguchi, Toda, and Ikeda have taught successive generations of Soka Gakkai members will concurrently be brought forth, is referred to in Soka Gakkai teachings as "human revolution." Ikeda expounds on this concept: "The term *human revolution* was first employed in the context of the Soka Gakkai by its second president, Josei Toda.... During his incarceration, he had a profound religious awakening, which led him to decide to dedicate his life to propagating Nichiren Buddhism. Mr. Toda called this inner transformation that he experienced 'human revolution.'" He further explained that achieving such inner transformation is "called 'attaining Buddhahood,' and human revolution is the process of engaging in Buddhist practice toward realizing that ultimate aim."[32] As Ikeda understands it, with chanting as the catalyst, this fundamental revolution in a person's life has a ripple effect on one's environment. Turner's situation demanded that she transform her environment.

Dealing with Ike Turner

Once Ike confirmed the location of Turner's hideout, he called Maria Lucien to ask if she would arrange a meeting between them. Turner agreed, having already resolved that, as she put it, no "matter what he said or did, I was never going back."[33] Ike picked her up from the Shorters' home on Lookout Mountain, and over coffee, as Ike sat holding his hat, Turner saw that he was afraid. "Real fear. I had always been under his thumb, but now I was strong, I was my own person, and he had never dealt with me on that level. He saw now that he had absolutely no control over me anymore, that I had outgrown my fear. And that scared him."[34] Even as she expressed feeling strong and seeing Ike's fear, Turner recognized the risk involved in such a meeting, and she took mitigating steps. For one, she tried to look as unattractive as possible. "I put on too much makeup, which was never my style, and deliberately wore an unflattering dress."[35] Throughout their relationship, Ike carefully controlled what clothing she bought and wore, both onstage and off. If she wore something he found unsuitable, it could provoke an argument or worse. Onstage, the Ikettes and members of the Kings of Rhythm would be fined against their compensation for unsuitable attire—sometimes finishing tours *owing* Ike money. If her attire, attitude, or performance was off in the slightest way, Ike would shout at Turner during the show, and then, after, she would be beaten. Ike also carefully curated wardrobes for his various girlfriends that he maintained while being married to Turner. Thus, looking unattractive was both an expression of Turner's state of freedom from Ike's control and a strategy for avoiding his violent gaze.

If carefully choosing an outfit to wear for the meeting was one strategy, carefully choosing her words was another. "I was always nice to him because I knew the rules: don't say *anything* that might trigger a fight."[36] Several fights between Ike and Tina were started because Ike disliked the way she responded to him. In 2013, she explained to Oprah that often Ike would ask what was on her mind and she would have to work to not have anything on her mind that would provoke a fight.[37] Their final fight in Dallas also began when Ike hit her for responding to him in a way that he found disagreeable. So, managing her responses during this conversation was of utmost importance. Turner's tactics worked, and Ike returned her to the Shorters' home without incident.

Back at Bolic Sound Studios, with it becoming increasingly clear that Turner was not returning, Ike unraveled. Ike Jr. remembers that his father stayed up "for fourteen days straight" and fell further into a cocaine dependency. Though Ike Jr., now a musician and recording engineer, was assisting his father in the studio, Ike beat him with a gun and sent him to the hospital.[38] Ronnie recalled that Ike began drinking and rerecording songs repeatedly, especially songs about going "down South, [to] get me another one like that other one."[39] Their business also suffered.

Ike booked the Revue for shows months, sometimes years, in advance. When Turner left in Dallas, Ike returned to Los Angeles and launched a desperate search for her, never bothering to cancel any of their planned concert dates. As dates were canceled, newspapers began to report on their "rumored split." A short article in the August 24, 1976, edition of the *Philadelphia Tribune*, typical of this period, related that "Reports are circling that there may be marital problems between the famed duo Ike and Tina Turner." According to the article, the director of the Temple University Music Festival had received a call from "Tina Turner's attorney informing him of the cancellation."[40] That Turner's attorney contacted them, and not a representative of Ike, is telling. Ann Cain, an assistant and erstwhile girlfriend of Ike's, recalled that promoters began calling Bolic Sound Studios "and filing lawsuits. Ike's way of dealing with all this was *not* to deal with it. He just went into his little studio and locked the door."[41] Ike's failure to cancel would have repercussions for Turner herself in their divorce proceedings.

After their meeting over coffee, Ike sent their four sons to live with Turner at the Shorters' home. Anticipating that she would no longer be able to live with Ana and Wayne with their sons, Ike also sent a thousand dollars to rent a house. However Ike may have seen his gesture, Turner saw it as a "dare, as if he was saying, 'Go ahead, try to make it out there on your own. I'll see you soon enough, begging for your old life.'"[42] Accepting Ike's dare, Turner used the money to rent a home on Sunset Crest Drive in Laurel Canyon, not far from Ana and Wayne. While small and simple, the house was enough for her and her sons to move forward. For Turner, this inevitably meant ensuring that she could remain financially independent of the Ike and Tina Turner moniker.

"I had to find a way to pay the creditors and support my family, while Ike watched from the comfort of our house and former lifestyle, hoping I would fail."[43] Immediately, Turner found herself facing lawsuits from concert promoters. Because Turner left the Revue in the middle of a tour, promoters held her responsible for the canceled concerts, which tarnished her reputation as a commercial entity. Though Turner had participated in "solo" projects, each deal had been brokered by Ike and she had still been a part of the Ike & Tina Turner Revue. Now, she was an unknown solo act.

Facing mounting bills and lawsuit fees, and desperate to remain independent, she called Rhonda Graam—former road manager for the Ike & Tina Turner Revue—toward the end of 1976. Turner asked if Graam would manage her and help her secure bookings. Knowing that Ike was keeping track of Turner's movements and the movements of anyone connected to her, Graam used the pseudonym "Shannon" to try to secure bookings for Turner. With no prospects for putting a show together, Graam booked Turner on television shows like *Hollywood Squares*, *The Brady Bunch*, and *Donnie and Marie*. Graam recalled that these shows were their only source of income. "She [Turner] was on food stamps and I was getting unemployment every two weeks, and between checks we'd charge things on my credit cards."[44] Although some of these appearances were humiliating for Turner—she remembers her sons teasing her for blunders made on *Hollywood Squares*—she tried to focus on survival. Speaking of this time, Turner later said:

I had to swallow my pride and do a lot of things to keep us afloat. I always tried to maintain my sense of humor. I called those days "Tina's Operation Oops," because there were so many "oops" when I was first figuring out how to be on my own. At a certain point, I released myself from the burden of getting everything right. I realized that I didn't have to be intimidated by not knowing, or hide my inexperience. I could simply say, "No, I don't know that," and promise myself that I would learn from my mistakes and do better next time. My only goal was to survive.[45]

The "burden of getting everything right" harkens back to Turner's child-hood struggles in school, where she imagined herself to be among the cat-egory of children labeled "not smart." Then, at Flagg Grove elementary school and on into high school, she had struggled to attain that elusive state of "getting everything right." But now, nearing the age of thirty-seven, she was on her own and releasing herself from that burden. And, with Graam's help, she was able to feel financially independent.

At the same time, through her friend Ann-Margret, she contacted di-vorce lawyer Arthur Leeds to take over her divorce petition. Though she filed her initial divorce petition only a few weeks after leaving Ike, Nate Tabor had been harassed and threatened relentlessly by Ike. After Ta-bor's departure, Turner needed the services of a more aggressive attor-ney. In her divorce petition, Turner asked for custody of her sons Craig and Ronnie, four thousand dollars in alimony, and one thousand dollars in child support.[46] A series of meetings held in Leeds's office involving Leeds, Ike, and Turner made it clear that Ike would not willingly meet her demands. Turner described her testimony in court: "I testified for about five minutes—just stated my name, the details of the marriage." In cham-bers, Turner also made clear to Leeds and the judge that should Ike decide to continue challenging her claims, she was "prepared to give everything away" if she had to. When the judge asked if she was certain about this, Turner replied without hesitation, "I'm *positive*, Judge."[47] While Turner did ask for her jewelry to be retrieved from Ike's safes at Bolic Sound Studios, Ike claimed to have no knowledge of the jewelry and so Turner dropped the request. For the time being, their divorce continued to drag on.

In the middle of their divorce proceedings, Ike asked Turner for an-other meeting—this time with Mike Stewart, head of the United Artists record label. "Ike was negotiating a new record deal, as we were not under contract to anyone at the time of the split. Mike asked me to come to his office to meet with Ike and discuss what was going to be done."[48] Through

Stewart, Ike offered to create better working conditions for her and allow her to remain independent if she would return to work with him. Under this arrangement, Turner would be managed by Stewart himself. Having Stewart as her manager was as good an idea as any, and she agreed to that. Turner, however, knew that working with Ike was a dangerous proposition. She explained to Stewart that she could not under any circumstances return to "that environment because it's dangerous. Ike will forget all about this meeting as soon as he's in the studio doing cocaine." She made clear to Stewart that "There would be no new record contract and no collaboration of any kind, professional or personal, with Ike Turner." And to Ike she made this clear: "We were finished."[49]

Ike's response? Intimidation. Rhonda Graam's home was twice set on fire, seemingly in retaliation for her support of Turner's solo efforts. After her car and home were shot into with a shotgun, Graam moved into Turner's home on Sunset Crest Drive, where her car was fired upon again and other cars were lit on fire outside the house. Fearing that the gunshots would continue, Graam and Turner's son Craig slept on the floor, with Turner sleeping in the walk-in closet. Just as she had slept in closets while staying with friends after leaving Ike, she was again, even in her own house, sleeping in closets because of Ike Turner.

With each incident, they called the police, who were by now becoming increasingly familiar with the Turners. Finally, a police officer came to the house to talk to Turner. What the officer told her frightened all of them. The officer had received a credible report that Ike Turner was "hiring a gunman to 'take [her] to the ballpark.'" While Turner "figured that Ike had probably just started this rumor himself, to scare" her, she was afraid nonetheless. "I could deal with Ike, but if he really did have a hitman after me . . . well, you can't deal with those guys." Detectives from a homicide squad visited Turner's attorney Arthur Leeds to inform him that they also received credible reports of threats made against him.[50]

Turner's immediate response was to travel with her gun, but on November 25, 1976—the day before her thirty-seventh birthday—the *Los Angeles Sentinel* reported that she had been arrested and booked for "allegedly carrying a concealed weapon."[51] The week before, Turner had been stopped for a traffic violation while on her way to a Buddhist chanting meeting. As she reached into her purse for her license, the officer saw her gun and arrested her. At the station, she explained her fear of Ike Turner and the supposed "hit" on her life. After the gun was confiscated, she was released the same day with a warning.[52]

The officers explained to Turner that they could not offer any protection until Ike or someone associated with him acted on these threats. They could only warn her to be careful. Her friends and associates, among them Mike Stewart as her manager, urged Turner to "lay low," and perhaps even leave the country if possible. So, as 1976 transitioned to 1977, and leaving her sons in the care of her sister, Alline, Turner traveled to Germany and remained hidden, once again cutting off contact with her family so that Ike could not find her. She stayed in Germany for approximately one month.[53]

Carol Dryer: Karma as Context

Eventually, Turner returned to the United States to face Ike Turner and her past. She found solace during this challenging time in chanting, returning to her practice of chanting two hours every morning and two hours every evening. She also continued her study of Soka Gakkai Buddhist concepts, such as "human revolution" and karma. The latter concept would prove to have a uniquely therapeutic value for Turner. Specifically, the idea that karma carried across lifetimes provided important context for her experiences in *this* life.

Karma is an important notion in all forms of Nichiren Buddhism, and indeed in all forms of Buddhism. Across the Buddhist world, karma functions as a powerful explanatory model for the circumstances of a person's life, or lives.[54] Nichiren, living in thirteenth-century Japan, saw evidence of karmic processes at work in the world around him. In a letter written to one of his followers, Nichiren explained that the repeated criticism he faced from governmental authorities in his day was a result of "my karma from past lives."[55] To another follower who had fallen ill, Nichiren wrote that the person's illness arose from previous karma and proceeded to explain the principle behind changing karma.[56] Indeed, for Nichiren, the primary function of discussing karma was to show how karma may be changed through practicing Buddhism in a manner consistent with how he understood the Lotus Sutra. He called this the principle of "lessening karmic retribution," explaining in another letter: "If one's heavy karma from the past is not expiated within this lifetime, one must undergo the sufferings of hell in the future, but if one experiences extreme hardship in this life [because of the Lotus Sutra], the sufferings of hell will vanish instantly."[57] Soka Gakkai teachings, especially those propounded by Daisaku Ikeda, draw upon Nichiren's teachings regarding the transformation of karma to form their understanding of karma. In his writings on karma, Ikeda explains that "The law of karma accounts for the circumstances of one's birth, one's individual nature and the differences among all living beings and their environments. . . . Buddhism teaches that the chain of cause and effect exists eternally; this accounts for the influence of karma amassed in prior lifetimes."[58] Ikeda goes on to explain that practicing Buddhism, specifically in the form of chanting *Nam-myoho-renge-kyo*, is the way to transform karma.

Turner accepted these understandings of karma, as evidenced by her extensive discussion of the concept in her memoir *Happiness Becomes You*.[59] However, she combined Soka Gakkai's teachings on karma with insights drawn from her enduring religious repertoire. In *I, Tina*, she names several psychics, including Ginny Matrone, Jacqueline Eastland, and Peter Hurkos, as practitioners she regularly consulted with.[60] One psychic in particular, though, Carol Ann Dryer, would have a lasting impact on Turner's understanding of her own karma; she explained to her what exact karma carried across her lifetimes to place her in the situation she now found herself in with Ike Turner.

Limited biographical details about psychic "soul reader" Carol Ann Dryer are available, although it is known that she was married to Ivan Dryer (1939–2017). Originally a filmmaker, Ivan Dryer was the creator of the original Laserium light shows in 1973 at the Griffith Observatory in Los Angeles.[61] An obituary in *LiveDesign Magazine* mentioned that in "recent years Dryer had cared for his convalescent wife, Carol," indicating that Carol Ann Dryer was ill in the final years of her life (she preceded Ivan Dryer in death).[62] Though she appeared on a number of television programs over the course of her career, the only known complete interview with Dryer appeared as "Seeing the Soul with Carol Ann Dryer," an episode of the *Thinking Allowed* television series. In this episode, with Jeffrey Mishlove as interviewer, Dryer claims she was born with psychic abilities, but in her answers to Mishlove's questions she betrays an intimate familiarity with

Jungian psychology and the work of Emmanuel Swedenborg.[63] She also references notions such as auras, chakras, and the popular work *A Course in Miracles*.[64] In other words, Dryer's knowledge base was drawn from key discourses in American metaphysical religion.

According to Dryer, all people have a "trinity within" them composed of the ego, soul, and spirit, each of which "has a part in your body: the heart is operated by the spirit; the soul operates through the will; and the ego operates through the intellect." "The spirit and the soul exist all throughout the universe, as well as in the body by your choice," Dryer clarified, but "the ego's only realm is here [in this life]." Echoing Peter Hurkos's description of his psychic abilities manifesting in the form of seeing images as if on a television screen, Dryer explained that she closes her eyes and can "see through that area of the spirit and the soul connected together, where I feel very deeply the other person—their feelings, their fears, their anxieties." For Dryer, a good psychic can "hook the images [of the spirit, soul, and ego] together with great ease or facility." Naturally, she considered herself to be just such a psychic. She saw this as the reason "Jungian analysts, which are a large body of my clientele, simply love to come in for a session with me." Ultimately, working with the soul and the spirit must "be done in a guided way, like meditation."[65] And such guided work is what she did with Tina Turner.

Turner learned about Dryer's work in the early seventies from singer Judy Cheeks, who had been an Ikette in the Ike & Tina Turner Revue and for whom Ike Turner had produced a record. Turner recalls Cheeks telling her that Dryer was "a soul reader."[66] Finally, in 1977, Turner was able to have her own session with Dryer. In their session, "Dryer related to Tina the saga of the great Egyptian Queen Hatshepsut," Loder explained in *I, Tina*. Hatshepsut was the fifth pharaoh of Egypt's Eighteenth Dynasty and daughter of Pharaoh Thutmose I. Much has been written about Hatshepsut's complex life and times, as she "married her half brother, who reigned for a brief eight years as Thutmose II."[67] At Thutmose II's death, since his successor Thutmose III was only ten years old, Hatshepsut "governed the empire as regent, and soon was proclaimed Pharaoh herself, dominating what subsequently became a joint reign with her stepson until her death two decades later."[68] Loder summarizes that "Dryer saw Tina as the warrior woman Hatshepsut, succeeding her brother-husband to power and ultimately outshining him, then dominating her stepson's reign."[69]

Turner recalls Dryer describing to her that "Hatshepsut had taken the throne from her brother because he was very perverted, and she knew that he would destroy Egypt." She went on, "But that I had had no right to take the throne from him because no one has a right to *take* from others, and so there was karma, guilt from that other lifetime, that I had to live through in this one."[70] Though, in Dryer's understanding, the spirit and soul range across multiple lifetimes, Turner herself would not have been able to remember this past life due to the traumas of her early life and her traumatic relationship with Ike. As Dryer explained to Jeffrey Mishlove: "The degree to which we can maintain that ability to know and see and experience our own soul level, is the degree of trauma that we have had in our lives, and if our origin was less traumatic, if our beginning was less traumatic, we have more memory."[71] Thus, remembering required the guided work that Dryer specialized in. Nevertheless, as Dryer began the tale, Turner did recall that she always felt a connection with Egypt. She remembered that one day she had seen a coffee-table book for sale in an airport titled *Ancient Egypt*. Reading the book on the airplane, she remembers feeling her pulse pounding. "And I didn't know why. I just knew there was a buzz, a connection, some feeling I'd never encountered before." Now, Dryer was explaining to her that this connection was in fact due to her past life in Egypt.[72] Dryer went further and unpacked the significance of the characters for Turner:

> Ike was the brother, of course, and this time I had to *let* him destroy his empire—which is what he finally did, lost everything he had. He had also vowed that he would torture me as I had tortured him in that other life— and he sure did deliver on that promise. When Carol told me all this, I started to cry. I had come through it. I had lived through all the pain and finally I was just about free of him. The lives with him were over. But according to Carol, the story of *my* life still had quite a bit to go.[73]

While Dryer's assessment of Turner's situation, placed in the context of Hatshepsut's story, had the potential to sound a note of despair, for Turner it was positive because she saw herself as nearing the end of that karmic struggle. Crucially, Dryer, just as the psychic in London did eleven years prior, gave Turner a context for her difficulties and provided an assurance that she would overcome them. Thus, the belief that she was Hatshepsut in her past life and the way that provided a viable explanation for her current life context had immense therapeutic value for Turner.

Just as the 1971 trip to Ghana she took with Ike and occasional performances at Black Power rallies never led to a corresponding interest in Pan-Africanism,[74] Turner's interest in Egypt never seems to have led her to a position of Afrocentrism as it did for some African American artists in the sixties and seventies.[75] Instead, Turner's interest held a personal, therapeutic value. Much of this therapeutic value could be seen to derive from the ways in which, as explained by sociologist of religion Courtney Bender, belief in past lives "place metaphysicals in multiple histories."[76] Bender's research focuses on metaphysical religion. Working in a primarily sociological vein, though, Bender's work centers the beliefs and behaviors of those who participate in metaphysical religious groups. She calls these people "metaphysicals." Tina Turner, maintaining her work with psychics like Dryer, alongside her practice of Soka Gakkai Nichiren Buddhism, would be considered a metaphysical in Bender's formulation. To Bender, for an adherent of metaphysical religion, adherence to ideas about past lives are "More than mere beliefs that provided philosophical answers to what happens to the soul after death," instead, "past lives mapped layers of story and history onto the present in ways that enlivened, deepened, and ultimately complicated current social relationships. Metaphysicals build and navigate tenuous but real social worlds through remembering, sensing, and experiencing past lives."[77] As Bender understands it, in the context of past life histories, "Difficult relationships, bad decisions about spouses or intimacies, intractable personality conflicts between family members, distrust and infidelity all become inflected with karmic meaning." In the process, each relationship "becomes an opportunity to work out karmic issues."[78] This is what Dryer's work enabled Turner to do: by placing her marriage to Ike Turner in a historical relationship to Hatshepsut, their relationship became "inflected with karmic meaning." Seeing the relationship in this way, under the guidance of Dryer, becomes a way to do the work that Bender sees as navigating "real social worlds" through acts of "remembering, sensing, and experiencing past lives."

But, in Soka Gakkai's understanding of karma, the significance of discussing karma is centered around its transformation. Thus, Turner's ascertainment of the karmic meanings of her marriage and impending divorce to

Ike Turner entails transforming that relationship in concrete ways. And indeed, as Bender explains, "To imagine, remember, and place oneself in relation to such a past life presents metaphysicals with a number of questions, some quite vexing, about their commitments to family in this life."[79]

Solo Tina

By 1977, Turner had already begun taking steps to revive her career. That year, Mike Stewart, her manager at United Artists, gave her an undisclosed amount of money to organize a band, dancers, and costumes to put together a show.[80] The money also went to hire producer Jack Good, choreographer Toni Basil, and costume designer Bob Mackie, all successful figures in the industry. Good was producer of the sixties' musical variety show *Shindig!* Basil began her career as a dancer on *Shindig!* before becoming a renowned choreographer and forming her own street dance troupe.[81] Mackie was most famous for designing extravagant, over-the-top costumes for Cher. Given the difficulties of securing bookings under the Tina Turner name, Rhonda Graam turned to the "cabaret circuit" of hotel and casinos, booking in places like Las Vegas, Lake Tahoe, and hotel chains like Caesars Palace, the Fairmont, and the Hilton. For these venues, it was decided that while Turner would utilize familiar songs from the Ike and Tina Turner catalogue, she would also capitalize on the success of disco. To this end, she incorporated hit disco songs like "Disco Inferno," by the Trammps, as well as songs like "Big Spender," drawn from jazzy stage musicals. She debuted this new show in Vancouver, Canada, before making her way down the West Coast of the United States and to Las Vegas, where press was on hand for her headlining "comeback" residencies.[82]

The August 3, 1977, edition of the weekly entertainment trade publication *Variety* reported that there was "nothing inherently new" about Turner's Caesars Palace Las Vegas debut, since Turner's "sexy volcanic force erupts with all the power and mesmerizing impact of former times, although the component aides and presentation are different." By "component aides," the reviewer meant to highlight the way Jack Good's producing and Bob Mackie's costuming replaced Ike Turner's control over the Ike & Tina Turner Revue's shows; "presentation" was a reference to Mackie's costumes, which presented "variants on the familiar cleavage and high pelvic cuts" of Turner's former stage costumes. The reviewer also mentions that, in addition to retaining covers of rock songs like "Honky Tonk Women," she also performed her "patented 'Proud Mary.'" This references the way in which Turner's spoken-word composition in the song's beginning and genre-crossing slow-to-fast style had become a signature for her, seven years after its release on Ike and Tina Turner's *Workin' Together* album. Among the musicians listed in her band was the piano player Kenny Moore (1952–1997).[83] Moore, a classically trained pianist, worked as a vocalist for gospel legend Rev. James Cleveland, and played piano for Aretha Franklin, Gladys Knight, and others. Moore remained with Turner's band until his death during Turner's 1996–1997 Wildest Dreams Tour.[84]

Speaking about her first solo concerts, Turner was honest about the show's difficulties. There were costume malfunctions; the audiences were different from what she was used to; and because of the canceled Ike & Tina Turner Revue tour, she was served lawsuit papers at each concert. Nonetheless, she "was independent for the very first time," and, she said, "[I] tried to hold on to that feeling, the excitement and optimism that propelled me every time I walked out on stage."[85] She explained that in her new shows she aimed to remain true to herself by not trying to sing "jazz or classical songs." She went on, "I sang rock 'n' roll, and R & B, and blues the whole time." Instead of changing musical styles, she changed the style of the show, to "get the new show to make a little bit more sense."[86] Though some may have found the show's aesthetic to be different than they remembered—a band in tuxedos and bow ties—Turner's show made sense "because that's where we were working—in the cabaret places that needed this type of production." She continued, "I got great reviews. I got standing ovations for the first time in my life. I don't remember standing ovations when I was with Ike. So I felt I was doing something right—and *I* was the one who did it."[87] For Turner, then, these shows were learning experiences that she could be proud of. Most importantly, the fact that she was doing this independently of Ike Turner was an accomplishment in itself. And this accomplishment was validated by her audiences. After the Las Vegas residency, the new show toured across the United States.

Bob Lucas's profile of the show in his January 5, 1978, *Jet* magazine cover story added an additional detail to the show. Lucas reported that Ike "was in the audience when she debuted at Caesar's Palace, but did not come to her dressing room after the first show that night." While Lucas does not say more about Ike's attendance at the show, he does write that Turner said that she was "on a friendly basis" with Ike and that "her four sons see their father often."[88] During this period and until their divorce was finalized in March of 1978, Ike continued to harass Turner as her divorce petition was fought in court. Yet, until she began to publicly reveal the violent details of their marriage and divorce in magazine profiles starting with Carl Arrington's 1981 *People* magazine story, Turner publicly downplayed the contentious nature of their separation.[89] Even as she minimized the details, she acknowledged that navigating her career and family was difficult.

"There were times when I felt so alone," Turner wrote. Much of this loneliness was her perception that yet again her mother had abandoned her. During the separation and divorce proceedings, Turner's fraught relationship with her mother, Zelma, only became more so. "Muh [sic] sided with Ike, if you can believe it. In her mind, he was always right because he had the big house, the Cadillac, the money. And, if you asked her, she definitely thought that he had all the talent." As Turner saw it, Zelma believed that Tina Turner needed Ike. She was at pains to describe what life with Ike was like and why she could never go back. Still, Turner explained, "No matter what I said Muh favored Ike and stayed close to him, almost as if she was *his* mother." Remembering that her mother had left her father, Richard, her, and Alline in Nutbush all those years ago, she concluded that while Zelma's reaction to her leaving Ike was painful, "it wasn't a surprise after so many years of being invisible to her." Nonetheless, while Turner toured the country, Zelma, Alline, and even Ann Cain came to help with her increasingly difficult sons.[90]

Though arrangements were made to have housekeepers care for the children and to have Zelma and Alline bring food for them, Turner could only do so much while touring. Ironically, though Turner and Ike were separated, life for the boys carried on much as it had while their parents were together: they saw very little of either of them. While Ike remained ensconced at Bolic Sound Studios, Turner was touring and performing. Amid this, Turner called Ann Cain for help.

According to Cain, Turner called her and told her she "was the only person she knew who could handle her boys." Turner also confided to Cain that her sons "were turning her house into a nightclub whenever she was working out of town."⁹¹ When she asked them to clean the home, they responded by telling her that they were "used to a housekeeper" and would not help clean up. She insisted, and since Ike Jr. in particular refused to clean, she kicked him out, explaining that she "was not going to live his life-style in [her] own house."⁹² Turner explained to Cain that, while her sons would have a home to stay in as long as she did, she was constantly concerned about them while she was working. She assured Cain that though she could not pay her for her services, one day she would compensate her.⁹³

In the meantime, Turner hoped that involving at least some of her sons in her new career would help. Turner hired Ike Turner Jr. to work as a sound engineer for her. But when Ike found out that his son was both working at Bolic Sound Studios and working for Turner, he forced Ike Jr. to choose between his parents, and thus Ike Jr. quit working for Turner. Ronnie Turner played bass, and she planned to incorporate him into her band. However, Turner discovered in a meeting with his teachers that Ronnie's drug problem was more serious than she knew. To help break his drug dependency, she sent him to a private school in Oregon for treatment. Though it was Ronnie who initially introduced Turner to Buddhist chanting, in Oregon he was introduced to Scientology, and to Turner he "seemed to really be cleaning up his life." A year later she brought him back to Los Angeles and enrolled him in an undisclosed Scientologist school. In part to accommodate him, Turner moved to a new, more spacious home in Sherman Oaks. Instead of helping her move, her sons were nowhere to be found. She *did* find Ronnie Turner in his room doing drugs and talking on the phone. Ronnie, like Ike Jr., was also kicked out.⁹⁴

This left Michael and Craig Turner at home. Turner noticed that Michael would "sit home every day and just play his guitar," and suspected that of all of them, Michael was the most affected by his parents' ongoing divorce. Eventually, Turner explained, "The doctor finally decided that Michael wanted to be with his father." So Michael went back to live with Ike. Craig worked and enlisted in the navy but remained close to Turner. Turner later acknowledged that she became "estranged from the other boys." But she reflected that, ultimately, "I think it had to be that way. Because they loved Bolic Sound, and they loved the image of Ike and the cars and the women. They needed to get to know what that life was really about, and what their father was really like. I already *knew*. So with Ronnie and Michael and Ike junior, I had no options. I had to work to support myself and to support them—but I couldn't support their habits and their laziness, too. They were used to that other kind of life, but that life was over for me." Turner concluded her reflection by saying that her attitude was "a matter of surviving" rather than about being strict with her sons.[95]

Even as Turner attended to each problem that arose with their sons, Ike Turner remained a constant, threatening presence. At times, Turner remembers, "Ike was still stalking me and often surfaced when I least expected him."[96] On one occasion, Ike met Turner's party at the airport as they were attempting to depart for a show.[97] On another occasion, she was harassed at home. Just as at her previous home, on Sunset Crest Drive in Laurel Canyon, once Ike discovered she had moved to the Sherman Oaks area of Los Angeles, the house was fired upon, and a fire was lit around one of the cars at the home. Again the police were called, and Ike Turner was suspected.[98] This incident was, for Turner, the proverbial straw that broke the camel's back. "That little incident did it for me. I really did need money then, because I had nothing but losses coming in. And I had worked for sixteen years to build up Ike and Tina Turner, and all that partnership had become. Now Ike had it all. It wasn't fair, but no amount of money was worth *this*. I just gave up."[99] Because of Ike's continued harassment, Turner decided that the time had come to drop most of her divorce claims and bring her divorce to a conclusion.

In court, Turner's attorney, Arthur Leeds, continued his aggressive pursuit of her divorce petition. Even as Leeds sought what he considered the full value of Turner's claims to Ike's assets, Ike repeatedly undervalued those same assets. These included clothes and jewelry, and properties throughout Southern California. At the same time, "In leaving him, Ike contended," as Loder explains, "Tina was taking with her the principal asset of their marriage: the 'good will' inherent in the entity of 'Ike and Tina Turner.' Ike valued the loss to him of this 'good will' at $750,000." Continued haggling over these claims and counterclaims had caused the divorce suit to persist from July 1976 to the fall of 1977. By November 1977, Turner had decided, against Leeds's objection, to drop all claims in her divorce petition. According to Leeds, in dropping her claims Ike "kept the studio, he kept his publishing companies, his four cars, the North Valley property—

he took all of the property, but none of the debt." Turner received the two cars that she had and "retained her writer's royalties from songs she had written, but Ike got the publishing royalties for both his compositions and hers." In the end, Leeds summarizes: "Tina walked out with what was on her back, essentially. But she said, 'My life's more important.'"[100] Crucially though, Turner also walked out with her name. When "A Fool in Love" was released under the name "Ike and Tina Turner," an entity was created that had never existed: Tina Turner. Since Ike created the moniker, he also trademarked it. In divorcing Ike, Turner also realized that she would need the trademark for her name in order to continue performing under it. Shrewdly, Turner asked for the trademark as a requisite for dropping all other claims in the divorce. The judge granted it, and finally, on March 29, 1978, their divorce was decreed final. Now, Turner was free to resume the resurrection of her career under the name Tina Turner.[101]

A Buddhist Blueprint for the Future

While Turner had performed throughout the year 1977, and even filmed a brief cameo appearance in the musical comedy film *Sgt. Pepper's Lonely Hearts Club Band*,[102] by her divorce in March 1978, she had not released any new music since 1975's *Acid Queen*. Nonetheless, in January 1978, Mike Stewart, Turner's manager at United Artists Records, began to work in earnest to generate a buzz around Turner in anticipation of an album release later that year.[103] In September, *Rough* (United Artists, 1978) was finally released. The album was produced by Bob Monaco and featured both original songs and covers of songs by Elton John, Ray Charles, and Bob Seger. Monaco had achieved success throughout the seventies, producing albums that blended funk, rhythm and blues, disco, and even jazz.[104] Later biographers have given the album mixed reviews, but when released, the album was positively reviewed by leading industry publications. A review in *Record World* called Turner's vocals "something to behold" and determined that "Bob Monaco has captured the essence of her unique song stylings" on the album.[105] *Cash Box* noted that as a result of the mix of styles, the album was "hot to go" for both album-oriented radio stations and black contemporary stations.[106] Finally, *Billboard* considered the album's musical backup "solid."[107] Thus, despite the lukewarm perception of later biographers, the music industry accepted the album and its mix of genres, just as they had Turner's previous genre-crossing efforts, *The Gospel according to Ike and Tina* and *Tina Turns the Country On.*

As the release of *Rough* came and went, Turner continued to perform across the United States and internationally. In each locale, her audience size varied considerably. But for Turner, "it didn't matter if five people came, or five hundred," because she "always believed that the audience was entitled to the same wonderful show," with her at her absolute best.[108] As her tour carried her across the United States, Australia, and Europe, Turner staked her performance reputation on this attitude. A show recorded at London's Apollo Theatre on March 25, 1979, is typical of Turner's performances during this era. The show was staged specifically for video recording, making it an ideal study of Turner's performance style in the early years of her solo career. Like the show at Caesars Palace Las Vegas, this performance featured choreography by Toni Basil and costumes by Bob Mackie. The show opens with Turner singing her cover of Elton John and Bernie Maupin's song "The Bitch Is Back," from the *Rough* album. The first two songs are performed without backup dancers, likely in an attempt to distinguish her own show from the shows of the Ike & Tina Turner Revue, which often opened with Turner and the Ikettes performing a dance routine. After the first song, Turner gives a monologue in which she presents a threefold typology of performers: "there are many different types of performers: you have the crooners, the comics, and the jokers." She classifies herself as neither a crooner nor a joker, but rather a "croaker." In so doing, she implies to the audience that she doesn't fit standard models— even if those models are of her own invention—of performers. She is in a league of her own. This leads her through a cover of the Native American rock band Redbone's 1970 song, "Crazy Cajun Cakewalk Band," which itself segues into Rod Stewart's "Hot Legs." The show proceeds through an array of songs, featuring the same genre mix as the *Rough* album. Some are original: "Nutbush City Limits" and "River Deep, Mountain High." Some are disco covers, like the Trammps's "Disco Inferno." She closes the show with a medley of more familiar covers from the Ike and Tina catalogue: "Proud Mary," "I Want to Take You Higher," and "Honky Tonk Women." Each song is performed in an equally diverse cabaret-style costume, designed by Mackie. What unifies the various song styles and costumes is

Turner's distinctive voice and dance style, performed with indefatigable energy. Key to this energy was Turner's Buddhist practice.

A month before the Apollo Theatre show, Turner was once again featured in a *Jet* cover story. This cover was different from previous stories, as it foregrounded her religious practice by featuring her posed on the cover in front of her elaborate *butsudan*, the Buddhist altar used by Soka Gakkai Buddhists. The cover reads: "Sex and Religion Keep Tina Turner Famous and Humble." Ostensibly, the article is about the way in which Turner uses sex appeal in a performative way for her public persona, and Buddhism in her "real," private life. Yet, the profile focuses almost exclusively on her Buddhist practice. The profile begins: "Clad only in a loosely tied robe, Tina Turner crosses the huge living room floor to the Buddhist shrine. A look of serenity crosses her features as she kneels, facing the East." With that, she demonstrates the practice: "'Nam-myo-ho-renge-kyo [*sic*] . . . nam-myo-ho-renge-kyo . . .' she chants over and over, hands clasped over the prayer beads looped around her fingers." It goes on to say, "And so begins the day for the *real* Tina Turner, behind the doors of her luxurious home in Studio City, a suburb north of Hollywood." In the article, Turner explains the Buddhist practice and its benefits, and displays, once again, her combinatory religious sensibilities when she is quoted as explaining that the doctrines of Nichiren Buddhism are "the same righteous teachings of the Bible." When discussing her children and divorce, she again conceals the difficulties with her sons by saying that they are independent and "not spoiled." She only alludes to Ike's previous control over her life by saying that her whole life had changed, but that the new Tina was exactly who she "wanted to be all the time, but sometimes when you cannot exercise your true self, these things don't come out until you are able to do it." She adds, "So now I can and I do."[109] Whereas previous magazine profiles had mentioned Turner's Buddhist practice or even quoted her discussion of Buddhist concepts, this *Jet* profile was one of the first to foreground her practice of Soka Gakkai Nichiren Buddhism. The article reinforces the public association of Turner's fame with Buddhism by juxtaposing images of Turner on stage and in front of her *butsudan* shrine and by juxtaposing Turner's perception of her own fame with her explanation of the benefits of practicing Buddhism.

Turner's Buddhist study and practice remained a priority even on tour. After arranging all practical details of a hotel stay, Turner's assistant on tour "always put her spiritual books by her bed." Then, he would "set up the necessary chanting corner with fresh fruit nearby."[110] More than a way to induce a personal sense of peace, chanting on tour was also a way to connect to her audiences. Turner later explained: "Since I began my solo career—thousands of concerts in dozens of countries—I have chanted and prayed before each show, focusing on the happiness of each person who came to see me. I visualized my audience and prayed that I could be whoever each person needed me to be that day in order to inspire their dreams, invigorate their hope, and recharge their souls. I prayed to spark in them a joyful revolution of the heart."[111] Taro Gold, a coauthor of *Happiness Becomes You*, further explained that she chanted up to an hour before each show.[112] Both the *Jet* profile and Turner's own description of her practice on tour were essential to reinforcing the public association between her as a professional artist and Buddhism. As Turner focused more on her Buddhist practice and the audiences viewing her show, she also began to consider anew her vision of her career.

When Turner left Ike and was staying with the Shorters, Wayne Shorter posed a series of questions to her that would prompt a deeper reflection of her life's goals. Now that she was on her own, Wayne asked her what she wanted in life. He clarified his question by asking, "If you could have anything your heart truly desires, what would you want? For yourself, for the people you love, for your community, for the world?" To this point, Turner had never been truly on her own and thus hadn't considered her own desires: "I didn't know how to answer that question. I was on my own for the first time and the future I wanted wasn't entirely in focus yet." Since she couldn't answer the question, Wayne encouraged Turner to create "a mission statement" for her life, which would "help set a clear direction."[113] This exchange between Wayne and Turner is noteworthy because of the way it echoes Soka Gakkai teachings about the power of creating "blueprints" for one's life.

Daisaku Ikeda explained the significance of creating such blueprints in *Learning from the Gosho: The Eternal Teachings of Nichiren Daishonin*, itself a collection of writings about Nichiren's letters. In this collection, Ikeda explains that after asking oneself questions about the future envisioned for oneself and what one wants to accomplish, we should "paint this vision of our lives in our hearts as specifically as possible. This 'painting' becomes the design for our future." He adds: "The more specific and detailed the blueprint we have in our hearts, the better. The point is to continue vividly painting the target we have and to advance toward that goal single-mindedly. Then, at each instant, the reality of our lives will gradually approach the painting that is our aspiration. Everything depends on what is in our hearts. Heartfelt prayers will definitely be answered."[114] In Soka Gakkai teachings, whatever is in a person's heart crystallizes into a prayer, as chanted before the *gohonzon*. In the process of "vividly painting the target," or creating a detailed plan for one's life, a person takes the first step toward accomplishing the fulfillment of his or her goals and dreams. As lofty and inspiring as Wayne's encouragement to Turner was, echoing as it did Ikeda's writings, it remained a normative prescription. At that time, Turner confided at a Buddhist discussion meeting: "Leaving—and divorcing—Ike proved to be more complicated than I had ever imagined. I was facing an army of lawyers filing lawsuits against me for walking out on concert and recording contracts I was supposed to do with Ike. Meanwhile, I was also being harassed by thugs Ike sent to intimidate me, whose tactics included setting fire to a car parked outside my house and firing bullets through my windows."[115] Thus, when Wayne initially posed his questions, Turner's practical circumstances prevented her from creating such a detailed blueprint.

Much in her life had transformed in the three years that passed since that conversation with Wayne. In the interim, she had finalized her divorce and begun rebuilding her career as a solo artist. Now, in 1979, she was able to begin painting a vision of her future. "Tina," as Loder explained, "was becoming restless with the state of her career. She was working regularly again, but always in cabaret.... She would soon be forty, and felt that her creative fires had yet to reach full flame. The cabaret circuit, particularly Vegas and Tahoe, paid good money—and money was a crucial concern."[116] In addition to Vegas and Tahoe, Turner's income was augmented by regularly touring abroad. But this was not enough: "Tina wanted more. She didn't like her new lounge-act image."[117] Instead, Turner was harboring a new dream. She "wanted to fill concert halls and arenas, like the Rolling Stones and Rod Stewart."[118] And she was well aware that her dream was "quite an ambition for a forty-year-old female singer" in a changing music business.[119]

After disco emerged as both a musical style and a multiracial counterculture in the late sixties' nightclubs of urban Philadelphia and New York, a range of recording artists achieved success with disco music in the seventies. These artists included Donna Summer, Gloria Gaynor, and even Michael Jackson. It also included groups like the Trammps; Earth, Wind, and Fire; the Bee Gees; ABBA; the Village People; Sister Sledge; and Rufus. The disco craze was also captured in films like *Saturday Night Fever*. To craft the disco sounds of these artists, groups, and movies, there arose disco producers like Giorgio Moroder and Bob Monaco. Monaco, as we have seen, produced distinctive albums that combined musical genres, and for this reason he was enlisted to produce Turner's first post-Ike solo album in 1978. Although Turner's second post-Ike album, *Love Explosion* (United Artists/Liberty, 1979), was also in the disco genre, by 1979 disco was already seeing a noticeable decline as new music trends emerged.[120]

At the same time, major changes were happening on the corporate side of the music business. After a series of failed business deals, United Artists Records was sold to Capitol/EMI Records. In the sale, many underselling artists were dropped from the label. When the sale was covered in a brief article in *Variety*, Turner was mentioned as one of the "soul acts" that would be retained.[121] Eventually, though, Turner departed from the label in the United States for reasons that are not entirely clear. Mike Stewart remained as her manager, and EMI kept her on the roster of artists in the UK. Suddenly without a record deal in the United States, Turner continued to work an international touring circuit.[122]

Rava Daly, one of the four dancers in Turner's stage show, knew Olivia Newton-John's English manager, Lee Kramer. Daly encouraged Turner to "talk to Lee and his associate, an Australian named Roger Davies, who had just come to America."[123] At the same time, representatives of Newton-John contacted Turner to solicit her for an ensemble appearance in Newton-John's television special *Olivia Newton-John: Hollywood Nights*. Turner met both Kramer and Davies during the taping of the special. Following Daly's advice, Turner contacted Kramer and sought advice from Stewart about how to approach a potential manager.[124] In the meantime, she prepared herself spiritually. Eddy Armani, Turner's assistant, recalls: "Tina sat in front of her altar chanting morning, noon, and night, willing Lee Kramer into her life. She consulted her psychic readers to see what they had to say. They all told her similar things, that she was going to be the biggest of stars, playing stadiums, never tiny venues again. They told her that she was going to [be] bigger than Mick Jagger."[125] With guidance from Stewart, and buoyed by chanting and psychic consultations, Turner arranged a meeting with Kramer and Davies.

New Management

Turner would later refer to their meeting, particularly meeting Roger Davies, as "that fateful meeting." Six years earlier, the *Nutbush City Limits* album had been a major success in Davies's native Australia. Thus, Davies knew who Tina Turner was, and he was vaguely aware that she was now a solo artist (though neither he, nor the public at large, knew the harrowing details of her life with Ike or her divorce). In Turner's estimation, Davies had expected her to "look much older," but her age was concealed by her wig, clothes, and styling. She also surmised from the look on his face during their meeting that he wasn't "all that impressed" with the music she brought to the meeting to demonstrate her recording potential. Remaining silent for much of the meeting, Davies asked her the same question Wayne Shorter had three years prior: "What do you want?" Unlike with Shorter, this time she had an answer: "I said, 'Well I just got a divorce. I'm in debt. I need a manager. I need a record company. I need records. And [by the way] I want to fill halls like the Rolling Stones and Rod Stewart.' There, I put all my cards on the table." Noting Davies's skepticism, she invited him and Kramer to see her perform in the Venetian Room at the Fairmont Hotel in San Francisco. Turner resolved that whether they came or not, she had "taken a step in the right direction" by meeting with them.[126]

Turner was scheduled for a two-week engagement at the Fairmont. Since Kramer and Davies had been invited to attend, it was crucial that the shows not suffer any of the technical difficulties that had plagued her debut shows in Vancouver and Las Vegas. She rehearsed with her band and dancers constantly. On the evening of the show, Turner conducted one final sound check to ensure that this potentially career-changing show was flawless. "'Testing, 1, 2, 3.' It all seemed routine until Tina stepped in," Armani wrote of that pre-show sound check in the Fairmont's Venetian Room. "I had never seen anyone conduct a soundcheck like her. She walked straight on the stage, picked up her microphone and said, 'Uh, okay, let's go. "River Deep, Mountain High."' Tina soundchecked as if she were performing to an audience. . . . It was like a show without the costumes and by the end of the song, the band members were dripping with perspiration."[127] For Turner, who likely had visualized an audience while chanting that evening, the sound check and rehearsal *were* a show. At showtime, she scanned the crowd hoping to see Davies and Kramer, "but they kept me waiting for two weeks. They didn't make it to San Francisco until the very last night of the show."[128]

Turner played two shows on that final night. Davies and Kramer attended both. Upon arriving at the Fairmont, Davies's first reaction was confusion: "We went into the Venetian Room, this big ballroom, and there were chandeliers and people in tuxedos. I said, 'This can't be the right room.' Then Tina's band came on, and they were all in tuxedos, too. I thought, 'This is very weird.'"[129] Nonetheless, "the first show," in Davies's estimation, was "great."[130] But the audience was staid, as they "sat comfortably at tables while they drank cocktails and watched the show."[131] To Davies the second show "was *better*. People were standing on tables; the chandeliers were shaking."[132] That show convinced him that underneath the cabaret act was a consummate performer. In short, Davies now believed in Turner herself.

Based on the success of the San Francisco shows, Kramer and Davies agreed to manage Turner. Her managerial relationship with Stewart ended immediately. Turner was still in debt to Stewart for financing her solo shows, and she owed back taxes and penalties to the Internal Revenue Service (IRS), so a financial arrangement was negotiated between the three men to pay both Stewart and the IRS.[133] With the financial arrangements made, Turner was signed as one of Roger Davies's acts.

South Africa and Racial Karma

To pay off her debt, Davies booked another international tour for Turner, with the aim of getting her out of the cabaret circuit in the United States. As Davies scheduled the tour, he received an offer from a promoter: $150,000 for a five-week tour. Enthusiasm for this offer was immediately tempered by the tour's location: apartheid South Africa. The 1940s and 1950s in South Africa saw the passage of a series of legislative acts institutionalizing racial segregation, beginning with the Prohibition of Mixed Marriages Act (1949), and arising out of Afrikaner nationalist ideologies.[134] Historian Saul Dubrow labels the period from the 1960s through the following decade a period of "high apartheid," a time when white supremacy and racial rule became synonymous.[135] In response to apartheid conditions, the African National Congress called for a "cultural and academic boycott" in 1958. Their calls gained international traction, and the United Nations initiated a series of resolutions and sanctions against the apartheid regime.[136] Regardless of the long-standing cultural boycott, a few artists ignored the boycott over the years for lucrative touring contracts. These included Queen, Cher, Frank Sinatra, Curtis Mayfield, Millie Jackson, and others. Millie Jackson, speaking of her reasons for touring South Africa despite the boycott, later explained that "American blacks who are forgotten here have the chance to go there and make some money." Referencing African American singer Brook Benton, Jackson further explained: "Brook Benton was over there when I was. When was the last time you heard from him? Brook Benton's not going to South Africa isn't going to solve any problems."[137] Jackson was also quoted saying, "Ghettoes are the same all around the world," in reference to the conditions of Black people in the township of Soweto.[138] Thus, at least for African American artists like Millie Jackson, defying an international boycott to perform in apartheid South Africa was a conscious choice. For Turner, the decision was a personal choice, with little reference to South Africa's sociopolitical situation.

Beyond knowing that South Africa was segregated, Turner claimed to have no further knowledge of the country's complex history. Davies did his best to explain that complexity to her, and the pros and cons of the deal. It was during apartheid, but she had lived through an apartheid in the United States: the Jim Crow South. She would get flack for it, but she had been dealing with flack ever since she left Ike Turner three years prior. The promoter promised that all her shows would have mixed audiences, so she agreed to the deal. She traveled to South Africa and did her shows in September 1980.[139] "It was the usual touring situation, so I didn't get to see much. I remember someone once said to me, 'Do you know what's happening in this country?' And I said, 'No.' Because I really didn't, beyond the basic fact that it was segregated. I didn't know how bad things really were. I had this new management, and no record company, and I was kind of caught up in my own problems."[140] Her focus was her career and the complexities of her personal life. As Turner performed in South Africa, she largely avoided making public statements about social or political issues. When asked if she would visit Soweto, Turner replied, "I evade problems."[141] Though Turner maintained this public stance, in private, she and her entourage experienced the discriminatory conditions on the ground in South Africa.

Rhonda Graam recalled that while their shows were racially mixed, there were incidents of discrimination against the group—as "one bus driver didn't want our two dancers, Annie and Lejeune, to get on his bus together because one was black and one was white." Graam continues by explaining that other than that experience, they "weren't involved with the racial situation."[142] Graam's recollections no doubt reflect her experience, especially as a white American, but it is unlikely that their integrated traveling group experienced no other discrimination. Turner's stage manager, Chip Lightman, was also white, as was dancer Ann (Annie) Behringer. The pianist Kenny Moore, Turner herself, bassist Ronnie Turner (Turner's son), and Eddy Hampton (Armani) were all Black. We may surmise that as the group traveled together, in apartheid South Africa, there were uncomfortable situations. Ronnie, like Graam, recalled that their shows were mixed, but he summarized his perception of South Africa by saying, "black people there had less than blacks even *usually* have. It was not the kind of place I would want to live."[143] The group was also not immune to more overt acts of racial discrimination.

Eddy Armani relayed to Turner his experience of being refused entry and service at a restaurant due to his being Black. Armani detailed Turner's response to him:

Ed, why do you think I spend so much time in my hotel suite? I'll only go out if the promoters are escorting us. Believe me, I'm not putting myself in a situation to be treated that way. . . . I've seen a lot of racism in my day. . . . You see, the thing to do is don't look too hard at it and don't think about it too much. This is their karma. They were brought back to live their lives this way. They all have something to learn from it and we have to leave them to it. This is not our country and it's none of our business. Let's just do our jobs and get out of here.[144]

In this response, Turner uses her understanding of karma—gleaned both from Buddhist teachings and from her work with Dryer—as a prism through which to view social issues like race.

Soka Gakkai Nichiren Buddhism promotes an understanding of karma that lends itself to personal and social transformation. That understanding is consonant with much of modernist Buddhist ethics, which sees karma, in both personal and collective forms, as a lens for moral reflection on the nature of personal and collective actions. Philosopher and Buddhist studies scholar Jay Garfield explains that in Buddhism, "Karma is not a system of reward and punishment: it has nothing to do with moral *desert*, it is not a supernatural connection between what one does and what happens to one. . . . Instead, it is simply the fact that who we are and what we experience is the consequence of past events, including actions, and the fact that the actions we perform now have effects in the future."[145] Garfield argues that this understanding should be kept in mind when considering Buddhist reflections on karma theory. While Buddhist literature commonly presents stories about how any given being's present body, life, or circumstances is the result of karma accumulated in the past, Garfield warns against misunderstanding the import of such stories. According to Garfield, if misunderstood, "karma could be taken as shoddy justification for inequality, oppression, excessive wealth, disability, etc."[146] Rather than take this perspective, Garfield urges that karma is a way of naming the Buddhist conviction that "The circumstances in which we find ourselves are similarly the product of a complex history of which we are only partial authors."[147] As an ethical concern, this conviction could then lead to a greater concern to undertake committed action for those who are less fortunate, to reflect upon ways to change systems of oppression, and so on.[148] Indeed, just such an understanding of karma has led to the emergence of Engaged Buddhism (or Socially Engaged Buddhism) movements in the twentieth and twenty-first centuries. These movements understand karma as a domain of ethical concern oriented toward social action in the world. These movements appeal to human rights discourse and to the importance of understanding the ways that systemic issues lead to both personal and collective suffering.[149]

Turner's understanding of karma in relation to the suffering of Black South Africans under apartheid differs both from Garfield's view outlined above and from that espoused in the writings of other Black Buddhists. Most Black Buddhist writers do not use karma as an explanation or justification for systemic racism. Instead, the transformative potential of Buddhist teachings is usually emphasized. For example, in *Dharma Matters: Women, Race, and Tantra,* Jan Willis—a Black Buddhist author who is a prominent scholar of Tibetan Buddhism—uses the Buddhist teaching of the Four Noble Truths, which name the ubiquity of suffering, to expound upon how the historical trauma of slavery gives people of color an understanding of suffering that white people could not have. Willis then emphasizes that, since the third noble truth speaks of the possibility for ending suffering and the fourth noble truth provides the path out of suffering, the suffering of historical traumas can be overcome.[150]

Karma does not appear in Willis's exposition and is de-emphasized in Black Buddhist writings, likely because of a keen recognition of the problem named by Garfield: the great potential for misunderstanding karma as providing a kind of cosmic justification for racism.[151] Turner's response to Armani undermines these understandings and reveals her hybrid conception of karma: "Ed, we are guests in this country. We are here working and when we are finished, we return home to our own freedom, our own lives and our own karma. We are not politicians, Ed, and we are not God. We can't change things here nor can we change the world. Let it go, Ed."[152] Even as Turner understood karma as a social force, on the level of transformation, she understood it as primarily personal. And this understanding enabled her to work in apartheid South Africa. In the end, the South African tour was, for Turner, as for other artists, a sound financial deal, even if not a sound social move. After her five-week tour of South Africa ended in October, the group returned to the United States, before resuming the tour in Australia and Southeast Asia.

Making Changes

Roger Davies joined the tour in Thailand. Though Davies saw that his subtle suggestions to Turner to change the show—"because I thought it was too disco, too Vegas"—had been taken, he grew frustrated with Turner's show, musicians, and entourage.[153] Considering her dream to perform rock 'n' roll music and fill stadiums, Turner's band provoked Davies's ire:

"By now, this band she had was starting to drive me crazy. She was paying them all far too much money; we seemed to be working just to pay the band. And they weren't rock 'n' roll, which I knew Tina needed to be."¹⁵⁴ Creatively, Turner had previously been associated with blues, rhythm and blues, soul, gospel, funk, and even disco and country styles, but now she aimed to be associated primarily with rock music. For Davies, his strategy was to work backward from Turner's dream of filling stadiums: filling stadiums required commercially successful, charting albums; albums required a record contract; and a recording contract required making Turner an attractive commodity to record labels and their predominantly white record executives. So, Davies explained to Turner their necessary next steps: "Listen, if we're ever gonna change this act, Tina, we've got to change everything—fire everybody. You've got to get rid of this band, get rid of the dancers, get rid of Rhonda, the sound guy, the lighting guy. You've gotta get young guys, make it rock 'n' roll. Get rid of these tuxedos and the silver-lamé sequins."¹⁵⁵ Turner agreed, and all members of her traveling team received notice that they were fired. Turner retained only Kenny Moore, by now the backbone of her show; Ann Behringer and Lejeune Richardson as dancers; Chip Lightman as road manager; and Eddy Armani as assistant. Turner then hired bassist Bob Feit, guitarist James Ralston, and drummer Jack Bruno, all younger than Turner, and white. Hiring younger, mostly white musicians was a conscious effort by Davies and Turner to appeal to the younger, predominantly white, rock 'n' roll audiences, record buyers, and executives.

In the United States, most of the concert dates Turner secured continued to be on the hotel and lounge cabaret circuit. Internationally, though, Turner could play in a variety of venues more suitable to her new show. This international focus was one of the most attractive aspects to her partnership with Davies. Turner appreciated that Davies "recognized the importance of building an audience in Europe." She explained that, in her view, "A lot of Americans in the music business didn't acknowledge that the rest of the world existed. Roger, probably because he was foreign, always thought globally. He had me working internationally, everywhere from Poland to Asia."¹⁵⁶ And their international focus was reflected in Turner's only record label representation at the time: Festival Records in Australia and EMI in England. However, reaching stadiums would still require a major recording contract. Despite Turner's perception of the parochial nature of the American music industry, a recording contract with a major label in the United States would bring the industry capital needed to reach her goals. So, Davies set about trying to secure her such a contract.

Davies's first strategy was to go to the press. In April of 1981, *Billboard* magazine noted that Turner was back in the recording studio for an as-yet-unannounced record release.[157] In these studio sessions, Turner followed the same format as the *Rough* and *Love Explosion* albums by recording contemporary covers of older songs, like the Rolling Stones' 1966 song "Out of Time."[158] Hoping that these recording sessions, combined with Turner's new show, would attract record label attention, Davies then had the press report on the *new* Tina Turner. Dennis Hunt, writing for the *Los Angeles Times*, proclaimed that rather than needing Ike to perform, Turner was "even better as a solo performer." Hunt noted that "The show is scaled down—with only five musicians and two female dancers—and is much more intimate." And he was careful to highlight, as per Davies's intention, that the "Las Vegas slickness, which always seemed to clash with her raunchy rhythm and blues style, is gone." Acknowledging that Turner largely performed abroad, Hunt wrote: "Since her split with Ike, Tina has spent most of her time touring foreign countries where she still has huge followings. In America in recent years, she hasn't had enough exposure to revitalize a career that faded in the mid-'70s while her relationship with Ike was crumbling." Finally, almost as an afterthought, but the crucial point for Davies's strategy, Hunt concluded: "The key to a big Turner comeback is a record contract. It's astounding that no label will sign an artist with her talent. If she performs frequently enough as well as she did last weekend, some record company is bound to take a chance on her."[159] The point was clear: Tina Turner is back, sans Ike and Vegas cabaret, and she is a viable commodity for a record deal.

While Hunt's *Los Angeles Times* article focused on Turner's show in relation to her record contract potential, Toronto's *Globe and Mail* centered the show's shift from rhythm and blues to rock. Paul McGrath's article begins on a humorous note, referencing Turner's energetic performance style: "Those scientists involved in the crucial search for alternative sources of energy have thus far overlooked whatever it is that makes Tina Turner move and sing the way she does." Though McGrath repeatedly refers to

Turner as a "veteran soul singer," he explains that her new show in April 1981 differs markedly from her show at the same venue (the Imperial Room of the Royal York Hotel in Toronto) the previous year.

> Her current show is somewhat different from last year's. The almost all-white band is more rock-oriented, and the selection of material has veered toward that style, most noticeably in the choice of the Rolling Stones' Jumpin' Jack Flash and Honky Tonk Women, songs by now in need of the hard, rough treatment she affords everything she puts her voice to. Her version of Nutbush City put Bob Seger's to shame, and her treatment of Proud Mary still ranks proudly with John Fogerty's original. The Beatles' Get Back, with Miss Turner and her attendant dancers shaking most lasciviously all in a row, was the show's pick-me-up, leading into the hot and heavy middle section.

McGrath seems unaware that Turner covered the same songs by these very artists both on record and in concert with the Ike & Tina Turner Revue. He also refers to her performance of "Nutbush City Limits" as a version of Bob Seger, forgetting that "Nutbush City Limits" is Turner's own composition that Seger was himself covering. In passing, he says that Turner's backing band is "not as slick" as her previous band and that the dancer-cum-backup singers' vocals "paled in comparison to their dancing." He does write, though, that pianist Kenny Moore's "gospel-tinged piano was the only remnant of the great rhythm and blues tradition that Miss Turner, bit by bit, seems to be abandoning in favor of straight rock music." Though McGrath is by turns laudatory and disparaging of the show, he nevertheless highlights what both Davies and Turner wish to make clear: Tina Turner is now a rock music act.[160]

To bolster the association of Turner with rock 'n' roll music, Davies's second strategy was to secure prestigious concert dates for Turner in the United States. For this, Davies took aim at New York City. Noting that Turner had not performed in one of the East Coast's major cultural capitals since her tenure with the Ike & Tina Turner Revue, Davies sought to make a splash in New York. He contacted Jerry Brandt, owner of the Ritz. Located at 119 East Eleventh Street in New York City's East Village, the Ritz had opened one year before in the historic Webster Hall venue. "And the Ritz was where everything started to happen for us. It was the hippest club in the city at the time."[161]

Brandt was enthusiastic about the prospects of Tina Turner performing at the Ritz as a return to New York City engagements. According to Davies, "He [Jerry Brandt] decided to take this on as a personal challenge. He took out full-page ads in *The Village Voice*, and he got every celebrity he knew to come along—Jagger came, Warhol, De Niro, Diana Ross, Mary Tyler Moore. . . . We sold out and wound up doing three nights there, S.R.O. [Standing Room Only]. The reviews were just unbelievable."[162] Some reviews, like Stephen Holden's *New York Times* review of the May 1981 shows, belie Davies's memory. Holden wrote, "Miss Turner presented the same bawdy female caricature that has endeared her to rock audiences." "Though she has a powerful voice, she often pushes it to a screeching frenzy" and, "Though she had plenty of gusto, what was missing was subtlety." In the end, though, even Holden acknowledged that Turner's performance style had a formula that worked for her, and he concluded his review by saying, "Miss Turner has obviously no intentions of tampering with the theatrical formula that made her a star."[163] While not a glowing review by any means, Holden's *New York Times* review was evidence that Davies's strategy was working, and a buzz was being created.

When Turner returned to the Ritz for four nights in September and October 1981, reviews were unanimously positive. Laura Foti wrote in *Variety* that, with her new shows, "Tina Turner is better than ever." At the end of her review, Foti added a line that must have pleased Roger Davies: "One note: Turner is without a record label, a situation that should be rectified without delay."[164] *Variety*'s review of these shows was even more telling when it emphasized the show's appeal to youthful rock audiences. "On a four-night stand in Gotham, the energetic, self-styled 'acid-queen' had no trouble winning over the young rock 'n' roll crowd at the East Village ballroom." "Although there was nothing new or unexpected in her show," the reviewer concluded, "Turner and her band generated a steadily building momentum and probably could have taken an extra encore with no objection from the whipped-up audience."[165] Predictably, there was indeed "nothing new" in Turner's show because she did not have an album of new material to promote, as she had no recording contract and no label backing. Thus, her show relied upon the same songs she had been performing, with some contemporary additions to augment the set list. Nonetheless, the show was calibrated to appeal to young rock audiences and the record label executives who paid such careful attention to their buying habits, a fact the reviewer clearly grasped.

Rock artists unequivocally took notice. Having seen Turner perform at the Ritz, Rod Stewart, veteran rock solo artist and frontman of the band Faces, invited Turner to perform a duet with him on NBC's *Saturday Night Live*.[166] Reviewers noticed that in their duet, Turner's look and hair bore more than a passing resemblance to Stewart's.[167] After seeing Turner perform with Rod Stewart, Keith Richards extended an offer to Turner and her band to be the opening act for three of the Rolling Stones arena concerts in November. At each show, on November 5, 6, and 7, 1981, Turner dueted with Mick Jagger on the Rolling Stones' song "Honky Tonk Women," to rousing applause.[168] The following month, Stewart again invited Turner to duet with him at the Los Angeles Forum. As planned by both Davies and Turner, she was increasingly becoming associated with, and being legitimized by, white, male rock 'n' roll audiences.[169]

With the attention of the press and a slate of high-profile rock performances behind Turner, Davies turned to his third strategy. In *My Love Story*, Turner recalled a conversation she had with Davies about the difficulties of finding a major label to sign her.

> I remember Roger saying, "Darling . . . Every door I walk through, I say 'Tina,' they say 'Ike.'" Record executives in America were brainwashed about Ike, who had a terrible reputation for being dangerous and unpredictable. Now his bad behavior was tainting me. Roger had never imagined it would be so hard to get a label, but he never gave up. Instead, he thought strategically, which is what made him a wonderful manager. He knew that there were many routes to a record contract. He was trying to figure out which one was right for me.[170]

One of those routes to a contract was courting record label attention through carefully worded statements in newspaper profiles. Another route was presenting her to young rock audiences and associating her with white, male rock artists. A third route, and perhaps the most crucial, was to break the public's association of Tina Turner with Ike. Thus, Davies's final strategy was to encourage Turner to begin publicly sharing the details of her marriage to and divorce from Ike Turner. She did this in a December 7, 1981, *People* profile.

Telling Tina Turner's Story

Carl Arrington did not know that he was a part of Davies's strategizing. Initially, his *People* profile of Tina Turner was intended to be, in his mind, "a simple comeback story." Indeed, 1981 was a year of rock artist comebacks, as media profiles focused on the musical "return" of artists like Rod Stewart[171] and the Rolling Stones.[172] Since he "didn't really know too much about the backstory," and since "nobody knew about the traumas that she went through," Arrington assumed that Turner, who had recently performed with both Stewart and the Stones, was another such return story. This assumption is reflected in the beginning of Arrington's profile of Turner.[173]

Opening with Turner's first experience touring with the Rolling Stones (in 1966), Arrington's profile seems to continue the by-now-familiar attempt to associate Turner with white rock 'n' roll pedigree, though he subverts the association by quoting Turner's explanation of how she "tried to teach him [Mick Jagger] some dances, because he'd just stand still onstage with the tambourine." Coyly confirming this, Mick Jagger is quoted as saying, "I learned a *lot* of things from Tina."[174] But, after this increasingly customary linkage of Turner with male rock 'n' roll artists, Arrington swiftly segues into a discussion of the dissolution of Ike and Tina's marriage. "Only now is Tina able to discuss what she claims were the harrowing events leading up to their split."[175] Turner then recounts the day in July 1976 when she left Ike. Abbreviating the narrative—she would later give it in detail in *I, Tina*—Turner explained that after Ike hit her "with the back of his hand," he beat her "the entire way from the airport to the hotel." She further described how when Ike would hit her, "he used *things* and not just his hands." Turner continued: "By the time we got to the hotel, the left side of my face was swollen like a monster's. I never cried, though. I laughed. No more of this." Turner concludes her tale of that harrowing day by declaring: "I felt proud. . . . I felt strong. I felt like Martin Luther King." Turner told Arrington, "When I left Ike, I was living a life of death. I didn't exist. I didn't fear him killing me when I left, because I was already dead. When I walked out, I didn't look back."[176] This account simplifies the emotional complexity of the narrative she would later give in *I, Tina* and *My Love Story*. In both autobiographies Turner speaks of the mixture of pride and fear she felt leaving Ike in Dallas and as she was hiding out with friends. Thus, even as she revealed her story for the first time to Arrington, she still withheld her innermost feelings. The rest of the profile captures the details of their meeting and the aftermath of their divorce. Arrington does note, however, that Ike Turner declined to be interviewed. Like most profiles of Turner, beginning with *Jet*'s February 1979 cover story, there is also a discussion of Turner's Buddhist practice. But Arrington adds that she and Ike "had dabbled with astrology and psychic phenomena" and that she "regularly has sessions with a psychic, Carol Dryer, who Tina says guided her spiritually through her liberation."[177] Arrington concludes the profile by quoting from Turner's first session with a psychic in 1966.[178] Unbeknownst to Carl Arrington, his simple "comeback story" on Turner would provide the model for nearly all subsequent profiles of Turner: highlighting her origins in Nutbush, Tennessee; her relationship with Ike Turner; her combinatory practice of Soka Gakkai Nichiren Buddhism and American metaphysical religion; and finally her association with rock 'n' roll.

If the narrative Arrington heard from Turner was more complicated than he ever expected, it was an act of courage for Turner to tell it to him. Nearly forty years later, in 2019, Turner said that before she told her story to Arrington, she consulted her psychic—likely Carol Dryer—and asked, "What's gonna happen?" This was because, as she explained: "I was afraid to put [the story] out because of what I might receive from Ike." The *People* profile was a mere five years after leaving Ike, and only three years after their divorce was finalized. Much of Ike's harassment had ceased by that point. So, she said, "[I] called close friends and everything; I didn't know if I should do *People* and publicly say it, you know, finally." She feared reprisal from Ike once the story was made public but courageously decided to share her story nonetheless.[179]

While the primary reason for Davies's encouragement to Turner to reveal her story to *People* was to disassociate her from Ike in the eyes of both the public and the record industry, it's possible to discern another motive on Turner's part. Soka Gakkai members are encouraged in discussion meetings to share "experiences" of their Buddhist practice. Akin to testifying, Soka Gakkai Nichiren Buddhists explain to new members and their guests how they have overcome seemingly unbeatable odds by chanting *Nam-myoho-renge-kyo* and participating in the Buddhist organization.[180] Doing so is seen both as encouraging to new members and as important proof of karmic transformation. In narrating her story to Carl Arrington and thus to the public, Turner was in effect giving her own experience, testifying to the liberative role of Buddhist practice (and other spiritual pursuits) in her life. That she was now divorced and working as an independent artist was proof that the karma of her relationship with Ike, at least insofar as their partnership went, was transformed.

After the *People* article appeared, Turner returned to the concert circuit and Davies hoped that the cumulative effect of his three-pronged strategy—press reports bolstering her association with rock 'n' roll and highlighting her need for a record label; prestigious concert dates at the Ritz in New York City; and publicly revealing the details of her marriage and divorce—would secure a record deal at a major record label. [181]

Conclusion

In the period from 1976 to 1981, Tina Turner worked on herself religiously, personally, and professionally to become "Tina." As a Soka Gakkai Nichiren Buddhist, Turner turned to her group of Buddhist "chanting women": Valerie Bishop, Matilda Buck, Susie Sempers, Maria Booker Lucien, and Ana Maria Shorter. With the latter, Ana Maria, and her husband, jazz saxophonist Wayne Shorter, Turner resided for an extended period of time and, there, she followed the Soka Gakkai Buddhist practice of chanting *Nam-myoho-renge-kyo* and reciting portions of the Lotus Sutra, in a twice-daily ritual known as *gongyo*. Turner and Ana Maria chanted up to four hours per day, helping Turner to prepare spiritually for the dissolution of her marriage. At the same time, Turner began attending NSA meetings, where she formally converted to Buddhism by receiving her own *gohonzon* and learned Buddhist doctrines. Chief among these doctrines were karma and the notion of past lives.

Displaying her combinatory religiosity, Turner combined her understanding of Soka Gakkai Nichiren Buddhist teachings with the work of psychic "soul reader" Carol Ann Dryer. From Dryer, she came to situate her violent marriage and complex separation from Ike Turner in the multilife context of a mythic past in ancient Egypt, wherein Ike was Pharaoh Thutmose II and Turner was Hatshepsut. Such contextualizing proved a therapeutic way for Turner to process the trauma of her marriage. In the process, Turner struggled to juggle her divorce proceedings, her sons, and a fledgling solo career.

Personally, she worked to divorce herself from Ike Turner. When she left Ike in a hotel in Dallas on July 3, 1976, she sought shelter with friends. First among them was Nate Tabor, a lawyer with whom she stayed and relied on to initiate the divorce proceedings that would dissolve both their marriage and their musical partnership. Eventually, attorney Arthur Leeds helped bring her divorce proceedings to a conclusion. During those proceedings, Turner worked to support herself and her sons. After her divorce, having won the legal right to her stage name "Tina Turner," Turner then worked on herself professionally, remaking herself into a solo artist.

She secured a new manager, Australian Roger Davies. With Davies, she shared a dream that seemed as wild as it was big: to become, as a Black Buddhist woman in her forties, a stadium-filling rock 'n' roll artist. Taking Turner's dream as his challenge, Davies concocted a strategy that included press, prestigious concert gigs, and revealing the details of Turner's past, all to court major record labels and coax them into signing Tina Turner as a solo musical act.

The result of this spiritual, personal, and professional work was a new *Tina*, poised on the precipice of an enormous commercial breakthrough. The *Private Dancer* album, from 1984, would catapult Turner into global stardom. First, though, she would have to again face the racism and sexism of the music business before she could accomplish many of her wildest dreams.

5

Wildest Dreams

I don't separate my work as a rock singer from prayer.
When I went onstage to make a living, I made people
happy with my work. The feedback was always that I in-
spired people to get out and help themselves to go forward,
to practice Buddhism. Everything has been very positive
and that's because of my spiritual practice.

—Tina Turner,
"What's Love Got to Do with It?
A Q and A with Tina Turner"

Alright! Sing it with me now," Turner breathlessly commanded an audience of 50,000 energetic fans at Amsterdam Arena. The Dutch
capital was a tour stop on Tina Turner's Wildest Dreams Tour 1996-1997.
Over three concert dates in September 1996, Turner played to a combined
audience of 150,000 people. These concerts in Amsterdam, captured in a
live video released as *Live in Amsterdam: Wildest Dreams Tour*,[1] were typical of shows on the tour. After performing "The Best," a song originally
appearing on the *Foreign Affair* album, which quickly became an anthem
for Turner, Turner engaged the audience in a sing-along. "Will you sing
it with me?" she asks rhetorically, cueing her fans to participate. "Simply
the best," Turner screams out, initiating a passionate call-and-response.
For just over a minute, it seems the entire audience fervently sings out. As
the audience sings each line of the chorus in turn, they have been pulled

into an experience crafted by Turner, an experience that is simultaneously entertaining and religious.

The entertainment aspect of a show like Turner's is clear enough. The set, video, lights, and sound—what music journalist Steve Moles called "the four elements" of a touring rock show—combined with the set list and choreography, were all carefully curated to present a theatrical spectacle that conveyed Turner's reputation for opulent, energetic stage shows. The concert as religious experience is embodied by Turner herself.

For Turner, as a Soka Gakkai Nichiren Buddhist, there is no distinction between pragmatic preparation for a concert—designing the set, curating the songs, and so on—and spiritual preparation. In Soka Gakkai teachings, the principle that "faith equals daily life" is stressed. In some of his letters, Nichiren would quote the following from Tiantai, the sixth-century patriarch and effective founder of Tiantai Buddhism: "No worldly affairs of life or work are ever contrary to the true reality."[2] In Soka Gakkai literature, the "true reality" referred to is understood to be a person's innate buddha-nature. Bringing forth this true reality of buddha-nature leads to success in a person's various daily endeavors. According to this understanding, then, "Our daily lives become the stage upon which we carry out a drama of deep" transformation.[3] In effect, for practitioners of Soka Gakkai Nichiren Buddhism, their endeavors become encoded with spiritual significance as they are trained to see their daily lives as a "stage" for their practice. For Turner, this means that her concert preparation and execution were a literal and figurative stage for her practice. This turns her concert into a religious experience, which the audience is brought into through their attendance and participation.

At a revival-type rock concert like Turner's, an audience sing-along becomes more than simply a moment of audience participation. It becomes, instead, a moment where Turner and her audience cocreate moments of religious experience. Thus, she transformed her rock concerts into arenas of religious and spiritual experience. In so doing, her performances articulate what might be called a wildest-dreams rock aesthetic. Such an aesthetic promotes a religious belief in the transformative power of dreams and possibilities; Turner's concerts become sites of "actual proof" (see chap. 3 above) that wildest dreams do come true.

The wildest-dreams rock aesthetic forms the experiential core of the commercial brand Tina Turner developed after leaving Ike Turner. This aesthetic subsequently contributed to her global success as a popular rock entertainer. In the United States, by the time of the Wildest Dreams Tour, her brand would be endorsed by both corporate America in a Hanes Hosiery campaign and by popular media in the person of media mogul Oprah Winfrey. Before these endorsements, though, Turner still had to capture the attention of the record industry and craft a commercially viable comeback.

On the Eve of *Private Dancer*

In the eight years that elapsed between leaving Ike Turner and the Ike & Tina Turner Revue, and her first commercially successful solo album, *Private Dancer* (Capitol/EMI, 1984), the song "Proud Mary" served as the frenetic climax to Turner's live performances. By the early eighties, Turner further expanded the ad-libbing that had served as a trademark characteristic of the 1970 hit. The version of this captured in the video *Tina Turner: Nice 'n' Rough*, filmed live at London's Hammersmith Odeon, is typical. Over the course of more than an hour, Turner works the audience into a frenzy, backed by a five-piece band, supporting vocals by Kenny Moore, and her two dancers, Ann Behringer and Lejeune Richardson, on a set designed by British rock-staging architect Mark Fisher. Dripping sweat in a glittering Bob Mackie costume with wings, Turner commands the band to "bring it down," to turn the music down so that she can speak to her audience. "People all over the world," she growls incredulously, "ask me, 'When am I gonna slow down?'" "You know what I tell 'em?" she asks, as Moore supplies the audience's curiosity: "What? What? What? What?" "I'm just gettin' started!" she finally answers.[4] Turner's spoken-word interlude is barely thirty seconds, but it perfectly captures her determination to let her viewers and audience (and those record executives watching with commercial interests in both) know that her best is yet to come. For her manager, Roger Davies, it was important to capitalize on this feeling that Turner's best years were still ahead of her.

Davies, having ended his business relationship with Lee Kramer, was now singularly focused on his two clients: Olivia Newton-John and Tina Turner. While Newton-John's career was already in full flight, Davies was fiercely determined to raise Turner's profile. In January 1982, she recorded two songs for the movie *Summer Lovers*. Turner's songs, "Johnny and

Mary" and "Crazy in the Night," were heard in the movie alongside the Pointer Sisters' "I'm So Excited." On the soundtrack, the songs were heard alongside the English new-wave band Heaven 17's song "Play to Win." Her appearance on the *Summer Lovers* soundtrack was followed by an in-person appearance as a presenter at the Twenty-Fourth Annual Grammy Awards in Los Angeles, in February.

Two members of Heaven 17, Ian Craig Marsh and Martyn Ware, left the band to form their own producing team: the British Electric Foundation (BEF). BEF maximized new technology in their recorded productions, using synthesizers and drum machines, rather than live musicians and instruments. For their first album, they sought to record modern, synthesized covers of popular songs from the sixties and seventies, with various artists singing over their electronically produced backing tracks. Marsh and Ware were interested in having Turner record the Temptations' 1970 hit "Ball of Confusion" and Sam Cooke's 1964 soul classic "A Change Is Gonna Come." The duo offered Davies and Turner two thousand dollars and first-class airline tickets to England to record the songs. Davies accepted the offer and brought Turner to England.[5]

"When we got there," Davies explained, "Tina found out the song was 'Ball of Confusion' [and 'A Change Is Gonna Come'] and she freaked out." With Davies, Turner had worked carefully since early 1981 to craft a show and a sound that would disassociate her from rhythm and blues and soul and thus forge a more solid association with rock 'n' roll music. Davies reinforced this association by his three-pronged strategy of press reviews, rock concert venues like the Ritz, and public revelations of the details of Turner's divorce from Ike Turner. To arrive in London to record new music with a production team purported to be on the cutting edge of new industry technology, only to find that it was all for the sake of a rhythm and blues song from 1970 and a soul song from 1964, felt like a step in the wrong direction.

According to Davies, Turner "was so afraid of being put back into any kind of category like 'oldies' or 'R and B.'" Nonetheless, since they had traveled and received payment, Turner recorded the songs. Marsh and Ware were so impressed with Turner's "one-take" vocals, her ability to sing an album-quality version of a song without the need to rerecord, that they made Davies "a standing offer to come back and do a record."[6] The result of their collaboration was released in Britain in April of 1982, on BEF's *Music of Quality and Distinction, Volume 1* (Virgin, 1982). Though a review in the *Guardian* called the release "the bizarrest album of the year,"[7] it did well in Britain—the only country it was released in. Davies and Turner had now, it seemed, reached a critical mass of visibility. Davies felt confident that he could now approach a major label for a record contract for Turner in the United States. The logical choice was Capitol Records, now a division of EMI in England, since Turner remained on EMI's roster of artists in the United Kingdom. Yet, Davies and Turner's rebranding efforts worked against them.

When concert dates around the United States were sparse in 1978 and 1979, Turner focused on performing internationally. In the United States, she was classified as a cabaret act and performed at venues like Caesars Palace in Las Vegas, and in the ballrooms of major hotel chains. Davies helped Turner to make changes to the show abroad and then sought to debut a new show, with the cabaret elements removed, at venues like the Ritz. Meanwhile, Turner still held international recording contracts with Festival Records in Australia and EMI in England. Thus, Capitol Records was not interested in her as an American act, seeing her instead as "another of the old [United Artists] acts that they'd already dropped from the label's roster."[8] Despite the building momentum, Turner remained without a record contract in the United States, and her dream of filling stadiums—which, again, required a record contract and a commercially successful album—seemed alarmingly distant, if not impossible. For the time being, Davies had no recourse but to continue strategizing and meeting with record executives while Turner continued touring.

Musical Bodhisattva

For Turner, though, her performance and Davies's business negotiations were only one tool. Her other tool was to return to her "mission statement," the blueprint of her aspirations to success. As Wayne Shorter had explained to Turner, it is the times when dreams seem impossible that having a "mission statement" for one's life and aspirations is most helpful. Turner summarized Shorter's guidance: "When life is difficult, returning to your mission will remind you of your purpose, your vow, and help raise your life condition. When our life condition is high enough, anything is possible—including the impossible." For Soka Gakkai Nichiren Buddhists, daily practice of chanting is the essential way to "raise your life condition" and clear away "all doubt from your mind."[9] It is worth quoting in full Turner's conceptualization of her thought process during difficult times, including this period prior to securing a major solo record deal.

> After I embraced Buddhism, I never doubted I would get where I wanted to go. But much of the time I had no idea how exactly I would get there. I left the "how" up to the universe and the mystical workings of my mind and soul. All along, I kept this encouragement from Daisaku Ikeda close to my heart: "One thing is certain: The power of belief, the power of thought, will move reality in the direction of what we believe and conceive of it. If you really believe you can do something, you can. That is a fact. When you clearly envision the outcome of victory, engrave it upon your heart, and are firmly convinced that you will attain it, your brain makes every effort to realize the mental image you have created. And then, through your unceasing efforts, that victory is finally made a reality." As I worked on mastering my mind in this way, and approached obstacles as catalysts for growth, continually changing poison into medicine without complaint, I experienced a deep-seated shift.[10]

While the concept of "changing poison into medicine" will be discussed in the next chapter, here it is important to say that for Turner, as for other Soka Gakkai Nichiren Buddhists, it refers specifically to using one's adverse circumstances—say, the gap between one's dreams and reality—as raw material for making a life change. It is also a fundamental principle in Soka Gakkai's understanding of the transformation of karma. Such spiritual guidance from Shorter and Ikeda forms the philosophical underpinning of Turner's wildest-dreams rock aesthetic, where the power of belief and practice are martialed to accomplish seemingly impossible dreams. Faith and practice thus provided spiritual support for the campaign to achieve a solo record contract.

Turner's efforts also included joining her fellow SGI-USA members for a "Buddhist peace festival" in October 1982. This festival, held on the National Mall in Washington, DC, to celebrate both Peace Day and NSA's twenty-fifth anniversary, was entitled "Aloha, We Love America."

George M. Williams, then general director of NSA, explained that the title was chosen because of the organization's "commitment to peace and harmony expressed by the Hawaiian word, 'aloha.'"[11] The festival continued NSA's tradition of holding large-scale conventions and festivals in the United States (at least once a year between 1968 and 1976) and, in Williams's words, was a demonstration of "their desire for a prosperous America and a peaceful world."[12] During the "Aloha, We Love America" festival, approximately ten thousand NSA members paraded down Washington's Constitution Avenue, "each carrying a full-sized American flag." Describing the event, staff writers from the *Washington Post* wrote that the "celebrants had come, mostly by bus, from all over the country." The report also noted that the festival was not without incident, since "Critics and former members of the group call it a cult, and counter-demonstrations were planned, including a protest staged Saturday night by eight members of the Citizens for Freedom Foundation, an anti-cult group from Chevy Chase."[13] The protests that met the festival in DC show that whatever NSA's wishes for a "prosperous America" may have been, the organization still struggled against negative portrayals.[14] The second day of the festival culminated in a concert featuring performances by Shorter, Herbie Hancock, and Turner. A photograph of Turner's performance shows her performing against a red-and-black SGI banner and backed by SGI-USA members, rather than her normal band and dancers. The photo is captioned: "I sang my heart out for the SGI Buddhist peace festival in Washington, D.C., 1982, where I vowed to always inspire hope through my music."[15] She further explained that in attending the festival and performing, she, Shorter, and Hancock "vowed to be musical Bodhisattvas: to create value in society by inspiring hope and peace through [their] artistic careers."[16] In making such a vow, Turner was consciously applying the religious ideal of the bodhisattva to her career as a rock entertainer.

Across many Buddhist traditions, bodhisattvas are understood to be beings who altruistically aspire toward awakening, the soteriological goal of Buddhism.[17] The practice of making vows is central to the bodhisattva ideal. In their broadest formulation, "bodhisattvas make four universal vows: (1) to save innumerable living beings, (2) to eradicate countless earthly desires, (3) to master immeasurable Buddhist teachings, and (4) to attain the supreme enlightenment."[18] The latter three vows are in service of the first vow, the vow to save countless beings. Most fundamentally, such salvific work takes the form of inspiring beings along the Buddhist path. In Soka Gakkai Nichiren Buddhism, drawing upon Nichiren's interpretation of Tiantai Buddhism, the bodhisattva ideal is understood to be the ninth of ten possible life-states. The ten life-states will be discussed in detail in the next chapter, but here it can be said that, as a life-state, the ideal of the bodhisattva describes "a state characterized by compassion in which one seeks enlightenment both for oneself and others. In this state, one finds satisfaction in devoting oneself to relieving the suffering of others and leading them to happiness."[19] This conceptualization of the bodhisattva and the practice of making vows is so central to Soka Gakkai Nichiren Buddhism that Daisaku Ikeda once wrote, "Prayer in Nichiren Buddhism means to chant daimoku [Nam-myoho-renge-kyo] based on a pledge or vow."[20] As a Soka Gakkai Nichiren Buddhist, Turner's assertion that in performing at the "Aloha, We Love America" festival she was making a vow "to be a musical Bodhisattva" must be understood in this context.

We have already seen that once Turner began performing as a solo artist, she would pray and chant for up to an hour before each show, praying for the happiness of her audience members. With that act, Turner was specifically linking her Buddhist chanting practice to her concert performances, another expression of the bodhisattva ideal. With her participation in the festival, she was taking this expression further still. She was now linking her Buddhist values, the ideal of the bodhisattva, to her artistic values, among fellow Buddhist artists. This joining of Buddhist values and ideals to practical career endeavors is a hallmark of Soka Gakkai Nichiren Buddhist praxis, and Turner would repeatedly display such linking in her writing and interviews.

Racism and Sexism in the Music Industry

After her performance at the October 1982 "Aloha, We Love America" festival, Turner resumed her touring schedule. And Davies continued seeking that elusive record deal. While Capitol Records in America wasn't interested in signing Turner, their international division noted her distinctive, modern interpretation of the Temptations' "Ball of Confusion" on BEF's *Music of Quality and Distinction, Volume 1*. They also noted that though the song was not released as a single in America, the song's video, filmed as a live performance, was added to MTV's video music rotation.[21] MTV premiered as an American cable channel on August 1, 1981. In the first two years of its existence, the channel was lambasted for featuring only a limited selection of Black artists, including Michael Jackson, Donna Summer, Whitney Houston, and Prince, among others. The addition of Turner's video to the channel's rotation made an impression, and Capitol's executives entered negotiations with Davies for a limited recording contract, assigning Turner to an in-house producer, John Carter.[22]

John S. Carter (1945–2011) began his career as a song lyricist before working in the "artist and repertoire" (A and R) department of Capitol Records.[23] In 1976, Carter inaugurated the position of Capitol Records director of artist acquisition.[24] Because of his experience writing songs, Carter also worked as a staff producer at the label. In this capacity, he worked with artists such as Bob Seger, the Steve Miller Band, and the Motels. Because Turner was assigned to Carter, he invested fifty thousand dollars in recording demo songs with her, using one song by the Motels, "Total Control," as one of these tracks.[25] Carter helped to negotiate a contract for Turner at Capitol. Finally, Davies's threefold strategy was beginning to bear fruit. A record deal with a major label—the crucial component of fulfilling Turner's dream of performing in sold-out stadiums as a headlining act, now religiously inflected as a bodhisattva vow—was finally at hand. That is, until changes at Capitol Records, and racism and sexism in the music business stalled her dream.

In *I, Tina*, Loder explains that "the actual hammering out of the Capitol contract took nine months, but by the spring of 1983, it was ready for signing."[26] Loder outlines how changes at the executive level caused Turner's record deal to stall. And indeed, in March, April, and May of 1983, Capitol Records underwent various personnel changes, as old executives were fired and new ones hired.[27] Newly hired executives were disinclined to honor deals made by former executives.[28] This was ostensibly the reason that Turner's record deal initially remained unsigned. The account in *I, Tina* continues by highlighting that another series of concerts at the Ritz and some (inadvertent) encouragement from David Bowie helped to convince executives at Capitol Records to finalize her contract. According to Davies, a label executive startled him with a call informing him that sixty-three executives were coming to the show at the Ritz. Davies elaborated:

Well, what it was, all the Capitol and EMI people from America and Europe were in New York for a listening session for David Bowie's new album, *Let's Dance* [EMI-America, 1983]. Bowie had just signed with EMI-America, a Capitol subsidiary here, and the listening party was a big event. Afterwards, they asked David what he was doing that night, and he told them, "I'm going to see my favorite female singer." They said, "Who's that?" He said, "Tina Turner." They went, "Tina Turner? Oh, yeah—she's on our label!" So they called me, I put them on the list, and they all came down: the executives, the A and R guys, the people from International. It was perfect for us. David brought Susan Sarandon, who'd starred with him in *The Hunger*, and he brought Keith Richards and John McEnroe—it was the weirdest combination of people. And the show that night was fantastic—Tina had the place standing on its head. Incredible. It was a real event, exactly what we needed.[29]

Turner continued Davies's account, describing how after the show that night, all these stars came backstage and posed for pictures with her. The photo session then turned into an all-night jam session in Keith Richards's hotel suite. During this jam session, she realized that rock 'n' roll artists like Richards and Bowie made their music new by going "back to all this old music that they loved—blues and R and B—and they would change it around and make something of their own out of it. Because the feeling that was in that old music was something they felt, too. But they made it new again."[30]

Bowie, like Mick Jagger, Keith Richards, and Rod Stewart, drew much inspiration from blues, gospel, rhythm and blues, and soul music. And like them, he considered Tina Turner to be a major influence. Indeed, Turner had known Bowie for a number of years at this point.[31] She recalled that in their conversations, as they built "a special friendship—a togetherness that came from mutual affection and admiration, and shared interests"— after the Ritz performance, he "could talk about art, religion, any topic."[32] Bowie and Turner shared mutual interests in Egypt, Buddhism, astrology, and mysticism.[33] Speaking of him in glowing terms, Turner said that when she thought of David, she thought of a beam of light. "He practically had a halo."[34] Beyond their mutual admiration, though, Bowie himself equivocated on the role he played in her comeback: "Oh, I'm not sure how much help I was; but, I certainly was enthusiastic about her when she went out on her own."³⁵ Nonetheless, according to Turner and Davies, after the star-power-and-record-executive-filled night at the Ritz, Capitol Records finalized Turner's record deal and greenlit work on a new album.

The emphasis on Bowie's role in both Davies's and Turner's recounting of events illustrates elements of their strategy of showcasing Turner at rock venues oriented toward young audiences and associating her with white, male rock artists. When Turner's *Private Dancer* album was released in 1984, media profiles would tell this story again and again, and it would finally appear in print when *I, Tina* was published in 1986. Across a variety of media, their account served to confirm for the reader—as Davies and Turner hoped—that she was a rock 'n' roll artist and that this was legitimated by a lineage of rock artists, including, but not limited to, David Bowie. At the same time, this account of events minimizes the lack of interest in her shown by executives at Capitol Records. When Turner related this tale in *I, Tina*, she was also only two years into her recording contract with Capitol Records and experiencing major popular success. Thus, she would be inclined to avoid offending her new record label.

However, in a 2009 interview—an audio clip from which is featured in *TINA*, the HBO Films Documentary—John Carter revealed that an executive's racist and sexist perception of Turner lay behind the unsigned record deal. Carter explained why the new management at Capitol Records dropped Turner from the label: "The new regime comes in and like any new regime, they got their own idea about what they wanna do." Carter described the exchange he had with a top executive: "So I flip out, I go downstairs, and I said, 'Hey, this is my act.' And the classic quote is, 'Carter, you signed this old nigger douchebag?' 'Yeah, Yeah, I did, and I'm really happy about it. Now pick up the phone and call Roger Davies.' He said, 'No fucking way.' And I get on my knees, and I said, 'I'm now gonna beg you, and I'm not gonna get up until you pick up the phone.' And there was a long stare down and he picks up the phone."³⁶ This exchange encapsulates both the discrimination that Turner faced as a Black woman in the music business and the legitimizing role that white men like Carter consequently had to play for Black artists like her. Knowing that she was facing racism from her own label, Turner herself would later share with Carl Arrington a thought experiment that she entertained. "Sometimes, I just play around with a little thought and dream and I say, 'What would happen if I had this fantastic album and they would put a different name on it and no picture?' I mean, just [an] abstract something. And I would just hide myself, right? And then come out with this black face on this album."[37] Perhaps to keep from crying, Turner laughs to Arrington as she concludes, "I'd love it!" A career that in 1983 was into its second decade, a reputation as an acclaimed performer, and associations with white rock artists who liberally drew inspiration from her work, and even imitated it—all were insufficient capital in a racist and sexist music industry, leaving Turner to wonder if it would be better if she hid herself rather than be a "black face" in the music industry.

Nonetheless, in John Carter's telling, the executive changed his mind but offered a major caveat: "Well, he says, 'Okay, she's back on the roster. You finish your record; but, you understand that we're gonna do nothing. That's all there is.'"[38] Turner and Davies, with Carter's support, were now free to continue recording, albeit without substantive support from the label.

Private Dancer

Capitol Records suggested that Turner utilize one of David Bowie's musicians as a producer and that she continue with the kind of material she was recording with Carter. But Davies felt the sound was inappropriate for her and pushed for Capitol to send Turner and him to England. This would enable them to capitalize on the production techniques of the new-wave production team BEF, whose members, Ian Craig Marsh and Martyn Ware, now constituted the band Heaven 17. Marsh and Ware were so impressed with Turner when they recorded "Ball of Confusion," that they made a standing offer to produce another single with Turner.[39] Davies intended to accept their offer, and since Turner was still signed with EMI in Britain, Davies called EMI's offices in London for support. EMI approved his plan.[40]

Working with Ware and Marsh, Turner agreed to cover Bowie's song "1984," since she and Ware and Marsh were Bowie fans. To augment the session, and returning to the formula they had used with success on *Music of Quality and Distinction, Volume 1,* Ware and Marsh convinced Turner to record a heavily synthesized cover of Al Green's 1971 soul song "Let's Stay Together." On this song, Turner brought together all her previous training to provide a distinctive, one-take delivery of the material. As Davies describes it, "Tina walked in and sang 'Let's Stay Together' live, in one take. It just *happened*. I got shivers down my back. . . . They went ahead and added all their little bits and pieces to it, and that take became the single."[41] While Ware and Marsh were once again impressed with Turner's "charm and professionalism,"[42] for Turner, it was a style of learning and performing music that extended back to Nutbush, Tennessee.

"The first time I hear a song," she explained, "I start singing along until I feel that I have it, exactly the way I did it as a child, when I listened to the radio. When I've absorbed it fully, I say, 'Okay, it's my song now, I own it,' and I'm ready to record. I go to the studio, step up to the microphone, and get it done."[43] This style of recording also harkens back to her days spent touring the Chitlin' Circuit with the Ike & Tina Turner Revue, where they would rehearse a song for hours on end. Later, when Ike Turner opened Bolic Sound Studios, he would make Turner sing the same songs over and over until he felt they were right. Thus, the professionalism that Ware and Marsh were commenting on was a discipline well honed over the course of her life and career.

EMI released "Let's Stay Together" as a single in England in November 1983, with an accompanying music video featuring Turner's dancers, Ann Behringer and Lejeune Richardson. The song entered *Billboard*'s music charts at number 36;[44] the following week it moved to number 16;[45] and by Christmas it had been in the top five of *Billboard*'s "Hits of the World" chart for Britain. To support the single, Davies scheduled Turner for appearances on the long-running British television show *Top of the Pops*, and concert performances at London's Ritz-like concert hall, the Venue. The show at the Venue was scheduled for three nights, starting on December 18, 1983,[46] but high demand caused the show to extend to eleven dates, followed by a thirty-date tour. To EMI, headquartered in London, the song was a resounding success. Capitol Records though, headquartered in Los Angeles—and committed to doing "nothing" to support the album, as John Carter was told—were not interested in the song for the American market and declined to release it.

However, a groundswell began to build around "Let's Stay Together" as import copies reached New York City, and the song was added to Black radio stations—like New York's WBLS—in January 1984.[47] At the same time, the single received mentions in the "Singles Review" section of *Billboard*, under the "Black Picks" category;[48] and the single was advertised in *Billboard* that month, classified as a "disco/dance" import.[49] *Cash Box* magazine reviewed the single as one of its "Feature Picks" in the "Black Contemporary" category: "Following Turner's recent fierce updating of the Temptations 'Ball Of Confusion' is a knockout rendition of the Al Green soul classic."[50] The reviewer went on to acknowledge the importance of the "romantic British synth funk production employed by Heaven 17's Martyn Ware and his [associate] Greg Walsh" in reining in Turner's "massive, deep throated alto."[51] The elements of the song that executives at Capitol Records disliked and deemed inappropriate for the American record market—its new-wave, synthesized production; and Turner's "wailing"—were the elements most highly praised by critics and industry reviewers.[52] By the end of January 1984, the song was on the list of "Most Added Records" on Black radio stations, and it entered *Billboard*'s "Hot 100."[53] In February 1984, "Let's Stay Together" was considered a hit in the United States:[54] *Billboard*'s Paul Grein wrote a piece titled "Tina Turner Rocks Back into Top 40";[55] Ed Blanche of the Associated Press, writing for the *Atlanta Constitution*, similarly proclaimed that the "Earth's Mother" was back.[56] Capitol Records in America could no longer afford to ignore *Tina Turner*, the Black woman that only months before they had decided was an "old nigger douchebag" worthy only of being dropped from their label's roster. Thus, Capitol Records demanded that Turner and Davies return to Los Angeles from England and record a full album to capitalize on the success of "Let's Stay Together." Together, Davies and Carter persuaded Capitol Records to allow Turner to finish her British tour and to record the requisite album in London. Capitol's executives relented and gave them one month to complete it. On such a tight time line, and combined with pressures from the record label, making *Private Dancer* became a personal, professional, and spiritual struggle for Turner.

I Might Have Been Queen

Personally, Turner was alone. Just as when she left Ike Turner, went into hiding, and remained isolated from her family and friends, she was once again separated from them all, maintaining only limited contact with her mother and sister, both of whom were in Los Angeles. Of her four sons during this time, she said: "My sons were at home, they were fine."[57] Of her friends, Turner explained: "Well, I didn't have that many friends in America."[58] Then she received an unexpected blow when Ann Behringer and Lejeune Richardson, her two dancers, quit when Turner could not afford to increase their pay after the success of "Let's Stay Together." To complete the album, Turner had to leave "everything and everybody behind. I needed every minute of my brain to map my life together."[59]

Professionally, Davies and Turner had one month to find songs for the album, producers to oversee the recording of songs, and professionals to take photos for the album's cover and design artwork. Davies found himself scrambling to source songs and producers, while Turner was still touring to support her successful single. Both frantically traversed London, meeting producers, rehearsing, and recording songs. Turner was unhappy with some of the song choices because she wanted to record rock music and saw many of the songs as soul and pop oriented. Davies and Turner had their biggest disagreement over a song written by Australian producer and songwriter Terry Britten. The song, "What's Love Got to Do with It?," was, to Turner's chagrin, a pop song.[60] "I didn't think it was my style. By that time," Turner recalled, "I felt that I had *become* all the songs that I was covering . . . that I had become rock 'n' roll. I had just never thought of singing pop."[61] As Davies grew more insistent that she had to at least try to record the song since time and song choices were scarce, the song began to evoke memories of her past with Ike where she was forced to sing songs she did not like: "I felt like I'm still singing stuff I don't want to sing; when I was with Ike, I was singing stuff I didn't want to sing, and here I am again."[62] In addition to causing a resurgence of traumatic memories, the song also precipitated a spiritual struggle within Turner.

In chapter 6 of *Happiness Becomes You*, Turner details how her song choices were "exercises in growth," since if the song became a hit, she would have to sing it repeatedly. Therefore, she explained, "Before committing to a song, I would visualize how I might perform it onstage. I imagine it from start to finish before recording a single word." By doing this, an act she considered to be "stepping outside my comfort zone," she was able to take ownership over her songs, "adding nuances that communicated a different meaning and subtext" to her audiences and expanding the song's potential, along with her own.[63] Expanding her own potential is a crucial spiritual concept for Turner, and such expansion exemplifies the Soka Ga-kkai Nichiren Buddhist notion of human revolution (see chap. 4 above). Recording "What's Love Got to Do with It?" was for Turner just such an act of human revolution. In the end, Turner did "the extra work" required to work with Terry Britten and record the song.[64] Nevertheless, "What's Love Got to Do with It?" was only one song. Combined with "Let's Stay Together" and "1984," both produced by Martyn Ware and Greg Walsh, Turner now had three songs for the album. They needed more.

At Davies's behest, Turner met with producer Rupert Hine and his song-writing partner Jeanette Obstoj. Turner narrated, especially to Obstoj, the story of her life that she first told to Arrington for *People* magazine in 1981. Obstoj paid close attention to the role spiritual beliefs played in Turner's life. In particular, she noted the prominence of Turner's belief in her past life as Hatshepsut. This belief placed her traumatic marriage to Ike Turner into the context of a therapeutic understanding of the past, the overcoming of which encouraged her dreams of future solo success. After listening to Turner, Obstoj, together with Hine and guitarist James West Oram, wrote the song "I Might Have Been Queen," produced by Rupert Hine.

"I'm a new pair of eyes / Every time I am born," Turner sings in the opening line of the song (and as the first track on the album, the open-ing line of the album)—immediately signifying to the attentive listener Turner's adherence to the Buddhist belief in rebirth. "An original mind / Because I just died," she continues, making clear to the listener what was only signified in the second line: in Buddhist belief, to be born, one must have first died. This cosmological cycle of birth and death, referred to as *samsara* in Buddhist doctrine, is considered to have no beginning.[65] En-compassing both the cosmic and the sociopolitical scope of rebirth, Turner sings about the new dawns and new empires that arise after dissolution. She displays the confidence gained through her Buddhist practice and her work with psychic Carol Ann Dryer, when she confidently reminds the lis-tener that she has ridden each wave throughout her lifetimes. Then, in the chorus, her voice rings with power as she soars through time and space to sing the song's title. When she sings of the rivers of time that carried her forward, we might imagine her speaking of the journey from ancient Egypt to the cotton fields of Nutbush, Tennessee, and now, to a recording studio in England making what may be the most crucial album of her life, *this* time around. Having taken us through her past, in the final verse she sings of the future, referencing her belief in the predictive efficacy of astrology. Then, Turner sings of looking down from on high and seeing no tragedies, which evokes the Soka Gakkai Nichiren Buddhist understanding of the awakened life-state, which is likened to a summit from which one is able to gaze on the world below with composure.[66] Taken together, the lyrics of "I Might Have Been Queen" capture Turner's spiritual understanding of the scope of her life, encompassing multiple lives in a broad sweep of history where the past is in context and the future is "no shock," thereby enabling Turner to face her present with composure.

In addition to "I Might Have Been Queen" as the first song, and "What's Love Got to Do with It?" as the second, *Private Dancer* contained seven other songs for a total of nine tracks (the European release included an additional song). The album had nine producers and presented Turner across a mix of musical genres, which would become standard for all her subsequent album releases. It took two weeks and $150,000 to produce.[67] At the end of April 1984, Davies submitted to EMI/Capitol Records the *Private Dancer* album and booked Turner as the opening act for Lionel Richie's four-month tour.[68]

EMI/Capitol Records released "What's Love Got to Do with It?" as the first single from *Private Dancer* in the first week of May 1984; *Private Dancer* was released on May 29, 1984.[69] A music video was filmed for the single in New York City's Greenwich Village neighborhood, showcasing an aesthetic that would become Turner's trademark: red lipstick, spiked blonde hair, leather skirt, and black high heels.[70] On the strength of the song and its accompanying music video, both "What's Love Got to Do with It?" and *Private Dancer* slowly climbed *Billboard*'s music charts over the summer of 1984. On July 25, 1984, *Private Dancer* was certified gold by the Recording Industry Association of America (RIAA); by August 21, the album was certified platinum and "What's Love Got to Do with It?," as a single, was itself certified gold.[71] In his *New York Times* review of the album, Stephen Holden noted that *Private Dancer* had become a top ten hit on music charts, and he proclaimed the album to be a "landmark . . . in the evolution of pop-soul music itself."[72] Evincing the album's mix of genres, other reviewers acknowledged the album's rock material.[73]

When Turner's tour with Lionel Richie ended that August, "What's Love Got to Do with It?" was number 2 on the "Hot 100" chart. Turner returned to

New York City to perform at the Ritz and do in-store promotions at the Village's Tower Records. While autographing records for fans at the store, Davies received a call from *Billboard* with an updated chart position: "What's Love Got to Do with It?" was number 1 on the "Hot 100" chart.[74] (On the same day, George Miller, codirector of the *Mad Max* movie franchise, offered Turner a costarring role in *Mad Max 3: Beyond Thunderdome*, about which more below.)[75] Turner finally had the elusive chart success that was necessary to achieve her dream of headlining sold-out stadium shows.

Rolling Stone magazine featured Turner on the cover of its October 11, 1984, edition, with a cover story by Kurt Loder. In Canada for a series of concert dates in fulfillment of contractual obligations to perform at a McDonald's convention—an obligation made before the success of *Private Dancer*—Turner spoke with Loder from her hotel suite in Montreal. At 3 a.m., Turner gave Loder a demonstration of her Buddhist practice, chanting *Nam-myoho-renge-kyo* repeatedly. After the demonstration, she explained the practice to Loder in the same language she had used previously: "[*Nam-myoho-renge-kyo* is] the mystical law of the universe. I'm saying a word, but it sounds like *hmmmnnn*. Is there anything that is without that? There's a hum in the motor of a car, in the windshield wipers, your refrigerator. An airplane goes *rowwmmmnnn*. Sometimes I just sit and listen to the sounds of the universe and to that hum that is just there."[76] In the article Turner acknowledges that a "cosmic turnaround" happened when she began sharing the difficult details of her past with Ike Turner, much of which is retold to *Rolling Stone* readers in the article.[77] At the end of the profile, though, Turner voices a new dream: to one day become a Buddhist teacher. "I'm gonna focus on [propagating Buddhism]. I think that's gonna be my message, that's why I'm here. And I think that's why I'm gonna be as powerful as I am. Because in order to get people to listen to you, you've got to be some kind of landmark, some kind of foundation. You don't listen to people that don't mean anything to you. You have to have something there to make people believe you. And so I think that's what's going on now. I'm getting their attention now, and then when I'm ready, they'll listen. And they'll hear."[78]

In Mahayana Buddhist traditions, Turner's intuition that her fame is a means or tool to get people's attention in order to teach them about Buddhism is known by the doctrinal concept of *upaya-kaushalya*, or "mastery of stratagems."[79] A doctrine of immense complexity, *upaya-kaushalya* is translated in the Soka Gakkai as "expedient means" and is defined as "The methods adopted to instruct people and lead them to enlightenment."[80] In other words, the chart success of *Private Dancer* and its singles served a twofold purpose for Turner. On the one hand, it was the critical commercial factor in determining her ability to headline a stadium tour. On the other, the resurgence in her popularity resulting from the album's success served as the expedient means to attract attention, so that one day she would be able to propagate religious teachings. Turner would not be ready to fully embody the role of religious teacher until retiring from performing in 2009. But at the end of 1984, *Private Dancer* was still on the music charts, and Turner was performing around the United States and Canada in fulfillment of prior concert obligations before traveling to Australia to costar with Mel Gibson in *Mad Max 3: Beyond Thunderdome*.[81]

Singles from *Private Dancer* continued to be released into 1985, and altogether seven of the album's nine (ten on the European release) songs were released as successful singles, most accompanied by music videos, including the *Billboard* number 1 hit, "What's Love Got to Do with It?" The album finished the year gold and platinum around the world, and triple platinum in the United States.[82] To continue promoting the album, Turner appeared on television and radio and in print throughout 1985, in a whirlwind of engagements.

In January 1985, Turner attended the American Music Awards ceremony and received both the Black Female Vocalist and the Black Female Video Artist awards.[83] After the ceremony, Turner joined more than forty other artists to record the song "We Are the World," as a part of the United Support of Artists for Africa (USA for Africa) charity effort for famine relief in Africa.[84] She then attended and performed at the Twenty-Seventh Annual Grammy Awards, held on February 26, 1985, where she collected three awards: Best Rock Vocal Performance, Female; Best Pop Vocal Performance, Female; and the coveted Record of the Year award, for the song "What's Love Got to Do with It?"[85]

In July, *Mad Max Beyond Thunderdome* debuted in theaters. Turner had two songs on the soundtrack, "One of the Living" (which won a Grammy in the Best Rock Vocal Performance, Female category at the Twenty-Eighth Annual Grammy Awards) and "We Don't Need Another Hero" (which peaked at number 2 on *Billboard*'s "Hot 100" chart). As part of the press for the movie, Arrington did another cover story on Turner for *People*. In it, he discussed the movie, Turner's Buddhist beliefs, and her use of psychics, homeopathy, and crystal therapy. Arrington also reported that the William Morrow publishing company had offered Turner $460,000 to publish her life story. Finally, Arrington noted that though Turner had long voiced a desire to act,[86] she turned down Steven Spielberg's offer to play the role of Shug Avery in his adaptation of Alice Walker's *The Color Purple*.[87] Turner would later explain that, only eight years after leaving Ike, *The Color Purple* was "uncomfortably close to the story of my life with Ike. . . . I didn't want to relive any of that nightmare ever again, even on screen."[88] The same month, Turner dueted with Mick Jagger at the Live Aid concert, in further support of USA for Africa efforts. In August, Turner was featured in another cover story, this time for *Life* magazine; the article once again discussed her Buddhist practice (with an accompanying photo of Turner in front of her *butsudan*) and lifestyle, noting that Turner had bought her mother, Zelma, a home in Los Angeles (confirming that though Turner had separated from her family to focus on the making and promoting of *Private Dancer*, she was still supporting at least some family members).[89]

Private Dancer's success also paved the way for the Private Dancer Tour 1985. In February 1985, the tour began in Helsinki, Finland, and continued through the end of the year, around Turner's other promotional efforts. It was Turner's first major tour as a solo, headlining artist. Two shows held in March 1985 at the National Exhibition Centre in Birmingham, England, were filmed for an HBO special in which Turner performed songs from the *Private Dancer* album. The show also featured duets with David Bowie and Canadian artist Bryan Adams (who was an opening act on the tour).[90] The tour saw Turner perform 180 shows, with an attendance totaling over two million people.[91] While not a stadium tour, and thus not yet the fulfillment of her dream, the show saw sold-out arenas in cities around the world and established her as a commercially successful, major headlining act.[92]

The Private Dancer Tour ended in Tokyo, Japan, with its final show on December 28, 1985. In Tokyo, Turner sat for an interview with *Seikyo Shimbun*, Soka Gakkai's daily newspaper in Japan. In addition to emphasizing the correlation between performing at NSA's 1982 "Aloha, We Love America" festival and her songs becoming "big hits," Turner reiterated to the interviewer that she chanted four hours each day during the difficult period of disentangling her life and career from Ike Turner. Intensive chanting, for Turner, produced what she called an "internal revolution"—an allusion to Soka Gakkai's principle of human revolution—that enabled her to "purify" her life. She identifies this purification as the reason she was able to identify Davies (and initially Lee Kramer too) as the right manager for her. The interviewer asked how she prepared mentally for her performances, and she responded that, while she doesn't prepare "in any particular way," she does use the focus and discipline drawn from her practice. "I concentrate my full power into what I should be doing at each moment. For example, whether I feel good or bad, or no matter what the situation, I decide, 'For the next hour, this is what I will do . . .' and throw my effort into what I should be doing. If I do this, then nothing can defeat me. Ultimately, to make up one's mind is everything." Though she had first said she did not prepare in any special way, she then tells the interviewer that she tries to spend "as much time as possible in a state of peace before going on." This included chanting *Nam-myoho-renge-kyo* for an hour before her performances. She acknowledges that her "intense performance schedule" left little time to study Buddhist teachings and attend NSA discussion meetings; however, she emphasizes that she continued to rely on Daisaku Ikeda's guidance about perseverance.[93] The interview concludes with Turner saying she is now chanting to meet directly with Ikeda, and with Turner assuring the readers of *Seikyo Shimbun* that she would like to return to Japan. Published on January 5, 1986, and coming at the end of the most commercially successful two years of her life to that point, the interview aptly summarizes how Turner saw the relationship between her practice of Soka Gakkai Nichiren Buddhism and her success.[94]

Break Every Rule and *Foreign Affair*

Between 1986 and 1991, Turner released *I, Tina* (New York: William Morrow and Co., 1986; written with Kurt Loder) and two successor albums to 1984's *Private Dancer*: *Break Every Rule* (Capitol Records, 1986) and *Foreign Affair* (Capitol Records, 1989). *I, Tina* and *Break Every Rule* both demonstrate Turner's growing sense of internationalism, which would be reflected in the title of the *Foreign Affair* album and her permanent move to Europe. In *I, Tina*, this sense of internationalism is most pronounced in the book's epilogue.

Throughout *I, Tina*, the reader glimpses an increasingly international focus as she and Ike Turner first travel to England in 1966, and subsequently tour throughout Europe (later adding Asia and Australia) each year. Then, once Turner becomes a solo artist, her tours carry her around the world, and she records *Private Dancer* in England. Yet, in the epilogue these glimpses are revealed more fully. "So now I sit in London," Turner says in the epilogue, "in the middle of spring and all its beauty." Since Davies and Turner planned to work on the next album in England and France, they relocated to a house in Holland Park, in the Kensington district of London. By reference to her belief in astrology, Turner mused that "every city holds an energy for certain people, where you can achieve anything positive because it's your place in the world. Well, London is mine."[95] Because "River Deep, Mountain High" was a major hit in England—even as it flopped in the United States—Turner considers her career to have started in London and, referring to *Private Dancer*, she concludes: "success has followed me here."[96] While writing about being in London in *I, Tina*'s epilogue, Turner was also recording her *Break Every Rule* album in Paris.[97]

As on the *Private Dancer* album, Turner was a "collaborator" in the composition process of *Break Every Rule*. Writer and popular culture critic Lisa A. Lewis distinguishes song composition, wherein someone writes either the lyrics or the music of a song, from the process of collaboration, wherein someone's thoughts or experiences form the basis of the song.[98] Writing about the song "I Might Have Been Queen," Lewis says that in relaying her life story and beliefs in reincarnation to Jeannette Obstoj, Turner was acting as a collaborator: "She did not write the songs, at least not according to the industry definition of songwriting. Yet, she was an important collaborator on several songs."[99] For *Break Every Rule*, Turner again shared her story and life experiences with the album's songwriters—Terry Britten and Graham Lyle (who also wrote "What's Love Got to Do with It?"), David Bowie, Bryan Adams, Rupert Hine and Jeannette Obstoj, Mark Knopfler, and Paul Brady[100]—and they used this as the raw material for crafting the song lyrics, lending the songs an autobiographical bent. Turner herself would say of the album, "Every track is about the last ten years since my days with Ike, describing what I feel and how I think. It's my life on vinyl."[101] Turner also collaborated by guiding the producer's choices in the crafting of songs. During the making of the album, Turner consciously guided the producers away from creating a gospel sound for the album's ballads. Rupert Hine intended to use a gospel choir to provide backing for Turner on the song "I'll Be Thunder." Turner, however, nixed the idea because, she said, "I don't want to go to church. I relate totally to what Patti LaBelle does, but I enjoy the fun of *not* being that serious."[102] Adding to the "fun" of the album were guest appearances by Phil Collins, Mark Knopfler, Eric Clapton, and Steve Winwood, again bolstering her association with white, male rock artists. The result of their collaborations was the critically acclaimed *Break Every Rule* album, released at the end of September 1986.[103] Certified platinum by the RIAA two months later, the album had been entirely produced and recorded in England and France.[104]

To support the album, Turner launched the four-leg Tina Turner Break Every Rule World Tour 1987/88. Rehearsals for the tour began in Munich, Germany,[105] where the tour's first show was played on March 4, 1987.[106] The European leg of the tour lasted through July 1987 and saw Turner break attendance records in thirteen countries across Europe, with some 1.8 million people seeing the show.[107] After Europe, the show toured the United States, where it was one of the highest-grossing tours of the year,[108] and Canada. South America comprised the third leg; the fourth leg combined Australia, New Zealand, Japan, and Southeast Asia. While the European leg was the most successful in terms of total attendance, it was on the South American leg that Turner's major dream to fill stadiums was finally fulfilled. Turner played a stadium show in Buenos Aires, Argentina, for an audience of approximately 60,000 people. Then the tour moved to Brazil for shows in São Paolo and Rio de Janeiro. On January 16, 1988, in Rio de Janeiro, Turner performed at Maracanã Stadium before 180,200 people. At the time, this was the largest paying crowd ever assembled for a solo artist.[109] The show was also broadcast live on HBO to an additional 26 million people. During the broadcast, Turner paused the show to acknowledge the moment: "You know, I had a wish . . . [to] fill a football stadium. I filled the biggest football stadium there is! Obrigado Rio, thank you!"[110] Altogether, the Tina Turner Break Every Rule World Tour 1987/88 played 230 concerts to 3.5 million people, across twenty-five countries.[111] Even as the Private Dancer Tour 1985 established Turner as a major arena rock artist, the Break

Every Rule World Tour established her as a commercially successful artist on a global scale, one who could fill stadiums. Her long-cherished career dream, to be a stadium concert act, was finally fulfilled. Davies and Turner had worked together from 1981 to transform her act into a rock 'n' roll show, secure a record contract, and disassociate her from Ike Turner, all in the service of securing the hit albums (*Private Dancer* and *Break Every Rule*) that would enable her to accomplish her wildest dream. She had also taken each opportunity to connect this dream to her practice of Soka Gakkai Nichiren Buddhism, chanting *Nam-myoho-renge-kyo* and praying that members of the record-buying public would attend her shows and become happy, which is to say she wanted her audience to experience the wildest-dreams rock aesthetic that her shows displayed.

The commercial success of these albums and tours meant that Turner was given more creative control on her next album, *Foreign Affair*. Recorded in New York, Paris, and London, the *Foreign Affair* album departed—at Turner's behest—from the formula of *Private Dancer* and *Break Every Rule*, which shared many of the same writers and producers. For this album, Turner said that she "wanted to record songs that people like Otis Redding, Sam Cooke and Marvin Gaye were singing back in the past."[112] To this end, Turner took the first producing credits of her solo career. Along with Davies, she served as the executive producer of the album. Turner coproduced and arranged the songs "Ask Me How I Feel" and "The Best." On the latter song, in particular, Turner crafted the song's signature opening ("the 'dun, da, da, dun, da, da' all of that");[113] had the songwriter change the key signature of the song; and had the writer add a bridge to the song.[114] She continued her collaborative role by working with the producers of the other ten songs to shape them and make them her own.

Turner's production credits and creative control also extended to the album's accompanying Foreign Affair World Tour 1990. She again worked with British stage architect Mark Fisher to design a set that featured a grand staircase for Turner to make her entrance, and a cherry picker to take her over the audience as she sang "Better Be Good to Me" during the show's climax. Turner herself served as musical director for the tour, to re-create live the song arrangements that she helped to craft on the album.[115] Turner also served as the main choreographer and brought back her dancers Ann Behringer and Lejeune Richardson. Behringer would later recall how before shows, the three of them would chant together.[116] The tour ran from April to November 1990, playing 125 shows across nineteen countries in Europe, to 3.5 million people.[117] The tour was a continuation of Turner's dream, since more than half of the venues were stadiums. But the tour is also notable in that despite being labeled a "world tour," the show only toured in Europe. Indeed, rather than simply the title of an album, *Foreign Affair* also captures the professional and personal changes occurring in Turner's life at this time. During this era, Turner shifted her focus almost exclusively toward Europe.

International Focus

Professionally, Turner began to orient her work toward her European audiences. This orientation began with the release of her Grammy-winning *Tina Live in Europe* (Capitol Records, 1988) compilation. The compilation captures performances from both the Private Dancer and Break Every Rule tours, including promotional concert performances. While these tours reached global audiences, the compilation focused only on the European legs of those tours. The liner notes reveal why this is so. In them, Turner writes of being onstage at New York's Madison Square Garden during the American leg of the Break Every Rule World Tour 1987/88. As she noticed someone in the audience who had been at some of her shows in Europe, she thought to herself, "Oh, how wonderful Europe really was!" She concludes the notes by sharing her feelings about Europe, echoing the same sentiments shared in the epilogue to *I, Tina*: "I honestly feel that my dream came true in Europe."[118] Therefore, the compilation focused on her European performances because she saw her dream as coming to fruition in Europe. She explicitly connects these sentiments back to 1966's "River Deep, Mountain High" being successful in England, even as it flopped in the United States. When combined with the *Foreign Affair* album and its European-only tour, Turner had now turned completely toward Europe, professionally. This professional turn toward Europe was mirrored in her private life.

To avoid media overexposure, after the Break Every Rule Tour Turner took a year off.[119] During that time, she developed her personal relationship with German record executive Erwin Bach. In *My Love Story*, titled in part to reflect how meeting Bach was the fulfillment of her lifelong search for love, Turner shared in detail how she met Bach and how they developed their relationship across continents.[120] Turner met Bach while traveling in Germany on the Private Dancer Tour. Since she was touring, they had few opportunities to see each other, but they remained in contact. Eventually, they began to spend time together between their professional commitments; by 1987, Turner was mentioning him by name in interviews;[121] and by 1990, magazine profiles were featuring photos of the couple at locales around Europe.[122] Turner's relationship with Bach influenced the next step in her turn toward Europe: she moved permanently from Los Angeles to London in 1988. She had decided that since she did not speak German, and thus could not immediately move to Germany, London "would be a good choice for an intermediate step." She went on, "I'd be closer to Erwin, and the city was already a second home to me."[123]

Taken together, in the period between 1986 and 1990, Turner's oeuvre—the epilogue to *I, Tina*; and the albums *Break Every Rule, Foreign Affair*, and *Tina Live in Europe*, with their accompanying promotional tours—and Turner's relationship with Bach and subsequent permanent relocation to Europe all combine to display a maturation of the internationalist sensibilities that awakened in her on her 1966 trip to England.

Regarding her professional orientation toward Europe, Turner claimed in interviews that this was because her later albums did not sell well in America. Presumably, Turner was referring to the fact that the *Foreign Affair* album peaked at number 31 on *Billboard*'s album chart (compared to numbers 3 and 4 for *Private Dancer* and *Break Every Rule*, respectively).[124] The album also failed to reach platinum sales in the United States (RIAA certified the album as gold), a fact that reviewers also noted.[125] Given the album's comparatively lackluster sales, it made sense for Turner to forgo an American leg of the Foreign Affair World Tour, focusing instead on touring European markets where the album did better commercially. At the same time, she claimed that a move to Europe made sense for her personal life because of her relationship with Bach. Yet Turner's comments in media profiles reveal still another reason for orienting her private and professional life toward Europe: racism.

In a 1985 radio interview with Lisa Robinson, Turner contrasted her experiences dating American men versus European men. "The European men [have] nothing about marrying a Black woman," Turner explained to

Robinson, "if he loves her and if he has chosen one for himself." She went on to say that, by contrast, "In America, it's almost shameful [for a white man to date a Black woman]. You gotta go through the mother . . . and you gotta go through society . . . it's still that old slavery thing that [the woman] is still Black. We're still niggers in America. I don't care how much a woman has claim to fame and what she is, she's still a nigger."[126] Turner's language here is strong, and may strike her listeners as offensive. However, Turner is relaying here, in a raw and honest manner, her own experiences. This undoubtedly had an influence on her decision to pursue a relationship with German-born Bach.

This racism accords with her professional experiences in the music business when Turner's nascent record deal with Capitol Records was nearly scuttled because of the racist and sexist perception of her by executives at the label. Turner also experienced racism and sexism in the movie industry. In 1988 and 1989, during her break, Turner attempted to develop another dream—that of having a sustained acting career. This dream was thwarted when Turner discovered that "it's not easy being black and a woman [in Hollywood]—that's two strikes against you automatically."[127] In *The Girl from Nutbush*, Turner explains her experience with the film industry with a strained smile: "Well, what I ran into is [that] there are very few parts for women, especially Blacks."[128] Finally, in a 1986 *Rolling Stone* article, Turner succinctly stated the phenomenological experience of what it's like to be a member of a minority group in America: "It hurts to be a minority. I am looked down upon because I'm black. It's forever. It's like a curse on you."[129] These comments display Turner's hyper-awareness of her social location as a Black woman in America.

Racial Diversity in SGI-USA

By contrast, the Buddhist discussion meetings that Turner attended in Los Angeles were one place where she was able to relax such hyper-awareness of her social location. From her tours in Europe with the Ike & Tina Turner Revue in the sixties, Turner had already felt herself to be "universal," to be beyond any single culture (see chap. 2 above). And when Turner wrote of Valerie Bishop, formally introducing her to "Nichiren Shoshu Buddhism" (that is to say, Soka Gakkai Nichiren Buddhism), Turner immediately noted the predominance of mixed-race couples who were engaged in the practice of chanting with the organization. Matilda Buck, Turner's Buddhist leader in the early days of her practice, also noted how people from "all walks of life" and a variety of different backgrounds would attend their Buddhist meetings (see chap. 3 above). The NSA/SGI-USA organization's propagation method of street *shakubuku*, discussed in chapter 3, combined with the organization's primarily urban locations attracted many people of color who eventually became committed members and leaders.

Owing to these efforts, African Americans came to compose a considerable number of SGI-USA's members. In 1969, political scientist James Allen Dator published *Sōka Gakkai, Builders of the Third Civilization: American and Japanese Members*, a sociological study of the Soka Gakkai organization in both Japan and the United States.[130] Dator also noted that African Americans constituted roughly one-sixth of the organization's membership.[131] By the time the NSA published its own account of its growth in George M. Williams's 1985 book, *Freedom and Influence*, the organization claimed that Black people composed 20 percent of its membership.[132] Many of these African Americans joined during NSA's *shakubuku* conversion drives in the late sixties and in the seventies.[133] Williams surmised that at least some African Americans joined the organization as a means to "challenge and overcome" their experiences of racial prejudice in the United States.[134] Regardless of their reasons for joining, African Americans have come to represent a sizable portion of present-day SGI-USA's membership. Their numbers have grown in the organization since at least 1962, as Dator's work showed. For this reason, scholars studying Buddhism in America have frequently noted that SGI-USA is one of the most diverse Buddhist organizations in America.[135] As a Soka Gakkai Nichiren Buddhist, then, Turner's experience of her Buddhist community as one where people of color predominate—holding leadership roles and positions of authority, as well as constituting a substantial portion of the membership body—necessarily differs from the experiences of racism and a lack of diversity in other American Buddhist communities, which other Black Buddhist authors like Jan Willis, Ruth King, and Reverend angel Kyodo Williams have written about.[136]

Nonetheless, for Turner, the constant experience of life in a country where your very existence is a "curse," and the attendant circumscription that Turner experienced in both her personal romantic life and her professional life as a recording artist and aspiring actor, reveals itself as another reason why Turner relocated to Europe, just as James Baldwin, Nina Simone, and other African American artists had already done. This period, then, from the 1986 release of both *I, Tina* and *Break Every Rule* to the completion of her Foreign Affair World Tour in 1990, saw the maturation of Turner's sense of internationalism. During this time, she accomplished her (wildest) dream of becoming a stadium-filling headline act, the realization of which she explicitly connected to her Buddhist practice. At the same time, she reoriented her personal and professional life toward Europe.

What's Love Got to Do with It?

Written with Kurt Loder and released on September 1, 1986, *I, Tina* expands upon the narrative that Turner began sharing in 1981. Across fifteen chapters, Turner shares her life story, taking the reader from her early years in Nutbush through to the commercial success of *Private Dancer*. The book features interviews with members of Turner's family (Zelma, Alline, cousins, and her sons), with Ike Turner, and with Turner's friends and business associates. Alongside their interviews, Loder provides necessary contextual information about music history and contemporaneous national events. In addition to giving intimate details about her life, *I, Tina* foregrounds both Turner's practice of Buddhism and her work with psychics in transforming her life. Explaining her rationale for writing the book, Turner would later say: "I wrote *I, Tina* as a response to all those people who at the biggest, most exciting time of my life, when my solo career was taking off, kept asking me about Ike. I thought, 'Is this guy gonna come back and haunt me forever?'"[137] Writing the book was an uncomfortable, and potentially dangerous, experience for Turner. When Turner first spoke to Carl Arrington about the harrowing circumstances surrounding her separation and divorce, she feared the potential consequences. At that time, in fall of 1981, Turner had only been divorced for three years, and much of the harassment she was receiving from Ike had finally ceased. Would publicly discussing the matter bring renewed harassment? When *I, Tina* was released in 1986, Turner again worried about the consequences, especially because Ike himself was attempting to revive his own career, releasing albums and giving interviews.[138]

Turner had heard from Ike sporadically over the years. "After I started working with Roger, Ike asked our sons to approach me about going out on the road with him one more time. He even spoke to Roger. . . . I couldn't bear the thought of standing on a stage with Ike, let alone consider singing his music." And yet, after the success of "What's Love Got to Do with It?" as a single, she never heard from Ike again.[139] In January 1989, Turner attended the fourth annual Rock and Roll Hall of Fame induction ceremony. She was inducting Phil Spector, producer of "River Deep, Mountain High." There, as she related to Mike Wallace during a *60 Minutes* interview, she took her seat in the audience, turned to look behind her, and "looked straight [into] Ike's face."[140] She continues: "It frightened me. . . . I just thought anything could happen; it wasn't safe at that point because this is when he was still heavily [into] drugs."[141] (Interestingly, when Wallace asks if she is still afraid of Ike, Turner immediately replies, "No, not afraid.") Other than this incident, she never saw Ike Turner again. When Ike and Tina Turner were inducted into the Rock and Roll Hall of Fame in 1991, Ike was in jail and Turner declined to attend the ceremony (Phil Spector inducted them and accepted the award on their behalf). But, in 1988, Disney bought the rights to *I, Tina* and announced its intention to turn the book into a major motion picture, with Turner as a consultant for the film.[142] Thus, she was required to tell the story once more.

Though Turner did not, as a part of her contract, have final script approval, she did look through drafts of the script with Brian Gibson and the film's producers. About the script she would later say, "[I] felt like they took the idea of my life and sort of wrote around it . . . the script that I read was far—quite far—from reality."[143] Nonetheless, after many drafts, the film's script was finalized, and the film proceeded. Work on the film began in the fall of 1992, with Brian Gibson (1944–2004) as director (his directing credits include *Poltergeist II* and *The Josephine Baker Story*). Angela Bassett was cast as Tina Turner; Laurence Fishburne was cast as Ike Turner. Michael Peters (1948–1994), famed for choreographing Michael Jackson's "Thriller" and "Beat It" music videos, signed on as the film's choreographer. While Fishburne watched old footage of Ike Turner and got a tutorial on Ike Turner's walking gait, Turner worked with Bassett on her costumes, makeup, choreography, and facial expressions on set.[144] Finally, *What's Love Got to Do with It?* was released in theaters on June 25, 1993.

The movie opened with a description of the Lotus Sutra, transitioning to a Baptist church where a young Turner is seen spiritedly singing. The film then follows the narrative of *I, Tina*: domestic strife at home leads her mother and father to leave. She eventually moves to St. Louis and there meets Ike Turner. They get married, move to Los Angeles, and amid their recording and performing schedule Ike grows increasingly erratic and abusive. Later, Bassett, as Turner, is depicted reciting *Nam-myoho-renge-kyo* in front of a *butsudan* after being introduced to the practice by a former Ikette. Behind the scenes of the movie, Turner had taught Angela Bassett how to chant, and each morning during filming, Turner herself would chant together with Brian Gibson, who was also a Nichiren Buddhist.[145] Bassett is Pentecostal and a member of the Church of God in Christ (Turner attended a Pentecostal church in Knoxville, Tennessee, as a child). That Turner and Bassett may have discussed their respective religious journeys while the latter was preparing for her role is an intriguing possibility because, if so, it provides an example of two Black women navigating religious difference and modeling a certain theological openness.

The movie's depiction of Turner's introduction to Buddhism highlights the liberties that the film took with the details of Turner's life. Where Turner was introduced to Buddhism in a series of encounters (chap. 3), the movie combines those encounters into a single composite character, represented by an ex-Ikette. Where Turner's son Craig was fathered by Kings of Rhythm saxophonist Raymond Hill, *What's Love Got to Do with It?* obscures this fact and gives the impression that Ike Turner was the father of two children with Turner. Finally, the film elides the fact that Turner moved back and forth between the homes of various friends after leaving Ike in Texas. Instead, the movie shows Turner living with the same composite character, who introduces her to Buddhism.[146] After Turner's escape, the movie then briefly sketches her divorce, meeting Roger Davies, and her comeback, ending with the release of "What's Love Got to Do with It?" and Turner's comeback performance at the Ritz nightclub. A cameo of Turner performing in Birmingham, England, on the Private Dancer Tour appears at the end.

For the film's soundtrack, Turner served as executive producer (along with Davies) and coproduced eight of the twelve songs on *What's Love Got to Do with It?* (Virgin, 1993). Many of these songs, including "A Fool in Love" and "It's Gonna Work Out Fine," were songs from her tenure with the Ike & Tina Turner Revue. For Turner, rerecording the songs was a traumatizing prospect: "I have not played an album of mine since I left Ike. And if I walk in somewhere and people are playing that stuff . . . it still scares me. I have flashbacks in my dreams. I'll wake up and still think I'm there."[147] She had also previously blocked her label from releasing Ike and Tina Turner material because, as she said, "I don't want my record company putting out that crap."[148] Thus, in the liner notes to the soundtrack Turner tersely remarked that the idea of rerecording songs from the Ike and Tina days did not thrill her, though she goes on to say that her band's enthusiasm during the recording process rubbed off on her.[149]

The movie was critically acclaimed,[150] receiving Academy Award and Golden Globe nominations, among other awards (Angela Bassett received the Golden Globe for Best Actress in a Motion Picture; she also received the NAACP Image Award for Outstanding Actress in a Motion Picture), and it was a box office success.[151] Reviews of *I, Tina*, on which the movie is based, had already highlighted how her book "offers hope to victims of spouse abuse."[152] The movie furthered this by showing, in graphic detail, the trauma she experienced and how she overcame it. In interviews, screenwriter Kate Lanier explained that the writing and production team "really clicked on the idea that Tina's story is like a heroic myth. . . . She set out on a quest, fought a dragon, and came through it successfully." She went on, "To me, it's unique to have a woman in this myth."[153] In bringing renewed public attention to Turner's experience of abuse and presenting her in an ultimately victorious light, *What's Love Got to Do with It?* furthered the triumphant-survivor narrative that had already become associated with her during the release of *I, Tina*.

And yet, the onscreen depiction of her traumas, including the abandonment by her parents and Ike Turner's abuse, was unwatchable for Turner. After describing the pain and embarrassment of having to talk about the details of her life again and again, Turner explained that she could not watch the movie. "I found the subject so upsetting," Turner remembered, "that I could never bring myself to watch *What's Love Got to Do with It*."[154] More than the movie's narrative license, Turner "didn't want to spend two hours reliving the nightmare [she'd] spent years trying to forget."[155] (Turner revealed in a 2000 interview that the stress of promoting the movie and recording the soundtrack caused her to get shingles.)[156] Further, Turner was rarely comfortable with how both the book and the movie made her into a heroine. In comments that echo Jimmy Thomas's statement that the Ike & Tina Turner Revue stayed out of conflicts and movements (see chap. 2), Turner explained: "It seems that I live a woman's liberated life but I was not aware of it because I'm not into movements. I was just surviving. That is the kind of woman I am."[157] Even still, Turner could recognize the work the film, in particular, did to bring awareness to abuse—"One story I recall: I was going through an airport when my movie came out. And there was a man who yelled out to me from across the room. He said, 'After seeing your movie, I will never beat my wife again!'"—and to Buddhism—"Everybody knows that I practice Buddhism, thanks to my movie. I think I planted many seeds with it."[158]

Indeed, *What's Love Got to Do with It?* centered Turner's religiosity in visual form for a global audience. By beginning in a Baptist church, the movie affirms for the audience that she has a familiar African American religious pedigree. But, by both foregrounding a one-line description of the image of the lotus in the mud as the movie opens and making her conversion to Buddhism the movie's pivot point, the movie reintroduced audiences to the place of Buddhism in the African American religious experience. Unsurprisingly, in interviews conducted to promote the movie, Turner discussed her practice frequently. Turner's explanation of her beliefs and practice in this extended excerpt from a 1993 *Vanity Fair* cover profile is typical:

I do something about my life besides eating and exercising and whatever. I contact my soul. I must stay in touch with my soul. That's my connection to the universe. . . . I'm a Buddhist-Baptist. My training is Baptist. And I can still relate to the Ten Commandments and to the Ten Worlds. It's all very close, as long as you contact the subconscious mind. That's where the coin of the Almighty is. . . . I don't care what they feel about me and my tight pants onstage, and my lips and my hair. I am a chanter. And everyone who knows anything about chanting knows you correct everything in your life by chanting every day.[159]

Like the movie, Turner here affirms that she received Baptist training, by which she seems to mean that she was thoroughly grounded in Baptist

Christian teachings, where the "Ten Commandments" stands as a syn-ecdoche for her Baptist education (likely because this was the doctrinal focus at Woodlawn Missionary Baptist Church when she and Robbie Ew-ing were baptized; see chap. 1 above). But she also affirms that she relates this to the Soka Gakkai Nichiren Buddhist concept of the "Ten Worlds" (see next chapter). Again, it is worth reiterating that these comments show that Turner's conversion to Soka Gakkai Nichiren Buddhism cannot be un-derstood as representing an exclusivist commitment to *one* religion above others. Indeed, given the combinatory nature of her religiosity, this could not be the case. Instead, her comments reveal that Turner incorporates *all* her religious training into her practice. Compare Turner's assertion of a Buddhist-Baptist identity here with Jan Willis's reflection on her own iden-tity as a "Baptist-Buddhist." Willis writes that she describes herself that way because she "call[s] on both traditions,"[160] and she "can use *Buddhist* methods to help [her] practice *Baptist* ideals."[161] Turner seems to express a similar point: by relating both Baptist and Buddhist doctrines, Turner can use the tools of one to express the ideals of the other. Importantly, Turner reveals that the connection for her is in the subconscious mind, a connection she would explore in her memoir *Happiness Becomes You* (see chap. 6 below). Finally, she reiterates, as she always did in interviews, that it was chanting everyday that changed her life.

Despite Turner's reluctance to tell her story again, and despite her inability to see that story depicted on screen in the major motion picture *What's Love Got to Do with It?*, she nonetheless promoted the movie and its soundtrack in media profiles and on tour. Turner embarked upon the ninety-seven date What's Love? Tour '93, beginning in June 1993 and ending in November of the same year. This was her first concert tour of North America since 1987 (she also played dates in Europe, Australia, and New Zealand). Together, the movie and soundtrack, media profiles and reviews, and the tour all solidified a multifaceted identity for Tina Turner in popular culture: Black woman, triumphant survivor, global artist, and African American Bud-dhist. For Turner's next projects, each of these identities would coalesce.

The Wildest-Dreams Rock Aesthetic

In April 1996, Turner released the *Wildest Dreams* album (Parlophone/Vir-gin, 1996; released in the United States in September). The thirteen-track (twelve in the US release) album was Turner's first album of all new material since 1989's *Foreign Affair* album. Drawn from a song on the album, the title *Wildest Dreams* encapsulated Turner's wildest-dreams message: the conviction that no matter one's background or past circumstances, one could imagine, create a blueprint, and accomplish even one's wildest dreams. This message was shared repeatedly throughout her success in the eighties, following the *Private Dancer* album, and was reinforced by the 1993 release of the movie *What's Love Got to Do with It?*, with its accompanying soundtrack and tour. Three years later, that message was now central to Turner's brand. To maximize her reach, another global concert tour was planned.

In preparation for Tina Turner's Wildest Dreams Tour 1996–1997, Turner spent four months rehearsing near Johannesburg, South Africa.[162] When the tour opened in Cape Town, South Africa, on April 16, 1996, at Newlands Cricket Stadium, three of the four major elements of a touring rock show that Moles named were wrong: the set was wrong because Turner was not centered in the iris of the "golden-eye" that formed the central set-piece; the lighting was too dark, obscuring the dancers and audience from Turner; and the audio mix coming through the sound wedges placed at the front of the stage, crucial to her ability to hear herself over the noise of the crowd, was muddled.[163] And so, though the show had just opened, rehearsals for the tour intensified.

In rehearsals, Turner worked with members of the design and staging team on each of the four elements of the show. As she had on three previous tours, she hired architect Mark Fisher to design the set. Previously, Fisher had designed a grand staircase for Turner's entrance and a cherry picker for the show's climax on the Foreign Affair World Tour 1990. Modified versions of both set pieces had been included on the What's Love? Tour '93. For the Wildest Dreams Tour, Fisher worked with Turner to design a terraced stage set with a golden, eye-shaped lighting rig, a reference to the 1995 James Bond *Goldeneye* film for which Turner had recorded the eponymous theme song. To replace the cherry picker, Fisher designed a motorized platform to take Turner into the audience during the show's climax. Turner worked with Christine Strand, Dave Natale, and LeRoy Bennett on the video, sound, and lighting, respectively. Alongside this, Turner worked with her musicians to arrange a set list of some twenty-three songs. The show's set list was paced to give the audience a sense of excitement first, then something mellow and moody, followed last by an explosive climax. "The music," Turner explained, "was organized in such a way to give the audience an emotional experience."[164] Finally, Turner worked with Micha Bergese and Andrew Mournehis on choreography for the tour's three dancers. But in addition to these practical preparations, a tour of this magnitude required Turner to prepare herself spiritually once again.

She had found that, she explained, "I can face anything—even the pressure of a huge concert tour—if I have chanted for half an hour, twice a day."[165] As she had for each previous tour, Turner developed a practice routine on tour that consisted of chanting and praying for up to an hour before each performance. Turner's practice affected those around her, perhaps none more so than Mournehis, the tour's choreographer.

Mournehis, from Melbourne, Australia, had auditioned as a choreographer for Turner in London before the tour. Once hired, Mournehis traveled with Turner as a member of the tour's production team. While in South Africa, Mournehis arrived early for his private rehearsals with Turner and saw her seated before her altar, chanting *Nam-myoho-renge-kyo*. Mournehis describes Turner's chanting as "literally reverberating through" him. When he pressed her for an explanation of what he had experienced, Turner told him: "You are awakening, Andrew . . . you are spiritually awakening." In the ensuing discussion, Mournehis remembers Turner giving him both a liturgical prayer book (likely an edition of *The Liturgy of the Soka Gakkai International*) for the practice and a copy of Deepak Chopra's *Seven Spiritual Laws of Success: A Practical Guide to the Fulfillment of Your Dreams*.[166] Turner herself never mentioned Chopra's book in any known source; however, she did write in *My Love Story* that she read Chopra's books and consulted with him directly while making the *Beyond* albums.[167] Chopra's work will be discussed in the next chapter, but even the subtitle of Chopra's book should make it clear that the themes he discusses would have been relevant to Turner's wildest-dreams brand message at that time. For Mournehis, both the liturgy and Chopra's book, given to him by Turner, provided the basis for a nascent spiritual practice.[168]

The result of all this preparation—both the pragmatic preparations of staging and rehearsing, and the spiritual preparation of chanting intently each day—was a well-crafted show for the audience. By the time Steve Moles saw the tour, over 120 concert dates after the tour's South Africa opening, he saw the set, video, lights, and sound as a "seamless whole."[169]

As a rock show, Turner's concert goes beyond those aesthetic elements. Turner's show also embodies the wildest-dreams rock aesthetic.

The wildest-dreams rock aesthetic is parallel to, and takes its inspiration from, scholar of philosophy Steve Odin's understanding of how Herbie Hancock and Wayne Shorter use Nichiren Buddhist philosophy in their practice of jazz improvisation. Odin explains that Hancock and Shorter formulate a "jazz aesthetics of spontaneous musical improvisation . . . based on the Nichiren Buddhist theory and practice of 'value creation' by tapping our Buddha nature as the source of infinite creative possibilities."[170] As explained in chapter 3 above, Soka Gakkai originated in the philosophical and educational theories of Tsunesaburo Makiguchi, the organization's first president. Primary among Makiguchi's theories was his theory of value creation, where value is understood as the philosophical principles of beauty, gain, and good.[171] In Soka Gakkai Nichiren Buddhism, bringing forth one's buddha-nature by engaging in the practices outlined by Nichiren enables one to actualize Makiguchi's theory of value creation. This is possible in Nichiren Buddhism because of the doctrine of *ichinen sanzen*, or "three thousand realms in a single moment of life." As the doctrine explains how it is possible for an ordinary being to experience Buddhahood, *ichinen sanzen* is the most important soteriological concept in Nichiren Buddhism. As Odin explains, "The doctrine of Buddha-nature as possessing 'three thousand realms in a single moment of life' signifies that each moment is a micro-cosmos of the macro-cosmos, such that everything is interconnected with everything else in the cosmic net of relationships. It is this doctrine of Buddha-nature as possessing 'three thousand realms in a single moment of life' that underlies the core of SGI Nichiren Buddhist teaching that each moment of life has unlimited creative possibilities." The *gohonzon* that Soka Gakkai Nichiren Buddhists chant to embodies this doctrine of *ichinen sanzen*, and chanting enables the practitioner to bring forth the unlimited creative possibilities that the doctrine expresses.

Odin argues that Hancock (and Shorter) "formulates a jazz aesthetics based on tapping Buddha-nature as the locus of unlimited possibilities by opening up to multiple new perspectives, that itself underlies the actualization of novel variations in the creative process of spontaneous improvisation, both in jazz and in life."[172] "This actualization of creative potentials in Buddha-nature," Odin continues, results in the maximum value creation as understood by Makiguchi. Thus, Hancock and Shorter use their Buddhist practice to engage in jazz improvisation as an actualization of Soka Gakkai Nichiren Buddhist principles. I use the terminology of "wildest-dreams rock aesthetic" to name the same phenomenon in Turner's concerts. Turner's spiritual preparation framed her concerts and enabled her to see them as an expression of her Buddhist practice in line with Soka Gakkai Nichiren Buddhist teachings. Turner uses her life story of triumph over adversity, doctrinal principles like *ichinen sanzen* and the transformation of karma, and her own Buddhist practice to craft the wildest-dreams message, which asserts the power of belief and practice to attain fulfillment. Because of this, in concert, Turner becomes a live embodiment of the wildest-dreams message. The wildest-dreams rock aesthetic, then, names the way Turner's wildest-dreams message is modeled and embodied by Turner in concert as a rock performer.

Beyond the doctrinal underpinnings of this idea, Turner's Buddhist mentor Daisaku Ikeda has offered more specific reflections on the relationship between performers and their performances. In a dialogue published with Herbie Hancock and Wayne Shorter, Ikeda expressed his view of the relationship between a performer, the performer's instrument, and communication with the audience. Ikeda wrote, "It is true that the same piece performed on the same instrument can sound completely different depending upon the spirit imparted by the performer. The performer's spirit has a mystical power to communicate emotion, something transcending mere technique." In the dialogue, Hancock responds to Ikeda's assertion with his conviction that as a saxophone player Wayne Shorter embodies this understanding and has just such a mystical communication with the audience: "When Wayne plays the saxophone, you hear Wayne. You don't hear the saxophone. The saxophone becomes the medium for hearing Wayne."[173] Shorter himself offers that "A great performance is a manifestation of an altruistic life condition, one that transcends the ego-driven pursuit of instant gratification, of the pursuit of money, power, and fame."[174] Thus, Hancock, Ikeda, and Shorter agree that performers are able to communicate their spirit, or their internal feelings, to the audience. Presumably this would be especially true if they prepare their spirit by engaging in spiritual practice before playing their instrument or performing. According to their understanding, Turner's preshow chanting routine would give her the "mystical power to communicate" with her audience. This mystical power to communicate is the mechanism that enables Turner's audiences at her concerts to experience the wildest-dreams rock aesthetic as a religious experience.

Such a conception of the relationship between performer, spiritual practice, and audience interaction is not limited to Soka Gakkai Nichiren Buddhists. Jason Bivins traces a similar understanding to the reflections of trumpeter Wadada Leo Smith. After converting to Islam in 1995, Smith structured "his life and music around Islamic practice."[175] Smith would pray and read the Qur'an for an hour before composing or practicing music. As Bivins explains, Smith held that "Islam helps him realize his musical principles at their fullest." Crucially, though, Bivins explains that Smith did not believe that his audiences needed "to embrace the specificity of his religion to experience joy or fulfillment"; instead, Smith held that if the music itself was embraced, then that musical event would in and of itself transform the listeners. Like Smith, Turner never espouses Buddhist beliefs during her show. Indeed, there is nothing *explicitly* religious about Turner's concerts: no religious insignia are displayed in the set or costuming; and the set list comprises songs that are largely devoid of religious doctrine, Buddhist or otherwise. Instead, both Smith and Turner seem to agree that through preparing oneself spiritually *before* the show, the performance itself becomes a transformative event for the audience. In line with Turner and the views expressed by Hancock, Ikeda, and Shorter, Bivins summarizes that for Smith, "The prophet or the artist can bring about a different way of being in the world."[176]

As transformative event, the concert—in Turner's case, specifically the rock concert—participates in the revivalist mode of religious experience in American religious history. American religions historian William McLoughlin argued that twentieth-century rock festivals, like Woodstock, maintain continuity with the religious revival meetings of the "great awakenings" of the eighteenth and nineteenth century. Some scholars have noted that revival meetings could exhibit a mixture of religious sensibilities. Some of the revival meetings that comprised the Great Awakenings, for example, the interactive dimensions of the meetings, especially between preacher and laity, display both the "Wesleyan [Methodist] emphasis on spiritual development as a communal (rather than a solitary) process and the traditional African emphasis on knowing the Spirit through the dynamic rhythmic interaction of individuals within a group."[177] The interactive dimensions of a rock concert, where the preacher and laity distinction is replaced by performer and audience, express these same dynamics of communal and rhythmic interaction between individuals. Just as these dynamics led to conversion and transformation during the Great Awakening revivals, music concerts too can be seen as sites of transformation, much as Wadada Leo Smith expresses. So pronounced are the similarities between revivals and music concerts that McLoughlin saw the proliferation of rock festivals and rock concerts as participating in a fourth great awakening.[178]

That audiences experienced Turner's concerts in this way is borne out by the recollections of Taro Gold. Gold attended Turner's concerts on the Wildest Dreams Tour and experienced firsthand the way that Turner's concerts became spiritual experiences for the audience members, with many crying and finding themselves inspired by Turner. As Gold described, "It was mystical and magical, and very real."[179] At that time, Turner's friends relayed to Gold that it was because of Turner's hour of chanting "for the true happiness of each audience member" before every show. Thus, to Gold, embedded in Turner's concerts was a palpable sense of religiosity that permeated the audience. Sean Jackson, a fan of Turner who also first saw her live on the Wildest Dreams Tour, concurs with Gold's sentiments. Jackson recalled that when he saw Turner in concert, he "felt spiritually connected" to Turner because he resonated with her inspirational narrative of triumphing over abuse and her embodiment of the power of belief. In other words, Jackson experienced the wildest-dream rock aesthetic as religious experience. The day after attending the concert, Jackson recalls feeling that the memory of seeing Turner was akin "to heaven."[180] Given both Jackson's experience and Gold's assertion that he frequently heard about and saw experiences like this at every concert he attended on the tour, it could be said that Turner's wildest-dreams message was indeed successfully communicated to her audiences.

Eventually, the Wildest Dreams Tour moved from South Africa to Europe, before going to Australia, New Zealand, and North America. Over sixteen months, Turner performed 255 concert dates to more than three million people across five continents. In magazine profiles in *Elle* and *Ebony*, she underscored the wildest-dreams message by emphasizing that she was herself living her wildest dreams.[181] Before the American leg of the tour, Turner made several US television appearances to promote the album and impending North American concerts. Among these, Turner's appearance on *The Oprah Winfrey Show* stands out.

Tina Turner and Oprah Winfrey

Turner's first appearance on *The Oprah Winfrey Show* aired February 21, 1997. By way of a superlative-laced introduction, Winfrey proclaimed that "legend" was the only word that could describe Turner, and she exclaimed that she had been waiting her whole life to interview Turner. Between performances of signature songs like "The Best" and "Let's Stay Together," Turner performed the title track from the *Wildest Dreams* album and sat for an interview. They covered topics that were by then standard fare: her early years picking cotton in Nutbush, her marriage and escape from Ike Turner, and her solo comeback. Turner reiterated that it was by contacting her subconscious mind, through chanting, that she was able to change her life (a perennial topic on *The Oprah Winfrey Show*). The episode also featured a tour of Turner's home in the South of France. The footage briefly showed her *butsudan*, at which she reminded the viewer that she chants morning and evening. Turner referred to the home as "heaven." She had moved from Los Angeles to London in 1988, then to Germany with her partner Erwin Bach, before finally moving to Zurich with him in 1994. She bought the French property amid these moves and had been steadily renovating it. Much of the interview with Winfrey and tour of the home was similar to her November 1996 appearance on *60 Minutes*, where she was interviewed by Mike Wallace. But this interview was unique in the way that Winfrey emphasized Turner's place as an *American* legend, as opposed to Wallace's focus on Turner's popularity in Europe. Winfrey's interview also discussed the movie *What's Love Got to Do with It?* and emphasized that Turner's story made her a role model for women. In doing so, and intersplicing it with footage of Turner's dream home and discussions of her subconscious mind-tapping Buddhist practice, the episode further makes Turner into one of the highest-profile African American Buddhists. Winfrey would later say that seeing Tina Turner live was akin to what people call getting the spirit in church.[182] Winfrey was not only affected by the religious experience of seeing Turner perform. She also seems to have seen Turner as something of an elder kindred spirit (Turner is Winfrey's senior by fifteen years), with whom she shared four interlocking affinities.

The first of these affinities is biographical. Like Turner, Winfrey was born in the South, in Kosciusko, Mississippi, a small town northeast of Jackson. Winfrey was initially raised by her maternal grandmother, who was primarily responsible for bringing her to church, like Turner's paternal grandmother. The early life of both women was marked by abuse, instability, and abandonment. Eventually, both would have to face racism and sexism in their respective careers to reach their desired levels of success. In this sense, Winfrey and Turner present as *sisters in the wilderness* who have known profound trauma and have overcome.

Yet, beyond these biographical commonalities, both women share a spiritual affinity. Both women exhibit a combinatory spiritual heritage. As Winfrey built a media empire centered around her own television talk show, *The Oprah Winfrey Show*, she attained a rarefied level of influence that served as a platform for and was in part constituted by her public spirituality. Religious studies scholar Kathryn Lofton has provided the most cogent analysis of Winfrey's religious and spiritual influences. Regarding Winfrey's spirituality, Lofton argues that aside from being raised within Afro-Protestant churches, "the spiritual genealogy of Winfrey's spiritual products" can be analyzed to reveal "shards of nineteenth-century experimental metaphysics, African American worship strategies, Eastern spirituality, and American free thought."[183] Turner, as discussed in the previous chapters, has much the same spiritual genealogy. Turner's religiosity combines Afro-Protestant Christianity (primarily Black Baptist, but with Black Pentecostal influence as well), Soka Gakkai Nichiren Buddhism, and an "experimental metaphysics" that participates in the stream of American metaphysical religion. Much as Turner classified herself as a spiritual seeker, so too could we classify Winfrey.[184] Through her identity as a spiritual seeker and as an influential public figure, Winfrey comes to function as something like a preacher, just as Turner aspires to be a religious teacher.[185]

The third affinity that Turner and Winfrey share is their respective presentations of a universal persona. Central to Winfrey's brand is her presentation as a relatable, universal persona. This persona is *not* raceless or genderless, for, as Lofton demonstrates, "If you watch or read the products of the Oprah Winfrey empire, you not only know Winfrey is *black* by her own description but you are also persistently made to believe that her blackness matters."[186] Nonetheless, socially in the context of her media platform, Winfrey has been careful to distance herself from any association with "the radicalism of Seventies feminism and sixties civil rights," Black Power sentiments, or any such movement; Winfrey performs a kind of Black accessibility and universality.[187] The same could be said for Tina Turner. Turner's simultaneous acknowledgment of herself as a Black woman *and* her felt sense of universality (see chap. 2 above); her roots in Black soul, gospel, and rhythm and blues *combined* with her own encouragement of public association of her with white, male rock artists; and her relocation to Europe because of commercial success *and* the stultifying effects of racism in the United States all mark Turner as simultaneously specifically Black and universally appealing. Like Winfrey, this appeal became a key feature of Turner's brand.

Finally, as a corollary to both women's identities as spiritual seekers, both Turner and Winfrey make religion and spirituality cornerstones of their commercial success, and, to that end, they promulgate the wildest-dreams message. They have publicly discussed their personal and professional highs and lows, and they have publicly shared their traumas. Rather than succumb to adversity, Winfrey and Turner both advocate for people's transformative capacity to envision and enact new possibilities for themselves. For Winfrey, this ability comes from the capacity to first learn from other spiritual teachings and traditions (often through reading, makeovers, consumption, and featuring spiritual teachers) and then act on what has been learned.[188] For Turner, this capacity is seen to stem from the innate buddha-nature of each person, as espoused in the teachings of Soka Gakkai Nichiren Buddhism (teachings that Turner augments with her reliance on psychics and astrology). Once this capacity is activated, a person can dream new possibilities and manifest those dreams. Winfrey and Turner present themselves as exemplifiers of this process. Winfrey herself would later say to Turner: "You don't just sing and dance. You represent possibility. When people see you performing, they know you've come up from the depths of despair. It means that however down a woman is, she can be like you."[189] In referencing Turner's performances, Winfrey alludes to the wildest-dreams rock aesthetic that Turner's concerts embody. Thus, central to the brand of both women is this religious belief in the power of wildest dreams, in the transformative power of possibility.

These four affinities account for the reason why, after Turner's first 1997 appearance on *The Oprah Winfrey Show*, Winfrey has labored to cement Turner's status as an American legend and to elevate Turner to the company of Black American greats. Lofton demonstrates that the highlighting and elevation of people were central aims in Oprah Winfrey's vision of her talk show.[190] Over the course of her show, Winfrey would highlight the importance of Maya Angelou, Toni Morrison, Coretta Scott King, and other prominent, illustrious African Americans.[191] Winfrey works to elevate Turner to their company because, as with them, her affinities with Turner render Turner on-brand. Since Turner is on-brand, Winfrey can relate to her. And if she can relate to Turner, then anyone in her vast network of influence can relate to Turner. That this is true is borne out by the easy rapport that Winfrey and Turner display on air, as the camera shows the smiling faces and nodding heads of their approving audience (one imagines that at least some of the guests—used to seeing Turner especially in the company of white men in the record industry—relish seeing the two ladies perform Black *sistahood*).

With endorsements from Oprah Winfrey and bolstered by appearances on *Larry King Live* (discussed in this book's introduction), *60 Minutes*, and other American television programs, Turner's Wildest Dreams Tour 1996–1997 was a success in America: (with Winfrey's help) it cemented Turner's status as an American icon. The tour cemented Turner's reputation as a commercially successful, headlining concert act, and it firmly associated Turner with the wildest-dreams rock aesthetic and the wildest-dreams message of the transformative power of dreaming.

Conclusion

"Raise your hands," Turner commands her audience during the finale to her filmed concert at Amsterdam Arena. "Sway to the music with me and as you leave this wonderful and beautiful venue, think about me and I'll think about you." Fifty thousand hands immediately go up and begin swaying as Turner begins to sing "On Silent Wings," a track from the *Wildest Dreams* album. As the skycam runs over the audience, the viewer of the concert video is afforded a meta-perspective and can observe the emotion on the face of many audience members as they stare at the stage transfixed, swaying solemnly to the music. This is the wildest-dreams rock aesthetic in effect. One imagines that as they watched Turner and swayed one final time, at least some of them felt what Oprah Winfrey, Taro Gold, and Sean Jackson felt when they saw the Wildest Dreams Tour: that they participated in a religious experience crafted and engendered by Tina Turner. Further, perhaps they grasped the message that the tour and all of Turner's concerts embodied: the transformative power of possibility encapsulated in the "wildest dreams" message. Turner honed this message over the course of her career as a solo entertainer.

From 1982 to 1984, Turner worked to overcome racism and sexism in the music industry and secure a major record deal. Securing such a deal was the crucial component in making the hit records that would enable her to fulfill her wildest dream of being the first Black woman to fill stadiums as a solo, headlining artist. She used her Buddhist practice, specifically chanting *Nam-myoho-renge-kyo* and studying Daisaku Ikeda's guidance on perseverance, to fuel her determination to succeed. The result was her multiplatinum *Private Dancer* album, the success of which paved the way for a headlining arena tour. This was followed by commercially successful albums, supported by headlining stadium tours, which saw her dream be fulfilled.

With the release first of *I, Tina* and then the biographical film *What's Love Got to Do with It?*, Turner's life story became a symbolic narrative of triumph over adversity. This narrative then became the central focus of Turner's image when her album and tour were named "Wildest Dreams," ostensibly because of a song on the album, but ultimately to capitalize on the wildest-dreams message of adversity overcome and dreams accomplished. On the ensuing concert tour, Turner worked with her production team to craft a show that embodied her brand and invited the audience into a rock-concert-cum-religious experience, with her at its center, and with Buddhism and metaphysical religion as its power source. By detailing her Buddhist practice and metaphysically inflected beliefs on mainstream television while promoting the album and tour, Turner became one of the highest-profile African American Buddhists, and thereby made a space for African American Buddhism as a part of American religious experience, even as Turner herself moved abroad and increasingly turned her focus toward Europe.

After a two-year break that saw Turner engaged in one-off projects, she returned with her *Twenty Four Seven* album (Parlophone, 1999; Virgin, 2000) and the subsequent Twenty-Four Seven World Tour 2000, which was the highest-grossing tour of the year in North America. That tour was followed by the Fiftieth Anniversary Concert Tour 2008–2009. The latter tour was billed as her final tour, celebrating fifty years in the music business (counting from her 1958 appearance as "Little Ann" on the song "Box Top"). Turner described her reason for retiring from live performances in *My Love Story*: "After working so hard for so many years, I was ready to stop. This was the moment to do it because I wanted to finish with my fans remembering me at my best. I didn't want them to come to a show in a year, or two years, and think *Oh, she used to be good*. I had a lot of pride and I've always had great timing. There's a wise expression, 'Leave the party before it's over.' I was ready to say goodbye to 'Proud Mary,' ready to hang up my dancing shoes, and ready to go home."[192]

This tour was her farewell to her fans and a capstone to her career. The Fiftieth Anniversary Concert Tour ended on May 5, 2009, in Sheffield, England. She sang her encore song, "Be Tender with Me, Baby," walked to each side of the stage, turned to walk backstage, turned and looked out at her audience, and waved good-bye one final time. With that, Turner had fulfilled her wildest dreams—"My wildest dream was to have this kind of success"[193]—and was now retired from live performing, at the age of sixty-nine.

One of Turner's wildest dreams had indeed come true: mainstream solo success, stadiums filled with adoring fans. Beyond the dream of mainstream success, there was one final wildest dream to fulfill: to become a religious teacher.

6

Beyond and Beyond

*When I'm ready, I will devote all my time to that—I'll tell
what I've learned. Many of you will listen, and some of
you will hear.*

—Tina Turner, *I, Tina*

Though for much of her life and career Tina Turner did not consider
herself a spiritual or religious teacher, the above epigraph, quoted
from the epilogue to her 1986 autobiography, *I, Tina*, shows that Turner
believed she would eventually be a religious teacher. Until her retirement
from live performing, Turner had limited herself to discussing her beliefs
and practices in interviews given amid the promotion of her work. Prior
to *I, Tina*, Turner stated that while success had been useful to her and her
loved ones, and while most of her "earthly dreams" had come true, she
knew that "singing and dancing weren't the fulfillment" of her destiny.
Instead, she wanted to teach about spirituality. She clarified, though, that
since her career was "still in bloom," she would not "confuse performing
and spiritual teaching."[1] And yet, she nonetheless hoped that *I, Tina* contained a message, that is, "The real power behind whatever success I have
now was something I found within myself—something that's in all of us,
I think, a little piece of God just waiting to be discovered."[2] She then offers
the prescription to her readers that they "purge" themselves of anything
holding them back, for the sake of liberating their true selves. So, she was in

fact teaching already. Yet, she did not explicitly consider herself a religious teacher until the release of the first *Beyond* album.

Beyond: Buddhist and Christian Prayers (UMG, 2009) was the first of several collaborative, interfaith albums that Turner would release under the auspices of the Beyond Music Foundation, cofounded by Regula Curti. Released between 2009 and 2018, these albums would see Turner begin to fulfill her final wildest dream of consciously stepping into the role of spiritual teacher. Then, in 2020, Turner released her third book, *Happiness Becomes You: A Guide to Changing Your Life for Good*, a coauthored memoir in the form of a self-help guide that uses her life experiences to elucidate religious (primarily Buddhist) principles. Together, the *Beyond* albums and *Happiness Becomes You* see Turner fully embody the role of religious teacher. Amid these projects, Turner experienced major changes in her personal life: Turner lost her mother, Zelma, her sister, Alline, and her son Craig Turner. In 2013, she married her longtime partner, Erwin Bach; also in 2013, Turner suffered a stroke, followed by intestinal cancer and kidney failure. Turner's reflections on these changes are captured in interviews given to promote *Beyond* and in the Buddhist memoir *Happiness Becomes You*.

Beyond and *Children Beyond*

Tina Turner was interviewed by Andrea Miller for the September 2011 issue of *Shambhala Sun* magazine to discuss the release of the first two *Beyond* albums: *Beyond (Gold Edition): Buddhist and Christian Prayers* and *Children Beyond* (UMG, 2011).[3] Turner explained to Miller that while she was "already on the journey of unity, of thinking about how there are religious wars and how someone has to help people know that God is to be found within, so that peace and harmony will evolve," she was invited to participate on the *Beyond* albums by Regula Curti.[4]

Regula Curti was born into a Swiss family and grew up singing and playing musical instruments. Later, she received her master's degree in music therapy and the expressive arts.[5] Though raised in a Protestant Christian family, Curti eventually studied Harbhajan Singh Khalsa's ("Yogi Bhajan") Kundalini Yoga in Thailand and India, and she was certified to teach in this tradition. Curti learned to sing and chant mantras, alongside the usage of sound for healing purposes from Khalsa's teachings.[6] In 2005, Curti and Dechen Shak-Dagsay, a Swiss singer born in Tibet, coorganized an interreligious dialogue between the Dalai Lama and Abbot Martin Werlen, abbot of Einsiedeln Abbey, a Benedictine monastery in Einsiedeln, Switzerland. At this event, Curti was struck by the emphasis that both figures put on remaining within the religious tradition one is raised in, rather than conversion to another religion. Curti then decided to explore the Christian prayers and hymns that she had grown up with. In 2007, Curti cofounded the Beyond Foundation with her husband to explore the healing and unitive elements of music.[7] At the same time, Curti and Shak-Dagsay began conceiving of an album joining Buddhist and Christian prayers together, with the idea of using the music to spur interreligious dialogue. Both realized that to reach a wider audience for their collaboration, they would need to add another singer with a wider reach to the project. Curti asked her friend Tina Turner if she would join the project.[8]

Curti met Turner six years prior to establishing the Beyond Foundation and Beyond Music Foundation, when the latter sought information about Beat Curti, Regula Curti's husband and the previous owner of Chateau Algonquin, Turner's home in Kusnacht, Switzerland.[9] Curti and Turner began a friendship around their mutual interests in music, religion, and spirituality. Turner recalls that Curti called her in the summer of 2008 and told her that she had heard Turner's voice in her "morning meditation and took that as a signal to ask" if Turner would contribute a spoken message to the album that she and Shak-Dagsay were developing.[10] Turner had seen a rainbow over Lake Zurich on the same morning that Curti called, which convinced her that "something deeply meaningful would come from this day." Turner further explained, "I believe in heavenly signs and good omens from Mother Nature. To me, rainbows symbolize peace, diversity, and awakenings," once again displaying the influence of her long-deceased maternal grandmother, Georgianna Flagg.[11] Influenced by these heavenly signs and remembering that, as she first disclosed in *I, Tina*, she aspired to be a spiritual teacher, Turner agreed to join the project and contribute a series of spoken-word messages.

Before beginning the Fiftieth Anniversary Concert Tour, Turner and Erwin Bach met with Deepak Chopra in Carlsbad, California, to consult about her contribution to Curti and Shak-Dagsay's album. Turner had read

Chopra's books, like *The Seven Spiritual Laws of Success*, and had "long admired his ability to explain multicultural spiritual concepts to a wider audience."[12] Chopra gave Turner a collection of "spiritual books" to read in preparation for writing her pieces for the album.[13] She then recorded her tracks for the album before going to Kansas City, Missouri, for the start of her tour. The album, *Beyond: Buddhist and Christian Prayers* (Universal Music Group, 2009), was released in Germany and Switzerland in June 2009. Turner contributed four pieces to the album: "Beyond: Spiritual Message by Tina Turner,"[14] and three spoken interludes. The *Beyond (Gold Edition): Buddhist and Christian Prayers* album (Universal Music Group, 2009/New Earth Records, 2010) was released in November of the same year in Germany and Switzerland, and in 2010 in the United States. The liner notes contained a message from Curti and Shak-Dagsay, in which the singers extol the virtues of each person praying "in his own tradition" and encourage their listeners to engage in a singing that "takes you beyond to a place where love and compassion grow."[15] Turner echoed these sentiments when she explained to Andrea Miller that *Beyond* was "an invitation" for people to open their hearts and become united.[16] The liner notes also contain endorsements from the Dalai Lama and Abbot Martin Werlen, whose interreligious dialogue sparked the idea of the album. Additionally, the gold edition contains three additional tracks featuring Turner chanting *Nam-myoho-renge-kyo* ("Sound of Mystic Law") and reciting Soka Gakkai International's liturgical practice of *gongyo* ("Purity of Mind" and "Power of Forgiveness").

Turner's first contribution, "Beyond: Spiritual Message by Tina Turner," comes three minutes and fifteen seconds into track 1. When Turner's voice comes in, she speaks in a lower register reminiscent of the opening lines of "Proud Mary," discussed in chapter 2 above. In the first lines, she says:

> Nothing lasts forever, no one lives forever,
> the flower that fades and dies, winter passes and
> spring comes, embrace the cycle of life, that is the
> greatest love.

Turner first presents to her listener the Buddhist principle of impermanence. She speaks of the cyclical nature of life, wherein "nothing lasts forever, no one lives forever." In both mainstream and Mahayana Buddhist traditions, existence is often said to be characterized or "marked" by three principles: impermanence (Pali: *anicca*; Sanskrit: *anitya*); unsatisfactoriness (Pali: *dukkha*; Sanskrit: *duhkha*); and no-self (Pali: *anatta*; Sanskrit: *anatman*).[17] Someone who understands these three marks is said to correctly understand the nature of existence. In referring to this principle, Turner is implicitly orienting her listener to a Buddhist view of life.

In the context of expressing to Miller the ways in which her Buddhist practice takes care of her, Turner reveals that these Buddhist teachings, specifically on impermanence, held special relevance to her. "I feel alone now," Turner confided to Miller, "my mother is gone, my sister is gone."[18] Turner's mother, Zelma, died in 1999, while Turner was in Europe promoting her *Twenty Four Seven* album. Though the two were not estranged, Turner's relationship with Zelma had remained strained. Turner perceived that her mother had sided with Ike during their divorce and its aftermath. To Turner, it seemed that while Zelma eventually enjoyed being the mother of a celebrity, she never truly accepted Turner herself as her daughter. Nonetheless, Turner took care of her mother's daily necessities, including buying and maintaining her home. Turner remembered that on one occasion she brought Zelma to her homes in the South of France and Zurich, and the visit became such a source of conflict that Turner threatened to send her back to Los Angeles. Their contentious relationship continued until Zelma died. "I was deeply affected by her death," Turner summarized, "in part because I mourned the relationship we should have had with each other but never did."[19] Turner chose not to attend her mother's church services so that the day would remain about Zelma, and not about Turner's celebrity presence.[20] But Ike attended, even offering to provide limousines for Turner's family. However, Turner did organize and attend her mother's cremation and the scattering of her ashes. In a concert celebrating her sixtieth birthday the following month, Turner dedicated the song "Talk to My Heart" to her mother.[21] Alline, Turner's sister whom she had remained close to, also died on September 4, 2010.

Though Turner does not mention Ike's death to Miller, Ike Turner died on December 12, 2007, of a cocaine overdose. At the time, Turner's only statement regarding his death was released through a spokesperson: "Tina is aware that Ike passed away earlier today. She has not had any contact with him in 35 years. No further comment will be made."[22] Turner herself would later write in *My Love Story* that she "felt strangely disconnected" upon hearing he had died, and that consequently she had understood that she had moved on.[23] This belies the fact that his death remains a complex subject for Turner. On other occasions she stated that discussing Ike brought nightmares, an experience Erwin Bach likened to Turner suffering a form of posttraumatic stress disorder.[24] Thus, while she may have felt nothing about his death, the memory of him was still a complicated subject for her.

All three deaths for Turner were alluded to by the Buddhist teaching of impermanence, which Turner encapsulated in the words "Nothing lasts forever, no one lives forever" in her spiritual message on *Beyond*. After these words, Turner next prescribes a series of practices for the listener:

> Start every day singing like the birds—singing
> takes you beyond, beyond, beyond, beyond.
> We all need a repeated discipline, a genuine
> training to let go our old habits of mind.

She emphasizes the need for "repeated discipline, a genuine training," and offers daily singing and prayer as examples of such discipline.[25] As per the contents of the album itself, this singing and praying need not necessarily be a formalized practice. Because each track on the album blends the singing of prayers from different traditions, the listener seems to be encouraged to do the same. What matters, from the standpoint of the message, is that it is done as a daily training. The result of such daily training is that "the head is clear," peace is brought back "to the soul," and the listener is taken "beyond." The daily training is the *how* behind Turner's wildest-dreams rock aesthetic. That is to say: if Turner's concerts embody and constitute the wildest-dreams rock aesthetic, Turner's prescription of daily training is the practical way that her audience can enact that aesthetic for themselves. At the end of the message, Turner summarizes by imploring her listener "to be in the present moment, to live in the beyond." Thus, over the course of the message, she introduces a Buddhist conception of the nature of life, prescribes a general daily practice, and summarizes the benefits of such a practice. Turner's usage of the spoken-word message format, combined with her familiar delivery style in the lower registers of her voice, recalls her most famous song, "Proud Mary." It also brings an echo of the chanted sermon discussed in chapter 1 above, familiar to Turner from her attendance at Black Baptist churches in Nutbush, Tennessee. Though she is teaching her audience a new message, it is still the same Turner familiar to them from her previous albums. This smooths the otherwise potentially jarring transition of hearing Turner the rock musician now teaching a message peppered with Buddhist themes in the context of atmospheric, "spiritual" music.

Beyond general prescriptions for daily practice, Turner contributes her personal practice to the album. "Purity of Mind" and "Power of Forgiveness" feature Turner's recitation of portions of chapter 2, "Expedient Means," of the Lotus Sutra, as presented in *The Liturgy of Soka Gakkai International*.[26] SGI president Daisaku Ikeda summarizes the meaning of the chapter's title, "Expedient Means," and the import of the passages Turner is reciting in his commentary on this chapter in the Lotus Sutra. Ikeda writes, "the term 'expedient means' refers to the skillful means or methods Buddhas employ to guide people to enlightenment. The 'Expedient Means' chapter extols the wisdom of the Buddha to thus instruct the people."[27] In other words, in Soka Gakkai's understanding, this portion of the Lotus Sutra tells of the Buddha's ability to teach others. According to the writings of Nichiren, understanding the import of the passage is more important than understanding the specific words or content.[28] Nichiren, basing himself on the teachings of Zhiyi and the Tiantai school of Chinese Buddhism, identified chapters 2 and 16 as the primary chapters of the text.[29]

Nichiren recommended that his followers include these two chapters in their daily practice. For Soka Gakkai Nichiren Buddhists, recitation of the *daimoku* and portions of these two chapters forms their twice daily liturgical practice of *gongyo*. That this is at least one practice Turner has in mind when she says "singing takes you beyond" is made clear in a 2011 interview with *Lion's Roar* magazine. In answer to the question "In what way is singing a spiritual practice?" Turner replies:

Nam-myoho-renge-kyo is a song. In the Soka Gakkai tradition we are taught how to sing it. It is a sound and a rhythm and it touches a place inside you. That place we try to reach is the subconscious mind. I believe that it is the highest place and, if you communicate with it, that is when you receive information on what to do. Singing a song can make you cry. Singing a song can make you happy. That's spirit—the spirit inside of you. If you look up "spiritual" in a dictionary, you will find that it is your nature, it is the person you are. When you walk into a room, a person might say, "Oh, she's got great spirit." Or you can walk into a room and someone will say that you don't have spirit because it's not visible. You're kind of off or negative. Meditation and praying changes your spirit into something positive. If it is already positive, it makes it better. I think that is the best answer I can give you right now.

For Turner, to recite *Nam-myoho-renge-kyo* is to sing a song. Of crucial importance is that such singing be done aloud. In an issue of the *World Tribune*, a trimonthly SGI-USA publication, it is explained that "sound and voice have great significance in Buddhism. Chanting Nam-myoho-renge-kyo, the act of voicing the wonderful sound of the Mystic Law, is the bridge that fuses our lives with the Law of the universe."[30] According to this understanding, using the voice to chant the sound of *daimoku* aloud causes a harmonizing or fusion of the individual's life with dharma—understood here as the "Law of the universe." Turner understands the subconscious mind as being the site of this fusion. Therefore singing, chanting, and recitation practices enable practitioners to contact their "subconscious mind," just as she explained to Larry King on *Larry King Live*.

This echoes the teaching of the "nine consciousnesses" in Soka Gakkai doctrine. In the Buddhist philosophical school known as Vijnanavada, or the "Consciousness Doctrine," consciousness is said to have eight or nine layers. The first five layers correspond to the five sensory organs of the eyes, ears, nose, tongue, and skin, along with their perceptions of sight, sounds, smells, taste, and touch, respectively. The sixth layer is the conscious mind, which organizes these perceptions, and which perceives mental phenomena. The seventh layer is the individual sense of self, which the Buddhist perspective regards as a mistaken sense. The eighth layer is known as the *alaya-vijnana*, or the "storehouse consciousness," so called because it is said to be the place where individual and collective karma is "stored."[31] Some Buddhist thinkers considered the eighth consciousness to be stained by karma, and thus posited a further, pure level of consciousness called the *amala-vijnana*, or "stainless consciousness." Soka Gakkai uses this schema to describe the integration of the physical and psychological components of all people. Soka Gakkai Nichiren Buddhists understand the ninth consciousness to be the subconscious mind. Ikeda explains that "Nichiren did not expound the nine consciousnesses concept, but he adopted its bottom line that the ninth consciousness [the stainless consciousness] is equal to Buddhahood."[32] In other words, for practitioners of Soka Gakkai Nichiren Buddhism, the particulars of the schema are less important than the fundamental point that the soteriological aim of Buddhist practice—Buddhahood—is synonymous with the ninth consciousness. The ninth consciousness is, for Turner, the space of beyond as mystical state. As Turner explained to Miller, "There is a stage in practice where you don't faint, you don't black out, but you are in a space."[33] When this space is reached, the conscious mind ceases its functioning and truth is received from the subconscious mind. Turner makes explicit that it is meditation practice (chanting *Nam-myoho-renge-kyo*) that opens this space that Turner calls "beyond." In referencing the subconscious mind and its transformation through singing and prayer, Turner alludes to these teachings for her listener on *Beyond*, and for readers of her interview in *Shambhala Sun*.

In 2011, Turner, Regula Curti, and Dechen Shak-Dagsay released their second collaborative album, *Children Beyond: Understanding through Singing* (Universal Music Group, 2011). On this album, they were joined by a group of thirty children from Zurich representing Buddhism, Christianity, Hinduism, Judaism, Islam, and Sikhism.[34] "The album contributes," the liner notes gloss, "to fostering the spiritual development of humans, especially of children. It contributes to creating tolerance and peace. Beyond means the world of sounds beyond dualities because the music and the singing of the prayers, supported by prayer postures, by gestures and by dance, are transcending the intellectual understanding."[35] The liner notes provide illustrations of the "prayer postures" that accompany each of the album's tracks. Rather than layering prayers and chants from each tradition on top of each other, as the previous album did, *Children*

Beyond allows each tradition a separate track. With Turner appearing on four out of sixteen tracks, this album saw her singing prayers, chants, and mantras from each of these traditions. Additionally, Turner wrote another spoken-word message, "Calling," which serves as the first track on the album.

As with the first *Beyond* album, *Children Beyond* opens with a spiritual message written by Turner. Thus, Turner's piece establishes the guiding message of *Children Beyond*. "Calling" begins with the voices of the thirty children intoning "*ong*," a sacred syllable in the Sikh Gurmukhi language. After a minute or so, Turner's voice comes in:

> When you sing—you do the right thing
> When you pray—you find the right way
> So when you sing—you do the right thing
> When you move—you find the right groove.[36]

This message offers a set of simple prescriptions to the album's children's chorus, and therefore to any child who would hear the track, which can be read as a condensed form of Turner's "Spiritual Message" on the first *Beyond* album. Turner tells the children to sing, pray, clean their mind, stay active ("When you move—you find the right groove"), and to remove barriers between people ("Break the wall—for peace to all"). Why staying active should occur in a list that is primarily about spiritual training is unclear. Though it could be related to the fact that Curti is a Kundalini Yoga teacher and would thus see movement as integral to a spiritual practice; this would then have influenced Turner's message. Unlike Turner's message on the first album, which imbeds a specifically Buddhist worldview, her message to children remains on a nonsectarian level. Rather than any specific religious practice, the children are given broad principles alongside their intended result. Turner's message then closes with her final injunction to the children to "forget it never." Closing in this way seems to imply that if this were the only track a child heard, the child would still get the import of the entire album.

Turner next appears on tracks 9 and 13. "Jai Da Da: Prayer of the Soul" is track 9, which the liner notes gloss as originating in Judaism and of a "universal" language. Cryptically the song is subtitled the "Prayer of the Soul," with the explanation that it should be sung "to strengthen your soul against sadness and helplessness."[37] Track 13 is a *"shanti* mantra," or "peace mantra," named by its first line: "Sarvesham Svastir Bhavatu: Mantra of Peace." The full mantra is sung in Sanskrit on the album:

> Om
> Sarvesham svastir bhavatu
> Sarvesham shantir bhavatu
> Sarvesham poornam bhavatu
> Sarvesham Mangalam bhavatu
> Om shanti, shanti, shanti.[38]

Shanti mantras are primarily found in the layer of Vedic literature called Upanishads, though they are found outside of this corpus as well. All *shanti* mantras are prayers or metrical verses that are recited to bring about peace and auspicious, fortunate circumstances, often for both the reciter and the reciter's environment. No translation is provided in *Children Beyond*'s liner notes for the "Sarvesham Svastir Bhavatu" mantra, nor is any indication of its origins, except to say that it is from "Hinduism." The mantra could be translated: "*Om.* May there be well-being for all. May there be peace for all. May there be abundance for all. May there be auspiciousness for all. *Om* peace, peace, peace."[39] On this track Turner's voice is particularly powerful, and she engages in an extended call-and-response with the children, as if Turner were leading them in recitation.

Finally, Turner appears on track 14, "Unity: Prayer of Unity." This is the most haunting track of the album, and in it Turner leads another call-and-response as she intones "amen," ascending the musical scale as she does so. After the call-and-response, Shak-Dagsay repeats *"sarva mangalam"* four times in response to the children's *"om."* Then, Curti sings a melismatic *"amin"* in response to the children's *"om shanti."* Unlike the previous *Beyond* album, where Turner's participation is limited to providing the guiding spiritual message and chanting, *Children Beyond* sees Turner represent her combinatory religious sensibilities on record by engaging with prayers drawn from multiple religious traditions to provide an example of interfaith harmony to children. Turner's prescriptive recommendations to the *Children Beyond* choir in her spiritual message and her demonstration of interfaith practice alongside Curti, Shak-Dagsay, and their other contributors can be seen as a way to provide children with the resources and teachings that she had to intuit on her own as a child from her grandmothers, from her experiences in Afro-Protestant churches, and from the wilderness.[40]

On both *Beyond (Gold Edition): Buddhist and Christian Prayers* and *Children Beyond: Understanding through Singing*, Turner is presented as a religious teacher imparting the teachings and practices that she herself has found to be transformative.

Love Within: Beyond and Awakening: Beyond

The third *Beyond* album, *Love Within: Beyond* (UMG, 2014), returns to the format of the first album, where prayers from different traditions are layered on each track. As indicated in the title, the theme is love, specifically the love of mothers and goddesses. For this album, an additional singer, Sawani Shende-Sathaye, joined the collaboration. Shende-Sathaye, from Pune, India, contributed prayers and mantras drawn from Hinduism. Turner again contributed a spiritual message to the album.

Turner's spiritual message begins with her referencing mythical time by saying, "In the beginning we all depend on attention and affection of our mother or other caring people."[41] Turner acknowledges on the track that for one reason or another one's mother may be indifferent or absent, as Zelma was, and thus attention and affection may be rendered by "other caring people." Such a caring person might be someone like Turner's maternal grandmother, Georgianna Flagg. Turner would later say that, along with Zelma, Flagg was always in her thoughts[42] and that she often went back to Flagg's home in her dreams.[43] As the spiritual message continues, Turner draws upon her own experiences to say: "Believing after all I have lived that love is within me and has never left me. I go beyond my history, beyond my life experience, my wounds and my sufferings, I go beyond, beyond."[44] Thus, with her message, Turner adds another dimension to what "beyond" means. More than beyond division into unity (the message of *Beyond (Gold): Buddhist and Christian Prayers*) and more than the mystical space of the subconscious mind, beyond also is the transcendence of a traumatic past.

"This music is a praise," Turner continues, "to all divine mothers, goddesses and saints, to the female power within all of us. . . . Go to the mother within you."[45] In singing of the mother within as a goddess, Turner is likely alluding to a previous professional experience she had where she was chosen to act the titular role in a planned Merchant-Ivory Productions film called *The Goddess.* The movie was to be directed by Ismail Merchant (1936–2005), scripted by Indian writer Suketu Mehta, and feature a soundtrack by tabla player Zakir Hussain. Merchant had seen Turner perform at Radio City Music Hall on the What's Love? Tour '93 and decided at that time that he would one day script her in a film.[46] In February 2004, Turner traveled with Merchant to India for a two-week tour to prepare for the role.

While in India, Turner gave an interview to Madhu Jain for *Outlook India,* in which she connected the suffering and poverty of modern-day Delhi, India, to the historical experiences of African Americans in the early twentieth century. She explains to Jain: "First I saw was what looked like suffering. . . . But then I said to myself, wait a minute, OK, I see what is happening. It is living back in time. Though I have to add there is no reason for it to be as bad as it is. There is so much possibility, given a chance. . . . We were like that once. It was a tough life. Martin Luther King said it can be done and it was."[47] Initially, Turner seems to primitivize the Indian people she observes in Delhi when she says they are "living back in time." Her further comments, though, make clear that she is grasping for a way to relate the current conditions she observes to her own experiences as a Black person growing up in the rural American South: "We were like that once." Turner's comments here evoke a perception of shared historical experience between African Americans and Indians, a perception that led figures like Howard Thurman and Martin Luther King Jr. to a place of solidarity with oppressed peoples around the world.[48] Even though Turner finds points of commonality between her life experiences and the experiences of people in India, she never expressed any particular sense of belonging in India (or any other part of Asia), unlike those feelings that she voices for Europe. Interestingly, her comments imply that she sees the civil rights movement, exemplified in the person of Martin Luther King Jr., as having fundamentally changed conditions for Black Americans. One is left to wonder whether this was the perspective she held while with the Ike & Tina Turner Revue, where she and the group refrained from explicit comments about social movements (see chap. 2 above). By her third day in India, Turner related to Jain that she "realized people were not suffering" as much as she had thought they were. Thus, as it was Turner's first trip to India, her impressions continued to evolve throughout her trip.

Turner also reflected on what the notion of a goddess meant to her. She explained to Jain, "In the USA, there is no female equivalent to god. . . . For me the goddess is positive. She has strength and the ability to help." She also relayed to Jain how she believed in the "cosmic energy of men and women" and that she felt that "what is in a woman is coming from the earth." These were feelings that she told Jain she intuited. And though people seemed to worship more in India, Turner saw that they ultimately took their problems to a god rather than directing themselves inward.[49] She concluded her interview with Jain, and her trip to India, by reflecting on the spiritual aspects of music. Though *The Goddess* was never made due to Ismail Merchant's untimely death in 2005, Turner's professional experiences traveling to India for the role likely planted seeds that would sprout in her spiritual message on *Love Within: Beyond*.

Turner also returned to her Black Baptist roots on the album by singing a verse of "Amazing Grace" in the first track, and by reciting the "Lord's Prayer" in the song "Almighty." She also returned to her own composition "I Am a Motherless Child" for the song "Mother Within"—the track being overlapped with Dechen Shak-Dagsay's recitation of a mantra, Sawani's singing a prayer in Hindi, and Curti's singing of the antiphon "Regina Coeli."

The fourth *Beyond* album, *Awakening: Beyond* (Beyond Singing, 2017), was released in November 2017. This album saw Dechen Shak-Dagsay be replaced by Ani Choying Drolma. On this album, Turner's only contribution appears on track 6, "Awakening Beyond—Part 1." On this track Turner offers an English recitation of the Mahayana Buddhist Heart Sutra, alongside another spiritual message. Her recitation of this sutra is notable because, though the sutra is one of the most famous in Buddhism and holds great importance across Mahayana Buddhist traditions, it does not hold any importance in Soka Gakkai Nichiren Buddhism, nor did Nichiren put any particular emphasis on the text.[50] Turner's limited participation on this album may have been due to ongoing health challenges (see below).

Taken together, these four albums represent Turner's conscious transformation into a religious authority figure. With the *Beyond* albums Turner (and her collaborators) seeks to create new dispositions in her listening audience. In stepping into the role of a religious teacher, Turner is asking her listeners—those who have bought her records and heard her live performances—to listen to her in a new way. She asks them to listen to her now as a practice of what anthropologist Charles Hirschkind calls "an exercise of ethical self-discipline" in his article "The Ethics of Listening."[51] Hirschkind analyzes the act of listening to recorded sermons by Muslims in Egypt. Building from Pierre Bourdieu's work on the notion of *habitus*, Hirschkind explains that practices such as listening to these recorded sermons "inculcate dispositions and modes of sensory experience," which is to say that such practices are a type of training that instills certain ideas and ways of experiencing, the particulars of which are determined by the content and context of the practice. Hirschkind summarizes that, among other benefits of listening to the tapes, "with repeated and attentive listening, they can also lead listeners to change their ways."[52] Parallels could also be drawn, perhaps closer to Turner's own background, to the commodification of Black sermonizing, in the form of recorded sermons of Black preachers that were played on the radio and sold as phonograph records during her early life. These sermon records could convey new ideas and social messages to their listeners.[53] Much like the recorded sermons, the cassette sermons Hirschkind studied could be listened to in a variety of situations, such as "while operating a café or barbershop, while driving a bus or taxis, or at home with one's family after returning from work."[54] Just as the cassette sermons and recorded sermons have the potential to transform their listeners through the practice of listening as an ethical discipline, Turner and her collaborators hope for similar transformations to take place in their listeners, as evidenced by the liner notes to *Beyond (Gold Edition): Buddhist and Christian Prayers*, *Children Beyond: Understanding through Singing*, *Love Within: Beyond*, and *Awakening: Beyond*. They hope to create listeners who pray daily and "go beyond" to deeper places inside of themselves.

Practices of "ethical listening" are also enjoined by many passages throughout the Buddhist canons. These passages also describe the benefits of such listening. An example from the Buddhist Pali canon declares,

"There are these five rewards in listening to the Dhamma. Which five? One hears what one has not heard before. One clarifies what one has heard before. One gets rid of doubt. One's views are made straight. One's mind grows serene."[55] The fifth benefit resonates with one of the stated aims of the *Beyond* albums: to bring peace or serenity. In the Lotus Sutra as well, several passages call upon practitioners to hear the text. Chapter 2 of the Lotus Sutra, discussed above, states, "If there are those who hear the [Buddhist teachings], then not a one will fail to attain buddhahood."[56] This explicitly links hearing and soteriology: if one hears the teaching, one will attain Buddhahood, the soteriological goal of practice for Turner as a Soka Gakkai Nichiren Buddhist. By this logic, listening to Turner chant the Lotus Sutra on *Beyond (Gold Edition)* assures that listeners will attain Buddhahood. The benefits of this hearing, however, do not only accrue to the hearer. It also benefits the one who causes the hearing. In Soka Gakkai's understanding, the act of teaching others is subsumed under the concept of "practice for self and practice for others." For Turner's Buddhist practice in particular, the act of teaching ultimately benefits oneself.

As a religious teacher with a combinatory religious repertoire, Turner does more than convey Buddhist doctrines and Christian hymns on the *Beyond* albums. She also draws from the stream of American metaphysical religion. The title of the albums, *Beyond*, is explicitly drawn from a quote attributed to the Persian poet and mystic Rumi: "Out beyond ideas of right doing and wrongdoing, there is a field. I'll meet you there."[57] The liner notes to the first album make clear that Rumi's words are the guiding metaphor for the entire project. Cultural historian Leigh Eric Schmidt has traced how Rumi has been "refracted" through the works of stalwarts of American spirituality and seeker culture, through figures such as Walt Whitman and Coleman Barks.[58] By making Rumi's notion of the beyond the central refrain of her own spiritual message, Turner shows her indebtedness to American metaphysical religion but places it into a global context by working with collaborators from Europe, Asia, and the Middle East (on *Awakening: Beyond*). Turner's indebtedness is also seen in her reliance upon Deepak Chopra's inspiration and writings to craft her own teachings. In his writings, Chopra, a onetime disciple of Maharishi Mahesh Yogi and his Transcendental Meditation teachings, blends New Thought ideas, Western hermeticism, Vedantic Hinduism, and other hallmarks of the stream of metaphysical religion that birthed New Age religiosity.[59] In speaking of the subconscious mind as a space beyond and a space of truth, Turner places herself in this lineage of American metaphysicalist teachers, even as she teaches Buddhist doctrines and sings prayers drawn from other religious traditions. Turner the teacher is every bit as combinatory as Turner the practitioner.

Love

In 2013, the year before *Love Within: Beyond* was released, Turner made two commitments: she formalized her international focus by becoming a Swiss national, and she married Erwin Bach. Turner had already decided that, having lived in Switzerland with Bach since 1994, she would live the rest of her life there. Turner took the oath of Swiss nationality on April 10, 2013, and signed a "Statement of Voluntary Relinquishment of U.S. Citizenship" on October 24, 2013.[60] Henceforth, Turner was to be referred to as an "American-born Swiss entertainer."

Between those two dates, Turner married Bach in a ceremony held at their Chateau Algonquin estate in Kusnacht, Switzerland. Bach's brother, Jurgen Bach, was the best man; Rhonda Graam served as Turner's maid of honor. Turner and Bach were married in front of a floral Tree of Life, with the front of the house decorated in what Turner called a "Garden of Eden" effect. That Turner and Bach had been married in a civil ceremony on July 4, 2013, almost to the day thirty-seven years earlier that she had left Ike Turner, lent further significance to their union. Turner later explained to Oprah Winfrey that, in meeting Bach, she was looking to give love to a person and looking to be loved. This is captured in the title of Turner's 2018 autobiography, *My Love Story*. Despite the joy of their wedding, Turner had felt slightly ill that day. Three months later, she had a stroke.[61]

In October 2013, Turner woke up to discover that she could not speak. By the time Bach took Turner to the hospital, the entire right side of her body was paralyzed. She spent ten days in the hospital, relearning to walk and use her right hand. Turner turned to Traditional Chinese Medicine (TCM) as part of her therapy, just as she had turned to homeopathy in the eighties to cure her of tuberculosis. A year after the stroke, after the release of *Love Within: Beyond*, Turner began suffering from crippling bouts of vertigo. She had also discovered that after years of living with high blood pressure, her kidneys were functioning at only 35 percent. In January 2016, she was diagnosed with intestinal cancer. And by July of the same year, low kidney function forced her onto dialysis. Turner spent nine months on dialysis. During that time she would again turn to Deepak Chopra's writings, especially Chopra's *Book of Secrets: Unlocking the Hidden Dimensions of Your Life* (2004), for guidance about preparing for the "next world." She also turned to Dante's *Divine Comedy*, drawing parallels between his description of the soul's journey to heaven and her own journey through trials and tribulations to awakening. Through all of this, her husband, Erwin Bach, remained at her side, demonstrating to her that the internal love she proclaimed on *Love Within: Beyond* was also mirrored to her externally. By the time *Awakening: Beyond* was released, Turner had received a kidney transplant, with Bach as the donor.[62]

Erwin Bach was and is undoubtedly the bright spot in Turner's story. But there has also been a shadow side to her love story. The afterword to *My Love Story* relates the story of her son Craig Turner's death by suicide on July 3, 2018. Turner described her son as, ultimately, a "troubled soul." In interviews throughout her career, Turner remained guarded on the subject of her children, only acknowledging that they had "problems."[63] She believes that Craig suffered throughout his life from loneliness and memories of his childhood, during which, due to the Ike & Tina Turner Revue's touring and recording schedule, he could not spend much time with his mother. Turner had spoken to her son the month before his death, and he seemed, by Turner's estimation, to be making progress in life. Nonetheless, Craig had died. Turner wrote that she was shocked at the planning that had gone into his suicide. She held a private memorial service for him in Los Angeles, replete with military honors, as Craig had been in the navy. There was also a Buddhist memorial service for Craig, officiated by Matilda Buck (see chap. 3 above).[64] Like those of Turner's mother, Zelma, Craig's ashes were spread over the Pacific Ocean, with Turner throwing a single rose into the water as her good-bye. She ends the afterword by saying that she wished she could have passed on some of her own strength to her son.[65] Four years later Turner's youngest son, Ronnie Turner, died after a short battle with cancer. Perhaps with the

Beyond albums, especially *Children Beyond: Understanding through Singing*, she sought to teach others that which she wished to teach her own children and family.

Happiness Becomes You

Beyond was the beginning of Turner transitioning to a role as a religious teacher. Her transition was completed with the release of *Happiness Becomes You: A Guide to Changing Your Life for Good*. In the introduction, Turner makes explicit that this book completes her turn to teaching when she writes, "I always wanted to be a teacher, but I believed I should wait for the moment when I had something important to say, when I was sure how to offer real wisdom. That time is now."[66] She coauthored the book with Regula Curti and Taro Gold, and it is written in the form of a self-help guide, using Turner's life experiences to illustrate Buddhist concepts.

In the afterword, dated August 8, 2020, Curti writes of her first time seeing Tina Turner live at the Zurich Convention Center in December of 1983. For Curti, who had grown up in a conservative society, seeing Turner perform live was a liberating experience. "Leaving the concert that night," Curti relays, "I let go of my sense of limitations. Never in my wildest dreams did I expect such a life-changing experience from a rock 'n' roll show—it was by far the greatest gift of inspiration I'd ever received from a performer."[67] Curti's life-changing experience at Turner's concert demonstrates how even then, in 1983, Turner had carefully calibrated the rock concert experience for her audience to be about both entertainment and a religious sense of possibilities for the fulfillment of an attendee's wildest dreams. This experience set Curti on the path of developing the confidence and resources needed to leave her own unfulfilling marriage, as Turner had done. When Curti finally met Turner, it was a literal dream come true, as she had dreamed of "a large, mirrorlike lake with stunning white flowers on the far shore" and had met Turner at Chateau Algonquin on Lake Zurich, which Turner had decorated with an array of white flowers.[68] Curti and Turner developed a friendship that would eventually lead to Turner's participation on the four Beyond Music Foundation albums discussed above. In 2014, Curti met Taro Gold in Switzerland.

Taro Gold was born into a Buddhist family and grew up between Kyoto, Japan; Australia; California; and Spain. As a child, Gold performed in Broadway musicals before studying at Soka University in Tokyo, a university founded by Soka Gakkai International president Daisaku Ikeda. While working on an MFA at the University of California, Los Angeles, Gold began to collate his journals and essays into a book of inspirational quotes titled *Open Your Mind, Open Your Life: A Book of Eastern Wisdom* (2002). Among other books, Gold also authored *Living Wabi Sabi: The True Beauty of Your Life* (2004).[69] The influence of both books is seen in *Happiness Becomes You*, which peppers each chapter with inspirational quotes drawn from Nichiren, Gandhi, Maya Angelou, and others. Turner herself would name *Living Wabi Sabi* as one of her favorite books.[70] Like Regula Curti, Gold felt a sense of serendipity in the "mystical intersections of Turner's life" with his own.[71] He recalls that he read an interview in the late eighties where Turner spoke of her dream to share her spiritual journey with the world, and he felt a voice saying to him that he would help her do so, one day. In 1994, he met Ana and Wayne Shorter, who shared stories with Gold about their time with Turner. They also shared that when people would seek to learn about Buddhism from Turner, she would send them to Ana and Wayne. Gold also developed a friendship with Turner's son Craig. After meeting Curti in 2014, they discussed Turner's dream of writing a book and drafted a proposal to help Turner convey her thoughts as a teacher. Once Turner overcame her health challenges, they began work on the book that became *Happiness Becomes You*.[72]

In the book's first chapter, "Nature," Turner relates the details of her life in Nutbush, Tennessee, much as she did in *I, Tina* and *My Love Story*. But, in *Happiness Becomes You*, the focus is on how her early adversities occurred against the backdrop of Nutbush's natural environment. This environment revealed to her "an unseen universal force" at work in the universe, even as racism and abandonment served as ever-present visible forces. In this chapter, too, she gives a brief overview of her life with Ike—an indication that whereas in previous books her sixteen-plus years with Ike took an outsized role, now they are relegated to their true place as only one portion of her larger life. The lesson that Turner wishes to convey in this chapter is the same as that which opened the movie *What's Love Got to Do with It?*: "The thicker the mud, the stronger the lotus that blooms from it, rising above the muck to reach the sun. The same is true for people. I know, because I did it. And I know you can, too."[73] She prefaces this with an assurance that her life has taught her that adversity is not inherently negative, depending upon what is done with that adversity.

In chapter 2 of *Happiness Becomes You*, Turner recounts her introduction to Soka Gakkai Nichiren Buddhism. She explains how, through studying the writings of Daisaku Ikeda, she learned the Buddhist concept of the "ten worlds." A concept of central soteriological value in Nichiren Buddhism, the ten worlds range from the lowest world of hell to the world of Buddhahood, the world of awakened beings.[74] The ten worlds are both ontological states of existence and experiential psychological states. Thus, a person in the world of hell, a state of abject suffering, would experience intense psychic distress; a person in the world of Buddhahood would experience spiritual joy. In Nichiren's teachings, each of the ten worlds is understood to contain the potential of the other worlds.[75] Since each world contains the potential of the other worlds, this means that even in a state of suffering (hell), a person can experience joy (Buddhahood). In *Unlocking the Mysteries of Birth and Death*, a book listed in the bibliography of Turner's book, Ikeda expounds upon the ten worlds and concludes that through chanting *Nam-myoho-renge-kyo* a person can bring forth the best of all of the ten worlds.[76] Turner likens these worlds to Abraham Maslow's hierarchy of needs, where the world of hell parallels the struggle to fulfill basic psychological needs and Buddhahood parallels Maslow's description of self-actualization.[77] Turner illustrates the ten worlds for her reader with examples drawn from "a lazy Sunday morning in 1977." For Turner, the lesson to be taken from that day and the ten worlds doctrinal schema is that the world people inhabit, which is to say their life condition, determines how they experience their circumstances.[78] In making sustained comparisons between the psychological theories of Abraham Maslow and Carl Jung, the book is also heavily inflected with the modern psychological learnings of Buddhist modernist discourse.[79]

The following chapter depicts Turner's conversion to Buddhism. She gives a brief history of Buddhism and of the Lotus Sutra's reception in nineteenth-century America, through the writings of American transcendentalists.[80] She explains *Nam-myoho-renge-kyo*, calling it the "anthem of angels," and provides a discussion of karma (see chap. 4 above). Turner's treatment of karma in this chapter, and throughout the book, differs significantly from the comments she made to her assistant while in South Africa in 1980. In South Africa, Turner had explained to her assistant that the racial apartheid there was a part of South Africa's collective karma. As such, she did not allow herself or members of her entourage to become entangled with or reflect at length on the situation. Their job was to successfully perform their concerts and return to their own karmic cultural contexts. In *Happiness Becomes You*, by contrast, Turner's discussion of karma is more in line with the understanding of Soka Gakkai Nichiren Buddhism. Namely, that the import of the doctrine of karma is that people can take meaningful, transformative action to change their karma. Turner writes, for example, that Buddhist teachings emphasize "that when a problem arises, we shouldn't view it as something we deserve because of our negative karma."[81] Throughout the book, Turner also discusses the relationship between teachings on karma and social realities. Thus, her views on karma show an evolution from the beginning of her Buddhist practice in the seventies to the writing of *Happiness Becomes You*. Regarding her own transformed karma, she declares that it was faith, born of chanting, that helped her to change her karma and successfully bridge the gap between her reality and her dreams.[82] Though she ends the chapter by saying someone does not have to chant like she does to become "truly happy," the implicit message is that what worked for Turner will work for her listeners (read: students).

Chapter 4 recapitulates Turner's understanding of Soka Gakkai's philosophy of mind, expressed in the nine-consciousness doctrine. Just as she found parallels between Maslow's hierarchy of needs and the ten worlds, here she draws parallels between Jungian psychology and the nine consciousnesses. Specifically, Turner sees pronounced similarities between Jung's idea of collective memory, Buddhist notions of collective karma, and the eighth consciousness, or subconscious mind.[83] Intuition arises from the eighth consciousness, and to her strong intuition Turner credits her ability to "tune in" or maintain a spiritual sense of what was happening behind her on concert stages even without seeing it.[84] This same eighth consciousness is where negative voices or negative psychological conditioning resides; for this, Turner revealed that when negative thoughts arose from her subconscious, she would consciously repeat eight positive thoughts. As racism and classism form part of the collective memory or karma of American society,[85] her negative thoughts included the internalization of experiences of discrimination in her personal and professional life. Turner reveals that it is the practice of tapping into the subconscious mind and purifying it, with purity being a characteristic of the ninth consciousness, that enabled her to overcome such discrimination.[86]

"Changing Poison into Medicine," the fifth chapter, is the core of the book. A phrase drawn from writings attributed to Nagarjuna, a second-century Buddhist philosopher, "changing poison into medicine," is another key doctrinal concept in Soka Gakkai Nichiren Buddhism. Soka Gakkai literature explains that "This phrase is often cited to show that any problem or suffering can be transformed eventually into the greatest happiness and fulfillment in life."[87] Turner recalls learning this concept while attending Buddhist meetings, immediately after leaving Ike in 1976. In one such meeting, after detailing the problems she was facing, an older Japanese woman named Kimiko explained to Turner that because she had so many problems, so much poison, she could turn her situation in a positive direction. In other words, she could change poison into medicine.[88] It was this principle, Turner discloses, that enabled her to face her difficult situation and overcome it. Illustrating the practical nature of the book, Turner again draws an example from her career to explain the concept. Before a show in New Zealand (likely occurring on the What's Love? Tour '93), Turner wakes up after a late party with a headache and food poisoning (and a hangover?). She felt herself too ill to perform, and there was a torrential rainstorm. Since her fans had paid to see the show, "made sacrifices to get tickets, travelled to the venue, and were willing to stand in the rain," she felt she could not cancel the show in good conscience. So, she chanted to transform the situation, to change poison into medicine, and after an hour of chanting she was able to perform one of her best shows.[89] The lesson gleaned from this: no matter how small or large the problem, it can be transformed for the better. So central is this message to Turner that she would go on to proclaim it as *the* theme of her life before audiences at the London, Hamburg, and Broadway premiers of *Tina: The Tina Turner Musical*. The remaining chapters of *Happiness*

Becomes You discuss human revolution (chap. 6; see chap. 4 above) and her interfaith *Beyond* albums (chap. 7).

The last chapter, "Homecoming," sees Turner address the importance of mental and physical health, alongside encouragement to use the teachings of the book to develop social and environmental ethics. About her son Craig's death by suicide, Turner writes, "it wasn't until his sudden death that I began to understand that Craig faced serious mental health challenges, ones he was not equipped to overcome on his own." This prompts her to reflect on the stigma around addressing mental health that prevents those in need from seeking (or receiving) help. This is especially true, Turner reflects, "for men, and I think it's even worse for Black men, like my son."[90] In coming to terms with the death of her son, Turner also reckons with the broader implications of a contemporary mental health crisis. Following the prescriptive nature of the book, Turner implores others to seek proper treatment if they or anyone they know is suffering on account of their mental health. Turner forestalls the criticism that in focusing on personal solutions and responsibility for mental health she is ignoring the structural causes of the mental health crisis by discussing "the fracturing of society" as a cause of the mental health crisis.

In Turner's understanding, the fractured nature of society also leads to racial, national, or religious division.[91] For Turner, such fragmentation can only be overcome by awakening to our shared identity as human beings: "I believe that only by awakening to this shared identity can we save ourselves, individually and collectively, from the problems we face around the world. We must urgently work together to find solutions that can transform the global poisons of systemic racism and homophobia, climate crisis, pandemics, loss of the Amazon jungle, factory farming of animals, fossil fuel consumption, nuclear weapons, plastic pollution, and more. The universal solution to all of the problems confronting humanity is for us to unite as one global team, honoring our truest roots as members of the same circle of life."[92] Here Turner shows that she understands *all* social, political, and environmental issues as having a singular root. That root is the fragmentation of society, rooted in division. Because the root is singular, Turner argues for a singular solution: awakening to our shared identity. These sentiments directly echo the teachings of Daisaku

Ikeda, who similarly argues that social division is the root cause of many of society's problems. Ikeda's understanding is most clearly evident in his response to the 1992 Los Angeles Riots, a long-form poem titled "Sun of Jiyu over a New Land." In one stanza of the poem Ikeda wrote: "As each group seeks its separate roots and origins, society fractures along a thousand fissure lines. When neighbors distance themselves from neighbors, continue your uncompromising quest for your truer roots in the deepest regions of your life. Seek out the primordial 'roots' of humankind."[93] The next two stanzas name these "primordial roots" as the life state of Jiyu (the bodhisattvas of the earth named in chapter 15 of the Lotus Sutra). If one reaches to these roots, Ikeda explains, then one will reach a place beyond divisions of borders, race, and gender and thereby find that "all become friends and comrades." The unmistakable echo between Turner's conviction that awakening to shared identity is the solution to the fragmentation at the root of societal problems and Ikeda's conviction that awakening to a deeper, religio-racial identity as bodhisattvas of the earth is the solution for the same,[94] shows that in *Happiness Becomes You* Turner is relying on the teachings of Soka Gakkai Nichiren Buddhism to explicitly address social concerns. This is a significant change for Turner because, as discussed above, throughout her career she often avoided social movements and, with rare exceptions, refrained from discussing social issues. That her discussion of these issues is placed in the final chapter of her book highlights that addressing social issues has become a primary concern for Turner.

Conclusion

Happiness Becomes You, then, presents Turner's teachings in a compact Buddhist memoir. The whole of the book can be seen as moving from Turner's personal transformation (chap. 1) to her consideration of societal or collective transformation (chaps. 7 and 8). Structuring *Happiness Becomes You* this way makes the book echo Turner's spiritual message on *Love Within: Beyond*. "I go beyond my history, beyond my live[d] experience, my wounds and my sufferings," Turner said in her spiritual message.[95] With *Happiness Becomes You*, she has now written what she spoke and sang on *Beyond*. Given the nature of the book, the presentation is necessarily prescriptive. Though peppered with assurances that a variety of religious and spiritual practices can help her readers to develop and fulfill their own wildest dreams, she is clear that, for her, chanting *Nam-myoho-renge-kyo* is the central node in her religious net, a net that includes Black Baptist Christianity, American metaphysical religion, and Soka Gakkai Nichiren Buddhism.[96]

With *Happiness Becomes You*, Turner joins the list of Black Buddhist teachers who have used the genre of memoir to express their Buddhist teachings, even as Turner's book veers firmly in the direction of self-help. *Happiness Becomes You* embodies a trend, noted by scholar Rima Vesely-Flad, in Black and feminist studies toward recognizing "the importance of prioritizing inner life while challenging violent institutions."[97] Incorporating the work of Kevin Quashie, Vesely-Flad argues that rather than overly emphasizing Black people's resistance to racially induced suffering, greater attention should be paid to the interior lives of Black people. In Vesely-Flad's analysis, such a focus reveals "a way of being in which an individual takes note of social forces and oppressive dynamics, including one's own experiences, but does not internalize the degrading messages inherent in those oppressive encounters."[98] Vesely-Flad's book, subtitled *The Practice of Stillness in the Movement for Liberation*, explores Buddhist practices that develop and reinforce this way of being. Vesely-Flad summarizes that her book "honors the long, slow process of Black people quieting their thoughts, delving into their own interior lives, and healing the fractures that have widened with intergenerational trauma and social degradation."[99] Turner's own book makes Buddhism and spiritual practice—prayer, chanting, quiet reflection, and observation of the natural world—central to both her own healing and liberation and central to her understanding of the possibilities for collective liberation. Therefore, as Black Buddhist writing, Turner's book participates in the trend noted by Vesely-Flad. Taken as whole, the book, though, is quintessentially Turner: in *Happiness Becomes You*, Turner teaches her reader, her students, to embody the same combinatory religiosity that she herself has propounded throughout her life and career.

Turner's teachings expressed across the four *Beyond* albums can also be seen to participate in this trend toward prioritizing interiority. In making "beyond"—to Turner both a personal space of quiet spiritual reflection and a social location transcending differences—the guiding metaphor of the albums, Turner (and her collaborators) prescribes spiritual practices of chanting, stillness, and reflection as remedies for social division. However, these practices do not preclude social action; instead, they ground social action. Activist Rosemarie Freeney Harding, briefly mentioned above in chapter 1, shared her observation that in social justice activism there is a mysticism that can be fostered. This is the African American mysticism of Harding herself and other civil rights activists like Howard Thurman. Regarding her work in the civil rights movement, Harding shared, "We experienced something extraordinary in the freedom movement, something that hinted at a tremendous potential for love and community and transformation that exists here in this scarred, spectacular country. For many of us, that 'something' touched us in the deepest part of our selves and challenged us in ways both personal and political."[100] This mysticism provided the bedrock for their activist work. On the *Beyond* albums and in *Happiness Becomes You*, Turner gestures in this direction with her teaching about the space *beyond* and her concluding reflections on awakening to shared humanity to heal social fragmentation, respectively. Thus, Turner as religious teacher joins a line of Black Buddhist teachers who employ Buddhist practices and teachings for personal and social liberation, and she joins a line of African American mystic activists who reach into a space beyond to ground their social activism.

Turner's first wildest dream was to fill stadiums as a solo, Black female rock 'n' roll artist. When she set out to rebuild her career after leaving Ike Turner in 1976, this dream seemed wild indeed. Through focusing on her religious training, she honed her vision, mustered her determination, and embarked on a series of increasingly larger world tours. She retired from live performing in 2009, having accomplished this dream. As she was accomplishing that dream, another dream came into focus. Turner wanted to teach others what she had learned. Between 2009 and 2020, Turner collaborated on *Beyond (Gold Edition): Buddhist and Christian Prayers*; *Children Beyond: Understanding through Singing*; *Love Within: Beyond*; and *Awakening: Beyond*, and wrote *Happiness Becomes You: A Guide to Changing*

Your Life for Good. Through these projects, Turner encapsulated the lessons drawn from her personal experiences, from a six-decade career in the music business, from a lifetime of religious practice, to present a mature synthesis of her Afro-Protestant, Buddhist, and American metaphysical religious training. Tina Turner had now fulfilled her final wildest dream to become a spiritual teacher.

Epilogue

Tina Turner debuted on a new stage on November 7, 2019. Her musical, *Tina: The Tina Turner Musical*, premiered on Broadway to a capacity crowd at the Lunt-Fontanne Theatre. The musical, much like Turner's memoirs and the movie *What's Love Got to Do with It?*, follows her early life, turbulent marriage to Ike Turner, personal tragedies, and ultimate triumph. As I do here, the musical places Turner's religiosity where it belongs, at the center of her story.

At every major juncture of Turner's life there was religion: she learned to dream in the cotton fields of Nutbush and found comfort in the natural, earthy spirituality of her maternal grandmother. This spirituality was itself rooted in a stream of Black southern religious culture that centered conjure, root work, dreams, visions, signs, and the wilderness experience. Through her paternal grandmother, she was educated in the strictures of rural, Black Baptist womanhood. In this context, she found her voice at Woodlawn Missionary Baptist Church and Spring Hill Baptist Church, even as she become aware of new performative possibilities for Black women in the Black Pentecostal movement. Six years into her relationship with Ike Turner she was deeply unhappy, suffering under the weight of Ike Turner's violent temper and controlling impulses. We may think of this time as another wilderness experience for Tina Turner. When I think of Turner's tenure with the Ike & Tina Turner Revue, I cannot help but be reminded of these words that Pearl Cleage wrote about her: "If we had seen the pain behind Tina Turner's powerhouse performances with the *Ike and Tina Turner Revue*, I like to believe we would have intervened, called for backup, and spirited our sister out of harm's way. But we didn't know, until she told us everything."[1] Of course, that didn't happen. Only those closest to the couple knew about his abuse, and for one reason or another they were powerless to stop it. By the time she began to tell her story, she had been separated from Ike Turner for five years. A friend in London brought her to a psychic who gave her crucial encouragement. This birthed an enduring reliance upon psychics, astrology, and ideas that we can call American metaphysical religion, a label that, as I use it, also includes the mystical and supernatural aspects of Black southern religious culture. Turner was then introduced to Soka Gakkai Nichiren Buddhism, through three encounters, initiated by her youngest son, Ronnie Turner. She combined the teachings of Buddhism with the guidance of one psychic in particular, Carol Ann Dryer, to process the trauma of her marriage to and divorce from Ike Turner. Along the way she chanted and formulated an ever-expansive dream for her future, which culminated in her successful commercial comeback in the eighties. Alongside her extensive musical oeuvre, Turner embarked upon some of the most extensive concert tours of the twentieth and twenty-first centuries. According to some estimates, she has sold more concert tickets than any solo performer in history. Turner has performed some of the greatest live concerts of the last two centuries, and two of her tours still hold concert attendance records. These performances were fueled by an intensive religious practice and set of beliefs, which blended Black Baptist Christianity, Soka Gakkai Nichiren Buddhism, and American metaphysical religious sensibilities. She finally retired in the twenty-first century as a global icon.

Turner moved to London, England, in 1988 and never resided in the United States again. In 2013, she became a Swiss national. However, as historian Henry Louis Gates Jr. wrote, "Still, Tina is indelibly American—and African American at that."[2] By this, Gates meant that Turner's upbringing and sensibilities are rooted in the experiences of Black Americans in the southern United States. Something similar is true of Turner's religious sensibilities. Turner inherits religious ideas that are drawn from Asia, Africa, and Europe, and she has transmitted those ideas across the globe on record-breaking world tours. In this sense, her religious sensibilities are best understood in a global context. Yet, the particular ways in which she combines three streams, Afro-Protestant Christianity, Buddhism, and (American) metaphysical religion, have deep historical roots and are quintessentially American—and African American at that.

Turner fulfilled her ultimate wildest dream of becoming a religious teacher, first by recording the *Beyond* albums and then by writing a memoir illustrating Buddhist teachings. Throughout her career, she had focused on the many: the mainstream, record-buying public. But, with these two projects, she turned her attention to the some who would hear. In the end, she's asking her audience to do what they've always done: listen to her. This time, though, she's asking them to listen in a new way; she's asking them to listen and be transformed. She's asking them to listen ethically. What Turner is teaching is best characterized as a hybrid religious sensibility. It stands both in the stream of American Buddhism, under the broad umbrella of the American branch of the Soka Gakkai International Buddhist organization, and in the tradition of American metaphysical religion, which encompasses a variety of religious tendencies, including astrology, utilization of psychics, and New Age beliefs. What is true of Tina Turner as a teacher is likely true of many others, just waiting to be discovered in American religious history. When we, as scholars, augment our work in the archives with detailed attention to popular culture, what other Black women might we find who use their religious repertoires to instruct us in a skillful combination of religious sensibilities?

Turner's death on May 24, 2023, lends new poignancy to her final public appearance in the United States. She traveled to New York City in November 2019 to attend the premier of her musical on Broadway. At the Broadway premier of *Tina: The Tina Turner Musical*, Tina Turner looked radiant. Wearing her trademark high heels and a gown outfitted with glittering Swarovski crystals, she entered the theater flanked by two of her biggest champions, American media mogul Oprah Winfrey and Turner's husband, Erwin Bach. At the end of the show, Turner herself took the stage and thanked the performers and the audience. With a smile, she reflected on her life, and offered her final Buddhist teaching: "This musical is my life . . . [and the] poison turned to medicine." Turner was expressing that her life, as shown in the musical and much discussed throughout her career, had been a series of hardships that she turned into positive benefits for herself. Through sharing the details of her story with the public, she also turned her hardships into positive benefit for others. Through telling her story, in often graphic detail, Tina Turner has taught countless people the world over how to triumph over their obstacles, how to change their own poison into medicine. As her passing brings renewed attention to her legacy, Turner's final message to her audience makes clear the significant role that religion played in her own life story. Some will listen, and indeed, some will hear.

A Note on Sources

In *Dancing in My Dreams: A Spiritual Biography of Tina Turner*, I rely heavily on Tina Turner's three autobiographies. I am not, however, limited to these sources. I also draw from media profiles, newspaper articles, and industry trade publications. As a public figure, Turner has left a veritable public archive of her own words in articles, interviews, and documentaries. In utilizing these sources, I follow the work of scholars of African American religious history like Vaughn A. Booker in taking seriously the potential for the resources of popular culture to reveal authentic expressions of religious authority, to index the performance of religious belief, and to provide exemplary models of religiosity for large public audiences.[1] To augment this material, I carried out fieldwork research in West Tennessee. I also conducted ethnographic interviews with those who knew Turner at crucial moments in her religious journey. This includes interviews with Robbie Ewing, who attended Woodlawn Missionary Baptist Church with Turner; Taro Gold, a coauthor of *Happiness Becomes You*; and Matilda Buck, onetime Soka Gakkai International–USA National Women's Leader. To analyze this material, I draw on insights from the discipline of history and subdisciplines of religious studies, including American metaphysical religion, African American religious history, womanist theology, and mysticism. By providing an analysis and genealogy of the religious ideas and traditions that constitute Turner's combinatory religious repertoire, I distinguish *Dancing in My Dreams: A Spiritual Biography of Tina Turner* from other published works on Turner's life—including her self-authored works. This analytical and genealogical work illuminates heretofore obscured religious threads in popularly available accounts of Tina Turner's religious beliefs and practices. This work also asks scholars of religion to think of religion outside of the boundaries of institutions and instead to attend to aesthetics, sensibility, and performance as religion. Beyond its utility for those familiar with Turner's life and career, this biography will be particularly valuable to scholars who work at the intersection of American religion and popular culture, to scholars studying the religious lives of Black women, to scholars interested in African American religious history, to scholars researching Black Buddhists and American Buddhism, and to scholars probing the history of Buddhism in the West.

Notes

Introduction

1. Tina Turner, interviewed by Larry King, CNN, *Larry King Live*, February 21, 1997, https://www.youtube.com/watch?v=UgtEeU_DDWY.

2. "Tina Turner—One Last Time Live (CBS TV Version)," YouTube, accessed May 10, 2022, https://www.youtube.com/watch?v=4S2QNwBWyNQ.

3. Ike Turner and others who knew Turner personally claim that Tina Turner was born with the name Martha Nell Bullock. For example, see "R&B Legend Ike Turner, 1931-2007," NPR, Fresh Air, December 14, 2007, https://www.npr.org/templates/story/story.php?storyId=17253727. As evidence they cite a signed contract, dated August 2, 1977, between Tina Turner and International Creative Management. Below the signature "Martha Nell Turner," it says "p/k/a [professionally known as] Tina Turner." Tina Turner herself has always maintained that she was born Anna Mae Bullock; this is confirmed by the research of Dr. Henry Louis Gates Jr. (private communication). Regarding the year of Turner's birth, a Tennessee Education Census schedule, dated April 12, 1948, lists Anna Mae Bullock's birthday as "November 26, 1940." Tina Turner maintains that she was born in 1939.

4. See, for example, Rosemarie Freeney Harding, "Hospitality, Haints, and Healing: A Southern African American Meaning of Religion," in *Deeper Shades of Purple: Womanism in Religion and Society*, ed. Stacey M. Floyd-Thomas (New York: New York University Press, 2006), 104-5.

5. Catherine Albanese, *A Republic of Mind and Spirit: A Cultural History of American Metaphysical Religion* (New Haven: Yale University Press, 2007).

6. On the notion of religious repertoires, see Justin Thomas McDaniel, *The Lovelorn Ghost and the Magical Monk: Practicing Buddhism in Modern Thailand* (New York: Columbia University Press, 2011), 9-13. See also Robert Ford Campany, *Making Transcendents: Aesthetics and Social Memory in Early Medieval China* (Honolulu: University of Hawaii Press, 2009); and Robert Ford Campany, "Religious Repertoires and Con-

testation: A Case Study Based on Buddhist Miracle Tales," *History of Religions* 52, no. 2 (November 2012): 99–141.

7. Lewis R. Rambo and Charles E. Farhadian, eds., *The Oxford Handbook of Religious Conversion* (New York: Oxford University Press, 2014), 4–7. Each essay in this volume nuances, challenges, or broadens the notion of conversion.

8. Some of the noteworthy publications are Curtis Evans, *The Burden of Black Religion* (New York: Oxford University Press, 2008); Sylvester A. Johnson, *African American Religions, 1500-2000: Colonialism, Democracy, and Freedom* (Cambridge: Cambridge University Press, 2015); Judith Weisenfeld, *New World A-Coming: Black Religion and Racial Identity during the Great Migration* (New York: New York University Press, 2017). For an earlier ethnographic study of Black religious groups outside of the "Black church" paradigm, see Arthur Huff Fauset, *Black Gods of the Metropolis: Negro Religious Cults in the Urban North* (Philadelphia: Philadelphia Anthropological Society, 1944). Albert J. Raboteau, *A Fire in the Bones: Reflections on African-American Religious History* (Boston: Beacon, 1995), goes beyond Afro-Protestantism to consider African American practice of Catholicism and African orisa religions. Some scholars have confirmed the importance of Afro-Protestantism while simultaneously challenging the monolithic Black church paradigm. See, for instance, Vaughn A. Booker, *Lift Every Voice and Swing: Black Musicians and Religious Culture in the Jazz Century* (New York: New York University Press, 2020).

9. See Anthony B. Pinn, *Embodiment and the New Shape of Black Theological Thought* (New York: New York University Press, 2010), xi.

10. Pinn, *Embodiment*, xi.

11. See, for example, Charles S. Prebish, *Luminous Passages: The Practice and Study of Buddhism in America* (Berkeley: University of California Press, 1999), which pays scant attention to African American Buddhists, even as it acknowledges the presence of Black Buddhists in a number of American Buddhist communities; Rick Fields, *How the Swans Came to the Lake: A Narrative History of Buddhism in America*, 3rd ed. (Boston: Shambhala Publications, 1992); Stephen Batchelor, *The Awakening of the West: The Encounter of Buddhism and the West* (Williamsville, NY: Echo Point Books and Media, 2011); and David L. McMahan, *The Making of Buddhist Modernism* (New York: Oxford University Press, 2008). McMahan's monograph does not purport to be a comprehensive history of Buddhism in America but seeks to detail key moments and discourses in the development of what some Buddhist studies scholars have labeled "Buddhist modernism." However, McMahan does not consider African American contributions to Buddhist modernist discourse. He also makes a choice to exclude Soka Gakkai International–USA, an organization that has been particularly successful with Black Buddhists. As Adeana McNicholl's 2018 article "Buddhism and Race" highlights, such exclusions demonstrate the way in which "Buddhist Studies scholars have been reluctant to account for how race and ethnicity, as social constructs, are fundamental constitutive factors to the identity formation of American Buddhists." See Adeana McNicholl, "Buddhism and Race," in *The Oxford Handbook of Religion and*

Race in American History, ed. Kathryn Gin Lum and Paul Harvey (New York: Oxford University Press, 2018), 223.

Chapter 1

1. Drawn from Robbie Ewing, telephone interview by the author, January 17, 2022. Ewing, née Brack, attended Woodlawn Missionary Baptist Church at the same time as Tina Turner and sang in the choir with her. As of this writing, Ewing has been a lifelong member of Woodlawn.

2. Alison Collis Greene, *No Depression in Heaven: The Great Depression, the New Deal, and the Transformation of Religion in the Delta* (New York: Oxford University Press, 2016), 11–32.

3. Sharon Norris, *Haywood County, Tennessee*, Black America Series (Charleston, SC: Arcadia Publishing, 2000), 7–10.

4. Henry Louis Gates Jr., *Stony the Road: Reconstruction, White Supremacy, and the Rise of Jim Crow* (London: Penguin, 2020), 9–17.

5. Paul Harvey, *Through the Storm, through the Night: A History of African American Christianity* (Lanham, MD: Rowman & Littlefield, 2011), 69. Hereafter, page references from this work will be given in parentheses in the text.

6. Evans E. Crawford, with Thomas H. Troeger, *The Hum: Call and Response in African American Preaching* (Nashville: Abingdon, 1995), 16.

7. Albert J. Raboteau, *A Fire in the Bones: Reflections on African-American Religious History* (Boston: Beacon, 1995), 143–44.

8. Crawford, *The Hum*, 71.

9. Crawford, *The Hum*, 56 and 70.

10. Paul Harvey, *Freedom's Coming: Religious Culture and the Shaping of the South from the Civil War through the Civil Rights Era* (Chapel Hill: University of North Carolina Press, 2005), 126.

11. Anthea Butler, *Women in the Church of God in Christ: Making a Sanctified World* (Chapel Hill: University of North Carolina Press, 2007), 2.

12. Butler, *Women in the Church of God in Christ*, 2.

13. Harvey, *Through the Storm*, 90–91.

14. See Evelyn Brooks Higginbotham, "The Politics of Respectability," in *Righteous Discontent: The Women's Movement in the Black Baptist Church, 1880–1920* (Cambridge, MA: Harvard University Press, 1994), chap. 7.

15. Higginbotham, "The Politics of Respectability," 187.

16. Yvonne P. Chireau, *Black Magic: Religion and the African American Conjuring Tradition* (Berkeley: University of California Press, 2006), 12. See also Harvey, *Freedom's Coming*, 120–23.

17. Chireau, *Black Magic*, 21.

18. Chireau, *Black Magic*, 20. Katrina Hazzard-Donald demonstrates through eth-

nographic work that such beliefs and practices persist into the twenty-first century. See Katrina Hazzard-Donald, *Mojo Workin': The Old African American Hoodoo System* (Urbana: University of Illinois Press, 2013), especially the introduction.

19. Tina Turner, *Happiness Becomes You: A Guide to Changing Your Life for Good* (New York: Atria Books, 2020), 5.

20. Norris, *Haywood County, Tennessee,* 9.

21. Tina Turner, with Kurt Loder, *I, Tina: My Life Story* (New York: Morrow, 1986), 19.

22. Tina Turner, *My Love Story* (New York: Penguin, 2019), 1–2.

23. *Oprah's Next Chapter,* season 2, episode 222, "Tina Turner," interview by Oprah Winfrey, featuring Tina Turner, aired August 25, 2013, in broadcast syndication.

24. Turner, *I, Tina,* 9.

25. Quoted in *Behind the Music,* season 1, episode 111, "Tina Turner: Behind the Music," written by Gay Rosenthal, featuring Tina Turner, aired March 5, 2000, on VH1.

26. Delores S. Williams, *Sisters in the Wilderness: The Challenge of Womanist God-Talk* (Maryknoll, NY: Orbis Books, 2013 [1993]), 96.

27. Williams, *Sisters in the Wilderness,* 97.

28. Williams, *Sisters in the Wilderness,* 108–15.

29. Turner, *Happiness Becomes You,* 13.

30. Turner, *I, Tina,* 13.

31. Madhu Jain, "Shakti's Postcards," *Outlook,* updated February 5, 2022, https://www.outlookindia.com/magazine/story/shaktis-postcards/223050.

32. Rosemarie Freeney Harding, with Rachel Elizabeth Harding, *Remnants: A Memoir of Spirit, Activism, and Mothering* (Durham, NC: Duke University Press, 2015), 12–13.

33. Harding, *Remnants,* 11.

34. Harding, *Remnants,* chap. 12.

35. Harding, *Remnants,* 13.

36. See Rosemarie Freeney Harding, "Hospitality, Haints, and Healing: A Southern African American Meaning of Religion," in *Deeper Shades of Purple: Womanism in Religion and Society,* ed. Stacey M. Floyd-Thomas (New York: New York University Press, 2006), 99 and 105.

37. Henry Louis Gates Jr., *In Search of Our Roots: How 19 Extraordinary African Americans Reclaimed Their Past* (New York: Skyhorse Publishing, 2017), 99.

38. Gates, *In Search of Our Roots,* 99–100.

39. Turner, *I, Tina,* 12.

40. Turner, *I, Tina,* 12.

41. Higginbotham, "The Politics of Respectability," 192.

42. Thomas Oscar Fuller, *History of the Negro Baptists of Tennessee* (Memphis: Haskins Print–Roger Williams College, 1936), 31.

43. Woodlawn Missionary Baptist Church, 150th anniversary, HJR 1026, 109th

General Assembly (2016), https://publications.tnsosfiles.com/acts/109/resolutions/
hjr1026.pdf.

44. Sharon Norris, "Hardin Smith," in *Tennessee Encyclopedia* (Tennessee Historical Society, 2018), https://tennesseeencyclopedia.net/entries/hardin-smith/.

45. Dorothy Granberry, "Black Community Leadership in a Rural Tennessee County, 1865-1903," *Journal of Negro History* 83, no. 4 (Autumn 1998): 252.

46. Norris, "Hardin Smith."

47. Gates, *In Search of Our Roots*, 83.

48. Turner, *I, Tina*, 12.

49. Robbie Ewing, telephone interview by the author, January 20, 2022.

50. For brief information on the tenure of each pastor since the church's founding, see "Historic Woodlawn Missionary Baptist Church: 155th Anniversary, Homecoming and Church Anniversary," May 23, 2021, no page numbers.

51. Crawford, *The Hum*, 86.

52. Sharon Norris, a historian of West Tennessee, claims that her research showed Turner was baptized at Spring Hill Baptist Church.

53. Turner, *Happiness Becomes You*, 8.

54. Gates, *In Search of Our Roots*, 83.

55. Chris Welch, *The Tina Turner Experience: The Illustrated Biography* (London: Virgin Books, 1994), 29.

56. Tina Turner, *My Love Story* (New York: Atris Books, 2018), 31.

57. Turner, *My Love Story*, 31.

58. Turner, *I, Tina*, 14.

59. Turner, *I, Tina*, 14.

60. *Zora Neale Hurston: Folklore, Memoirs, and Other Writings*, ed. Cheryl A. Wall (New York: Library of America, 1995), 901-5.

61. Harvey, *Through the Storm*, 88.

62. See Harvey, *Freedom's Coming*, 142-48. For Spirit possession in Holiness Pentecostal churches, see Cheryl J. Sanders, *Saints in Exile: The Holiness-Pentecostal Experience in African American Religion and Culture* (New York: Oxford University Press, 1996), 59-63.

63. See Chireau, *Black Magic*, 107-13, and Harvey, *Through the Storm*, 92-94.

64. Chireau, *Black Magic*, 109.

65. Sanders, *Saints in Exile*, 64-67.

66. Harvey, *Freedom's Coming*, 147.

67. Butler, *Women in the Church of God in Christ*, 4-5.

68. Jerma A. Jackson, *Singing in My Soul: Black Gospel Music in a Secular Age* (Chapel Hill: University of North Carolina Press, 2004), 25.

69. Butler, *Women in the Church of God in Christ*, 7.

70. Butler, *Women in the Church of God in Christ*, 3.

71. Turner, *I, Tina*, 14-15.

72. Gates, *In Search of Our Roots*, 92.

73. Tina Turner Heritage Days, accessed October 5, 2022, https://www.tinaturner heritagedays.com/flagg-grove-school.

74. Turner, *My Love Story*, 28.

75. Turner, *I, Tina*, 32,

76. Turner, *My Love Story*, 29.

77. Turner, *My Love Story*, 29.

78. Turner, *I, Tina*, 21.

79. Turner, *I, Tina*, 27.

80. Turner, *I, Tina*, 27.

81. Norris, *Haywood County, Tennessee*, 21-22.

82. Welch, *The Tina Turner Experience*, 30.

83. Turner, *I, Tina*, 29.

84. Anne-Leslie Owens, "WDIA," in *Tennessee Encyclopedia* (Tennessee Historical Society, 2018), https://tennesseeencyclopedia.net/entries/wdia/.

85. Maureen Mahon, *Black Diamond Queens: African American Women and Rock and Roll* (Durham, NC: Duke University Press).

86. Turner, *I, Tina*, 28-29.

87. For the most forceful corrective to the secularity of the blues, see James H. Cone, *The Spirituals and the Blues: An Interpretation* (New York: Orbis Books, 1992 [1972]).

88. See Nick Salvatore, *Singing in a Strange Land: C. L. Franklin, the Black Church, and the Transformation of America* (Urbana: University of Illinois Press, 2006), 64.

89. Turner, *I, Tina*, 29.

90. Harvey, *Through the Storm*, 102-3.

91. Paul Harvey, *Southern Religion in the World: Three Stories* (Athens: University of Georgia Press, 2019), 74.

92. Tina Turner, writer and vocalist, "I Am a Motherless Child," Blue Thumb Records BTS5, track 7 on side A of *Outta Season*, 1969. Two different blues songs and the late nineteenth-century spiritual "Motherless Child" share the same title.

93. Yolanda Pierce, *In My Grandmother's House: Black Women, Faith, and the Stories We Inherit* (Minneapolis: Broadleaf Books, 2021), xvii.

Chapter 2

1. Tina Turner, with Kurt Loder, *I, Tina: My Life Story* (New York: Morrow, 1986), 106.

2. Tina Turner, *I, Tina*, 102; Chris Welch, *The Tina Turner Experience: The Illustrated Biography* (London: Virgin Books, 1994), 104-13.

3. Tina Turner, *I, Tina*, 39-40.

4. On Clarksdale, see Ike Turner, with Nigel Cawthorne, *Takin' Back My Name: The Confessions of Ike Turner* (London: Virgin Books, 1999), 5.

5. Ike Turner, *Takin' Back My Name*, 5.

6. Nick Salvatore, *Singing in a Strange Land: C. L. Franklin, the Black Church, and the Transformation of America* (Urbana: University of Illinois Press, 2006), 64. This is still the case today: up Yazoo Street from Centennial Baptist Church, on the aptly named "Blues Alley" Street, is the Delta Blues Museum, located in the old freight train depot.

7. Salvatore, *Singing in a Strange Land*, 64.

8. Salvatore, *Singing in a Strange Land*, 64-65.

9. See chap. 1 in Salvatore, *Singing in a Strange Land*.

10. Ike Turner, *Takin' Back My Name*, 6-7.

11. Ike Turner, *Takin' Back My Name*, 18.

12. State of Mississippi, "Statement of Gov. Barbour on Passing of Blues Legend Pinetop Perkins," press release, March 22, 2011, https://www.charlestonchronicle.net /news/2011/mar/3.22barbouronpinetopperkins.html.

13. Quoted in Andrew S. Hughes, "Handing on the Blues; with Documentary, Pinetop Perkins' 'Lessons' Won't Be Lost to Future Generations," *South Bend (IN) Tribune*, March 15, 2002.

14. Ike Turner, *Takin' Back My Name*, 20-22; "Ike Turner & Pinetop Perkins: Student and Teacher," *Elmore Magazine*, November 1, 2006.

15. John M. Giggie, *After Redemption: Jim Crow and the Transformation of African American Religion in the Delta, 1875-1915* (New York: Oxford University Press, 2008), 25.

16. Giggie, *After Redemption*, 51-53; Lerone A. Martin, *Preaching on Wax: The Phonograph and the Shaping of Modern African American Religion* (New York: New York University Press, 2014), 91-124.

17. Yvonne P. Chireau, *Black Magic: Religion and the African American Conjuring Tradition* (Berkeley: University of California Press, 2006), 144-45.

18. Giggie, *After Redemption*, 55; Chireau, *Black Magic*, 148. Blues artists' mimicry of preachers could often be a source of tension between these artists and the preachers they mocked. For a discussion of these issues and the importance of the mythology of the devil to blues music, see Adam Gussow, *Beyond the Crossroads: The Devil and the Blues Tradition* (Chapel Hill: University of North Carolina Press, 2017).

19. Chireau, *Black Magic*, 145.

20. Chireau, *Black Magic*, 146-47.

21. Chireau, *Black Magic*, 148.

22. Historian Alison Greene remarks: "Delta religion was no more complete without the blues than without churches, each an antagonist and accompanist to the other." See Alison Collis Greene, *No Depression in Heaven: The Great Depression, the New Deal, and the Transformation of Religion in the Delta* (New York: Oxford University Press, 2016), 47.

23. "Ike Turner & Pinetop Perkins: Student and Teacher"; Ike Turner, *Takin' Back My Name*, 2-5; Welch, *The Tina Turner Experience*, 36; Tina Turner, *I, Tina*, 43-45. For

a discussion of how Black recording artists were often cheated in record deals, see Martin, *Preaching on Wax*.

24. Ike Turner, *Takin' Back My Name*, 44-48.

25. Tina Turner, *I, Tina*, 46-47.

26. Tina Turner, *I, Tina*, 47.

27. See, for example, the 1956 newspaper clipping that mentions Ike Turner being arrested for carrying a gun and refers to him as "pistol-whipping": "Trial of Rock 'n Roll Singer Postponed," *Atlanta Daily World*, November 28, 1956.

28. Tina Turner, *I, Tina*, 49.

29. Ike Turner, *Takin' Back My Name*, 59.

30. Ike Turner, *Takin' Back My Name*, 59.

31. Ike Turner, *Takin' Back My Name*, 62.

32. See Mark Bego, *Tina Turner: Break Every Rule* (Lanham, MD: Rowman & Littlefield, 2003), 63, and Ike Turner, *Takin' Back My Name*, 62. See also Tina Turner, *I, Tina*, 62.

33. Jerma A. Jackson's *Singing in My Soul: Black Gospel Music in a Secular Age* (Chapel Hill: University of North Carolina Press, 2004) provides an excellent overview of Sister Rosetta Tharpe's life. See also Gayle F. Wald's biography of Tharpe, *Shout, Sister, Shout! The Untold Story of Rock-and-Roll Trailblazer Sister Rosetta Tharpe* (Boston: Beacon, 2007), and Paul Harvey, *Southern Religion in the World: Three Stories* (Athens: University of Georgia Press, 2019).

34. Turner relates this story in a number of sources, including on an episode of *Oprah's Next Chapter*. See *Oprah's Next Chapter*, season 2, episode 222, "Tina Turner," interview by Oprah Winfrey, featuring Tina Turner, aired August 25, 2013, in broadcast syndication. Turner related that this was a new experience for her because she had never seen nor experienced someone being *beaten*. With her mother and father, she saw them *fight*—with her mother fighting back. See the discussion in Tina Turner, *My Love Story* (New York: Penguin, 2019), 44.

35. Tina Turner, *My Love Story*, 43.

36. Tina Turner, *My Love Story*, 39.

37. Tina Turner, *My Love Story*, 80.

38. The term "Chitlin' Circuit" and the social and cultural histories that it attempts to label and describe are a complex issue. The name was originally applied to the circuit of largely white-owned theaters for African Americans performing on the vaudeville circuit, under the auspices of the Theatre Owners Booking Association. For a detailed discussion of the Theatre Owners Booking Association and the Chitlin' Circuit, see Henry Louis Gates Jr., "The Chitlin Circuit," in *African American Performance and Theater History: A Critical Reader*, ed. Harry J. Elam Jr. and David Krasner (New York: Oxford University Press, 2001), 132-48. For a discussion of the perilous nature of the Chitlin' Circuit for Black women performers, see Daphne Brooks's discussion of jazz pianist Mary Lou Williams, in *Liner Notes for the Revolution: The Intellectual Life*

of Black Feminist Sound (Cambridge, MA: Belknap Press of Harvard University Press, 2021), 96-98. See also Brooks's discussion of the circuit on 91, 271, 333, 361, and 381.

39. Author's private collection.

40. See Salvatore, *Singing in a Strange Land*, 201-2.

41. Quoted in Welch, *The Tina Turner Experience*, 58.

42. Ike Turner, *Takin' Back My Name*, 75-80; see also chap. 7 in Tina Turner, *I, Tina*.

43. Ike Turner, *Takin' Back My Name*, 102; see 102-4 for Ike Turner's discussion of the Black Panther concert.

44. Ike Turner, *Takin' Back My Name*, 101.

45. See Tracy Fessenden, *Religion around Billie Holiday* (University Park: Pennsylvania State University Press, 2018), 51-53. See also Danielle Fosler-Lussier, *Music in America's Cold War Diplomacy* (Berkeley: University of California Press, 2015), and Lisa E. Davenport, *Jazz Diplomacy: Promoting America in the Cold War Era* (Jackson: University Press of Mississippi, 2013).

46. This concert's staging and promotion outside of State Department channels served as a counterpoint to the State Department's efforts. See Penny Von Eschen, *Satchmo Blows Up the World: Jazz Ambassadors Play the Cold War* (Cambridge, MA: Harvard University Press, 2006), 225.

47. Quoted in Welch, *The Tina Turner Experience*, 72.

48. Welch, *The Tina Turner Experience*, 72.

49. For an overview of Phil Spector's life and his cultural impact on American popular music, see Sean MacLeod, *Phil Spector: Sound of the Sixties* (Lanham, MD: Rowman & Littlefield, 2017).

50. Robert Palmer, "Phil Spector—Master of the 60's Sound," *New York Times*, March 20, 1977.

51. Quoted in Tina Turner, *I, Tina*, 93.

52. Krasnow details the terms of Phil Spector and Ike Turner's deal in Tina Turner, *I, Tina*, 92-93. See also discussion of their arrangement in Maureen Mahon, *Black Diamond Queens: African American Women and Rock and Roll* (Durham, NC: Duke University Press), 248-49.

53. Tina Turner, *I, Tina*, 95.

54. Tina Turner, *My Love Story*, 48-50.

55. Further details of the recording session are described in Tina Turner, *I, Tina*, 96-98.

56. MacLeod, *Phil Spector*, 124. See also Mahon's analysis of the structure of the song and its blend of pop and rhythm and blues: Mahon, *Black Diamond Queens*, 250. See also Craig Werner, *A Change Is Gonna Come: Music, Race & the Soul of America*, rev. ed. (Ann Arbor: University of Michigan Press, 2006), 37-40.

57. Leroy Patterson, "Ike and Tina Turner: Husband-Wife Team Reaches Top," *Ebony*, May 1971, 92-93. Other artists have had similar perceptions of both the record industry and American radio. Emily Lordi quotes Minnie Riperton saying of her solo

work in the sixties, "[It] wasn't what you'd call black music so therefore nobody knew what to do with it. I mean, in the record industry if you were black you were black and you couldn't be anything else. At that time you were Negroes, you weren't even human beings. That's the way it was then, that's the way it is now." See Emily Lordi, *The Meaning of Soul: Black Music and Resilience Since the 1960s* (Durham, NC: Duke University Press, 2020), 118.

58. Mahon, *Black Diamond Queens*, 252. On the "British Invasion," see Welch, *The Tina Turner Experience*, 101-4. See also Harvey Rachlin, *Song and System: The Making of American Pop Music* (Lanham, MD: Rowman & Littlefield, 2020), 102; and see chap. 2 of Stephen Tow, *London, Reign over Me: How England's Capital Built Classic Rock* (Lanham, MD: Rowman & Littlefield, 2020).

59. Tina Turner, *My Love Story*, 65.

60. See discussion of Georgianna Flagg in chap. 1.

61. Tina Turner, *I, Tina*, 106.

62. Tina Turner, *I, Tina*, 106.

63. Tina Turner, *I, Tina*, 106-7. As discussed in chap. 1, Tina Turner is *not* of significant "mixed blood," as revealed to her in the research of Henry Louis Gates Jr.

64. For a discussion of artists who moved to France and the notion of "racial catholicity" underlying conceptions of Black universalism, see chap. 3 of Josef Sorett, *Spirit in the Dark: A Religious History of Racial Aesthetics* (New York: Oxford University Press, 2016).

65. Turner became a Swiss citizen in 2013, revoking her US citizenship in the process; see Tina Turner, *My Love Story*, 195-97.

66. Carol McGraw, "Peter Hurkos; Detective Who Used Psychic Powers," obituary, *Los Angeles Times*, June 12, 1988.

67. Norma Lee Browning, *The Psychic World of Peter Hurkos* (New York: Doubleday, 1970).

68. "Peter Hurkos, 77, a Psychic Used by Police," obituary, *New York Times*, June 2, 1988.

69. Ike Turner, *Takin' Back My Name*, 98-99. However, Ike admits that Hurkos was neither able to locate the money nor identify who stole it.

70. Alicia Puglionesi, *Common Phantoms: An American History of Psychic Science* (Stanford, CA: Stanford University Press, 2020), 22.

71. Puglionesi, *Common Phantoms*, 2-3.

72. Puglionesi, *Common Phantoms*, 12.

73. Puglionesi, *Common Phantoms*, 9.

74. See Paul Harvey, *Freedom's Coming: Religious Culture and the Shaping of the South from the Civil War through the Civil Rights Era* (Chapel Hill: University of North Carolina Press, 2005), 111-20.

75. Ike Turner's introduction to cocaine and his subsequent drug dependency are detailed in chap. 14 of Ike Turner, *Takin' Back My Name*.

76. The circumstances surrounding Turner's suicide attempt are described in

chap. 9 of Tina Turner, *I, Tina*, 108–18. All quotes in this paragraph come from that chapter. Ike claims that she attempted suicide several times and considered these as forms of attention seeking; see Ike Turner, *Takin' Back My Name*, 135–40.

77. In live performances of this song, Ike and Tina graphically mimicked sexual gestures and sounds. These performances were derided by critics as "pornographic," and Turner herself became so ashamed of the song that in a 1996 *60 Minutes* profile she plugged her ears and refused to listen to a recording of her performance.

78. Mahon analyzes the Turners' turn to rock music and the cultural legacy of Tina Turner as a rock artist in chap. 8 of Mahon, *Black Diamond Queens*; see especially the section "Covering Rock," 252–65.

79. Tina Turner, *I, Tina*, 120.

80. On John Fogerty, see Werner, *A Change Is Gonna Come*, 151–57.

81. Mahon, *Black Diamond Queens*, 258.

82. Ike and Tina Turner, "I Am a Motherless Child," AZLyrics, accessed October 7, 2022, https://www.azlyrics.com/lyrics/iketinaturner/iamamotherlesschild.html. Emphasis added.

83. Ike and Tina Turner, "Nutbush City Limits," Genius, accessed October 7, 2022, https://genius.com/Ike-and-tina-turner-nutbush-city-limits-lyrics.

84. Ike and Tina Turner, "Proud Mary," Genius, accessed October 7, 2022, https://genius.com/Ike-and-tina-turner-proud-mary-lyrics.

85. Emily Lordi, *Black Resonance: Iconic Women Singers and African American Literature* (New Brunswick, NJ: Rutgers University Press, 2013), 10–11.

86. Audre Lorde, "Poetry Is Not a Luxury," in *Sister Outsider* (Berkeley, CA: Crossing, 2007 [1984]), 36–39.

87. "Tina Turner," Recording Academy Grammy Awards, accessed October 7, 2022, https://www.grammy.com/grammys/artists/tina-turner/7641.

88. Mahon, *Black Diamond Queens*, 258.

89. Werner, *A Change Is Gonna Come*, 155.

90. W. E. B. Du Bois, *The Souls of Black Folk* (reprint, New York: New American Library, 1993), as cited in Wallace Best, *Passionately Human, No Less Divine: Religion and Culture in Black Chicago, 1915-1952* (Princeton: Princeton University Press, 2007), 99.

91. Best, *Passionately Human*, 99.

92. Best, *Passionately Human*, 97.

93. Most maintain that the name, pronounced like Bullock, is an homage to Tina. Ike claims he made up the name because it sounded unique; see Ike Turner, *Takin' Back My Name*, 125.

94. Tina Turner, *My Love Story*, 91. Tina Turner's introduction to Soka Gakkai Nichiren Buddhism and its discipline of chanting will be discussed in the next chapter.

95. Tina Turner, *I, Tina*, 136.

96. Tina Turner, *I, Tina*, 138.

97. LaShawn Harris, *Sex Workers, Psychics, and Numbers Runners: Black Women in New York City's Underground Economy* (Urbana: University of Illinois Press, 2016), 96.

98. Tina Turner, *My Love Story*, 87.

99. Tina Turner, *I, Tina*, 138.

100. Jane Iwamura, *Virtual Orientalism: Asian Religions and American Popular Culture* (New York: Oxford University Press, 2011), 112.

101. Chireau, *Black Magic*, 139.

102. Chireau, *Black Magic*, 141-42. See also Harris, *Sex Workers*, 96-104.

103. Sorett, *Spirit in the Dark*, 162-66.

104. Religious studies scholar Lois Ann Lorentzen explains: "California saw non-traditional religions emerge from the 1960s counterculture and hippie subculture. By the end of the 1970s, New Age was a big tent that included a range of spiritual practices and beliefs. Difficult to define, it is a decentralized, heterogeneous spiritual movement that includes beliefs in divine energy, pantheism, auras, healing, alternative medicine, and the idea that social change requires deep psychic and consciousness change. Practices include channeling, crystals, meditation, astrology, divining . . . , holistic healing, and music. Multiple roots or resources for New Age philosophy include Wicca, neo-paganism, Theosophy, Hinduism, and Buddhism." See Lois Ann Lorentzen, "Golden State of Grace? A Lifetime Scholar of Religion Surveys California Spirituality," *Bloom* 5, no. 4 (Winter 2015): 26.

105. Catherine L. Albanese, *A Republic of Mind and Spirit: A Cultural History of American Metaphysical Religion* (New Haven: Yale University Press, 2007), 5.

106. See chap. 1.

107. Albanese, *Republic of Mind and Spirit*, 5-6.

108. Albanese, *Republic of Mind and Spirit*, 6. In metaphysical religion, Albanese sees the prevalence of varieties of correspondence theories that posit that "The human world and mind replicate—either ideally, formerly, or actually—a larger, often more whole and integrated universe, so that the material world is organically linked to a spiritual."

109. See Albanese, *Republic of Mind and Spirit*, 12.

110. Albanese, *Republic of Mind and Spirit*, 9. Here, Albanese is building on the work of Leonard Norman Primiano. See Albanese, 518n9.

111. I use "religious repertoire" in the sense outlined by Justin McDaniel, *The Lovelorn Ghost and the Magical Monk: Practicing Buddhism in Modern Thailand* (New York: Columbia University Press, 2014), 9-12.

Chapter 3

1. Tina Turner, *Happiness Becomes You: A Guide to Changing Your Life for Good* (New York: Atria Books, 2020), 18.

2. Tina Turner, *Happiness Becomes You*, 19.

3. Tina Turner, *My Love Story* (New York: Penguin, 2019), 55.

4. Tina Turner, *My Love Story*, 55-56.

5. Turner describes these efforts in Tina Turner, *My Love Story*, 81–82.

6. Tina Turner, with Kurt Loder, *I, Tina: My Life Story* (New York: Morrow, 1986), 134.

7. *TINA*, directed by Dan Lindsay and T. J. Martin (New York: HBO Documentary Films, 2021).

8. Tina Turner, *I, Tina*, 133.

9. Tina Turner, *My Love Story*, 87; see also Tina Turner, *Happiness Becomes You*, 19. Turner also recounts this story in an interview for the Swiss magazine *Bilanz*: Stefan Barmettler, "Tina Turner und Regula Curti: Mein Erfolg ist der Beweis," *Bilanz*, December 13, 2011, https://www.handelszeitung.ch/geld/tina-turner-und-regu la-curti-mein-erfolg-ist-der-beweis. The relevant passage reads as follows: "Turner: Eines Tages kam mein jüngster Sohn mit einer Gebetskette aus Holz nach Hause und erzählte mir begeistert, sie spende Kraft und mache Wünsche wahr. Da wurde ich stutzig. Zuerst die Toningenieure, dann mein Bub, und alle wiesen mich auf dasselbe hin: Unternimm etwas, geh deinen eigenen Weg."

10. Tina Turner, *Happiness Becomes You*, 19.

11. For a brief biography of Tsunesaburo Makiguchi, see "Biography," Tsunesaburo Makiguchi, accessed October 10, 2022, https://www.tmakiguchi.org/biography. html. For a discussion of Makiguchi's life, works, and the founding of Soka Kyoiku Gakkai, see Levi McLaughlin, *Soka Gakkai's Human Revolution: The Rise of a Mimetic Nation in Modern Japan* (Honolulu: University of Hawaii Press, 2019), 39–44. See also Dayle M. Bethel, *Makiguchi: The Value Creator* (New York: Weatherhill, 1994 [1973]).

12. Unfortunately, there is no complete English-language biography of Josei Toda. Daisaku Ikeda, Toda's disciple and the third president of Soka Gakkai, authored *Ningen Kakumei* (The Human Revolution), a twelve-volume novelized account of Toda's life and the founding of Soka Gakkai. This work was translated into English and published as a two-book abridged set: Daisaku Ikeda, *The Human Revolution*, trans. Soka Gakkai, 2 vols. (Santa Monica, CA: World Tribune Press, 2004). For a brief biography of Josei Toda's life and tenure as second Soka Gakkai president, see McLaughlin, *Soka Gakkai's Human Revolution*, 44–53. See also chap. 3 in Richard Seager, *Encountering the Dharma: Daisaku Ikeda, Soka Gakkai, and the Globalization of Buddhist Humanism* (Berkeley: University of California Press, 2006).

13. For an overview of Nichiren's life, see the introduction in *Selected Writings of Nichiren*, ed. Philip B. Yampolsky, trans. Burton Watson and others (New York: Columbia University Press, 1990), 1–10. See also Jacqueline I. Stone, *Original Enlightenment and the Transformation of Medieval Japanese Buddhism* (Honolulu: University of Hawaii Press, 1999), 242–63.

14. On the Kamakura era, see Stone, *Original Enlightenment*, 55–62.

15. Ralph H. Craig III, "Grace, Symbol, and Liturgy," *Buddhist-Christian Studies* 38 (2018): 269. For a detailed account of Nichiren's teaching and its relationship to other developments in medieval Japanese Buddhism, see part 3 of Stone, *Original Enlightenment*, 239–355.

16. McLaughlin, *Soka Gakkai's Human Revolution*, 43.

17. McLaughlin, *Soka Gakkai's Human Revolution*, 44-48.

18. Seager, *Encountering the Dharma*, 53. See also McLaughlin, *Soka Gakkai's Human Revolution*, 48.

19. Ikeda, *The Human Revolution*, 2:962.

20. For data on Soka Gakkai's membership in Japan at the time, see McLaughlin, *Soka Gakkai's Human Revolution*, 53. See also Kiyoaki Murata, *Japan's New Buddhism: An Objective Account of Soka Gakkai* (Tokyo: Weatherhill, 1971), 114. In a private communication with the author, McLaughlin said it is unclear precisely how well the number of households the organization claims corresponds to the number of individual members it has.

21. Ikeda refers to his studies with Josei Toda as "Toda University." See Daisaku Ikeda, *The Wisdom for Creating Happiness and Peace: Selections from the Works of Daisaku Ikeda*, vol. 3 (Santa Monica, CA: World Tribune Press, 2020), 228-31.

22. McLaughlin, *Soka Gakkai's Human Revolution*, 55.

23. McLaughlin, *Soka Gakkai's Human Revolution*, 55. Seager sees the three presidents as epitomizing modern Japanese history: "Makiguchi is the critical and cosmopolitan thrust of the Meiji Restoration; Toda, the hope and energy of postwar occupation and reconstruction; Ikeda the global success story of Japan's postwar social and economic miracle." Seager, *Encountering the Dharma*, 87.

24. Phillip Hammond and David Machacek, *Soka Gakkai in America: Accommodation and Conversion* (New York: Oxford University Press, 1999), 24. These women are often called "Pioneer Women" in Soka Gakkai International's literature. For a typical example of these women, see the story of early SGI-USA/NSA member Sachiko Takata Bailey, in Sachiko Takata Bailey, *Winter Always Turns to Spring: A Memoir* (Victoria, BC: Friesen Press, 2013).

25. Hammond and Machacek, *Soka Gakkai in America*, 25.

26. Hammond and Machacek, *Soka Gakkai in America*, 25.

27. George M. Williams, *Freedom and Influence: The Role of Religion in American Society* (Santa Monica, CA: World Tribune Press, 1985), 4.

28. James Allen Dator, *Sōka Gakkai, Builders of the Third Civilization: American and Japanese Members* (Seattle: University of Washington Press, 1969), 15. In this book, Dator utilizes issues of *Seikyo Shimbun* and interviews with Soka Gakkai members to build a profile of the organization.

29. Dator, *Sōka Gakkai*, 21.

30. Williams, *Freedom and Influence*, 156-57.

31. *The Soka Gakkai Dictionary of Buddhism*, s.v. "shoju," accessed October 29, 2022, https://www.nichirenlibrary.org/en/dic/Content/S/148.

32. *The Soka Gakkai Dictionary of Buddhism*, s.v. "shakubuku."

33. For an overview of proselytization efforts under Josei Toda's leadership and the organization's entry into Japanese politics, see McLaughlin, *Soka Gakkai's Human Revolution*, 48-58.

34. For comprehensive treatments of the history of Buddhism in America, see Christopher S. Queen and Duncan Ryūken Williams, eds., *American Buddhism: Methods and Findings in Recent Scholarship* (Surrey, UK: Curzon, 1999); Rick Fields, *How the Swans Came to the Lake* (Boston: Shambhala Publications, 1992); and Adeana McNicholl, "Being Buddha, Staying Woke," *Journal of the American Academy of Religion* 86, no. 4 (December 2018).

35. Williams, *Freedom and Influence*, 183.

36. Hammond and Machacek, *Soka Gakkai in America*, 100–101.

37. Hammond and Machacek, *Soka Gakkai in America*, 101.

38. Tina Turner, *Happiness Becomes You*, 19.

39. Tina Turner, *Happiness Becomes You*, 19.

40. Catherine L. Albanese, *A Republic of Mind and Spirit: A Cultural History of American Metaphysical Religion* (New Haven: Yale University Press, 2007), 49. Hereafter, page references from this work will be given in parentheses in the text.

41. "Hot 100," *Billboard*, November 17, 1973.

42. Dennis Hunt, "Pop Album Briefs: Nutbush City Limits," *Los Angeles Times*, December 2, 1973.

43. "Top Album Picks: Pop," *Billboard*, November 24, 1973.

44. The song was originally credited to Ike Turner, but later releases clarify that the song was written by both Ike and Tina. The BMI music-licensing record credits the song to Tina Turner.

45. Tina Turner, *I, Tina*, 137–38.

46. The European release of the *What's Love Got to Do with It?* soundtrack calls the song "Tina's Wish."

47. Tina Turner, *I, Tina*, 138.

48. Tina Turner, *I, Tina*, 138.

49. Tina Turner, *I, Tina*, 139.

50. Herbie Hancock and Lisa Dickey, *Possibilities* (New York: Viking, 2014), 154.

51. Matilda Buck, telephone interviews by the author, June 16, 2021; July 9, 2021.

52. Tina Turner, *Happiness Becomes You*, 41.

53. Tina Turner, *I, Tina*, 139.

54. Tina Turner, *My Love Story*, 88.

55. Tina Turner, *Happiness Becomes You*, 42.

56. *The Writings of Nichiren Daishonin*, vol. 1 (Tokyo: Soka Gakkai, 1999), 599.

57. Seager, *Encountering the Dharma*, 78. Seager further explains that this concept has a long history in Japanese Buddhism. About the notion of benefit in Japanese Buddhism, see Ian Reader and George Tanabe, *Practically Religious: Worldly Benefits and the Common Religion of Japan* (Honolulu: University of Hawaii Press, 1998).

58. Tina Turner, *My Love Story*, 88.

59. Tina Turner, *I, Tina*, 140.

60. Fabio Rambelli, "Home Buddhas: Historical Processes and Modes of Repre-

sentation of the Sacred in the Japanese Buddhist Family Altar (*Butsudan*)," *Japanese Religions* 35, nos. 1 and 2 (2010): 64–67.

61. See, for example, the explanation in *The Nichiren Shoshu Sokagakkai*, 3rd ed. (Tokyo: Seikyo, 1966), 214–15.

62. McLaughlin, *Soka Gakkai's Human Revolution*, 117.

63. Tina Turner, *Happiness Becomes You*, 42.

64. *Behind the Music*, season 1, episode 111, "Tina Turner: Behind the Music," written by Gay Rosenthal, featuring Tina Turner, aired March 5, 2000, on VH1.

65. Tina Turner, *I, Tina*, 140.

66. Tina Turner, *I, Tina*, 140.

67. Tina Turner, *Happiness Becomes You*, 44.

68. Mark Bego, *Tina Turner: Break Every Rule* (Lanham, MD: Rowman & Little-field, 2003), 124.

69. "Hits of the Week," *Record World*, May 4, 1974.

70. "Album Reviews," *Cash Box*, May 4, 1974.

71. Tina Turner, *I, Tina*, 141.

72. Geoffrey F. Brown, "Tina Turner Talks about Ike and 'Tommy,'" *Jet*, April 24, 1975, 60–61.

73. Brown, "Tina Turner Talks," 62.

74. Brown, "Tina Turner Talks," 63.

75. For Ikeda's commentary on principles of correspondence, see Daisaku Ikeda, in conversation with Masayoshi Kiguchi and Eiichi Shimura, *Buddhism and the Cosmos* (London and Sydney: Macdonald & Co., 1985), 30–31.

76. Robert Windeler, "Tina Turner Sizzles in a Solo Act," *People Weekly*, May 5, 1975, 34.

77. Tina Turner, *I, Tina*, 143.

78. Tina Turner, *I, Tina*, 145.

79. *TINA*.

80. Tina Turner, *I, Tina*, 143.

81. Tina Turner, *I, Tina*, 147.

82. Tina Turner, *I, Tina*, 148.

83. Ike Turner, with Nigel Cawthorne, *Takin' Back My Name: The Confessions of Ike Turner* (London: Virgin Books, 1999), 98–99.

84. "Vegas Showrooms Back on Regular Schedule," *Los Angeles Times*, April 1, 1976; "Talent: Temple's Music Festival to Run during Summer," *Billboard*, June 5, 1976; "Grand Prix, Ike, Tina in Show," *Chicago Tribune*, June 17, 1976; and Sherry Martin, "Sherry Martin: MJ's New York Time Is for the Free and Spirited," *Memphis Tri-State Defender*, June 19, 1976.

85. Tina Turner, *I, Tina*, 148.

86. Tina Turner, *I, Tina*, 150.

87. Tina Turner, *I, Tina*, 151. In *My Love Story*, Turner claims that the incident with the chocolate happened *after* they arrived in Dallas, rather than before they left

Los Angeles. Here, I rely on the account in *I, Tina*; below, I rely on the account in *My Love Story*.

88. Tina Turner, *My Love Story*, 92–93.

Chapter 4

1. Tina Turner, *My Love Story* (New York: Penguin, 2019), 99.
2. Tina Turner, with Kurt Loder, *I, Tina: My Life Story* (New York: Morrow, 1986), 153.
3. All quotes from Turner, *I, Tina*, 153–54.
4. Turner, *I, Tina*, 160.
5. Eddy Hampton Armani, *The Real T.: My 22 Years with Tina Turner* (London: Blake Publishing, 1998), 52. Armani's account is an unauthorized biography.
6. Turner, *My Love Story*, 99.
7. Oprah Winfrey, "Oprah Talks to Tina Turner," *O, the Oprah Magazine*, May 2005, https://www.oprah.com/omagazine/oprahs-interview-with-tina-turner.
8. Turner, *My Love Story*, 99.
9. Turner, *My Love Story*, 100.
10. Private communication with author.
11. Turner, *I, Tina*, 155.
12. Turner, *My Love Story*, 100.
13. Michelle Mercer, *Footprints: The Life and Work of Wayne Shorter* (New York: Penguin, 2007), 192.
14. Mercer, *Footprints*, 193.
15. Turner, *I, Tina*, 156.
16. Turner, *My Love Story*, 107.
17. Turner, *I, Tina*, 156. See also Turner, *My Love Story*, 100.
18. Turner, *I, Tina*, 157.
19. Mercer, *Footprints*, 193.
20. All quotes above from Matilda Buck, telephone interviews by the author, June 16, 2021; July 9, 2021.
21. See discussion of membership in James Allen Dator, *Sōka Gakkai, Builders of the Third Civilization: American and Japanese Members* (Seattle: University of Washington Press, 1969), 5n3.
22. Peter N. Gregory, "Describing the Elephant: Buddhism in America," *Religion and American Culture: A Journal of Interpretation* 11, no. 2 (Summer 2001): 237. Gregory provides an in-depth discussion of the "two Buddhisms" typology of understanding Buddhism in America. In brief, this model argued that there were two distinct (but sometimes overlapping) Buddhist communities in the United States, an immigrant or Asian American Buddhism on the one hand, and a predominantly white convert Buddhist community on the other. This typology has been rightly and cogently criticized on a number of points, most salient among them: the way it reduces the variety and

complexity of Asian and Asian American Buddhist experience; and the way it minimizes (or excludes entirely) Black and Brown Buddhists in American Buddhist history. For the first point, Chenxing Han, *Be the Refuge: Raising the Voices of Asian American Buddhists* (Berkeley, CA: North Atlantic Books, 2021), is an excellent place to start. For the latter point, see Jan Nattier, "Who Is a Buddhist? Charting the Landscape of Buddhist America," in *The Faces of Buddhism in America*, ed. Charles S. Prebish and Kenneth K. Tanaka (Berkeley: University of California Press, 1998), 183–95.

23. Gregory, "Describing the Elephant," 242.

24. Han, *Be the Refuge*, 131.

25. Han, *Be the Refuge*, 133.

26. Rima Vesely-Flad, *Black Buddhists and the Black Radical Tradition: The Practice of Stillness in the Movement for Liberation* (New York: New York University Press, 2022), 127.

27. Vesely-Flad, *Black Buddhists*, 128.

28. Taro Gold, telephone interview by the author, July 26, 2021.

29. Turner speaks about her experiences at these meetings in Tina Turner, *Happiness Becomes You: A Guide to Changing Your Life for Good* (New York: Atria Books, 2020), 94.

30. Daisaku Ikeda, *The Heart of the Lotus Sutra: Lectures on the "Expedient Means" and "Life Span" Chapters* (Santa Monica, CA: World Tribune Press, 2013), 112–13.

31. *The Soka Gakkai Dictionary of Buddhism*, s.v. "karma," accessed October 29, 2022, https://www.nichirenlibrary.org/en/dic/Content/K/35.

32. Daisaku Ikeda, *The Wisdom for Creating Happiness and Peace: Selections from the Works of Daisaku Ikeda*, part 2, *Human Revolution* (Santa Monica, CA: World Tribune Press, 2017), 24.

33. Turner, *My Love Story*, 101.

34. Turner, *I, Tina*, 158.

35. Turner, *My Love Story*, 101.

36. Turner, *My Love Story*, 101.

37. *Oprah's Next Chapter*, season 2, episode 222, "Tina Turner," interview by Oprah Winfrey, featuring Tina Turner, aired August 25, 2013, in broadcast syndication.

38. Turner, *I, Tina*, 158.

39. Turner, *I, Tina*, 159.

40. Elaine Welles, "Ike, Tina Turner Cancel Temple Concert Because 'of Marital Problems,'" *Philadelphia Tribune*, August 24, 1976, 1 and 21.

41. Turner, *I, Tina*, 159.

42. Turner, *My Love Story*, 102.

43. Turner, *My Love Story*, 102.

44. Quoted in Turner, *I, Tina*, 160.

45. Turner, *My Love Story*, 105.

46. Turner, *I, Tina*, 161.

47. Turner, *I, Tina*, 161.

48. Turner, *I, Tina*, 161–62.

49. Turner, *My Love Story*, 106–7.

50. All quotes from Turner, *I, Tina*, 162. See also Turner, *My Love Story*, 107.

51. "Tina Turner Arrested," *Los Angeles Sentinel*, November 25, 1976, D2.

52. These events are related in Turner, *My Love Story*, 108. See also Turner, *I, Tina*, 162–63.

53. Armani, *The Real T.*, 62–64.

54. For an explanation of how the notion of karma functions across Buddhist traditions, how the notion ties into other Buddhist concepts, and a comparative understanding of karma across Indian religious traditions, see John S. Strong, *Buddhisms: An Introduction* (London: Oneworld Publications, 2015), 115–25.

55. *The Writings of Nichiren Daishonin*, vol. 1 (Tokyo: Soka Gakkai, 1999), 405.

56. See *The Writings of Nichiren Daishonin*, 1:631–34.

57. *The Writings of Nichiren Daishonin*, 1:199.

58. Daisaku Ikeda, *Unlocking the Mysteries of Birth and Death . . . and Everything Between: A Buddhist View of Life*, 2nd ed. (Santa Monica, CA: Middle Way, 2003), 26–27.

59. For example, see Turner, *Happiness Becomes You*, 51–54.

60. Turner, *I, Tina*, 167.

61. "Ivan Dryer, 1939–2017," International Laser Display Association, accessed September 14, 2021, https://www.ilda.com/ivandryer.html.

62. "Ivan Dryer, Laserium Founder and Laser Show Pioneer, Dies at 78," *LiveDesign Magazine*, August 2, 2017, https://www.livedesignonline.com/business-people-news/ivan-dryer-laserium-founder-and-laser-show-pioneer-dies-at-78.

63. For an overview of Emmanuel Swedenborg's life, see Catherine L. Albanese, *A Republic of Mind and Spirit: A Cultural History of American Metaphysical Religion* (New Haven: Yale University Press, 2007), 140–44.

64. "Seeing the Soul with Carol Ann Dryer," *Thinking Allowed with Jeffrey Mishlove*, directed by Arthur Bloch (1988; Oakland, CA: Thinking Allowed Productions, 2011), DVD.

65. All quotes from "Seeing the Soul with Carol Ann Dryer."

66. Turner, *I, Tina*, 167.

67. See Emily Teeter, "Museum Review: Hatshepsut and Her World," *American Journal of Archaeology* 110, no. 4 (October 2006): 649–35, for a summary of Hatshepsut's life and representations of her in the context of a review of two museum exhibits. Anthony Spalinger, "Drama in History: Exemplars from Mid Dynasty XVIII," *Studien zur Altägyptischen Kultur* 24 (1997): 269–300, provides a historical discussion of both Hatshepsut and Thutmose III, with a focus on the literary and historical context of their reigns. Spalinger also provides extensive footnotes on relevant sources.

68. Turner, *I, Tina*, 168.

69. Turner, *I, Tina*, 168. This connects Turner to other Black artists in the sixties and seventies who looked to ancient Egypt, Egyptology, and African heritage. See, for example, John Szwed's discussion of the place of conceptions of Egypt in the life and

art of Afro-futurist and Jazz artist Sun Ra, in *Space Is the Place: The Lives and Times of Sun Ra* (Durham, NC: Duke University Press, 2020). See also Jason C. Bivins, *Spirits Rejoice! Jazz and American Religion* (New York: Oxford University Press, 2015), 68–70.

70. Turner, *I, Tina*, 168.

71. "Seeing the Soul with Carol Ann Dryer."

72. This story is related in Turner, *I, Tina*, 167–68.

73. Turner, *I, Tina*, 168.

74. For a succinct definition of Pan-Africanism, see Richard Brent Turner, *Soundtrack to a Movement: African American Islam, Jazz, and Black Internationalism* (New York: New York University Press, 2021), 6–7. Ronald H. Fritze, *Egyptomania: A History of Fascination, Obsession, and Fantasy* (reprint, London: Reaktion Books, 2017), chap. 11, provides a popular history of African American interest in Egypt. See also Fritze's overview of Hatshepsut's reign, 43–44.

75. The most famous example of Afrocentrism was jazz artist Sun Ra (1914–1993). Sun Ra is also considered to be the founder of Afro-futurism. For an extensive biography of Sun Ra, see Szwed, *Space Is the Place*. For a broader discussion of Afrocentrism and African American (jazz) artists, see Bivins, *Spirits Rejoice!*, 67–68.

76. Courtney Bender, *The New Metaphysicals: Spirituality and the American Religious Imagination* (Chicago: University of Chicago Press, 2010), 152.

77. Bender, *The New Metaphysicals*, 121.

78. Bender, *The New Metaphysicals*, 142. Bender calls these relationships across lifetimes the "mystic family" and writes that "the mystic family experienced imperfectly from life to life provides a powerful but quite different space to therapeutically question and reorient relationships as important steps toward redemption of the whole." See Bender, 143.

79. Bender, *The New Metaphysicals*, 121.

80. Armani claims that this amount was $150,000; see Armani, *The Real T.*, 67. This is unverified.

81. Known as the Lockers. Basil would also go on to record the 1982 hit "Mickey."

82. The first show in Vancouver was replete with humorous technical difficulties. See Turner, *I, Tina*, 163–64.

83. All quotes from "New Acts: Tina Turner," *Variety*, Wednesday, August 3, 1977, 70.

84. "Deaths: Kenneth L. Moore," *Billboard*, May 3, 1997, 36.

85. Turner, *My Love Story*, 109.

86. Turner, *I, Tina*, 164.

87. Turner, *I, Tina*, 164. Though in *My Love Story*, she wrote that her first standing ovation was in Europe with Ike.

88. Bob Lucas, "New Year, New Tina, New Title," *Jet*, January 5, 1978, 23–24.

89. Lucas also profiled Tina in a July 1977 cover story; there he does mention that Tina was booked for carrying a gun "because of an unpleasant divorce from her

husband, Ike." See Bob Lucas, "Trials and Triumphs Test Tina Turner," *Jet*, July 28, 1977, 59.

90. All quotes from Turner, *My Love Story*, 109.

91. Quoted in Turner, *I, Tina*, 167.

92. Turner, *I, Tina*, 171–72.

93. Turner, *I, Tina*, 167.

94. Turner, *I, Tina*, 172.

95. All quotes from Turner, *I, Tina*, 172.

96. Turner, *My Love Story*, 110.

97. This incident is described in Turner, *My Love Story*, 110–11.

98. Turner, *I, Tina*, 165.

99. Turner, *I, Tina*, 166.

100. All quotes taken from Turner, *I, Tina*, 169.

101. Turner, *My Love Story*, 112. Interestingly, the earliest "first use" listed for the trademarked "Tina Turner" is 1978, the same year Ike and Tina Turner's divorce was finalized. See https://tmsearch.uspto.gov/bin/showfield?f=doc&state =4810:xrhvo4.5.3.

102. The film was produced by Robert Stigwood, who also produced *Tommy*. See a review of the film in Frank Meyer, "Music Records: High-Priced Choir Makes Film Bow with 'Sgt. Pepper,'" *Variety*, December 21, 1977, 61 and 65.

103. Bill Lane, "Tina Turner Goes Solo," *Memphis Tri-State Defender*, January 28, 1978, 7.

104. Previously, this mix of genres was also fully displayed on the funk band Rufus's gold-selling second album, *Rags to Rufus* (ABC, 1974). In 2003, Chaka Khan released her autobiography, *Chaka! Through the Fire* (New York: Rodale Books, 2003). Khan writes that Ike Turner flew Rufus to Los Angeles to record them at Bolic Sound Studios. According to Khan, Ike was interested in making her either a replacement for Turner or, at the very least, an Ikette. Khan was a member of Rufus until 1983.

105. "Record World Album Picks," *Record World*, October 21, 1978, 20.

106. "Album Reviews," *Cash Box*, October 7, 1978, 20.

107. "Billboard's Top Album Picks," *Billboard*, October 7, 1978, 82.

108. Turner, *My Love Story*, 109.

109. "Sex and Religion Keep Tina Turner Famous and Humble," *Jet*, February 15, 1979, 60–63.

110. Armani, *The Real T.*, 144.

111. Turner, *Happiness Becomes You*, 124–25.

112. Quoted in Turner, *Happiness Becomes You*, 197.

113. Turner, *Happiness Becomes You*, 107.

114. Both quotes from Daisaku Ikeda, *Learning from the Gosho: The Eternal Teachings of Nichiren Daishonin* (Santa Monica, CA: World Tribune Press, 1997), 129. Ikeda is commenting on Nichiren's writing, "Letter to the Mother of Oto." See *The Writings of Nichiren Daishonin*, vol. 2 (Tokyo: Soka Gakkai, 2006), 1030–31. In the letter,

Nichiren praises the mother of one of his disciples for traveling a long distance to see him. Nichiren likens this to the patriarchs of his tradition who traveled great distances to learn about Buddhist teachings. Specifically, he states that this is evidence of a person's devotion. In his commentary, Ikeda uses the example of the mother as an opportunity to discuss the nature of a person's heart or spirit (and thus the person's determination) based on a passage of another Buddhist sutra and the doctrinal concept of *ichinen sanzen*.

115. Turner, *Happiness Becomes You*, 94.

116. Turner, *I, Tina*, 173.

117. Turner, *I, Tina*, 173.

118. Turner, *My Love Story*, 115.

119. Turner, *My Love Story*, 115.

120. For a cogent history of disco, see Peter Shapiro, *Turn the Beat Around: The Secret History of Disco* (New York: Faber & Faber, 2005).

121. "Capitol to Retain Only Top Artists from UA Diskery," *Variety*, March 28, 1979, 84.

122. Turner, *I, Tina*, 173.

123. Turner, *My Love Story*, 115.

124. Turner, *I, Tina*, 173; Armani, *The Real T.*, 125-26.

125. Armani, *The Real T.*, 126.

126. This meeting is described in Turner, *My Love Story*, 115-16. All quotes therein; brackets original. See also Turner, *I, Tina*, 175-76.

127. Armani, *The Real T.*, 127.

128. Turner, *My Love Story*, 117.

129. Quoted in Turner, *I, Tina*, 176.

130. Quoted in *Behind the Music*, season 1, episode 111, "Tina Turner: Behind the Music," written by Gay Rosenthal, featuring Tina Turner, aired March 5, 2000, on VH1.

131. Turner, *My Love Story*, 117.

132. Quoted in Turner, *I, Tina*, 176.

133. Turner, *I, Tina*, 175; Armani, *The Real T.*, 128.

134. Saul Dubrow, "Afrikaner Nationalism, Apartheid and the Conceptualization of 'Race,'" *Journal of African History* 33, no. 2 (1992): 209-37.

135. Saul Dubrow, "Racial Irredentism, Ethnogenesis, and White Supremacy in High-Apartheid South Africa," *Kronos*, no. 41 (November 2015): 237.

136. A list of UN actions against the South African apartheid regime can be found here: "The UN: Partner in the Struggle against Apartheid," United Nations in South Africa, accessed September 7, 2021, https://southafrica.un.org/en/about/about-the-un.

137. Quoted in Christopher Connelly, "Apartheid Rock," *Rolling Stone*, June 10, 1982, https://www.rollingstone.com/music/music-news/apartheid-rock-108260/.

138. Quoted in Militant Blacks, "Entertainers Told to Stay Away from South Africa," *Korea Times*, November 29, 1980, 4.

139. In *I, Tina*, Turner claims that the South Africa tour took place in 1979. However, press reports are unanimous in reporting that the shows took place in September and October of 1980. See, for example, two press reports: "International: Tina Turner Advert Row," *Billboard*, September 20, 1980, 67, and "Turner Wins over Press, Fans in S. Africa Tour," *Variety*, October 1, 1980, 112. It is possible that Turner toured South Africa in both 1979 and 1980, but I have found no evidence that she ever performed in the country in 1979.

140. Turner, *I, Tina*, 177.

141. Quoted in Blacks, "Entertainers Told to Stay Away," 4.

142. Quoted in Turner, *I, Tina*, 178.

143. Quoted in Turner, *I, Tina*, 178.

144. Quoted in Armani, *The Real T.*, 148.

145. Jay L. Garfield, *Buddhist Ethics: A Philosophical Exploration* (New York: Oxford University Press, 2022), 174.

146. Garfield, *Buddhist Ethics*, 175.

147. Garfield, *Buddhist Ethics*, 175.

148. Garfield, *Buddhist Ethics*, 175-78. See also Garfield's discussion of action theory and karma on 14-17.

149. See Garfield, *Buddhist Ethics*, chap. 12. See also Christopher S. Queen, ed., *Engaged Buddhism in the West* (Boston: Wisdom Publications, 2000), and Sallie B. King, *Being Benevolence: The Social Ethics of Engaged Buddhism* (Honolulu: University of Hawaii Press, 2005).

150. Jan Willis, *Dharma Matters: Women, Race, and Tantra* (Somerville, MA: Wisdom Publications, 2020), 126-30. Religious studies scholar Rima Vesely-Flad has researched the usage of Buddhist teaching for healing historical and systemic traumas in twentieth- and twenty-first-century writings by Black Buddhists; see Vesely-Flad, *Black Buddhists and the Black Radical Tradition*.

151. Note should be taken, however, of Larry Ward's usage of karma to explain race in the United States. See Larry Ward, *America's Racial Karma: An Invitation to Heal* (Berkeley, CA: Parallax, 2020).

152. Quoted in Armani, *The Real T.*, 149.

153. Quoted in Turner, *I, Tina*, 178.

154. Quoted in Turner, *I, Tina*, 178-79.

155. Quoted in Turner, *I, Tina*, 179. See also Turner, *My Love Story*, 118.

156. Turner, *My Love Story*, 118.

157. "Sound Business: Studio Track," *Billboard*, April 4, 1981, 77.

158. Turner, *I, Tina*, 180.

159. Dennis Hunt, "Rhythm 'n' Raunch a la Tina Turner," *Los Angeles Times*, April 8, 1981, H7.

160. Paul McGrath, "Tina Still Has the Patent on Sexy Soul Fireworks," *Toronto Globe and Mail*, April 21, 1981, 18.

161. Roger Davies, quoted in Turner, *I, Tina*, 181.

162. Quoted in Turner, *I, Tina*, 181.

163. Stephen Holden, "Pop: Tina Turner at the Ritz, the Mae West of Rock Music," *New York Times*, May 14, 1981, C15.

164. Laura Foti, "Talent in Action: Tina Turner," *Variety*, October 24, 1981, 34.

165. Rich, "Concert Reviews: Tina Turner," *Variety*, November 4, 1981, 66.

166. Stewart often cited Tina Turner as an early influence. According to Paul Nelson and Lester Bangs, in the mid-1960s Stewart performed as a member of a British soul outfit—the Soul Agents—that aimed to be a "white soul revue" modeled on the likes of the Ike & Tina Turner Revue. See Paul Nelson and Lester Bangs, *Rod Stewart* (New York: Delilah Books, 1981), 61.

167. Robert Palmer, "The Pop Life: Is Rod Stewart Cured of the Illness of Success and Back . . . ," *New York Times*, October 28, 1981, C19.

168. John Rockwell, "Pop: The Stones at Play," *New York Times*, November 7, 1981, 1.9.

169. Maureen Mahon, "TMT 232: Maureen Mahon," interview with boice, *Talk Music Talk with boice*, podcast audio, August 4, 2021, https://open.spotify.com/episode/6pIqgIDHBWBBIFpRDLKLuv?si=eR-lZS9DT2iBX_ovA7B7Eg&dl_branch=1&nd=1.

170. Turner, *My Love Story*, 118–19.

171. See Palmer, "The Pop Life," C19.

172. Rockwell, "Pop," 1.9.

173. Carl Arrington, quoted in *TINA*, directed by Dan Lindsay and T. J. Martin (New York: HBO Documentary Films, 2021).

174. Quoted in Carl Arrington, "Tina Turner, the Woman Who Taught Mick Jagger to Dance, Is on the Prowl Again," *People*, December 7, 1981.

175. Arrington, "Tina Turner."

176. Quotes in Arrington, "Tina Turner." July 1, 1976, is given as the day she left Ike, but in all other sources Tina, and others, have consistently maintained that it was July 3, 1976.

177. Arrington, "Tina Turner."

178. See above, chap. 2.

179. All quotes from *TINA*.

180. For a collection of such experiences, see Zan Gaudioso and Greg Martin, *The Buddha Next Door: Ordinary People, Extraordinary Stories* (Santa Monica, CA: Middleway, 2007).

181. A report in the *Korea Times* discusses Tina performing in Poland when Carl Arrington's *People* profile was on newsstands. See "Singer Turner Delights Poles," *Korea Times*, December 7, 1981, 5.

Chapter 5

1. *Live in Amsterdam*, directed by David Mallet (Eagle Rock Entertainment, [1996] 1999), DVD.

2. See *The Writings of Nichiren Daishonin*, vol. 1 (Tokyo: Soka Gakkai, 1999), 905.

3. SGI-USA, *An Introduction to Buddhism*, 2nd ed. (Santa Monica, CA: SGI-USA, 2016), 36.

4. *Tina Turner: Nice 'n' Rough*, directed by David Mallet (Thorn/EMI Music Video, 1982), VHS.

5. Tina Turner, with Kurt Loder, *I, Tina: My Life Story* (New York: Morrow, 1986), 185.

6. Quoted in Turner, *I, Tina*, 185.

7. Robin Denselow, "The Band's on the Run," *Guardian*, April 12, 1982, 9.

8. Turner, *I, Tina*, 185.

9. Tina Turner, *Happiness Becomes You: A Guide to Changing Your Life for Good* (New York: Atria Books, 2020), 108.

10. Turner, *Happiness Becomes You*, 109. Here she is quoting Daisaku Ikeda, *My Dear Friends in America: Collected Addresses to the SGI-USA Since 1990*, 3rd ed. (Santa Monica, CA: World Tribune Press, 2012), 258. This quote of Ikeda's parallels the discussion in chap. 4 above.

11. George M. Williams, *Freedom and Influence: The Role of Religion in American Society* (Santa Monica, CA: World Tribune Press, 1985), 160.

12. Williams, *Freedom and Influence*, 161.

13. Sara Rimer and Elsa L. Walsh, "Buddhists Parade; Peace Day Celebrated by Women's Group," *Washington Post*, October 11, 1982, C1.

14. See Ted Sell, "Militant Japanese Sect Seeks New Recruits," *Los Angeles Times*, September 21, 1962, 23; Nancy J. Adler, "Soka Gakkai Pray for a Richer Life," *New York Times*, March 3, 1968, 8; and Kim Klein, "Nichiren Shoshu, Rah! Rah! Rah! Inner Peace, Happiness, Hooray! The Power of the Chant," *Washington Post*, December 27, 1970, G1.

15. Turner, *Happiness Becomes You*, photograph between 100 and 102.

16. Turner, *Happiness Becomes You*, 105.

17. Or such beings are *already* awakened and they perform salvific deeds for the sake of other beings. See Rupert Gethin, *The Foundations of Buddhism* (Oxford: Oxford University Press, 1998), 226–31.

18. *The Soka Gakkai Dictionary of Buddhism*, s.v. "bodhisattva," accessed October 29, 2022, https://www.nichirenlibrary.org/en/dic/Content/B/40.

19. *The Soka Gakkai Dictionary of Buddhism*, s.v. "bodhisattva."

20. Daisaku Ikeda, *The New Human Revolution*, vol. 1 (Santa Monica, CA: World Tribune Press, 1995), 244.

21. See Jacob Hoye, *MTV Uncensored* (New York: Pocket Books, 2001); Margena A.

Christian, "Why It Took MTV So Long to Play Black Music Videos," *Jet*, October 9, 2006, 16-18 and 53-54; and Alan Wells, "Black Artists in American Popular Music, 1955-1985," *Phylon* 48, no. 4 (1987): 309-16.

22. Jack Lloyd, "Entertainment: Tina Turner Is Still a Rock Queen," *Philadelphia Inquirer*, January 14, 1983, E26.

23. "Co-writer of 'Incense' Lyrics," *Los Angeles Times*, May 27, 2011, AA6.

24. "Music Records: Perry Named V.P. of Capitol A&R," *Variety*, June 2, 1976, 57; "General News: Executive Turntable," *Billboard*, June 5, 1976, 6.

25. Turner, *I, Tina*, 185.

26. Turner, *I, Tina*, 185.

27. See reporting in "News: Executive Turntable," *Billboard*, March 12, 1983, 4; "News: Executive Turntable," *Billboard*, April 2, 1983, 4; and "News: Executive Turntable," *Billboard*, May 28, 1983, 4.

28. Turner, *I, Tina*, 185-86.

29. Quoted in Turner, *I, Tina*, 186.

30. Turner, *I, Tina*, 187. See also Tina Turner, *My Love Story* (New York: Penguin, 2019), 120-23.

31. With Bowie, Turner recorded the song "Tonight" for Bowie's *Tonight* album (EMI America, 1984).

32. Turner, *My Love Story*, 132.

33. Timothy White, "David Bowie," *Musician*, May 1, 1983, 59 and 60.

34. Turner, *My Love Story*, 132.

35. Quoted in *The Girl from Nutbush*, directed by Chris Cowey (Picture Music International, 1992), VHS.

36. John Carter, quoted in *TINA*, directed by Dan Lindsay and T. J. Martin (New York: HBO Documentary Films, 2021).

37. Quoted in *TINA*.

38. *TINA*. In a statement provided to entertainment news website TheWrap, a spokesperson from Capitol Records sought to distance the company from these comments: "The incident that John Carter describes in the HBO documentary, 'Tina,' would have occurred 40 years ago when Capitol was under different ownership and management, and we're only now learning of those reprehensible and appalling comments." The spokesperson goes on to say: "Capitol Music Group is proud of our association with Tina Turner and the role we play in ensuring her music will continue to inspire new generations for decades to come." See Ross A. Lincoln and Andrea Towers, "Capitol Records Condemns 'Reprehensible' Former Exec Who Called Tina Turner N-Word (Exclusive)," *TheWrap*, March 29, 2021, https://www.thewrap.com/capitol-records-condemns-reprehensible-former-exec-who-called-tina-turner-n-word-exclusive/.

39. Mark Bego, *Tina Turner: Break Every Rule* (Lanham, MD: Rowman & Littlefield, 2003), 158.

40. Turner, *I, Tina*, 188.

41. Quoted in Turner, *I, Tina*, 189.

42. Quoted in Bego, *Tina Turner*, 158.

43. Turner, *My Love Story*, 122.

44. "Hits of the World," *Billboard*, November 26, 1983, 56.

45. "Hits of the World," *Billboard*, December 3, 1983, 54.

46. "Light Entertainment News: Venue Nights," *The Stage and Television Today*, November 24, 1983, 3.

47. "Singles Radio Action," *Billboard*, January 21, 1984, 19. See also Turner, *I, Tina*, 191.

48. "Singles Reviews: Black," *Billboard*, January 14, 1984, 63.

49. "Advertisement," *Billboard*, January 21, 1984, 45.

50. "Feature Picks," *Cash Box*, January 14, 1984, 9.

51. "Feature Picks," 9. See also "Music Records: Record Reviews—Singles," *Variety*, February 1, 1984, 128.

52. See Turner, *I, Tina*, 189.

53. See "Radio: Most Added Records," *Billboard*, January 28, 1984, 16, and "Hot 100," *Billboard*, January 28, 1984, 72.

54. Turner, *I, Tina*, 191.

55. Paul Grein, "Talent and Venues: Tina Turner Rocks Back into Top 40," *Billboard*, February 25, 1984, 41 and 48.

56. Ed Blanche, "Tina Turner: The Earth Mother's Back," *Atlanta Constitution*, February 18, 1984, D34.

57. Blanche, "Tina Turner."

58. Quoted in *TINA*.

59. See Turner, *My Love Story*, 123.

60. For a more complete picture of the production of the album, see Turner, *I, Tina*, 191–94, and Turner, *My Love Story*, 123–27.

61. Quoted in Turner, *I, Tina*, 193.

62. Quoted in "Tina Turner Interview 20/1/1985 with Lisa Robinson," uploaded by SaraJ, May 13, 2017, https://youtu.be/7DHwCXwRzL8.

63. All quotes from Turner, *Happiness Becomes You*, 116–17.

64. Turner, *Happiness Becomes You*, 117.

65. On *samsara*, see Gethin, *The Foundations of Buddhism*, 27 and 64.

66. See Ikeda, *My Dear Friends in America*, 34–35.

67. See Turner, *I, Tina*, 194.

68. "Lionel Richie: Tour Dates Set," *Los Angeles Sentinel*, April 19, 1984, B5.

69. Turner, *I, Tina*, 195.

70. Turner, *My Love Story*, 126.

71. "Search: Tina Turner," RIAA, accessed September 26, 2021, https://www.riaa.com/gold-platinum/?tab_active=default-award&se=Tina+Turner#search_section.

72. Stephen Holden, "Tina Turner Turns a Page in the Evolution of Pop-Soul," *New York Times*, August 26, 1984, H22.

73. See, for example, Carl Mathews, "Private Dancer," *Baltimore Afro-American*, August 18, 1984, 11.

74. Turner, *I, Tina*, 196. Paul Grein, "News: Chartbeat," *Billboard*, September 1, 1984, 6. See also "Chart History: Tina Turner," *Billboard*, Prometheus Global Media, accessed February 17, 2020, https://www.billboard.com/music/tina-turner /chart-history/HSI/song/334033.

75. "Near-$13-Mil 'Mad Max 3' Set to Roll with Gibson, Tina Turner," *Variety*, September 5, 1984, 7 and 30.

76. Quoted in Kurt Loder, "Sole Survivor," *Rolling Stone*, October 11, 1984, 19.

77. Loder, "Sole Survivor," 20.

78. Quoted in Loder, "Sole Survivor," 60.

79. See *Vimalakīrtinirdeśa: The Teaching of Vimalakīrti*, trans. from Sanskrit by Luis Gómez and Paul Harrison (Berkeley, CA: Mangalam, 2022), 169.

80. *The Soka Gakkai Dictionary of Buddhism*, s.v. "expedient means." For a full discussion of this doctrine, see Paul Williams, *Mahāyāna Buddhism: The Doctrinal Foundations*, 2nd ed. (London: Routledge, 2009), 150-57.

81. Turner, *I, Tina*, 197.

82. "Tina Turner," *Billboard*, December 22, 1984, 2.

83. "Search: Tina Turner," *American Music Awards*, accessed September 27, 2021, https://www.theamas.com/winners-database/?winnerKeyword=Tina+Turner &winnerYear=.

84. USA for Africa was initially spearheaded by Harry Belafonte. Belafonte himself was inspired by the efforts of charity supergroup Band Aid, led by Irish musician and activist Bob Geldof. For a detailed overview of the purpose, recording, and impact of "We Are the World," see Jaap Kooijman, *Fabricating the Absolute Fake: America in Contemporary Pop Culture*, rev. ed. (Amsterdam: Amsterdam University Press, 2013), 23-42.

85. "Artist: Tina Turner," Recording Academy Grammy Awards, accessed September 27, 2021, https://www.grammy.com/grammys/artists/tina-turner/7641.

86. See Geoffrey F. Brown, "Tina Turner Talks about Ike and 'Tommy,'" *Jet*, April 24, 1975, 61.

87. Carl Arrington, "Cover: Thunder Dame," *People*, July 15, 1985, 44-46 and 49-50.

88. Turner, *My Love Story*, 127. See also Steven Spielberg's comments in Joe Baltake, "Why Book Made Spielberg See Purple," *Philadelphia Daily News*, December 17, 1985, 45.

89. Nancy Griffin, "Tina," *Life*, August 1985, 23-28.

90. With Bryan Adams, Tina recorded the song "It's Only Love" for Adams's *Reckless* album (A&M, 1984).

91. Turner, *My Love Story*, 143.

92. William Gin, tour book production, *Tina: Private Dancer Tour 1985* (USA: 1985).

The tour book covers only the American leg of the tour, thus the concert dates listed are incomplete.

93. Taro Gold noted that Tina relied particularly on the collection of Ikeda's guidance contained in Daisaku Ikeda, *Guidance Memo*, trans. George M. Williams (Santa Monica, CA: World Tribune Press, 1975). This collection contains a number of quotes by Ikeda related to perseverance. See, for example, 73, 74, and 97. Taro Gold, telephone interview by the author, July 26, 2021.

94. "Behind Tina Turner's Dynamic Comeback and New Fame," *Seikyo Shimbun*, January 5, 1986.

95. Turner, *I, Tina*, 202.

96. Turner, *I, Tina*, 202.

97. Bego, *Tina Turner*, 190. See also liner notes for Tina Turner, *Break Every Rule*, Capitol Records, 1986, CD. For details on the making of the album, see Mark Rowland, "Tina Turner Ain't Funky Anymore," *Musician* 96 (October 1986).

98. See Lisa A. Lewis, *Gender Politics and MTV: Voicing the Difference* (Philadelphia: Temple University Press, 1990).

99. Lewis, *Gender Politics and MTV*, 78.

100. Liner notes for Tina Turner, *Break Every Rule*, 4, 9, 10, 11, and 12.

101. Quoted in Elizabeth Sporkin, "Star: Tina Turner," *Ladies' Home Journal*, April 1987, 39.

102. Quoted in Rowland, "Tina Turner Ain't Funky Anymore," 74.

103. See, for example, Daniel Brogan's *Chicago Tribune* album review: "Turner Outdoes 'Dancer' with 'Break Every Rule' LP," *Chicago Tribune*, September 12, 1986, N_A75.

104. "Search: Tina Turner," RIAA, accessed October 1, 2021, https://www.riaa .com/gold-platinum/?tab_active=default-award&se=Tina+Turner#search_section.

105. See Peter Jones, "Tina Turner: Record-Breaking European Tour Stands as Lasting Tribute," *Billboard*, August 15, 1987, T-22.

106. Stylorouge, programme design, *Tina Turner Break Every Rule World Tour 1987/88* (USA: Teamwork Productions, 1987), 1.

107. The countries were Germany, Holland, England, Switzerland, Belgium, Norway, Sweden, Spain, Italy, Austria, France, Ireland, and Denmark. See Jones, "Tina Turner," T-22.

108. See Robert Hillburn, "U2's $35-Million Gross Is Highest for '87 Tour," *Los Angeles Times*, January 23, 1988, EOC1.

109. See Charles Shaar Murray, "The Long Goodbye," Q, April 1988, 52–60.

110. *Rio '88: Tina Turner*, directed by Roberto Talmo (New York: EV Classics, 2001 [1988]), DVD.

111. Murray, "The Long Goodbye," 52. See also "Tina Turner's Farewell Tour Breaks Every Record," *Los Angeles Sentinel*, April 21, 1988, B7. While promoting the tour, Turner claimed that this would be her farewell tour. She repeated this claim about each of the subsequent five tours she embarked upon.

112. Tina Turner, liner notes for *Foreign Affair* (2021 Remastered Boxset), Tina Turner, Parlophone, 2021 [Capitol, 1989], no page numbers.

113. Quoted in Roger Scott, "Foreign Affair Track by Track with Tina," liner notes for *Foreign Affair*.

114. See Jason Draper, "Foreign Affair: Behind Tina Turner's Commitment to Being the Best," *Dig!*, July 16, 2021, https://www.thisisdig.com/feature/foreign-affair -tina-turner-album-holly-knight-interview/.

115. See Glenn Sakamoto, tour book design, *Tina Turner Foreign Affair World Tour 1990* (England, 1990), no page numbers.

116. See Andrew McGibbon, *I Was Douglas Adams's Flatmate: And Other Encounters with Legends* (London: Faber & Faber, 2011), 135.

117. See Chris Welch, *The Tina Turner Experience: The Illustrated Biography* (London: Virgin Books, 1994), 189.

118. Tina Turner, liner notes for *Tina Live in Europe*, Tina Turner, Capitol, 1988, CD, no page numbers.

119. Murray, "The Long Goodbye," 59. Moyra Caldecott, a British writer of historical fiction, claimed in her memoir *Multi-Dimensional Life* that in October 1988 Turner traveled with her to Egypt. See Moyra Caldecott, *Multi-Dimensional Life: A Writer on the Process of Writing* (Bath, UK: Bladud Books, 2007), 105-25. I have been unable to find any information to verify this, but Turner did acknowledge in interviews that she spent time traveling during her year off. For example, see Lynn Norment, "Rich, Free and in Control: The 'Foreign Affairs' of Tina Turner," *Ebony*, November 1989, 168.

120. See Turner, *My Love Story*, 145-56.

121. For example, see Lisa Robinson, "People Are Talking About: Music; Lisa, It's for You . . . It's Tina Turner!" *Vogue* 177, no. 5 (May 1, 1987): 94.

122. See "Tina Turner: 50 and Foxy with New LP, New Boyfriend," *Jet*, January 15, 1990, 56-59.

123. Turner, *My Love Story*, 156. However, Tina did subsequently move to Germany with Erwin.

124. "Chart History: Tina Turner," *Billboard*, accessed October 3, 2021, https://www.billboard.com/music/tina-turner/chart-history/TCL/song/309714.

125. "Search: Tina Turner," RIAA, accessed October 1, 2021, https://www.riaa .com/gold-platinum/?tab_active=default-award&se=Tina+Turner#search_section. For a review, see Greg Kot, "'Foreign Affair' Lets Turner Head Home," *Chicago Tribune*, September 17, 1989, J6.

126. Quoted in "Tina Turner Interview 20/1/1985 with Lisa Robinson."

127. Quoted in Iain Blair, "Toned-Down Tina," *Chicago Tribune*, September 17, 1989, J6.

128. Quoted in *The Girl from Nutbush*, directed by Chris Cowey (Picture Music International, 1992), VHS.

129. Quoted in Nancy Collins, "The Rolling Stone Interview: Tina Turner," *Rolling Stone* 485 (October 1986): 49.

130. Dator drew his data from a survey of 114 issues of Soka Gakkai's organ publication, the *Seikyo News*. *Seikyo Times* was published from May 15, 1962, to September 28, 1965, running 148 issues in that time frame. Dator points out that *Seikyo News* was superseded by *Seikyo Times*, and the latter was then superseded by *World Tribune*. From the issues he surveyed, Dator pulled two hundred testimonials of American members, from which he concluded "that the 'typical' American member is a white male in his twenties or thirties, in the military but of less than officer rank, married to a Japanese [woman] who was a member of the Sōka Gakkai before they met, converted by his wife, and . . . of Roman Catholic or lower-class Protestant background." See James Allen Dator, *Sōka Gakkai, Builders of the Third Civilization: American and Japanese Members* (Seattle: University of Washington Press, 1969), 31-32.

131. Dator, *Sōka Gakkai*, 32. See also Richard Seager, *Encountering the Dharma: Daisaku Ikeda, Soka Gakkai, and the Globalization of Buddhist Humanism* (Berkeley: University of California Press, 2006), 146-47.

132. Williams, *Freedom and Influence*, 186.

133. Major newspapers reported on the success of NSA's conversion efforts, often with inflated membership numbers. For example, see Klein, "Nichiren Shoshu," G1.

134. Williams, *Freedom and Influence*, 187. See also Seager, *Encountering the Dharma*, 147-49.

135. See, for example, Jan Willis, *Dharma Matters: Women, Race, and Tantra* (Somerville, MA: Wisdom Publications, 2020), 96-97; David W. Chappell, "Racial Diversity in the Soka Gakkai," in *Engaged Buddhism in the West*, ed. Christopher S. Queen (Somerville, MA: Wisdom Publications, 2000), 184-217; and Rima Vesely-Flad, *Black Buddhists and the Black Radical Tradition: The Practice of Stillness in the Movement for Liberation* (New York: New York University Press, 2022), 279n1.

136. These authors' writings can be found in many sources. Among the most compelling: Willis, *Dharma Matters*, chaps. 7 and 8; Ruth King, "Wholeness Is No Trifling Matter: Race, Refuge, and Faith," in *Black and Buddhist: What Buddhism Can Teach Us about Race, Resilience, Transformation, and Freedom*, ed. Pamela Ayo Yetunde and Cheryl A. Giles (Boulder, CO: Shambhala, 2020), 150-74; Zenju Earthlyn Manuel, *The Way of Tenderness: Awakening through Race, Sexuality, and Gender* (Boston: Wisdom Publications, 2015); and Rev. angel Kyodo Williams, Lama Rod Owens, and Jasmine Syedullah, *Radical Dharma: Talking Race, Love, and Liberation* (Berkeley, CA: North Atlantic Books, 2016).

137. Quoted in Welch, *The Tina Turner Experience*, 194.

138. See the profile of Ike Turner in Edward Kiersh, "Ike's Story," *Spin*, August 1985, https://www.spin.com/2015/06/ikes-story-1985-feature-ike-tina-turner/.

139. Turner, *My Love Story*, 139.

140. Tina Turner, interviewed by Mike Wallace, *60 Minutes*, November 10, 1996, video.

141. Turner, interviewed by Wallace.

142. See, "Tina Turner," *Variety*, April 20, 1988, 141.

143. Quoted in Bego, *Tina Turner*, 207; Gerry Hirshey, "Woman Warrior at 53, the Amazing Tina Turner Just Keeps on Rollin,'" *GQ*, June 1993.

144. On the making of the film, see Aldore Collier, "'What's Love Got to Do with It,'" *Ebony*, July 1993, 110-12.

145. Taro Gold, telephone interview by the author, July 26, 2021.

146. *What's Love Got to Do with It?*'s narrative licenses are helpfully summarized in Donald Brackett, *Tumult: The Incredible Life and Music of Tina Turner* (Guilford, CT: Backbeat Books, 2020), 148-53.

147. Quoted in Mark Rowland, "Tina's Tag Team," *Musicians*, no. 96 (October 1986): 78.

148. Quoted in "Interview Tina Turner: Private Answers," *Vox*, April 1, 1992, 17.

149. Liner notes for *What's Love Got to Do With It?*, Tina Turner, Virgin 1993, CD.

150. For reviews, see Janet Maslin, "Review/Film: What's Love Got to Do with It; Tina Turner's Tale: Living Life with Ike and Then without Him," *New York Times*, June 9, 1993, C15; "Review: What's Love Got to Do with It," *Afro-American Red Star*, June 5, 1993, B6; and Kenneth Turan, "'Love': Playing It Nice and Rough; Exceptional Acting Powers Story of Up and Downs of Ike and Tina Turner," *Los Angeles Times*, June 9, 1993, F1.

151. See Leonard Klady, "Top 100 Pix Take $8 Bil Globally," *Variety*, January 3, 1994, 42.

152. See "Tina's New Book Offers Hope to Victims of Spouse Abuse," *Baltimore Afro-American*, October 4, 1986, 11.

153. Quoted in "Review: What's Love Got to Do with It," *Afro-American Red Star*.

154. Turner, *My Love Story*, 166.

155. Turner, *My Love Story*, 166. See also her comments made during a press conference for the movie, shown in *TINA*.

156. Jana Lynne White, "The Speak Easy Interview: Tina Turner," uploaded by Jack James, June 7, 2021, https://www.youtube.com/watch?v=-EciVhTjF8Y.

157. Welch, *The Tina Turner Experience*, 168.

158. "The Queen of Hope: Tina Turner," *Living Buddhism*, August 1, 2018, 10.

159. Maureen Orth, "The Lady Has Legs," *Vanity Fair*, 1993, https://archive.vanityfair.com/article/1993/5/the-lady-has-legs.

160. Jan Willis, *Dreaming Me: Black, Baptist, and Buddhist—One Woman's Spiritual Journey* (Boston: Wisdom Publications, 2008), 338-39.

161. Willis, *Dharma Matters*, 127.

162. It is unknown why she chose to rehearse the tour in South Africa. It was likely cost-effective to do so. This was the reason for rehearsing the Break Every Rule World Tour 1987/88 in Germany. See Jones, "Tina Turner," T-22.

163. See Holly Millea, "Tina Turner Happy at Last," *Elle*, August 1996, 151-52.

164. Turner, *My Love Story*, 159.

165. Quoted in Robin Eggar, "Tina Turner," *London Daily Express*, November 17, 1996, 31.

166. Deepak Chopra, *The Seven Spiritual Laws of Success: A Practical Guide to the Fulfillment of Your Dreams* (New York: Harmony, 1994).

167. See Turner, *My Love Story*, 22-23 and 186.

168. Mournehis relayed this story in a podcast interview. See Andrew Mournehis, interview with Daniel Tucker, "Divine Grace," *Spiritual Tradie* (podcast), January 2018, https://open.spotify.com/episode/1UFY2zWSCf6k ab6KXJ5hCT?si=pciRNpTgRfOjY64fnLWKaA&dl_branch=1.

169. Steve Moles, "Four for Tina and the Queen of Rock's Wildest Dreams Tour," *TCI* 31, no. 3 (March 1997): 45.

170. Steve Odin, "Nichiren Buddhism in the Contemporary Jazz Improvisation of Herbie Hancock and Wayne Shorter," *Polish Journal of Aesthetics* 54, no. 3 (2019): 65.

171. Odin, "Nichiren Buddhism," 71-72.

172. Odin, "Nichiren Buddhism," 76.

173. Herbie Hancock, Daisaku Ikeda, and Wayne Shorter, *Reaching Beyond: Improvisations on Jazz, Buddhism, and a Joyful Life* (Santa Monica, CA: World Tribune Press, 2017), 58.

174. Hancock, Ikeda, and Shorter, *Reaching Beyond*, 68.

175. Jason C. Bivins, *Spirits Rejoice! Jazz and American Religion* (New York: Oxford University Press, 2015), 245.

176. All quotes from Bivins, *Spirits Rejoice!*, 246.

177. See Ann Taves, *Fits, Trances, and Visions: Experience Religion and Explaining Experience from Wesley to James* (Princeton: Princeton University Press, 1999), 103.

178. William G. McLoughlin, *Revivals, Awakenings, and Reform* (Chicago: University of Chicago Press, 1978), 208-11. See also the discussion of McLoughlin in Robin Sylvan, *Traces of the Spirit: The Religious Dimension of Popular Music* (New York: New York University Press, 2002), 70. Sylvan is drawing on McLoughlin, 1-23. For more on religious experience and performance during the awakenings, see Taves, 76-117.

179. Quoted in Turner, *Happiness Becomes You*, 195.

180. Private communication with the author.

181. Millea, "Tina Turner Happy at Last," 151-54, and Lynn Norment, "Living My Wildest Dream: Tina Turner," *Ebony*, September 1996, 38-40 and 42-44.

182. Oprah Winfrey, quoted in *TINA*.

183. Kathryn Lofton, *Oprah: The Gospel of an Icon* (Berkeley: University of California Press, 2011), 58-59.

184. Lofton parses the combinatory, interconnected threads of Winfrey's spirituality: Lofton, *Oprah*, 51-81.

185. See Lofton, *Oprah*, 118-47.

186. Lofton, *Oprah*, 127.

187. Lofton, *Oprah*, 127-28.

188. Lofton's book deals with each of these strategies. See especially Lofton, *Oprah*, chaps 1; 3; and 5.

189. Oprah Winfrey, quoted in Turner, *My Love Story*, 167.

190. Lofton, *Oprah*, 4.

191. Winfrey's esteem for these figures is demonstrated by her inclusion of them, and Turner, in her 2005 Legends Ball celebration.

192. Turner, *My Love Story*, 189.

193. Turner, *My Love Story*, 165.

Chapter 6

1. Tina Turner, with Kurt Loder, *I, Tina: My Life Story* (New York: Morrow, 1986), 202.

2. Turner, *I, Tina*, 199.

3. *Shambhala Sun* changed its name to *Lion's Roar* in January 2016.

4. Andrea Miller, "Tina Turner: What's Love Got to Do with It?," *Lion's Roar*, March 7, 2016, https://www.lionsroar.com/tina-turner-whats-love-got-to-do-with -it/. Originally appearing in *Shambhala Sun*, 2011.

5. Angel Romero, "Interview with Regula Curti, Founder of the Beyond Foundation and Beyond Music Project," *World Music Central*, March 3, 2018, https://world musiccentral.org/2018/03/03/interview-with-regula-curti-founder-of-the-beyond -foundation-and-beyond-music-project/.

6. Victor Fuhrman, "Regula Curti: Awakening Beyond," *OMTimes*, accessed October 13, 2022, https://omtimes.com/2017/11/regula-curti-awakening-beyond/.

7. Fuhrman, "Regula Curti."

8. Romero, "Interview with Regula Curti, Founder of the Beyond Foundation and Beyond Music Project."

9. Tina Turner, *Happiness Becomes You: A Guide to Changing Your Life for Good* (New York: Atria Books, 2020), 194.

10. Norbert Classen, "Tina Turner Goes 'Beyond,'" *Newsage*, September/October 2009, 13.

11. Turner, *Happiness Becomes You*, 139.

12. Turner, *Happiness Becomes You*, 148.

13. See Turner, *Happiness Becomes You*, 149, for a description of Turner's composition process, inspired by the books Chopra gave her.

14. Tina Turner, spiritual message, "Beyond," Tina Turner, Gunther Mende-Kim, Pit Loew, Dechen Shak-Dagsay, Regula Curti, recorded 2009, Universal Music Switzerland, track 1 on *Beyond: Buddhist and Christian Prayers*, 2009, digital. The album notes cite Rumi and Deepak Chopra as influences.

15. Regula Curti and Dechen Shak-Dagsay, "The Singers Message," liner notes for *Beyond (Gold Edition): Buddhist and Christian Prayers*, Universal Music Group, 2009.

16. Miller, "Tina Turner."

17. For references to these characteristics in mainstream Buddhist sources, see Bhikkhu Bodhi, *In the Buddha's Words* (Boston: Wisdom Publications, 2000), 306–9. For a discussion of the three characteristics with reference to both mainstream and

Mahāyāna Buddhist sources, see John S. Strong, *Buddhisms* (London: One World Publications, 2015), 127–29.

18. Miller, "Tina Turner."

19. Tina Turner, *My Love Story* (New York: Penguin, 2019), 179.

20. This was a controversial decision. See Doug Camilli, "Turner Passes on Mother's Funeral," *Montreal Gazette*, October 20, 1999, B12, and Liz Hodgson, "Turner Snubs Mum's Funeral," *South China Morning Post*, October 20, 1999, 16.

21. See Turner, *My Love Story*, 176–79, for a full discussion of Tina's relationship with Zelma and the latter's death.

22. Michele Schweitzer, quoted in Mumbi Moody and Robert Jablon, "Ike Turner, Former Husband of Tina, Dies," *Bennington (VT) Banner*, December 13, 2007.

23. Turner, *My Love Story*, 186.

24. See *TINA*, directed by Dan Lindsay and T. J. Martin (New York: HBO Documentary Films, 2021).

25. Buddhist traditions have a range of words for such training practices, including the frequently used *bhavana*, which covers a range of meanings, such as "meditation," "forming in the mind," and "contemplation."

26. *The Liturgy of the Soka Gakkai International* (Santa Monica, CA: World Tribune Press, 2015), 1–5.

27. Daisaku Ikeda, *The Heart of the Lotus Sutra: Lectures on the "Expedient Means" and "Life Span" Chapters* (Santa Monica, CA: World Tribune Press, 2013), 21.

28. See, for example, his discussion of chanting without having a discursive understanding of meaning, in *Selected Writings of Nichiren*, ed. Philip B. Yampolsky, trans. Burton Watson and others (New York: Columbia University Press, 1990), 307–11.

29. For an outline of chapter 2 of the Lotus Sutra and the interpretations of Zhiyi and Nichiren, see Donald S. Lopez Jr. and Jacqueline I. Stone, *Two Buddhas Seated Side by Side* (Princeton: Princeton University Press, 2019), chap. 2. For chap. 16, see Lopez and Stone, chap. 16.

30. "Why Chant Out Loud?," *World Tribune*, June 9, 2017.

31. See Strong, *Buddhisms*, 272–77, for an overview of these layers of mind. For an in-depth introduction to this philosophical school and its origins, see the introduction in Asaṅga, *A Compendium of the Mahāyāna: Asaṅga's Mahāyānasaṃgraga and Its Indian and Tibetan Commentaries*, trans. Karl Brunnhölzl, vol. 1 (Boulder, CO: Snow Lion, 2018).

32. Daisaku Ikeda, *Unlocking the Mysteries of Birth and Death*, 2nd ed. (Santa Monica, CA: Middleway, 2003).

33. Miller, "Tina Turner."

34. Fuhrman, "Regula Curti."

35. Regula Curti, Tina Turner, and Dechen Shak-Dagsay, "Children Beyond: Beyond Dualities," liner notes for *Children Beyond: Understanding through Singing*, Universal Music Group, 2011.

36. Tina Turner, "Calling by Tina," liner notes for *Children Beyond*.

37. "Jai Da Da," liner notes for *Children Beyond*.

38. "Sarvesham Svastir Bhavatu," liner notes for *Children Beyond*.

39. In transliterated Sanskrit: "om˙. sarves˙ām svastir bhavatu. sarves˙ām śāntir bhavatu. sarves˙ām pūrn˙am bhavatu. sarves˙ām man˙galam bhavatu. om˙ śāntih˙ śāntih˙ śāntih˙." The precise origins of the mantra are unknown, but it may be loosely derived from the *Br˙hadāran˙yaka Upanis˙ad*. Author's own translation.

40. See Turner, *Happiness Becomes You*, 175.

41. Tina Turner, "Love Within: Spiritual Message by Tina Turner," *Love Within: Beyond*, UMG, 2014, CD.

42. Turner, *My Love Story*, 179.

43. Henry Louis Gates Jr., *In Search of Our Roots: How 19 Extraordinary African Americans Reclaimed Their Past* (New York: Skyhorse Publishing, 2017), 91.

44. Turner, "Love Within."

45. Turner, "Love Within."

46. "Tina Turner, 64, Reinvents Herself as Screen Goddess," *Times of India*, February 17, 2004, 2. Merchant was criticized by the UK-based Hindu Human Rights organization for casting Tina Turner, a rock singer, in the role of a sacred goddess. Lisa Tsering, "Ismail Merchant Responds to Hindu Protests," *India-West*, March 19, 2004, C26, provides an overview of the controversy and Merchant's response.

47. Turner, quoted in Madhu Jain, "Shakti's Postcards," *Outlook Magazine*, February 23, 2004, https://www.outlookindia.com/magazine/story/shaktis -postcards/223050.

48. For example, see Paul Harvey's discussion of Howard Thurman's trip to India in Paul Harvey, *Howard Thurman and the Disinherited* (Grand Rapids: Eerdmans, 2020), chap. 2.

49. Turner, quoted in Jain, "Shakti's Postcards."

50. For an introduction to the Heart Sutra, see Donald S. Lopez Jr., *Elaborations on Emptiness: Uses of the Heart Sūtra* (Princeton: Princeton University Press, 1996), 3–18. For a detailed exploration of the Mahayana doctrines underlying the Heart Sutra, see Paul Williams, *Mahāyāna Buddhism: The Doctrinal Foundations*, 2nd ed. (New York: Routledge, 2009), 45–62.

51. Charles Hirschkind, "The Ethics of Listening: Cassette-Sermon Audition in Contemporary Egypt," *American Ethnologist* 28, no. 3 (2001): 624.

52. Hirschkind, "The Ethics of Listening," 626–27.

53. See Tracy Fessenden, *Religion around Billie Holiday* (University Park: Pennsylvania State University Press, 2018), 18–26; Vaughn A. Booker, "An Authentic Record of My Race," *Religion and American Culture: A Journal of Interpretation* 25, no. 1 (Winter 2015): 21–25; and Lerone Martin, *Preaching on Wax* (New York: NYU Press, 2014).

54. See Hirschkind, "The Ethics of Listening," 625.

55. Thanissaro Bhikkhu, "Dhammassavana Sutta: Listening to the Dhamma," *Access to Insight*, 1997, https://www.accesstoinsight.org/tipitaka/an/an05/an05.202 .than.html.

56. *The Lotus Sutra and Its Opening and Closing Sutras*, trans. Burton Watson (Tokyo: Soka Gakkai, 2004), 75.

57. Fuhrman, "Regula Curti."

58. Leigh Eric Schmidt, *Restless Souls: The Making of American Spirituality* (New York: HarperSanFrancisco, 2005), 140–41.

59. See Catherine L. Albanese, *A Republic of Mind and Spirit: A Cultural History of American Metaphysical Religion* (New Haven: Yale University Press, 2007), 447–48.

60. Al Kamen, "Tina Turner Formally 'Relinquishes' U.S. Citizenship," *Washington Post*, November 12, 2013, https://www-washingtonpost-com.stanford.idm.oclc .org/in-the-loop/wp/2013/11/12/tina-turner-formally-relinquishes-u-s-citizenship/. See also Turner, *My Love Story*, 194–97.

61. For details of Tina and Erwin Bach's marriage, see Turner, *My Love Story*, 5–18.

62. Turner, *My Love Story*, 198–217.

63. See, for example, Tina Turner, interviewed by Mike Wallace, *60 Minutes*, November 10, 1996, video.

64. Private communication with the author.

65. All material drawn from Turner, *My Love Story*, 241–45.

66. Turner, *Happiness Becomes You*, ix–x.

67. Quoted in Turner, *Happiness Becomes You*, 191.

68. Turner, *Happiness Becomes You*, 194.

69. Taro Gold, *Open Your Mind, Open Your Life: A Book of Eastern Wisdom* (Kansas City, MO: Andrews McMeel Publishing, 2002); *Living Wabi Sabi: The True Beauty of Your Life* (Kansas City, MO: Andrews McMeel Publishing, 2004). See also Taro Gold, "Life," 2021, https://tarogold.com/life/.

70. "Tina Turner: By the Book," *New York Times (Online)*, October 18, 2018.

71. Turner, *Happiness Becomes You*, 196.

72. All information drawn from Turner, *Happiness Becomes You*, afterword.

73. Turner, *Happiness Becomes You*, 3.

74. See *The Soka Gakkai Dictionary of Buddhism*, s.v. "ten worlds," accessed October 29, 2022, https://www.nichirenlibrary.org/en/dic/Content/T/82.

75. For a full explication of the ten worlds in Nichiren's thought, see the discussion of the ten realms in Lopez and Stone, *Two Buddhas Seated Side by Side*.

76. See Ikeda, *Unlocking the Mysteries*, 123–26.

77. Turner, *Happiness Becomes You*, 33–34.

78. Turner, *Happiness Becomes You*, 31.

79. On Buddhist modernism, see David McMahan, *The Making of Buddhist Modernism* (New York: Oxford University Press, 2008). See also Ira Helderman, *Prescribing the Dharma: Psychotherapists, Buddhist Traditions, and Defining Religion* (Chapel Hill: University of North Carolina Press, 2019).

80. Turner, *Happiness Becomes You*, 47. For this history, see Donald S. Lopez Jr., *The Lotus Sutra: A Biography* (Princeton: Princeton University Press, 2016), chaps. 5 and 6.

81. Turner, *Happiness Becomes You*, 97.

82. Turner, *Happiness Becomes You*, 57.

83. Turner, *Happiness Becomes You*, 64.

84. Turner, *Happiness Becomes You*, 69.

85. Larry Ward, *America's Racial Karma: An Invitation to Heal* (Berkeley, CA: Parallax, 2020), 24–42.

86. Turner, *Happiness Becomes You*, 80–85.

87. *The Soka Gakkai Dictionary of Buddhism*, s.v. "changing poison into medicine."

88. Turner, *Happiness Becomes You*, 92–96.

89. Turner, *Happiness Becomes You*, 98–99.

90. Turner, *Happiness Becomes You*, 176.

91. Turner, *Happiness Becomes You*, 181.

92. Turner, *Happiness Becomes You*, 182.

93. Daisaku Ikeda, "Commemorating the 25th Anniversary of 'The Sun of Jiyu over a New Land,'" *World Tribune*, accessed April 30, 2022, https://www.worldtribune.org/2017/11/sun-jiyu-new-land-2/.

94. For the term "religio-racial," see Judith Weisenfeld, *New World A-Coming: Black Religion and Racial Identity during the Great Migration* (New York: New York University Press, 2016), 5–13.

95. Turner, "Love Within."

96. For example, see Turner, *Happiness Becomes You*, 35–36.

97. Rima Vesely-Flad, *Black Buddhists and the Black Radical Tradition: The Practice of Stillness in the Movement for Liberation* (New York: New York University Press, 2022), 8.

98. Vesely-Flad, *Black Buddhists*, 9–10.

99. Vesely-Flad, *Black Buddhists*, 11.

100. Rosemarie Freeney Harding, with Rachel Elizabeth Harding, *Remnants: A Memoir of Spirit, Activism, and Mothering* (Durham, NC: Duke University Press, 2015), 168.

Epilogue

1. Pearl Cleage, with Zaron W. Burnett Jr., *We Speak Your Names: A Celebration* (New York: One World Books, 2005), 39.

2. Henry Louis Gates Jr., *In Search of Our Roots: How 19 Extraordinary African Americans Reclaimed Their Past* (New York: Skyhorse Publishing, 2017), 80.

A Note on Sources

1. Vaughn A. Booker, *Lift Every Voice and Swing: Black Musicians and Religious Culture in the Jazz Century* (New York: New York University Press, 2020), 21.

Index

abuse: in Ike's upbringing, 48; and *I, Tina*, 173–75; and Oprah Winfrey, 184; Turner marriage defined by, 1, 6, 10, 42–43, 49, 56–57, 64, 73, 94–98, 108, 182, 218; in Zelma and Richard's marriage, 18

Acid Queen (Tina Turner), 92, 122

Adams, Bryan, 162, 164

Adiele, Faith, 9

aesthetics: Black Pentecostal, 30; Georgianna Flagg's, 20, 39; Ike Turner's, 48; Native American, 21–22; Turner's fashion, 159; Turner's solo concert, 118, 194; wildest-dreams rock, 144–45, 148, 166, 176–87, 194

Africa (African), 69, 104, 182; Pan-Africanism, 116. *See also* South Africa

African American (African Americans): ancestry, 20–22; and American Society for Psychical Research, 60; Great Migration, 68; and India, 201; in Memphis, 33; radio, 36–37; and Reconstruction, 14–16; religious history, 8–10, 14–16, 45, 175; in St. Louis, 43; and transportation, 45–46; travel abroad, 58; and white music businessmen, 46–47; women, 15, 19–24, 29, 37, 40, 173, 217, 219. *See also* Black southern religious culture

Afro-Protestant Christianity, 8–9, 15–16,

29–30, 38, 64–65, 70–72, 116, 184, 200, 216, 219

alcohol (drinking), 23, 25, 33–34, 47, 108

"Aloha, We Love America" (festival), 148–50, 162

American Society for Psychical Research (ASPR), 60

Ann-Margret, 90–92, 110

Argentina, 165

Arrington, Carl, 119, 139–41, 153–54, 158, 162, 171

Asia, 69, 134, 164, 201, 204, 218; Asian religions, 8, 68; Southeast Asia, 58, 94, 133, 165

Asian Americans, 105

astrology, 2, 7, 68, 81–82, 140, 152, 159, 164, 185, 218–19

auras, 114

Australia: Andrew Mournehis, 178; Festival Records, 134, 147; Ike & Tina Turner Revue tour, 58, 73, 94; *Mad Max 3*, 161; Roger Davies, 127–28, 142; Taro Gold, 208; Terry Britten, 157; Turner solo concerts, 123, 133–34, 164–65, 176, 182

authority (religious), 9, 15–16, 29, 83, 170, 203

awakening (spiritual), 55, 76, 107, 178, 181–82, 191, 206, 212–15

Bach, Erwin, 167–69, 183, 190–91, 194, 205–6, 219

Bach, Jurgen, 205
Baker, LaVern, 36–38
Baldwin, James, 58, 171
Baptist: Baptist Home Mission Society, 24; in *I, Tina*, 173, 175; National Baptist Convention, 14–15; theology, 30. *See also* Black Baptist; Centennial Baptist Church; Spring Hill Baptist Church; Woodlawn Missionary Baptist Church
Basil, Toni, 117, 123
Bassett, Angela, 4, 172–74
Behringer, Ann (Annie), 131, 134, 145, 155, 157, 166
Berry, Chuck, 43
Beyond: Buddhist and Christian Prayers (Tina Turner), 190–93
Beyond Foundation, 4, 191
Beyond (Gold Edition): Buddhist and Christian Prayers (Tina Turner), 190, 192, 200, 203–4, 215
Beyond Music Foundation, 190–91, 207
Bible, 2, 15–16, 19, 23, 26, 30, 66, 81, 92, 124
Bihari, Joe, 47
Bishop, Valerie, 72–73, 83–91, 98, 104, 141, 169
Black. *See* African American (African Americans)
Black Baptist: Ike & Tina Turner Revue, 65, 67, 90; respectability politics, 23–25, 40; Turner's early life, 7–8, 13–16, 19, 22–23, 27–30, 56, 69–70, 86, 195; Turner's religiosity, 2, 184, 214, 218; Turner's solo career, 202; womanhood, 217. *See also* Jackson, Mahalia
Black Buddhists, 8–9, 106, 133, 142, 170, 176, 183, 187, 214–15
Black church, 8, 14–16, 40, 64–65
Black Pentecostal, 6, 28–30, 38–40, 49, 184, 217
Black southern religious culture, 6–8, 14–16, 21–22, 28, 39, 46, 66, 72, 217–18
blues (music): and the Chitlin' Circuit, 51; in England, 55; and the Ike & Tina Turner Revue, 62–65, 118; Ike Turner

and, 43–51; Tina Turner and, 34–41, 122, 134–36, 146, 152, 185
bodhisattva, 147–51, 213
Bolic Sound Studios, 65, 73–74, 84, 93, 95, 101, 108, 110, 119–20, 155, 187
Bond, Roy, 32–35
Bootsie Whitelow String Band, 36, 38, 50
Bowie, David, 151–54, 162, 164
Brady, Paul, 164
Brandt, Jerry, 136–37
Brazil, 77, 165
Break Every Rule (Tina Turner), 163–68, 171
Brenston, Jackie, 47
British Electric Foundation (BEF), 146, 154
Britten, Terry, 157–58, 164
Bruno, Jack, 134
Buck, Matilda, 104, 141, 170, 206
Buddha (Buddhahood), 75–76, 87, 106–7, 179, 195, 197, 204, 209; as Shakyamuni, 75
Buddhism: altars (*butsudans*), 87–88, 124, 127, 162, 173, 178, 183; *amala-vijnana*, 196–97; author positionality, 5; canon, 203–4; David Bowie and, 152; Engaged Buddhism, 132; ethical listening, 203–4; in *Happiness Becomes You*, 207–16; human revolution, 80, 107, 112, 158, 163, 212; impermanence, 192–94; and improvisation, 179–80; on *Larry King Live*, 1–3; literature, 93, 132, 144, 199, 211; Mahayana, 160–61, 193, 202; memorial service, 206; no distinction between spiritual and practical, 144; rebirth, 158; Tendai, 75; Ten Worlds, 175, 209–10; Tiantai, 144, 150, 195; Turner attributes her success to, 163, 171; Turner's Buddhist blueprint, 122–28; *upaya-kaushalya*, 160–61. *See also Beyond: Buddhist and Christian Prayers* (Tina Turner); Black Buddhists; chant (chanting); Soka

Gakkai Nichiren Buddhism; Turner, Tina: religious teacher

Bullock, Alex, Jr., 22-25, 34

Bullock, Alline: after Turner divorce, 95, 101, 112, 119; death, 190, 193; and *I, Tina*, 171; lives with grandparents, 13, 23, 27, 30; and Tina, 25, 33-35, 43; and Zelma, 18

Bullock, Anna Mae. *See* Turner, Tina

Bullock, Floyd (Richard), 11-12, 17-19, 22-24, 27, 33, 35, 119

Bullock, Roxanna, 13, 19, 22-25, 28, 30-35, 39, 56

Bullock, Zelma: death, 190, 193, 206; divorce, 33; and hair, 18-19; and *I, Tina*, 171; and Pentecostalism, 27-28; Turner's early life, 11-12, 17-23, 35; and Turner's life after leaving home, 56, 101, 119, 162, 200

Burroughs, Nancy (Nannie), 15, 19, 24

butsudan, 87-88, 124, 162, 173, 183

Cain, Ann, 108, 119-20

Caldwell, A. J., 26

Capitol/EMI Records, 127, 147, 150-56, 159, 169

Carter, John S., 151-56

Centennial Baptist Church, 44-45

chakras, 2, 114

chant (chanting): for albums, 196-99, 204; Christian sermons, 14-15, 26, 45, 195; and creativity, 179; discussed with Larry King, 1-2; following Turner's divorce, 101-7, 112-13, 125-29; group, 80-81; and internal revolution, 163; and *I, Tina*, 173-76; and karma, 210; for Kurt Loder, 160; Nichiren teachings on, 75; and performance, 150, 167, 178, 180, 211; Turner empowered by, 93-98; Turner's chanting friends, 84-88, 91, 141; Turner's introduction to, 73-74, 120; Turner's practice, 8. *See also Nam-myoho-renge-kyo*

Charles, Ray, 49, 53, 122

Chess Records, 47

Children Beyond: Understanding through

Singing (Tina Turner), 190, 197-200, 203, 206-7, 215

China (Chinese), 94, 195, 205

Chitlin' Circuit, 51, 100, 105

Chopra, Deepak, 178, 191-92, 204, 206

choreography, 117, 123, 144, 166, 172, 178

Christian. *See* Afro-Protestant Christianity; *under denominations by name*

Church of God in Christ (COGIC), 28-29, 38, 173

civil rights movement, 17, 51-52, 67, 185, 201, 215

Clapton, Eric, 91, 165

cleanliness, 15-16, 23-26, 40, 102, 120

Collins, Phil, 165

concerts: attendance records, 2, 218; Canadian, 160-61; and chanting, 125, 144; festival, 149-50; filmed, 186-87; global, 177-79; Ike & Tina Turner Revue, 50, 52, 61, 98, 108-9; and karma, 210; Live Aid, 162; and the Ritz, 136-38, 141, 146-47, 151-53, 160, 173; Rolling Stones, 42, 138; sites of religiosity, 2-4, 9, 181-82, 187, 207; stadium, 142-43, 165-66, 186; Turner's early solo career, 126, 134, 136, 141, 146-47, 155; Turner "served" papers at, 118. *See also* aesthetics: wildest-dreams rock; *under individual tours by name*

conjuring, 6, 16, 28, 46, 66, 68, 217

conversion: Christian, 28; and concerts, 182; Soka Gokkai aims, 74-78, 85-86, 98, 170; Turner's, 1, 7-10, 56, 71-74, 104-7, 141, 175-76, 209-10

Cooke, Sam, 49, 146, 166

costume (outfit), 107, 117-19, 123, 129, 145, 172, 181, 219

country (music), 36-37, 46, 65, 90, 92, 98, 123, 134

cultural universalism, 55-58

Currie, Evelyn, 34

Currie, Josephus Cecil, 20, 22

Currie, Margaret, 33

Curti, Regula, 190-92, 197, 202, 207-8

Dalai Lama, 191–92
Daly, Rava, 127
dance (dancer): backup, 50, 73, 117, 123, 127–28, 131, 134–36, 145, 149, 155, 157, 178; and Buddhism, 197; holy dance, 27–30, 64; routine, 123; Turner's style, 124
dance (music), 37–41
Dator, James Allen, 78, 170
Davies, Roger, 127–30, 133–42, 145–47, 150–60, 163–66, 173
disco, 117, 122–23, 127, 133–34, 156
divination, 16, 46, 66–67
Drolma, Ani Choying, 202
drugs, 91, 95, 120, 172. *See also* Turner, Ike Wister: cocaine use
Dryer, Carol, 112–16, 132, 140, 142, 158, 218

EMI Records, 127, 134, 147, 152–55, 159
England (London): 123, 154–58, 183, 211; and astrology, 81–82; British rock musicians, 55, 152; Briton, 127, 145, 166; Ike & Tina Turner Revue and, 42, 55–62, 70, 94, 164; psychics in, 42, 115, 218; Turner moves to, 183, 218; Turner solo career, 123, 134, 145–47, 154–58, 162–68, 173, 178, 188, 211, 218
Europe (European): album release, 159, 161; and Buddhism, 78, 187; commercial music success in, 82, 134, 152, 183, 193; DNA, 21; and metaphysical religion, 69, 81, 204, 218; and psychical research, 60; spiritualism, 68; tours to, 3, 24, 56–58, 61, 73, 94, 123, 164–69, 176, 182; Turner moves to, 1, 171, 185
Ewing, Robbie Brack, 25–26, 176

Feit, Bob, 134
Fiftieth Anniversary Concert Tour 2008–2009, 3–4, 188, 191
Fisher, Mark, 145, 166, 177
Flagg, Georgianna, 6–7, 13, 20–23, 31, 34–35, 39, 55–56, 191, 200, 217
Foreign Affair (Tina Turner), 143, 163, 166–68, 177

Foreign Affair World Tour, 168, 171, 177
Franklin, Aretha, 51–52, 89, 95, 118
Franklin, C. L., 44
frenzy, 15, 26, 64–65
funk, 63, 83, 122, 134, 156

Gates, Henry Louis, Jr., 21–22, 27, 31, 218
Gates, J. M., 45
Gaye, Marvin, 166
Germany, 56–58, 61, 70, 85, 94, 112, 165, 167–69, 183, 192
Ghana, 52, 116
Goddess, The, 201–2
gohonzon, 7–8, 75–77, 87, 103–6, 126, 141, 179
Gold, Taro, 125, 182, 187, 207–8
gongyo (Purity of Mind and Power of Forgiveness), 2, 77, 101, 141, 192, 195
Good, Jack, 117
gospel (music): 89–90, 98, 118; Ike & Tina Turner Revue, 65, 89–90, 98, 118, 123; Turner's early life, 12, 26, 36–41; Turner's solo career, 134, 136, 152, 165, 185; and Turner's stylistic development, 49, 51, 63
Gospel according to Ike and Tina, The (Ike and Tina Turner), 89, 123
Graam, Rhonda, 95, 101, 109–11, 117, 131, 205
grandmother theology, 40, 55
Green, Al, 154, 156
Gruen, Bob, 94
guitar (guitarists), 29, 37–40, 43, 46–48, 62, 83, 120, 134, 158

hair, 18, 20, 23, 36, 40, 58, 138, 159, 175
Hampton, Eddy (Armani), 131
Hancock, Herbie, 85, 149, 179–81
Happiness Becomes You: A Guide to Changing Your Life for Good (Tina Turner), 4, 6, 30, 73, 99, 113, 125, 157, 176, 190, 207–16
Harbhajan Sing Khalsa, 190
Hare Krishna, 104
Hatshepsut, 2, 10, 114–16, 142, 152, 158
healers, 21, 46, 66, 68

healing, 16, 28, 46, 55, 68, 191, 214
heaven, 39, 63, 182-83, 191, 206
Hill, Raymond, 50, 173
Hinduism, 197-200, 205
Hine, Rupert, 158, 164-65
Holiness Pentecostal Church, 27-31, 38, 40, 49, 65
Holland (the Netherlands), 58, 143, 186
hoodoo, 6, 66
hooks, bell, 9
Hopkins, B. T., 26
Houston, Whitney, 151
Howlin' Wolf, 45
Hurkos, Peter, 58-62, 66-67, 72, 83, 95, 113-14

I, Tina (Tina Turner), release, 163-64, 171-74, 187
Ike & Tina Turner Revue: autobiographical songs, 39; on catalogue, 117, 123; Chitlin' Circuit, 51-53; *Come Together*, 62-65; groupies, 72; origins, 5-6; and Phil Spector, 53-55; professional life (1973-1975), 82-84; professional life (1974-1976), 89-94; tours, 56-58, 61-62, 70, 94, 164, 169, 206; *Workin' Together*, 63-65, 118. *See also* Bolic Sound Studios
Ikeda, Daisaku: and blueprints, 125-26; and Buddhahood, 106-7; early ministry, 77-81, 88; and expedient means, 195; and *ichinen sanzen*, 92; and karma, 113; and nine consciousnesses, 197; and performance, 180-81; and perseverance, 163, 187; and prayer, 150; and social issues, 213; ten worlds, 209; and wildest-dreams aesthetic, 148
Ikettes, 50, 52, 61, 73, 93, 103, 107, 114, 123, 173
India, 20, 23, 68, 190, 200-202
Indonesia, 95
Islam (Muslims), 181, 197, 203

Jackson, Katherine, 4
Jackson, Mahalia, 38-39, 49, 63

Jackson, Michael, 127, 151, 172
Jackson, Millie, 130
Jackson, Sean, 182, 184, 187
Jagger, Mick, 128, 137-39, 152, 162
James, William, 60
Japan (Japanese), 58, 73-79, 105, 112, 162-65, 170, 208, 211
jazz, 37-38, 52, 85, 89, 117-18, 122, 141, 179-80
Jim Crow, 5, 17, 130
John, Elton, 90, 122-23
Johnson, Mel, 100
Judaism (Jew), 85, 197-98
juke joints, 33-34, 44-45, 50
Jungian philosophy, 114, 209-10

karma: and Buddhahood, 106; and Buddhism, 112-17; and family care, 101; racial, 129-33; and social division, 211; storage, 197; transformation of, 148, 180; Turner discusses, 209-10; and Turner's solo career, 141
King, B. B., 36-39, 43-48
King, Coretta Scott, 186
King, Larry, 1-3, 7, 10, 186, 196
King, Ruth, 9, 170
Kings of Rhythm, 43, 46-48, 70, 83, 107, 173
Knight, Gladys, 118
Knopfler, Mark, 164-65
Kramer, Lee, 127-29, 145, 163

Las Vegas residency concerts, 73, 95, 117-18, 123, 126, 128, 133, 135, 147
Laveau, Marie (Voodoo Queen), 46
Leeds, Arthur, 110-11, 121-22, 142
Lightman, Chip, 131, 134
Little Milton, 43
Little Richard, 49
Live in Amsterdam: Wildest Dreams Tour (Tina Turner), 143
Loder, Kurt, 37-38, 47-48, 57, 61-62, 74, 84, 94, 114, 121, 126, 151, 160, 163, 171
Lotus Sutra (*Saddharma-pundarika-sutra*), 75-76, 112-13, 141, 173, 195, 204, 209, 213

Love Explosion, 127, 135
Love Within: Beyond (Tina Turner), 200–206, 213, 215
Lucien, Maria Booker, 89, 101–4, 107, 141

Mackie, Bob, 117, 123, 145
Mad Max 3: Beyond Thunderdome, 160–61
magic, 16, 46, 68, 182
Makiguchi, Tsunesaburo, 74–77, 80, 86, 88, 105–6, 179–80
Manuel, Zenju Earthlyn, 9, 106
Marsh, Ian Craig, 146, 154–55
Mason, Charles Harrison, 28–29
Merchant, Ismail, 201–2
metaphysical religion: defined, 66–71; Dryer and, 114–17; Oprah Winfrey and, 184, 187; and psychics, 60; Turner and, 2, 7–9, 72, 81–82, 92, 117, 140, 214–19; and Turner's music, 204–5; vernacular religion, 69–70
Methodist (Wesleyan), 181
Middle East, 73, 204
Miller, George, 160
Monaco, Bob, 122, 127
Montgomery, Robbie, 103
Moore, Kenny, 118, 131, 134–36, 145
Mormonism, 82
Mournehis, Andrew, 178
Mrs. Blake, 27–30
Muddy Waters, 45, 95
My Love Story (Tina Turner), 6, 73, 85, 96, 138, 140, 167, 178, 188, 194, 205–8
mysticism: African American, 6–8, 18, 21–22, 72, 82, 215, 218; Buddhist, 81, 185, 148, 152, 160, 197, 200, 208; Georgianna Flagg's, 39–40, 55; wildest-dreams aesthetic, 180–82

Nam-myoho-renge-kyo: on albums, 192, 197; as anthem of angels, 209; and metaphysical religions, 91, 214; and performance, 163, 166, 173; and Ronnie Turner, 74; Soka Gokai teachings on, 75, 106, 113, 150; as song, 196;

Sound of Mystic Law, 192, 196; and Tina Turner's conversion, 104; Tina Turner demonstrates, 2, 124, 141, 160, 178; Tina Turner empowered by, 93, 98, 187, 209; Tina Turner introduced to, 85
National Baptist Convention, 14–15
Native American, 20–22, 60, 82, 123
New Age, 82, 205, 219
New Thought, 204–5
Newton-John, Olivia, 127, 145
New Zealand, 165, 176, 182, 211
Nichiren Shoshu Buddhism. *See* Soka Gakkai Nichiren Buddhism
Nichiren Shoshu Soka Gakkai of America (NSA). *See* Soka Gakkai International–USA (SGI-USA)
Nutbush, Tennessee: early life, 5–6, 10–13, 16–20, 23–24, 33–36, 83, 100, 119, 140, 158, 171, 183, 208; education in, 31–32; religion in, 24–30, 40, 69, 83, 155, 195, 217. *See also Nutbush City Limits* (Tina Turner); Turner songs: "Nutbush City Limits"
Nutbush City Limits (Tina Turner), 82–84, 89, 97, 128

Obstoj, Jeanette, 158, 164
occult practices, 72, 85
Oram, James West, 158
Outta Season, 38, 61, 64, 83
Owens, Lama Rod, 9

Perkins, Joe Willie "Pinetop," 44–47
Phillips, Sam, 46–47
piano, 12, 26, 44–48, 85, 118, 131, 136
pop (music), 6, 37, 41, 53, 55, 82, 90, 145–46, 157–61
praise (music), 201
prayer: on *Larry King Live*, 2; the Lord's Prayer, 66, 86, 202; prayer beads, 74, 85, 87, 124; prayer book, 89; "Tina's Prayer," 84, 97; in Turner's early life, 23–30, 40, 56; Turner's practice during solo career, 125–26, 150, 166, 178, 205, 214; in Turner's solo career catalogue,

194–200; Wadado Leo Smith and, 181. *See also Beyond: Buddhist and Christian Prayers* (Tina Turner)

Prince, 151

Private Dancer (Tina Turner), 3, 6, 142, 145, 153–68, 171, 177, 187

Private Dancer Tour, 162, 165–68, 173

psychics: psychic readers, 66, 68, 84, 127; Turner consults, 42–43, 56–62, 70, 82–84, 113–16, 128, 218; and Turner's metaphysical religion, 7, 66–72, 81, 86, 141, 162, 171, 185, 219. *See also* Dryer, Carol; Hurkos, Peter

race (racial): boundaries, 17, 43–44; and civil rights, 51–52, 67, 132; diversity in SGI-USA, 169–71; division, 210, 213; identity, 213; inequality, 14; mixed-race couples, 170; multiracial, 127; music, 38; racial karma, 129–33; violence, 44, 214

racism, 5, 24, 58, 131, 133, 142, 150–54, 168–70, 184–87, 208, 211–12

radio, 3, 5, 36–38, 41, 45–46, 50, 55, 122, 155–56, 161, 203

railroad, 43, 45

Ralston, James, 134

rape, 93–94

Rawls, Lou, 95

Reconstruction, 14, 31

recording studios: Bolic Sound Studios, 65–66, 73, 84, 87, 93, 95, 101, 103, 108, 110–11, 119–21, 124; Sun, 46–47; Turner and, 135, 155, 158; Turner's movement restricted to, 81

religious teacher. *See* Turner, Tina: religious teacher

respectability, 16, 19, 23–25, 28–30, 40, 48

rhythm and blues (R&B), 38, 41, 43, 47, 51, 54–55, 62–65, 122, 134–36, 146, 152, 185

Richards, Keith, 138, 152

Richardson, Lejeune, 93, 134, 145, 155, 157, 166

Richie, Lionel, 159

Righteous Brothers, 53

ring shout, 14, 28–29

Ritz, the, 136–38, 141, 146–47, 151–55, 160, 173

River Deep, Mountain High (Tina Turner), 42, 90, 93

rock 'n' roll (music): Best Rock Vocal Performance Award, 161; Black Diamond Queens, 37; British rock musicians, 55, 152; concert, 144–46, 187; Ike & Tina Turner Revue, 62–65; Ike Turner as pioneer, 5, 41, 43, 47–48; male artists, 138–39, 153, 165, 185, 215; Rock and Roll Hall of Fame, 172; Rosetta Tharpe, 38; Tina Turner as queen of, 49; Tina Turner solo career, 118, 123, 133–42, 149, 153–54, 157, 159, 165–66, 195, 207, 215; wildest-dreams aesthetic, 144–45, 148, 166, 176–87, 194

Rolling Stones, 42, 55–56, 62, 92, 126, 128, 135–39

root work, 16, 40, 217

Rough (Tina Turner), 122–23, 135

Sadanaga, Masayasu, 78

sanctified. *See* Holiness Pentecostal Church

Sanskrit, 193, 199

Scientology, 120

Seger, Bob, 122, 136, 151

segregation, 17, 43, 45, 51, 55, 130. *See also* Jim Crow

Sempers, Susie, 103, 141

sermons, 12–16, 26, 44–46, 65, 195, 203

sexism, 142, 150–54, 169, 184, 187

Seymour, William, 28

Shak-Dagsay, Dechen, 191–92, 197–202

shakubuku, 74, 77–81, 85–88, 104, 170

Shende-Sathaye, Sawani, 200

Shonin, Nichiren (Nichiren the Sage), 75

Shorter, Ana Maria, 85, 89, 94, 101–4, 107–9, 125, 141, 208

Shorter, Wayne, 85, 89, 101–4, 107–9, 125, 128, 141, 147–49, 179–81, 208

signs, 6, 16, 21, 27–28, 40, 60, 191, 217
Sikhism, 197–98
Simone, Nina, 58, 171
slavery (enslaved people), 13–16, 22, 24, 29, 31, 36, 133, 169
Smith, Hardin, 6, 14, 24–25
Smith, Wadada Leo, 181–82
Soka Gakkai International–USA (SGI-USA): and American culture, 80–81; American General Chapter, 79; Buddhist Peace Festival, 148–49; and conversion efforts, 86, 170; *daimoku*, 75, 150, 195–96; founding and beliefs, 74–81; Overseas Branch, 78; racial diversity in, 169–71; *The Liturgy of the Soka Gakkai International*, 2, 178, 195; Turner and, 7, 85, 104, 141, 163; twenty-fifth-anniversary concert, 148–49, 162; and Valerie Bishop, 84–85, 88, 99, 169; *World Tribune*, 196. *See also* Ikeda, Daisaku; Soka Gakkai Nichiren Buddhism
Soka Gakkai Nichiren Buddhism: "actual proof," 86–87, 144; buddha-nature, 12; faith equated with daily life, 144; *gohonzon*, 7–8, 75–77, 87, 103–6, 126, 141, 179; and *ichinen sanzen*, 179; as Nichiren Shoshu Buddhism, 75–76, 85, 169; nine con-sciousnesses, 196–97, 210; origins, 74–84; *Soka Kyoiku Gakkai* (Value-Creating Education Society), 74; Soka University, 208; three secret laws, 75; Turner's empowerment through, 92–94; Turner's identification with, 9; Turner's introduction to, 7–8. *See also* Buddhism; chant (chanting); conver-sion; karma
soul (music), 51–52, 61–63, 82–83, 90–91, 95, 134, 136, 146, 152–59, 185
soul (religious term), 67, 70, 113–16, 125, 127, 148, 175, 194, 198–99, 206
sound vibration, 2
South Africa, 2, 129–33, 177–78, 182, 210
Spector, Phil, 53–55, 70, 172

spirit (Holy Spirit): catching the, 5, 26–29; and Christian worship, 26; and Dryer, 114–15; Ikeda's teachings on, 180; and performance, 182–83; and prayer, 196; and supernatural, 16, 21, 66–67, 106
spiritualism (spiritualists), 59–60, 68
spirituals, 14, 37, 39
Spring Hill Baptist Church, 6, 12, 24, 30–33, 37, 40, 69, 83, 217
Stewart, Mike, 110–12, 117, 122, 127–29
Stewart, Rod, 123, 126, 128, 138–39, 152
subconscious, 1–2, 175–76, 183, 196–97, 200, 205, 210–11
Sufism, 85
suicide, 61, 206, 212
Summer, Donna, 127, 151
Summer Lovers, 145–46
supernaturalism (supernatural), 6–9, 16, 21–22, 28–29, 39–40, 46, 60, 66–72, 82, 132, 218
Swedenborg, Emmanuel, 114
Sweet Rhode Island Red (Ike and Tina Turner), 90
Switzerland, 58, 183, 190–92, 193, 197, 205, 207, 218

Tabor, Nate, 100–101, 110, 142
Thailand, 133, 190
Tharpe, Rosetta, 38, 49
Thomas, Jimmy, 51–52, 61, 175
Tina: The Tina Turner Musical (Tina Turner), 6, 211, 217, 219
Tina Live in Europe (Tina Turner), 167–68
TINA (Tina Turner), 74, 93–94, 153
Tina Turner: Nice 'n' Rough (Tina Turner), 145
Tina Turner Break Every Rule World Tour 1987/1988, 165–67
Tina Turner One Last Time Live (Tina Turner), 4
Tina Turns the Country On (Tina Turner), 90, 92, 123
Toda, Josei, 74–80, 86, 88, 96, 105–7
Tommy, 65, 90–93

Transcendental Meditation, 85, 204–5
Turner, Craig Raymond, 50, 73–74, 101–2, 110–11, 120, 173, 190, 206, 208, 212
Turner, Ike, Jr., 73, 92, 101, 108, 120–21
Turner, Ike Wister: in *Behind the Music*, 88; and the blues, 42–48; cocaine use, 61, 65–66, 84, 91, 93, 96, 108, 111, 193; death, 193–94; divorce process, 99–104, 107–12, 121–22; early relationship with Tina Turner, 48–51; forced Tina to sing songs she didn't want to, 157; prevents Tina's Buddhist practice, 7, 85–89; at Rock and Roll Hall of Fame, 172; as rock pioneer, 41; Tina leaves, 95–98; Tina narrates life with, 139–42, 158, 160, 162
Turner, Izear Luster, 44–45
Turner, Michael, 50, 73–74, 101–2, 120–21
Turner, Ronnie: drug abuse, 120–21; early life, 50; following Turners' divorce, 101–4, 108, 110; in Inglewood, 88; introduces Tina to Buddhism, 72–74, 81, 84, 86, 104, 218; musician, 120, 131
Turner, Tina: American Music Awards, 161; as authority figure, 9, 203; as Buddhist-Baptist, 30, 175–76; cancer, 190, 206; in church choirs, 5, 12–13, 25–27, 30–31, 34, 36, 40; and cotton, 5, 13–14, 17–18, 36–38, 43, 183, 217; cousins, 22, 25, 33–35, 171; discusses MLK, 139, 201; DNA ancestry, 21–22; does not see Ike after 1991, 172; dyslexia, 32; early education, 31–32; early relationship with Ike, 48–50; and feminism, 94, 185; first encounters with Buddhism, 73–74; Hanes campaign, 145; independence, 57, 62, 66, 92–98, 109–11, 118, 141; international focus, 134, 164, 167–69, 205; *Jet* profiles, 91–92, 98, 124–25; leaves Ike, 96–97; as "Little Ann," 48–49, 70, 188; and London, 42, 56–57, 61–62, 91, 115, 123, 145–46, 154–57, 164–68, 178, 183, 211, 218; marries Erwin Bach, 190; marries Ike Turner, 50; "one take" delivery, 146, 154–55; Operation Oops, 109–10; origins of Tina name, 49–50; personal dreams, 3; picnic performances, 5, 13, 36–37, 41, 50, 63; platinum (multiplatinum) albums, 2–3, 159, 161, 165, 168, 187; religious teacher, 4–5, 9, 161, 184, 188–90, 200, 203–4, 207, 215, 219; in Ripley, Tennessee, 32–35, 50; Rock and Roll Hall of Fame, 172; as spiritual seeker, 67–72, 97, 184–85, 204; and sports, 32–33; in St. Louis, 5, 35–41, 43, 47–48, 56, 83, 95, 100, 173; stroke, 32, 190, 205; Swiss citizenship, 205; on television, 1–4, 42, 53, 56, 91–92, 109, 113–14, 127, 155, 161, 183, 186–87; third encounter with Buddhism, 84–89; universal persona, 184–85; unwanted pregnancy, 18–19; vocals, 40, 49, 53–55, 70, 122, 146
Turner songs: "A Change Is Gonna Come," 146; "A Fool in Love," 5, 49–50, 53–54, 57, 70, 122; "Almighty," 202; "Amazing Grace," 12, 30, 89, 202; "Ask Me How I Feel," 166; "Ball of Confusion," 146, 150, 154, 158; "Better Be Good to Me," 166; "Bold Soul Sister," 61; "Crazy in the Night," 145; "I Am a Motherless Child," 38–39, 61–63, 202; "I Might Have Been Queen," 156–59, 164; "I'll Be Thunder," 165; "I've Been Loving You Too Long," 61; "Johnny and Mary," 145–46; "Let's Stay Together," 154–58, 183; "Make Me Over (Tina's Prayer)," 83–84, 97; "Mother Within," 202; "Nutbush City Limits," 4–5, 25, 62–63, 67, 83, 97, 123, 136; "On Silent Wings," 186; "Proud Mary," 5, 62–66, 118, 123, 136, 145, 188, 192, 195; "River Deep, Mountain High," 5, 53–55, 66, 70, 123, 129, 164, 167, 172; "The Best," 143, 166, 183;

"What's Love Got to Do with It?" 143, 157–61, 164, 172

Twenty-Four Seven (Tina Turner), 193

Twenty-Four Seven World Tour 2000, 3–4, 188

United Artists Records, 110, 117, 122, 127, 147

United Kingdom (UK), 55, 127, 147

USA for Africa, 161–62

Vijnanavada (Consciousness Doctrine), 196

Walsh, Greg, 156, 158

Ware, Martyn, 146, 154–56, 158

Werlen, Abbott Martin, 191–92

What's Love Got to Do with It? (film), 3–6, 30, 171–77, 183, 187, 208, 217

What's Love Tour '93, 176, 177, 201, 211

white: artists, 138, 153–54, 165, 185–86; and the Chitlin' Circuit, 51–52; church, 24, 30; clubs, 43, 47; executives, 134; interracial relationships, 169; landholders, 14, 17, 22; music, 37, 64; music fans, 62, 138; musicians, 134, 136; and psychical research, 60; radio stations, 36, 55; supremacy, 16, 130; Turner works for, 35; women, 44

Wickham, Vicki, 42–43, 56, 72

wilderness experience, 18–19, 60, 184, 200, 217

Wildest Dreams (Tina Turner), 143, 176–77, 183, 186–87

Williams, Elbert, 17, 79, 149, 170

Williams, George M., 78–79, 88, 149, 170

Williams, Kyodo, 9

Williamson, Sonny Boy, II, 36, 39, 45

Willis, Jan, 9, 133, 170, 176

Winfrey, Oprah, 3–4, 18, 101, 145, 183–87, 205, 219

Winwood, Steve, 165

womanism, 19, 40

Woodlawn Missionary Baptist Church, 6, 11–14, 23–26, 28, 33, 36–37, 40, 69, 83, 176, 217

yoga, 190, 198, 204

Titles published in the

LIBRARY OF RELIGIOUS BIOGRAPHY SERIES

Orestes A. Brownson: American Religious Weathervane
by Patrick W. Carey

The Puritan as Yankee: A Life of Horace Bushnell
by Robert Bruce Mullin

A Life of Alexander Campbell
by Douglas A. Foster

Duty and Destiny: The Life and Faith of Winston Churchill
by Gary Scott Smith

Emblem of Faith Untouched: A Short Life of Thomas Cranmer
by Leslie Williams

Her Heart Can See: The Life and Hymns of Fanny J. Crosby
by Edith L. Blumhofer

Emily Dickinson and the Art of Belief
by Roger Lundin

God's Cold Warrior: The Life and Faith of John Foster Dulles
by John D. Wilsey

A Short Life of Jonathan Edwards
by George M. Marsden

The Religious Journey of Dwight D. Eisenhower: Duty, God, and Country
by Jack M. Holl

Charles G. Finney and the Spirit of American Evangelicalism
by Charles E. Hambrick-Stowe

William Ewart Gladstone: Faith and Politics in Victorian Britain
by David Bebbington

One Soul at a Time: The Story of Billy Graham
by Grant Wacker

An Odd Cross to Bear: A Biography of Ruth Bell Graham
by Anne Blue Wills

*A Heart Lost in Wonder: The Life and Faith of **Gerard Manley Hopkins***
by Catharine Randall

*Sworn on the Altar of God: A Religious Biography of **Thomas Jefferson***
by Edwin S. Gaustad

*The Miracle Lady: **Katherine Kuhlman**
and the Transformation of Charismatic Christianity*
by Amy Collier Artman

Abraham Kuyper: *Modern Calvinist, Christian Democrat*
by James D. Bratt

*The Religious Life of **Robert E. Lee***
by R. David Cox

Abraham Lincoln: *Redeemer President*
by Allen C. Guelzo

Charles Lindbergh: *A Religious Biography of America's Most Infamous Pilot*
by Christopher Gehrz

*The First American Evangelical: A Short Life of **Cotton Mather***
by Rick Kennedy

Aimee Semple McPherson: *Everybody's Sister*
by Edith L. Blumhofer

*Mother of Modern Evangelicalism: The Life and Legacy of **Henrietta Mears***
by Arlin Migliazzo

*Damning Words: The Life and Religious Times of **H. L. Mencken***
by D. G. Hart

Thomas Merton *and the Monastic Vision*
by Lawrence S. Cunningham

*God's Strange Work: **William Miller** and the End of the World*
by David L. Rowe

Blaise Pascal: *Reasons of the Heart*
by Marvin R. O'Connell

*Occupy Until I Come: **A. T. Pierson** and the Evangelization of the World*
by Dana L. Robert

*The Kingdom Is Always but Coming: A Life of **Walter Rauschenbusch***
by Christopher H. Evans

***Oral Roberts** and the Rise of the Prosperity Gospel*
by Jonathan Root

*Strength for the Fight: The Life and Faith of **Jackie Robinson***
by Gary Scott Smith

*A Christian and a Democrat: A Religious Life of **Franklin D. Roosevelt***
by John F. Woolverton with James D. Bratt

***Francis Schaeffer** and the Shaping of Evangelical America*
by Barry Hankins

***Harriet Beecher Stowe:** A Spiritual Life*
by Nancy Koester

***Billy Sunday** and the Redemption of Urban America*
by Lyle W. Dorsett

***Howard Thurman** and the Disinherited: A Religious Biography*
by Paul Harvey

*We Will Be Free: The Life and Faith of **Sojourner Truth***
by Nancy Koester

*Dancing in My Dreams: A Religious Biography of **Tina Turner***
by Ralph H. Craig III

*Assist Me to Proclaim: The Life and Hymns of **Charles Wesley***
by John R. Tyson

*Prophetess of Health: A Study of **Ellen G. White***
by Ronald L. Numbers

***George Whitefield:** Evangelist for God and Empire*
by Peter Y. Choi

*The Divine Dramatist: **George Whitefield** and
the Rise of Modern Evangelicalism*
by Harry S. Stout

*Liberty of Conscience: **Roger Williams** in America*
by Edwin S. Gaustad